# AMERICAN FORCE

A COUNCIL ON FOREIGN RELATIONS BOOK

# AMERICAN FORCE

## Dangers, Delusions, and Dilemmas in National Security

RICHARD K. BETTS

COLUMBIA UNIVERSITY PRESS    *New York*

Columbia University Press
*Publishers Since 1893*
New York    Chichester, West Sussex

Copyright © 2012 Columbia University Press
All rights reserved

Library of Congress Cataloging-in-Publication Data
Betts, Richard K., 1947–
    American force : dangers, delusions, and dilemmas in national security / Richard K. Betts.
        p. cm. — (A Council on Foreign Relations book)
    Includes bibliographical references and index.
    ISBN 978-0-231-15122-1 (cloth : alk. paper) — ISBN 978-0-231-52188-8 (ebk.)
    1. United States—Foreign relations.    2. United States—Foreign relations—1945–1989.
3. United States—Foreign relations—1989–    4. United States—History, Military—20th century.
5. United States—Military policy.    6. National security—United States.    I. Title.    II. Series.
    JZ1480. B49 2011,
    355.00973'09045—dc22

                                                                                    2011014659

Casebound editions of Columbia University Press books are printed
on permanent and durable acid-free paper.
Printed in the United States of America

c 10 9 8 7 6 5 4 3 2 1

References to Internet Web sites (URLs) were accurate at the time of writing. Neither the author nor Columbia University Press is responsible for URLs that may have expired or changed since the manuscript was prepared.

For a man I never knew, and those like him:
1st Lieutenant Andrew J. Bacevich Jr., U.S. Army, 1st Cavalry Division
Killed in action in Salah Ad Din Province, Iraq, May 13, 2007.
Soldiers don't get to pick their wars.

Western belief in the universality of Western culture suffers from three problems: it is false; it is immoral; and it is dangerous.
—Samuel P. Huntington, *The Clash of Civilizations and the Remaking of World Order*

It isn't fashionable to say so, but the United States of America is the most dangerous military power in the history of the world.
—Walter Russell Mead, *Special Providence*

A short jump is certainly easier than a long one: but no one wanting to get across a wide ditch would begin by jumping half-way.
—Carl von Clausewitz, *On War*

# CONTENTS

# PREFACE

This book's skepticism about emphasis on military force in U.S. foreign policy is hardly unique, but it is different from the sort found regularly on the leftward end of the American political spectrum. It comes from someone with a history of arguing for strong military forces and energetic competition for influence in regional military equations throughout the world. The reasons for those arguments, however, ended abruptly near the end of the twentieth century.

The book reflects the thinking of a Cold War hawk and post–Cold War dove, or, to be accurate, thinking that tilted respectively but inconsistently in those directions; and my recent dovishness is of a crusty sort. During the Cold War my views were usually just to the right of the Democratic Party's center, halfway between Walter Mondale and Henry Jackson. Since the Cold War my foreign policy opinions tend to be just to the left of the party's center, barely closer to John Kerry than to Dennis Kucinich. The difference is not due to a change of heart or intellectual inconsistency, but simply to the end of the Cold War. The epochal importance of that ending was well recognized, but its strategic implications were misread. In the Cold War the combination of Soviet military power in Europe and Marxist ideological appeal to populations everywhere made it imperative to contest the communist opposition forcefully; the future political organization of the world really was at stake. Threats so far in the twenty-first century, however, are just not in the same league. The role of American force in American foreign policy should have been sharply recast but was not.

In the vocabulary of American domestic politics I would be called a liberal or moderate, but this book is conservative in the literal sense. It argues for caution and restraint, not isolation, and for decisive force when force is used. Ardent liberals will consider the book primitive and blinkered, mired in old thinking about power and military competition, and if they glide over the qualifications in my arguments about intervention, inhumane. Neoconservatives will consider it dangerously complacent, failing to appreciate the severity of the twenty-first century's new dangers. I hope that practitioners will not consider it glib. I do freely indulge the luxury of the critic who labors without the burden of responsibility, but I hope that language in the book does not sound arrogant; I have only tried to make my points in a manner as forthright, pungent, and arresting as possible.

Of course it is far easier to diagnose what is wrong or what will not work than to forge and implement a policy that is both right and feasible. I have no confidence that I would always have done better on the problems discussed in the chapters that follow. If any of the criticisms here reek of the naïve simplification that often goes with academic detachment, I plead guilty: apart from infrequent consulting, my only personal experiences in government were short and long ago, and my very brief experience as a military officer never took me closer to danger than Fort Benning, Georgia. If parts of the book seem grumpy and negative, they should be understood within this apology at the outset.

And yet, I do admit to a motive of some impatience. People died because of hesitancy in application of force in the Balkans and elsewhere, and many more because of reckless adventurism in Iraq. Some ventures were initiated by my fellow Democrats, others by Republicans, but in most cases support spanned the spectrum. Too many policymakers want to use force for good purposes but either refuse to face the reality that using military force requires killing or accept that fact all too readily and without enough anxiety.

The chapters that follow touch on many but not all important issues in contemporary national security policy, and they are essays, arguments of opinion. They rest on my assessment of what seems the most relevant evidence, but they are not exercises in systematic, original, methodologically fastidious research. The essays can be read independently, but the book has a coherent theme, and four of the chapters (1, 2, 7, and 12) have never before been published in any form in books or journals. The other chapters draw on essays that were published in previous years, but they have been heavily revised and updated and incorporate much new material. The cores come from the following articles. Chapter 3: "The Delusion of Impartial

Intervention," *Foreign Affairs* 73, no. 6 (November/December 1994) and "The Lesser Evil," *The National Interest* no. 64 (Summer 2001); chapter 4: "The New Threat of Mass Destruction," *Foreign Affairs* 77, no. 1 (January/ February 1998); chapter 5: "The Soft Underbelly of American Primacy," *Political Science Quarterly* 117, no. 1 (Spring 2002); chapter 6: "Striking First," *Ethics & International Affairs* 17, no. 1 (2003); chapter 9: "Are Civil-Military Relations Still a Problem?" in *American Civil-Military Relations*, ed. Suzanne C. Nielsen and Don M. Snider (Baltimore: Johns Hopkins University Press, 2009); chapter 10: "Is Strategy an Illusion?" *International Security* 25, no. 2 (Fall 2000); chapter 11: "A Disciplined Defense," *Foreign Affairs* 86, no. 6 (November/December 2007). Chapter 8 draws on "The Three Faces of NATO," *The National Interest* no. 100 (March/April 2009) and, with the exception of the lines by Thomas Christensen noted in the text, the sections written by me in Richard K. Betts and Thomas J. Christensen, "China: Getting the Questions Right," *The National Interest* no. 62 (Winter 2000/01); my whole discussion of China here benefits greatly from the rest of Christensen's contributions to that original article, but he does not necessarily endorse everything said in this chapter. Chapter 2 draws on a paper distributed by the Princeton Project on National Security but otherwise unpublished: "U.S. National Security Strategy: Lenses and Landmarks," November 2004.

I thank James Wirtz of the Naval Postgraduate School and Loch Johnson of the University of Georgia for helpful reviews of the proposal and first rough draft of the book, and Anita O'Brien for skilful editing of the manuscript. At Columbia University Press Peter Dimock prodded me gently but persistently to do this book, and Anne Routon oversaw the project. Richard N. Haass and James M. Lindsay at the Council on Foreign Relations deserve gratitude for open-mindedness in sponsoring this as a CFR Book.

As always I am grateful to my family—my wife, Adela M. Bolet, and children, Elena Christine, Michael Francis, and Diego Fitzpatrick Betts—for making life happy in so many ways that prevented me from completing this work much earlier. Like other books I have formally dedicated to them, this one is naturally for them too. The formal dedication of this book, however, is to 1st Lieutenant Andrew J. Bacevich Jr., killed in Iraq in 2007, as one representative of the tragic best in this country's tradition of service to national security: the people who have to implement the grand designs of visionary political leaders, the people who go into the point of the spear, sent by those who do not have to bear the cost of their decisions themselves and who often do not send anyone from their own families to bear the cost. Bacevich was a soldier from a soldier's family. His father, Andrew Bacevich Senior, will not agree with everything in this book but shares some of its concerns with even stronger feelings than mine. Having more than paid his own dues in many years of military service, he has since been a relentless and articulate critic of the uses of American force. I never had the chance to know Bacevich Junior, am only slightly acquainted with Senior, and do not claim to speak for either, but I believe that American force will be used better, and not used carelessly, if policymakers take more care with people like the former and listen harder to those like the latter.

# AMERICAN FORCE

# PART I. THE POST–COLD WAR HIATUS

# 1

## INTRODUCTION
### FROM COLD WAR TO HOT PEACE

When the United States became more secure it became more forceful. Since the Cold War ended it has spent far more than any other country or coalition to build armed forces; it has sent forces into combat more frequently than it did in the era of much bigger threats to national security; and it has done so much more often than any other country. The United States has been, quite simply, "the most militarily active state in the world."[1] To many in the mainstream of American politics this is as it should be because the United States has the right and responsibility to lead the world—or push it—in the right direction. To others, more alarmed by the pattern, U.S. behavior has evolved into "permanent war."[2]

Some of this belligerence was imposed on the United States by Al Qaeda on September 11, 2001, but the terrorist threat cannot account for the bulk of blood and treasure expended in the use of force over the past two decades. In the first half of the post–Cold War era, until complications in Iraq and Afghanistan, American national security policy was driven not by threats but by opportunities—or rather what an overambitious consensus in the foreign policy elite mistakenly saw as opportunities. Instead of countering immediate dangers, American policy aimed to stabilize the world in order to prevent dangers from arising. There is no evidence, however, that this activism short-circuited more dangers than it generated. And at the same time, American force has been ambivalent, trying to do too much with too little. Policy elites who wanted to make the world right sometimes held back for fear that costly ventures would lack public support. Sometimes they have chosen the worst of both worlds, compromising between all-out effort and doing nothing at all, but with the result of action that is both costly and indecisive.

The use of force is the most extreme instrument of foreign policy, and it is what preoccupies the planners of national security policy. Americans like to believe that the United States does not resort to force lightly, and that when it does, it does so only defensively. Whatever the motives, or however justified force may be in principle, it is hard to control and exploit effectively in practice. Many who want to use American force for good purposes focus too much on motives, too much on the ends rather than the means. They lack sufficient awareness of how limitations of the means complicate and often derail the ends.

The news is not all bad. Some of the American uses of force in recent years were necessary, proper, and effective, and some of the mistakes are clear only in the luxury of critics' hindsight. The record of judgment and action is inconsistent and not thoroughly explained by any simple theory. The negative part of the record, however, was mostly due to a bad combination of material power, moral conceit, and middling effort. American leaders—both Democrats and Republicans—tried to do a lot, with excessive confidence in their ability to understand and control developments, but they wanted to do it all on the cheap. All too often they wound up surprised when the price turned out to be expensive. They liked to use force frequently but not intensely, when the reverse combination would have been wiser. Too often they found that force proves ineffective if applied sparingly. How did this combination of forcefulness and hesitancy happen?

When the end of the Cold War swept away the epochal threat to Western democracy, the United States had a choice: to relax or to advance. A naïve realist would have expected the first, a comfortable retirement from military exertion. The disappearance of military threat with the collapse of the only other superpower, and of political threat with the worldwide collapse of the only competitive ideology, provided unprecedented national security—at least in the strict sense of the term. (National security is distinguished from "human" security, the wider span of concerns—for example, environmental health—that may well be more important in the end.) The single significant exception to this benign situation in international politics was the potential for interruption of oil supplies, but exporters would have no incentive to exploit that option except in retaliation for American meddling in their interests. Otherwise, the threats left on the post–Cold War roster were indirect rather than immediate, local not global, threats not to vital material interests of the United States but to moral interests, or the interests of other countries' citizens. Such threats may sometimes warrant American action, but they are mainly matters of charity and human decency, not national security.

As it was, the United States chose the second option—expansion—but hesitantly. American leaders chose not to conceive of security in the strict sense of territorial integrity, political autonomy, and economic viability, but in the broader sense of a congenial world filled with ideological kindred devoted to optimizing economic exchange and resolving disputes through the rule of law. In this view, security ultimately requires extending the West's preferred world order. This ambitious alternative would push other societies toward organizing themselves and behaving according to the right values, and would suppress disorders that threatened the security not just of Americans but of foreign populations. This latter-day domino theory aimed to prevent threats from emerging by preventing local pathologies from metastasizing and eventually reaching Americans at home.

On balance, this has been the wrong choice. In the dozen-year hiatus between the opening of the Berlin Wall and Al Qaeda's assaults on September 11, the United States experienced a holiday of sorts from the traditional rough-and-tumble of international conflict. It failed to take advantage of an excellent security situation in this period to manage a transition to a balance of power and modus vivendi with major states. Instead, Washington pushed to exploit unipolarity and dabble in attempts to stabilize and reform countries beset by violence. Some of the initiatives beginning in the 1990s that flowed from the urge to forge world order, promote democracy, and prevent bad behavior made sense, but it proved difficult to keep the sensible moves within bounds and avoid imbroglios that cost more to get out of than they were worth. In the 1990s Washington also indulged an instinct for the capillaries, losing sight of the priority of relations with major powers that are more important than the messes in minor countries on which efforts fixated.[3]

Then came September 11th. National security policy reacted energetically, and for awhile quite sensibly. Flushed with premature confidence from apparent victory in Afghanistan, however, George W. Bush seized the wrong opportunity and confused counterterrorism with war against Iraq. This venture gravely damaged American interests, worsening threats rather than relieving them. Even if the eventual outcome in Iraq proves reasonably stable, the cost will have far exceeded the benefit.

The frequency of resort to force came out of an elite consensus of strange bedfellows: conservative nationalists unapologetically happy to pump up

America's number one status and get in the face of foreigners; cosmopolitan liberals anxious to make the world a cooperative marketplace in the mold of our own country; and neoconservative zealots aiming to do both. Explicit opposition was weak and limited to anti-interventionist paleoconservatives and liberals, minorities in both parties at least until disappointments piled up. Opposition was latent in the greater skepticism of much of the mass public all along, skepticism that would only be activated by costly failure—which made the more ambitious interventionists reluctant to push their visions except in cases where it seemed they might succeed with modest effort.

It would be a mistake to exaggerate the failures of post–Cold War uses of force or the unrealism of foreign policy leaders' planning principles. It is always easier to diagnose a mistake than to prescribe a reliable cure. It is especially unfair for critics to shake their fingers self-righteously when, unlike officials in the world of action, they have the luxury of hindsight and lack the responsibility for making things work in real life. Unfair as they may be, the essays that follow will dwell on mistakes and misconceptions rather than policies that did not stumble.

The idea that U.S. foreign policy has overreached is hardly novel at this point; indeed it is even commonplace since the ordeals in Iraq and Afghanistan. The impulse to overreach preceded these ventures, however, and is resilient. Criticism of post–Cold War military activism is not beating a dead horse because the impulse never recedes indefinitely. Americans want to accomplish much at low cost and are even willing to pay high costs for big stakes. High costs were accepted in the twentieth century because the stakes were the survival and security of Western liberal democracy in the face of successive challenges from great powers and transnational ideologies. That long experience of worldwide struggle established habits that colored the approach to the world after victory, and that can revive when recent setbacks fade from attention.

The chapters that follow explore the Cold War background and several of the main issues and cases that preoccupied national security policy after the collapse of communism. They do not present a tightly integrated analysis that weaves all conclusions into a single theme but should be read as independent excursions that share some common concerns. To appreciate the case for getting policy priorities on a different track it helps to clarify the genuinely important dangers the United States faces, recognize the delusions that have driven some repeated mistakes, and confront the dilemmas that limit how well even sensible choices can produce good outcomes.

## DANGERS

Americans face many potential threats to their safety, the worst of which may lie beyond the realm of national security properly conceived. Collapse of the international financial system is one disaster that is no longer unimaginable. Scientists can point to a number of potential natural catastrophes that could gravely damage human life—environmental devastation, uncontrolled pandemic disease, massive destruction from collision with asteroids, and so on. The risk of at least one such development is actually far greater than politicians and policymakers appreciate.[4] Related to natural disasters would be deliberate devastation inflicted by superempowered individuals or tyrants who make use of malign byproducts of bioengineering, hyperdeveloped artificial intelligence, and other technological advances.[5] Some of these overlap with issues of national security, but if the term has any meaning, national security must refer to the more specific category of military vulnerability and threats to the nation's political autonomy and fundamental economic viability.

In the strict sense of national security the United States has faced far fewer dangers in recent years than it did before the 1990s, or than it may face some years from now. This should be obvious, yet a surprising number of policymakers and commentators, especially among liberals and neoconservatives, seem not to grasp the point. Now more than two decades since the Berlin Wall opened, and under the immediate emotional impact of Al Qaeda's fanaticism, many Americans have forgotten—or are too young to remember—the tremendously different nature and scale of the threats to "the American way of life" that energized permanent peacetime mobilization.

In the first half of the twentieth century radical nationalist ideologies, fused with great power military capabilities—German fascism and Japanese militarism—threatened the independence of the Western democracies and the huge countries of Russia and China, caused the deaths of fifty to seventy million people, and destroyed most of Eurasia. In the second half of that century a universalist ideology, backed by Soviet and Chinese power, made a prolonged bid for the hearts and minds of people throughout the world.

Although young people today may think that the fear of a now-defunct faith taking over the world must have been overwrought, Marxism-Leninism thrived and advanced in many regions. Communism was quite unlike radical Islam today, which is a mobilizing force and model for social organization only in culture areas where the religion is already historically rooted. Rather it was an ideal with appeal and political clout to varying degrees in virtually every part of the world (except, perhaps, the United States). Until close to the end it was not inevitable that communists would lose the Cold War. In that context muscular American activism to compete for control of political and military developments abroad made great sense.

The end of the Cold War blessed the United States with the least dangerous outside world in living memory. That does not mean that recent dangers are small, or that they may not become awesome before long, but that they are more modest than the ones that shaped the modern American national security establishment. It means that since the Berlin Wall opened, Washington has faced nettlesome medium powers but no hostile great power, nor—with the single exception of a potential collective Arab oil embargo—any country or coalition with the power to threaten vital interests even if it became hostile. With the related exception of revolutionary Islamism (an exception whose potency should not be exaggerated), military and political threats today are local, not global, and have scant potential for contagion beyond their neighborhoods.

This window of extraordinary security could remain open for a long time, but not forever, if only because American primacy will not last forever. There are plausible threats on the horizon that are in the same league with those of the twentieth century, and some are discussed later in the book. Some of the conceivable dangers were immanent in the disputes and crises of the past two decades that are examined in the essays that follow. The difference in the post–Cold War world, however, was that policymakers had the freedom to devote most of their attention to matters that were of mild importance compared with the challenges of the past and, potentially, of the future.

## Delusions

Some mistaken resorts to force are traceable to enthusiasms common in American liberalism, enthusiasms that were liberated by the collapse of the bipolarity that had constrained them. (Liberalism here does not refer to the colloquial meaning of left-of-center in contemporary domestic politics. Rather it means the classic tradition venerating freedom, political equality, and economic openness that encompasses all of American politics and includes those we call conservatives and neoconservatives.) These enthusiasms have fed on three sets of misconceptions.

*Liberal universalism and the habit of empire.* Americans have usually thought of their political order as exceptional, but a model for what the world should become. Many of us tend to assume that deep inside every foreigner of good will must be an American struggling to get out. If other countries are given a fair chance, American exceptionalism should evolve into universal Americanism, or at least Western liberal democracy of some sort in tune with the United States. This has been the underlying political agenda in globalization to many in the U.S. foreign policy establishment, including majorities of both political parties.

The idea of an "empire of liberty" goes back to Thomas Jefferson, but for most of U.S. history this hubris was held in check by the limits of American power and the inclination to promote the American model outside of North America by example rather than by force. A century ago nationalism and crusading liberalism were given a mutually reinforcing boost by Theodore Roosevelt and Woodrow Wilson. Then, after 1945, Americans became accustomed to leading the "free world," and within the West a liberal empire became institutionalized over the course of four decades. By the end of the Cold War Washington had developed the habit of empire and turned from defending it to expanding it. The right and responsibility to advance democracy and human rights where possible were taken for granted, although there was much less agreement on whether this should be done if it required sacrifice.

The extent to which national security became tacitly identified with empire is reflected in how the structure of government defined organizations responsible for national security almost completely in terms of operation far from home rather than at our own shoreline. The National Security Council (NSC) and Department of Defense concerned themselves exclusively with defense lines far forward, on other continents, and the protection of allies, not direct defense of U.S. borders. Military forces were organized for combat in terms of a worldwide set of unified commands, each one with a huge headquarters and bureaucracy, overseeing a given foreign region (EUCOM for Europe, PACOM for Asia, CENTCOM for the Middle East, SOUTHCOM for Latin America, and AFRICOM for Africa), and each with a four-star military proconsul overshadowing U.S. ambassadors in the area. When terrorists brought foreign attacks to the continental United States for the first time since the War of 1812, brand new organizations were created to handle the threat—a Homeland Security Council, as if the security of the United States itself was not already in the portfolio of the NSC; a new military NORTHCOM for North America, as if the U.S. armed forces had not previously been concerned with operating on home territory; and a new Department of Homeland Security, as if protection of the homeland was not the responsibility of the Department of Defense. No other country in the world, not even the former European imperial powers, has a military structure organized so thoroughly in terms of functions so far from home.

*War as policing.* For some time after the collapse of the Soviet Union and Marxist ideology, unipolarity obscured the crucial difference between war and law enforcement. In a liberal world order the rule of law is the norm, and in a unipolar world the chief enforcer is far more powerful than any violator. In contrast to the Cold War, when the Universal Declaration of Human Rights and the United Nations Charter were recognized as pious but impotent norms that took a back seat to the competition for allies, those who rejected the rule of these documents came to be considered lawless and subject to discipline. To many policymakers, especially after the first Bush administration in the early 1990s, U.S. military force was an instrument that could be used to impose law, democratic norms, and world order—in effect, the United States could be "globocop." This role might be played in concert with the "international community," via the United Nations or the North Atlantic Treaty Organization (NATO), but participation in collective actions did not derail the misconception that force should usually be used lightly because that idea is now even more ingrained in allied governments.

Some attempts to use force in this multilateral and limited manner—such as in the second phase of the Somalia intervention in 1993, "pinprick" punishments in Bosnia before 1995, or the initial assault on Serbia in 1999—proved ineffectual or surprisingly costly. This was because U.S. and NATO forces found themselves acting not as police suppressing individuals or small groups, but in acts of war, confronting organized mass resistance by force of arms. This was discomfiting to those who unleash force for humanitarian reasons because they do not like the idea of killing people and breaking things even for good purposes. They hope for clean application of force without casualties, or at least combat in which only the guilty are destroyed and large numbers of civilian deaths are an aberration.

War, in contrast, inevitably hurts the innocent as well—and as anyone who has studied or experienced war will insist to those who hope otherwise, the stress is on *inevitably*. Deliberate targeting of civilians may be prevented, but the nature of real war is that accidental collateral damage is a regular cost of doing business. Accidental death and destruction can be reduced by improved technology or restraints on strategy, but it cannot yet be eliminated in any war of consequence. Law enforcement aims to protect the rights and interests of individuals by apprehending transgressors and holding them to account for their crimes, and letting the guilty go free rather than unfairly harm an individual innocent. In war, the ultimate communitarian enterprise, the priorities are reversed; many individual interests are sacrificed for the nation's collective interest. Soldiers die for their countrymen, not themselves, and civilians caught in cross fires are simply out of luck. This fundamental empirical difference between policing and war is not easily grasped by people of good will. Before unleashing force they need to recognize that war by its nature entails terrible injustice to many individuals, and that acceptance of that injustice as the lesser evil is implicit in any decision to send the military into combat.

Force undertaken as police action that turns into real war is a distasteful shock to politicians who expect that force can be used without injustice. The most salient characteristic of war as distinguished from policing is that it involves *killing*. If politicians are to authorize war they must endorse killing. Many are reluctant to admit this. As a result, U.S. leaders have sometimes unleashed force, then recoiled from results and held back from decisive resolution of the issue. In short, they sometimes did not grasp what war is and stumbled into it irresponsibly.

*Control on the cheap and primacy with purity.* Confusing police action with war is a symptom of general underestimation of the price of using force effectively and exploiting primacy to reshape the world. Underestimation was fatefully encouraged by the stunning success that marked the transition to the post–Cold War world: the 1991 war against Iraq. This was a powerful exception to the rule, an overwhelming, easy victory at low cost, executed under virtually complete control of the United States. That huge success, however, was due to sober restraint. George H. W. Bush (hereafter, Bush I) did not succumb to victory disease and did not grab for more gains than the liberation of Kuwait and reduction of Iraqi power—a cautious strategy to which his son should have kept.

To impose justice, stability, and cooperation on oppressed or ungoverned nations is usually a tall order. It is hardly ever done cheaply, especially against nationalist resistance. If accomplishing the task in some given case is likely to require twenty years of effort, hundreds of thousands of forces, and hundreds of billions of dollars, it is reckless to start the effort if one is only willing to commit less. Or if the strategic objective is just to coerce an adversary, it is usually a mistake to apply force abstemiously rather than with overwhelming power. Coercion is hard to accomplish without instilling overwhelming fear. As Clausewitz says, "A short jump is easier than a long one: but no one wanting to get across a wide ditch would begin by jumping half-way."[6]

The logic of democracy, however, provides all too many reasons for jumping halfway. Either extreme alternative—inaction or overwhelming force—poses severe costs. Compromise is the natural political solution to ambivalence, the way to avoid facing either of those costs fully, at least in the short term. At the time decisions on force are made, avoiding the immediate extreme costs seems the most pressing necessity, and the long-term costs of indecisive war do not seem to be the necessary result of compromise. The long-term costs do not become evident until the compromise option is tried and fails, often after the authorities who make the decision have passed from the scene and handed the problem to successors.

Force and coercion are brutal by definition. Military effectiveness thus requires some measure of deliberate and willing brutality. Even then, the vagaries of politics, organization, culture, and individual leadership can derail a carefully constructed strategy. Any significant resort to force will hurt people on a large scale, without definite assurance of achieving its purpose. For these reasons force should be used less frequently, with better reason, and with more conscious willingness to pay a high price than it has been in many cases since the Cold War.

## DILEMMAS

Force is rarely better than a blunt instrument. There is no consistent formula for success, and many strategies risk counterproductive results. As with many of the most difficult challenges in politics, leaders facing the question of force are too often damned if they do and damned if they don't, and too often reduced to working for the lesser evil. Among the dilemmas considered from different angles in all the essays that follow, several stand out.

*Prudence or paralysis.* Deciding to kill people and destroy things for some political purpose—which is what a decision to use military force is about—must be a momentous choice. There are three potential outcomes from application of force, only one of which is better than refraining: the results can prove (1) effective, achieving the political objective; (2) ineffective, but leaving things no worse than the status quo ante; or (3) worse than ineffective (counterproductive). The currency of death and destruction, and inevitable uncertainty about what the results will be, mean that, although force need not always be the last resort, the presumption should usually be against it unless the alternatives are unambiguously worse.

While action poses risks, however, inaction does too. Just as policymakers can never be certain that combat will make the situation better, they cannot be certain that refraining will not make it worse. Sober sensitivity to the drawbacks of force may underwrite excessive passivity. There are few cases in which policymakers can know with confidence that the results of war will be not only positive but low in cost; otherwise, the targets of force would usually concede without a fight. So a decision on force is a gamble, but there are no accepted rules for judging the odds of success, or accepted standards for what odds are too low to justify the gamble.

*Counterterrorism and unconventional warfare: attrition or antagonism?* Straightforward conventional wars like the first against Iraq in 1991 may kill many soldiers, but often the victims are mostly soldiers, who are always considered legitimate targets. Unconventional, irregular, or asymmetric warfare, in contrast, takes place in the midst of civilian populations, and collateral damage is usually extensive—and it is unconventional warfare that is most common in the unipolar world. Civilian casualties anger and alienate precisely the people whose loyalty is the main stake in the conflict. Holding back from combat because of the risk of accidental civilian casualties, however, gives insurgents or terrorists running room and respite from attrition and raises the combat risks to American soldiers. Even strenuous efforts to avoid collateral damage often fail, as mixed results from stringent U.S. rules of engagement in Afghanistan showed after the move to a revised counterinsurgency strategy.

This problem poses the risk of strategic judo—that rebels may use the strength of American military power against its purpose.[7] Combat action that is effective in direct attrition of the enemy but which mobilizes more locals against the American cause defeats itself. There is yet no sure standard for estimating how to strike the balance of risk between ineffective and counterproductive employment of military options.

*Overwhelming force or small footprint?* This dilemma follows from the last. Force is most effective in direct suppression of opposition when it is massive and overpowering. Force used in small doses or hesitantly may fail to conquer, prolonging indecisive combat and thereby additional carnage. Or if the aim is coercion, force may fail by imposing insufficient costs and signaling weakness to enemy decision-makers. Overwhelming force is likely to make conventional war shorter, and sometimes less destructive in the end. As the problem of strategic judo indicates, however, in unconventional warfare the odds of winning the allegiance of a local population may decline with the size of a military presence and the scale of military operations. Minimizing alien intrusion and applying no more force than absolutely necessary may raise the odds of political success. Some situations fall between either category, leaving the tradeoff hard to calculate.

*Humanitarian projects: consistent or capricious selection?* Some cases of humanitarian emergency, such as starvation in Somalia in 1992, seem so easily relieved by minimal military effort that moral interests mandate a decision to act. Or others, such as the genocide in Rwanda in 1994, are so horribly egregious that holding back from intervention is inhumanly callous. The first type, however, can evolve into more difficult ventures, as happened in the attempt to impose political order in Somalia after the food relief, and the gravity of the second type may not be evident at the outset. Between these extremes, moreover, lie a huge number of humanitarian crises of varying severity. The United States cannot act against all of them but should not foreswear acting in all of them. A simple standard for selection in principle is to act where the benefits are high and costs low. But this is often hard to know in advance, so choosing some cases for intervention but not others may be arbitrary. Policymakers may justify their selection on grounds that they know the right case when they see it, but such a standard is an instinct, not a strategy.

*Deterrence or provocation?* The most important uncertainty in dealing with adversaries is the "security dilemma"—determining whether they are evil aggressors bent on conquest or coercion, or defensive powers who prefer the status quo but feel insecure and arm or exert pressure as a precaution. The first must be deterred or defeated; the second may be better handled by reassurance. After Sarajevo in 1914 European governments rushed to combat when reciprocal restraint and sensitivity to the security dilemma might have avoided the catastrophe that followed; in 1938 at Munich the British and French avoided that mistake but made the opposite one, failing to recognize the unlimited aggression in Hitler's plans.

How can policymakers know for sure which type of adversary they face? If the diagnosis is wrong, the United States risks either being exploited by an aggressor it mistakenly thinks is defensive or provoking an unnecessary conflict with a peacefully motivated opponent that it treats as an aggressor. In coming years the question of diagnosis will be crucial in regard to China. Excessive emphasis on deterrence could make conflict a self-fulfilling prophecy as China chafes and pushes back; insufficient emphasis on deterrence could make China more opportunistic, adventurous, and willing to risk conflict.

*Application of force: formulas or flexibility?* There is a chasm between policy decision and military implementation. The complexity of any important strategic situation—technical limitations of modern military instruments and support structures, political context on both sides of a confrontation, quality and strength of an adversary's capabilities and will, unique opportunities or obstacles that emerge as a case develops, problems in communication, and so on—makes it extremely difficult to keep military action in line with policy objectives. Policymakers who lack military expertise and military technocrats who lack political sensitivity can all too easily proceed without making their moves consistent with each other's imperatives and constraints. Military professionals, keenly aware of how blunt an instrument military force is and how hard it is to control, crave clarity and simplicity in strategy and prefer to rely on tried and true drill-book formulas for combat effectiveness. Their priority is to minimize friction, avoid surprises, and keep control of military outcomes. They want war plans that account for all actions through all phases from beginning to a clearly defined end, so that they can do their jobs by the numbers. Politicians, in contrast crave flexibility, tentativeness, and adaptability of military operations, so they can raise or lower aims as conditions permit, take advantage of opportunities as they emerge, or back away from problems if they run into trouble. These natural differences in orientation and responsibility create permanent tension between those who decide to use force and those who carry out the decision.

*Priorities: benefits or costs?* If an interest is vital, the United States should invest blood and treasure to protect it with little regard for limits. Although rhetoric always cites any interest as vital, however, few truly are; "vital" literally means *necessary to life*. For most interests the main policy question about committing force is the balance of costs and benefits when neither are extreme. Hawks usually care most about benefits, doves most about costs. Neither benefits nor costs, however, are easily estimated in advance.

Benefits are hard to calculate because they depend on counterfactual assumptions (what would have happened if the policy implemented had been different), or because they involve subjective judgments about effects on foreign governments' policies and motivations, or because they involve unquantifiable moral interests. Costs are hard to estimate for the same reasons, and because it is impossible to know for sure how much blood and treasure must be spent to achieve the purpose. The most fundamental material costs, however, are quite clearly denominated in numbers: casualties and dollars expended. Sometimes costs prove happily lower than anticipated, as in the 1991 Persian Gulf War. More often they are higher than anticipated, as in Somalia, Kosovo, the second war against Iraq, and Afghanistan after 2002.

Such miscalculations follow easily from focusing on the balance of power rather than the balance of stakes. American primacy highlights the overwhelming disparity of power between Washington and whatever opponents it engages. On their home turf, however, the locals have a far higher stake in the outcome, and thus more incentive to bleed for their cause. These contests can then become limited conflicts for the United States but total wars for the locals, escalating into more than Washington bargained for.

*Control without control.* The use of force has a political object, so when Washington uses force it is with the aim of controlling a political outcome. As the only superpower operating in the post–Cold War world, the United States has had objectives that have not been simply matters of self-defense, as are those of most normal countries that do not aspire to control more than their own territory and political autonomy. Rather, the United States has aimed to shape world order and protect or reform other countries. A prime ingredient in this agenda is promotion of democracy in countries in which American forces intervene. All too often, however, these two objectives—shaping outcomes according to an American vision and democratization—work against each other. If democratization is achieved, Washington loses control of policy decisions and implementation in the country. Local politicians may or may not move their societies in directions consistent with American judgments of proper reform. At the same time that the United States loses control, it gets stuck with blame for what happens in the country as long as U.S. intervention continues. Thus the independent Afghan government that followed the ouster of the Taliban descended into catastrophic corruption, incompetence, and double-dealing, and many Afghans blamed American intervention for the mess in their country.

As long as the United States plays the role of superpower it is vulnerable to blame whether it promotes democracy or not, because a superpower has to do political and military business with all sorts of regimes. For decades Washington supported the government of Hosni Mubarak in Egypt, then scrambled to repudiate it when popular revolution broke out. Shifting gears to support revolution makes sense when there is hope that it can prove benign, and support for democracy is necessary despite the risks that it will come back to bite. But the United States will be criticized for sins of control even when it does not control, and lack of control doubles the risk when American military forces are entangled in direct efforts to pacify local conflicts.

The essays in this book explore these issues and elaborate on skepticism about American force. This should not obscure the reality that force is sometimes used for the right reasons and with satisfactory results. I am a genuine admirer of the American armed forces and their accomplishments and am happy when they are employed by political authorities who know what they are doing. The good news should not be no news, but the good news is not the focus of this book.

The underlying argument in the book is not consistent and unequivocal, as it should be were it to offer a powerful theory; hard problems in real life never admit of simple solutions without exception or qualification. But the essays that follow oppose most of the message of officials and analysts who support American efforts to build (either unilaterally or multilaterally) a liberal empire. The main targets are the presidential administrations of Bill Clinton and George W. Bush (Bush II); I am less critical of Bush I, whose team was a bit more prudent, or Barack Obama, who inherited the worst messes he had to confront, and who at least had the good sense to oppose the worst decision since the Vietnam War, the invasion of Iraq. Pundits or scholars on the wrong side of issues in the chapters that follow are most of the prominent neoconservatives, liberal hawks, and fervent multilateralists, many of whom would be outraged to be lumped together, but who for their different reasons have favored the use of armed forces to further expansive rather than just narrow conceptions of security. My arguments are more in tune with those of Andrew Bacevich, Barry Posen, Stephen Walt, Christopher Layne, Eric Nordlinger, Lawrence Korb, and other realist doves, cautious liberals, and paleoconservatives.[8]

The essays in this book touch on a variety of issues and cases, but the point of departure is one conviction: a hawkish stance on national security policy made good sense in the Cold War, but winning that war should have made a bigger difference than it did. There should have been a bigger relief from military activism after the epochal global threat to liberal democracy and American interests went away. To put that case in context, the next chapter surveys the background from which the twenty-first-century security environment came and the evolution of American strategy for the use of force that established important habits of mind that lived on after the dangers that caused them.

# 2 | POLICY MILESTONES
## COLD WAR ROOTS OF CONSENSUS

One main criticism of American overreaching since the Cold War, coming from paleoconservatives and liberal realists, is that genuine national interests do not require expensive activism, and such activism begs for pushback from foreigners who do not want Americans meddling in their business. A different criticism, from mainstream liberals, is that neoconservative zealots tore U.S. policy away from multilateralism and the binding to international institutions that made U.S. leadership both legitimate and effective in the second half of the twentieth century. Until the chastening events of Iraq, the second view was much closer to elite conventional wisdom than was the first.

The following survey of the Cold War background of recent policy casts doubt on the second view. On essential national security strategy, at least, there was much less genuine binding of U.S. prerogatives to international mechanisms of cooperation than institutionalist folklore holds. Differences in interpretation have been due in part to whether attention focuses on economic and diplomatic issues or military and strategic concerns, and on binding arrangements in principle or the qualifications attached to them in practice.

The balance of evidence is not absolutely clear and sometimes amounts to a glass half-full, mostly because the differences of belief and behavior of actual officials have been only matters of degree. Some emphasize multilateral cooperation; others emphasize unilateral freedom of action. With brief exceptions, however, those on both sides have sought some measure of what the others emphasize. Those concerned above all with marshalling military power against adversaries have also valued multilateral cooperation and integration of the Western alliance because such arrangements would maximize Western power and military efficiency, and those whose prime concern was the inner political solidarity of the Western alliance have still sought American freedom of action.

Politics does not stop at the water's edge, but meaningful differences are less than meet the eye. When differences in diplomatic method are put aside, both approaches have usually aimed to come out in the same place. Rather than seeing a choice between nationalism and internationalism, makers of national security strategy have usually conflated them, assuming a natural identity of interest between Americans and other right-thinking societies. Even to liberals, multilateralism has usually been a vehicle for American control (rationalized as leadership), not an alternative to it, and international institutions have been seen as enablers for American visions rather than a constraint on them. Whenever a choice did emerge between asserting American aims and deferring to allied preferences, the former almost always won out.

Early in the Cold War Dwight Eisenhower was a great promoter of transnational institutions, but for selfish American reasons. He pushed European integration as a means toward replacing bipolarity with two Western power blocs to counter the Communist East, and he did this primarily to reduce the American military burden. This aim was abandoned after 1960 as Kennedy and his successors pushed permanent American leadership, cemented by permanent military presence in Europe.[1] When bipolarity ended, in turn, the United States did not just remain engaged in the old Western alliance but pumped it up as the vanguard of political globalization. Yet this was still multilateralism under American tutelage, with American primacy uncompromised and, most Americans assumed, welcomed.

To see how policy metamorphosed after the Cold War from defense of the West to extension of the West, the following pages survey conceptual underpinnings of national security strategy; landmarks in the most general level, grand strategy; problems in translating grand strategy into workable programs at the operational level; and the net importance of unilateral as opposed to multilateral approaches to strategy. To illustrate themes as well as to lay out crucial points in history, each section features a different aspect of NATO, the most important and enduring vehicle of American strategy.

## The Power of Order or the Order of Power?

After the 1940s there was a basic consensus on two overarching objectives of national security policy: (1) development of a liberal political and economic world order, and (2) containment and deterrence of communist power. Two other objectives became important in more recent times: (3) assured access to Middle Eastern oil, and (4) attrition of anti-American terrorists. The first of these objectives, liberal world order, is endorsed rhetorically by all and engages the passions of many in the elites who pay attention to foreign affairs. In actual strategy, however, it has been significant only when its requirements have been consistent with those of the capacity for force and coercion.

The reverse is not true; force and coercion have sometimes been used in ways inconsistent with liberal visions. The mission of cooperative world order is endorsed by all in principle. In practice, it does not take precedence over the development and assertion of American power. Curiously, this remains as true in the twenty-first century as in the Cold War. The requiem for national sovereignty declared by theorists of globalization has proved to be premature. In national security, if not in other aspects of foreign policy, American policymakers have promoted cooperative world order as long as the order does things the American way.

For most of the Cold War the distinction between world order and other security objectives did not matter. The diffuse objectives were complementary, the strategies for pursuing them were simply added together, and controversies were about secondary issues rather than fundamental aims. Isolationists and Marxists were stranded on the fringes of political debate, mainstream conservatives and liberals were all internationalists, and the importance of alliances to the anticommunist cause suppressed tension between nationalism and multilateralism. This was the Cold War consensus. Partisans argued about which aims should get more attention at the margin and about the relative importance of economic, political, and military means for building security, but, with the exception of the 1970s, not about fundamental aims.

Beneath the unifying consensus, however, lay a split in conceptions of what national security is about. One conception is broad, cosmopolitan, and focused on developing international institutions and mechanisms of peaceful cooperation. This conception does not distinguish national security policy very clearly from the rest of foreign policy. The other conception is narrow, nationalist, and focused on maintaining sovereignty, military power, and leverage against adversaries.[2] (Disclosure: My own views are eclectic but closer to the narrow conception.)

The broad view accepts military power as a necessity but sees it as reduced in importance after the era of world wars and buries it among a raft of other interests, such as economic prosperity, human rights, and environmental health, that are identified as elements of security.[3] This view is muted in wartime but surges back each time war ends. In this view "global governance" (in effect, the political globalization of liberalism) provides a better guarantee of American safety than does assertion of sovereign prerogatives; the most important strategies are those that maximize economic and political cooperation; and military force is best used in a system of collective security.

This view coincides with confidence that the United States has ample military security. At least for most of the time since the British burned the White House, this notion has been quite reasonable, given the blessing of huge ocean moats to the east and west and weak neighbors to the north and south. In the broad view, the main function of the U.S. military should be, in effect, policing against breaches of international law or human rights abroad. Strenuous cultivation of capability to wage large-scale war, the traditional function of military power, shows Old Thinking rooted in obsolete fixation on the balance of power among states and risks being wasteful or counterproductive.

Few of those rooted in the narrow power politics perspective pay more than glancing attention to institutions for diplomatic cooperation such as the United Nations, Organization for Security and Cooperation in Europe (OSCE), Organization of American States (OAS), or Association of Southeast Asian Nations (ASEAN), if they do not overlook them altogether. Global governance enthusiasts, in contrast, avoid focusing on specifically national security, or the institutions most associated with it. Take, for example, John Ruggie's book *Winning the Peace*. It has two chapters on security policy since 1945, entitled "Competitive Security" and "Cooperative Security," but both chapters are actually about cooperative security. The one that allegedly addresses competitive security ignores the issues that dominated the attention of policymakers, saying virtually nothing about military arrangements for deterrence and defense, war plans, or nuclear strategy. While focusing on institutions that were at most secondary concerns to

American policymakers, such as the European Atomic Energy Community (EURATOM), it ignores the main institutions founded in the same period to underwrite national security, which absorbed far more attention and resources, such as the Department of Defense, Strategic Air Command, or Central Intelligence Agency (CIA). Half of the chapter is about the United Nations, and the discussion of NATO is entirely about its political construction, not the development of its military functions.[4]

"Security," unmodified by the adjective "national," does indeed have a broad meaning.[5] Indeed, in the long run issues of "human" security like environmental health may be the most important. In the narrow view, however, *national* security properly conceived cannot be the same as *foreign policy*, which is about everything of interest to the United States in the outside world. National security is part of foreign policy—the part focused on preserving sovereignty and protecting the country from conquest, destruction, or coercion. The crucial ingredient in strategy is military power, and the principal requirement is not to engage in policing but to be ready for war. Police functions imply preponderant power and comparative ease of enforcement by the international majority against deviant governments or groups if the will to act can be found. War is far more challenging. It implies conflict between adversaries who both believe that their capability or strategy gives them a chance to win.

The narrow view in no way denies the importance of political cooperation with other countries or of economic interdependence, it just sees them as separate arenas, or as secondary elements of strategy for security. International institutions and cooperation are most valuable to the extent that they support American interests and facilitate the marshalling and use of power. Those attentive to power are unmoved by arguments that modern interdependence makes the priority of sovereignty passé because "when the crunch comes, states remake the rules by which other actors operate," and "to be sovereign and to be dependent are not contradictory conditions." Rather, "to say that a state is sovereign means that it decides for itself how it will cope with its internal and external problems."[6]

Nor should national security be automatically identified with international security, although it almost always is in American political discourse. The interest of the American nation may or may not coincide with the security of other nations, desirable as others' security may be. Many in the foreign policy elite do not accept this distinction, and it has seldom been reflected in policy over the past sixty years, but it is well understood by the large segments of the general public that Walter Russell Mead dubs "Jeffersonian" and "Jacksonian." Indeed, the mass public tends to be more unapologetically nationalistic than the attentive foreign policy elite.[7] In the sixteen elections since World War II voters selected a presidential candidate who was clearly less nationalistic than his opponent only twice, in 1964 and 2008. (And in those cases Johnson and Obama presented themselves as reliable patriots but appeared less fervent only because Goldwater and McCain seemed more extreme.) Because truly national security is genuinely popular with the mass public, liberal rhetoric tends to fold all foreign policy goals into that category rather than recognize national security as a distinct subset of concerns about political independence, control of territory, physical safety from attack, and basic economic viability.

Across the political spectrum American elites do tend to conflate U.S. national security with international security. For liberals this means that what is good for the world is good for the United States, and for conservatives it means that what is good for the United States is good for the world. This is not merely a cute nuance of difference, but a significant difference in attitudes and priorities. In practice, however, the policy implied is often the same for both assumptions. The conflation of national interest and international order flows from the economic conceptions and political culture that define American identity. As Louis Hartz wrote, liberalism (in the classical sense) so thoroughly suffuses our society that Americans do not even recognize it as an ideology rather than the self-evident natural order of things.[8]

As long as the costs of conflation are low, this assumed identification is logical and popular. When costs rise to unexpected levels—as, for example, in the late stages of the Indochina war, the 1983 intervention in Beirut, the 1993 intervention in Somalia, or the wars in Iraq and Afghanistan—the difference between national interest and interest in world order explodes into view. By 2010 half of respondents in one Pew Research Center poll signed on to the proposition that the United States "should mind its own business internationally and let other countries get along the best they can on their own."[9]

## THE ENDURING PRIORITY OF MILITARY INSTRUMENTS

Strategy is not a policy objective. It is a *plan* for using capabilities to *achieve* policy objectives. The capabilities deployed are primarily economic, military, and secret political instruments. Strategies are to objectives what means are to ends. Pundits often confuse the difference and speak of objectives and strategies interchangeably. They focus on the aspirations of strategy more than on the actions required to achieve them, on strategy in theory more than in practice. Even political leaders usually stop short of following strategic decisions through to the end and concentrate on charting a course they expect minions to find ways to implement. The chasm between decision and implementation is the main reason statesmen disappoint themselves.

Strategy in *theory* is whatever the government's political leaders believe it to be, which is usually something very general if not vague. This is often called grand strategy. Strategy in *practice* is what the government's professional diplomats, soldiers, and intelligence officers actually produce in specific programs, plans, and operations. As in most of life, the levels of theory and practice in strategy are not always aligned.

Politicians and their principal lieutenants concentrate on grand strategy, general ideas for coordinating resources, alliances, and operations in a general vision. Political leaders also have a natural stake in pleasing many constituencies, so official declarations err on the side of inclusiveness. The annual report mandated by Congress, *National Security Strategy of the United States*, has sometimes been a Christmas tree on which every interest group hangs its foreign policy concerns. This report rarely says much that really illuminates national security strategy, although it sometimes provides a useful bumper-sticker version of official ideas.

The driver's manual version of strategy, for where the rubber meets the road, comes closer to the level of analysis in Clausewitz's conception, which defines strategy as "the use of engagements for the object of the war."[10] Strategy at this level translates aspirations into specific concrete initiatives, but in practice translation is sometimes garbled. Worse, operational imperatives may take on a life of their own and produce an emergent strategy different from what political leaders explicitly plot.

What instruments of policy are most important for security? Priorities depend on what arena is the center ring. The broad view of security emphasizes the economic and ideological realms and the narrow view emphasizes the military. This difference in focus shapes the concepts that both apply to understanding the international system. Those focused on political economy cited the early Cold War period as one of U.S. hegemony because of American economic strength. Specialists in strategic studies, in contrast, defined the international structure then as bipolarity. They never dreamed of using the word "hegemony" to describe the American global position until the collapse of the Soviet pole (although they could recognize American hegemony *within* the Western alliance). For those focused on security rather than prosperity, high politics and strategy were about deterring adversaries and influencing neutrals who might tilt either way in the global struggle between opposed socioeconomic systems. This meant concentrating strategically on those adversaries and neutrals—the Second World of communism and the Third World of less developed and aspiring new nations—that together had most of the world's people, land, and natural resources. American economic power was most relevant for generating political influence, and especially military capability.

The broad economy-oriented view of security, in contrast, fastened on relations with First World allies, the countries that have most of the world's money. In this view the United States had global hegemony in the earlier period because of its economic dominance, and that hegemony eroded as other economies recovered and grew after World War II. Military power was of interest not as the essential concern of foreign policy but as a background condition, shielding the economic and political development that was the important story.[11] Indeed, liberal theorists of international politics argued that growing interdependence made force obsolescent but they had little to say about what military policy should be or when, where, or how force should be unleashed. Yet although economic and diplomatic instruments of strategy have always been important, and were at the forefront in the late 1940s, for most of the time it is the planning and managing of force and coercion that has been at the center of national security policy. Surprisingly, this still proved true after the Cold War. What demonstrates the persistent dominance of military concerns?

First, government structure. The National Security Act of 1947, the foundation that still organizes government for this subject, established brandnew institutions focused primarily on dealing with the danger of war: the Department of Defense, Central Intelligence Agency, and National Security Council. Periodic reorganizations of these institutions—for example, the Defense Department Reorganization Act of 1958, the Goldwater-Nichols bill of 1986, establishment of the Department of Homeland Security after September 11th, and the Intelligence Reform and Terrorism Prevention Act of 2004, which reorganized the intelligence community—have always received far more attention than changes in the apparatus for making and implementing international economic policy.

Second, resource allocation. Defense and intelligence budgets are where the overwhelming bulk of national resources for foreign affairs have gone: many trillions of dollars since World War II, dwarfing expenditures for foreign development assistance, the United Nations, public diplomacy, or other nonmilitary aspects of foreign policy.

Third, rules of engagement. In the realm of security, the United States tends to conform law to policy rather than the reverse. That is, government interpretations of law are made to accord with strategic imperatives and preferred instruments, or, when deemed necessary, laws or legal institutions other than those of the United States itself are simply disregarded. The most extreme example was the rationalization of torturous interrogation techniques by Bush administration lawyers after September 11th, but less extreme examples abound. The most important long-standing evidence of the priority of policy is the institutionalization of intelligence operations. Although intelligence collection and covert political intervention throughout the past half-century have followed U.S. law with few exceptions, they routinely violate the laws of other countries through operations in those countries.[12]

Fourth, the regular refocusing prompted by crises. Challenges to strategic emphasis on military power usually wear longer in rhetoric than in actual strategy. Liberal views of security priorities have been periodically ascendant, only to be regularly shoved aside by forcible jolts—the Soviet invasion of Afghanistan, Iraq's conquest of Kuwait, Al Qaeda's assault on the Twin Towers and Pentagon. "In placid times, statesmen and commentators employ the rich vocabulary of clichés that cluster around the notion of global interdependence. Like a flash of lightning, crises reveal the landscape's real features."[13]

The persistent importance of the military dimension does not result just from periodic jolts. Americans evidently like having and using military power, even when the need for it plummets. The pace of high defense spending continued long after what originally drove it (the Soviet Union's five million men under arms and thousands of nuclear weapons) ceased to be a threat, and when counters to the new principal threat (secretive terrorist groups) lay more in intelligence and unconventional special operations than in regular military forces. A decade into the twenty-first century the

United States spends almost 5 percent of gross domestic product (GDP) on defense. This is less than during the Cold War, but it yields an absolute amount that is close to half of all military spending in the world.

The survey that follows begins with important strategic initiatives in the economic and political realms and then concentrates on the military dimension of strategy. At the level of grand strategy the story is straightforward, as initiatives such as the Truman Doctrine, Marshall Plan, NATO, rapprochement with China, arms control with the Soviet Union, and NATO expansion were clear commitments to pursue clear goals. Grand strategy does not show much, however, about what strategy actually accomplishes. When we move to more specific initiatives meant to give practical force to lofty changes of direction, the story becomes more complicated. Alliance diplomacy, domestic politics, bureaucratic processes, and civil–military relations confuse the translation of general strategic concepts into actual plans and capabilities. In real life the glittering rhetoric of bold strategic innovation often overlays confusion, hesitancy, and inertia. The evolution of NATO's strategy of "flexible response" illustrates this tricky reality and serves as a reminder to beware of the prevalent tendency to confuse objectives with strategy, and strategic principles with operational practice.

## COLD WAR MILESTONES: GRAND STRATEGY

Throughout the Cold War economic and political instruments were secondary but significant elements in U.S. strategy: financial aid to buttress pro-Western governments, and information programs to combat the appeal of communist ideology. In the very earliest stage of the Cold War, however, before the war scare of 1948, economic and political approaches dominated grand strategy. For those who identified U.S. national security with liberal world order, the founding acts and longest-lasting initiatives occurred even before the Cold War. The Bretton Woods conference of 1944 formed new economic institutions—the International Monetary Fund and the World Bank—to create stable exchange rates and more international trade, while the establishment of the United Nations in 1945 aimed to preserve peace politically through a quasi-collective security system based on a concert of great powers. For those focused on the balance of power, the prime economic initiative was the Marshall Plan, which fortified allies by stabilizing their societies. The prime political strategy was not reliance on collective security or overt propaganda, but the girding of alliances and exploitation of covert political interventions in countries faced with strong communist movements.[14]

After U.S. policy toward the USSR hardened in 1946, national security planners were uncertain about whether the Soviet threat was primarily military or ideological. In early 1947 the Truman Doctrine launched support of Greece and Turkey against internal and external communist pressure. The Marshall Plan then supplied capital to revitalize European economies. The State Department pushed postwar plans for a liberal international economic system in order to avoid repeating the history of the interwar period.[15] If, as Robert Pollard says, "the key element" of policy in the early Cold War was "reliance upon economic power to achieve strategic aims," this followed a prime rule of strategy in the broadest sense: rely on comparative advantage, fight on favorable terms. But the Marshall Plan was followed by decades in which military instruments dominated national security strategy. The economic arena was central only temporarily in 1947 because of the expectation, soon dashed, that a Soviet military threat was not imminent and could be checked by the American atomic monopoly.[16]

The most novel departure in strategy before the full militarization of the Cold War was the plan to influence internal political developments in foreign countries by clandestine means. In December 1947 the National Security Council approved the document known as NSC 4/A, the first formal plan for American covert psychological operations, just as the NSC was advising the president on how to oppose the influence of the Italian Communist Party. The incompatibility of this instrument with formal international norms was well recognized, as indicated by the reluctance of government departments to give it a home. George Kennan wanted the State Department to control covert operations, but Secretary of State George Marshall vetoed that arrangement. Director of Central Intelligence Roscoe Hillenkoetter also resisted but got stuck with it; responsibility for the function was vested in the new CIA. Half a year later the NSC endorsed NSC 10/2, which went beyond secret propaganda to political and economic intervention: funding parties in foreign elections, economic warfare, and paramilitary assistance to underground movements inside the communist bloc.[17] Thus began the history of covert action as a staple of strategy, a compromise option between sending the marines or doing nothing in response to unwelcome developments abroad. Covert action projects quickly became extensive and routine, used throughout the world. It was the routinization of this instrument of secret coercion that gave clearest meaning to the term "Cold War."

The war scare of 1948, prompted by the blockade of Berlin and the communist coup in Czechoslovakia, as well as the Soviet detonation of a nuclear weapon in 1949, ended confidence that the Soviet offensive would be only ideological, rather than military. The year 1949 brought the most significant and enduring strategic innovation of the Cold War: establishment of the North Atlantic Treaty Organization. NATO superseded the 1948 Brussels Treaty of alliance among Britain, France, and the Benelux countries. Although earlier verbal commitments had been given by James Byrnes in Stuttgart in 1946 and by Truman and Marshall in 1948, NATO committed the United States by treaty to the defense of Western Europe in an "entangling alliance" for the first time in peacetime history.

The automaticity of American commitment via article 5 was the main point of the North Atlantic Treaty, the sharpest departure from American tradition, and the most controversial. Wary senators seized on article 11's assurance that treaty provisions would be implemented by the parties "in accordance with their respective constitutional processes" as an escape hatch.[18] Often forgotten in later years, article 11 is a reminder that the United States bound itself, but not irrevocably. In the beginning NATO remained a traditional "guaranty pact," an American promise to come into the fray in the event of war. Only later did it become a uniquely integrated organization with U.S. forces deployed in strength on the front line before war, and an articulated multinational command structure functioning in peacetime.[19] When this happened, however, it was under strict American control, and it happened more for military reasons than for the political reasons that liberals emphasize. The political reasons were also of a different sort that are quite unfamiliar to those who celebrate the Atlantic union today.

Evolution into a genuinely institutionalized alliance, as distinct from traditional ad hoc or transient compacts, was what made NATO such an innovation in strategy. To get to that unprecedented degree of transnational military institutionalization and peacetime mobilization required a novel idea for grand strategy, and a jolt to give the idea legs. The novel idea again came from the State Department's Policy Planning Staff, this time under Paul Nitze, in the document known as NSC 68. The Korean War provided the jolt. When Nitze's predecessor George Kennan authored the "X" article that coined the term "containment," he had in mind not military but political containment. He even opposed establishing NATO as a multilateral alliance.[20] This was because Kennan, although known as a consummate realist, had a lifelong distaste for the military and did not understand the operational need for military integration in peacetime.

Nitze's paper left Kennan's reservations in the dust and called for a new departure in American history: the fielding of large forces in being for peacetime readiness, instead of the traditional reliance on mobilization after the outbreak of war.[21] This focused the issue: "Could a democracy arm to deter or could it only arm to respond?"[22] The actual text of NSC 68, however, was mostly rhetoric, and President Truman reacted by asking for more information on the programs and costs implied. Given the need to increase taxes, and the pressure on other public spending programs that major growth in military budgets would impose, there was no formal decision to forge ahead with NSC 68's recommendations. Then the North Korean attack two months after submission of the paper galvanized the government. Despite the fact that a fair-sized war was under way in Asia, however, the resulting buildup was concentrated in NATO capabilities in Europe and nuclear striking forces.[23]

NATO's multinational command structure, unprecedented in peacetime, served two purposes. First was the efficient pooling of military power to provide readiness against what was assumed to be overwhelming Soviet superiority in conventional forces, an aim that endured to the end of the Cold War. The second purpose was to lay the groundwork for U.S. withdrawal from primary responsibility for European defense. This aim was far more significant than current memory recognizes.

The military reasons for promoting transnational integration were simple. In the event of war, the only hope for defending the inner-German border against hordes of Soviet armored divisions poised within a few hundred kilometers of the Rhine and the English Channel depended on perfect coordination of military deployments and operational doctrine and plans, and reliable mechanisms for the immediate exercise of centralized command—and this all needed to be in place *before war began* if there was to be a chance of holding the line in combat. At the same time, the American commitment to multilateralism was less than absolute. Although the alliance was integrated, integration did not mean equality. The principle was established that the Supreme Allied Commander, Europe (SACEUR) would always be an American. For the Europeans this deal made for binding of the United States to their defense, but only symbolically, because for the

Americans the deal institutionalized their control of the central function of the organization. Military integration also provided the crucial means for politically rationalizing the rearmament of West Germany—the necessary condition for building a hefty NATO force and for limiting the military load the United States would have to bear in the alliance.[24] Encasing West German forces within the institutionalized multinational command structure reduced the potential threat to the other states of Western Europe.

In short, the unprecedented size of the perceived threat from the East meant that a militarily effective NATO had to be a highly articulated, institutionalized NATO. Thus NATO was a thoroughly conservative institution as much as a liberal one. For liberals, however, organizational integration was an end in itself, institutional cement for political unity. It would create a security community, not just through European integration but through wider transatlantic integration, entwining the two sides of the Atlantic. NATO's significance in this view was more political than military, and more for keeping the U.S. role prominent than for helping it to recede.

For Dwight Eisenhower, however, the new institutional arrangements would cope with military vulnerability in a way that would allow the United States to extricate itself from the main responsibility for European defense. He made numerous statements to this effect, as when he was finishing his assignment as SACEUR in 1952: "'if in ten years, all American troops stationed in Europe have not been returned to the United States, then this whole project'—meaning the whole NATO effort—'will have failed.'"[25] Later presidents were more interested in maintaining American dominance in the alliance, and the Europeans also remained adamant about keeping U.S. power fully fused with NATO. By the 1960s permanence of U.S. deployment became accepted (although debate over the scale and conditions recurred in the 1970s with the Mansfield Amendment).

The reasons for integration that were strategic as distinct from diplomatic were highlighted by the very different development of defense arrangements on the other side of the world. When war raged in Korea while peace continued in Europe, why was the NATO model for building a security community not applied to Northeast Asia? For several reasons, but in no small part because, unlike in Europe, a military imperative did not underwrite the political impulse for integration. Integration was not needed for military purposes and would require a collaboration among diverse polities far more awkward than was possible in Europe. Geography obviated the operational need for integration. Unlike Germany and France, Japan was shielded by a buffer of water from Soviet invasion, and Korea was a peninsula with a short front that was far less of a challenge to defend than the inner German border. This situation in turn made it easier to resolve the regional political anxieties about Japanese power, since a strong Japanese military was not needed for defense of vulnerable allies in the same way that German power was needed in Europe. The United States concluded a peace treaty in which Japan embraced a demilitarized status virtually unprecedented for a great power. The reality was not as dramatic as the pacifist principle established in the peace constitution since soon after it was imposed the Korean War changed American thinking and Washington pushed Tokyo to develop "self-defense forces" that were no different from normal militaries, except in principle. Nevertheless the principle, and the limits on actual rearmament, contained Japan as effectively as integration in NATO contained the Federal Republic of Germany (FRG). In Northeast Asia the United States managed its security relations bilaterally with Korea and Japan and did not need a "NEATO" for the region.

In Southeast Asia, however, John Foster Dulles's enthusiasm for the principle of collective security did lead the United States to try to apply the NATO model. The Eisenhower administration celebrated the formation of the Southeast Asia Treaty Organization (SEATO) as Indochina was partitioned after the French defeat at Dien Bien Phu. Today SEATO sounds like a footnote in history, but it is a cautionary footnote for those enthralled with the idea of international institutions for their own sake. SEATO went along with the Australia, New Zealand, United States (ANZUS) Pact in the South Pacific, the Rio Pact in Latin America, and the Baghdad Pact and Central Treaty Organization (CENTO) in the Middle East, a proliferation of anticommunist treaties dubbed "Pactomania" by skeptics at the time. In sharp contrast to NATO, however, none of these other organizations proved significant because they performed no genuine military function. SEATO was the closest analogue to NATO, but it turned out to be an empty institution. Substituting lofty political declarations for genuine common cause in strategy, SEATO was a paper alliance that proved impotent in the unfolding of the major conflict within its area, the Indochina War of the 1960s. By 1975 SEATO was defunct, but it had not been completely harmless. Though the organization was not involved, its logic was tied to the long string of decisions that entangled the United States in commitment to a noncommunist government in South Vietnam and a pattern of de facto American unilateralism covered by a fig leaf of token multilateral support—a phenomenon seen again after 2003 in the war in Iraq.

In terms of grand strategy, nothing important changed for the fifteen years after 1954, although containment was played out in a few harrowing crises, many adjustments in particular strategies and programs, and a prolonged war in Indochina. The consensus on resisting communist "wars of national liberation" did underwrite one departure in specific military strategy, the Kennedy administration's promulgation of counterinsurgency doctrine, beginning officially with National Security Action Memorandum (NSAM) 2 in 1961.[26] Kennedy sponsored a higher profile for unconventional warfare training and counterguerrilla operations, symbolized in the invigoration of Army Special Forces and intensification of CIA paramilitary programs. This guidance, however, did not take hold within the American military. By 1965 the war became a conventional one. After years of inconclusive military investment and the shock of the 1968 Tet Offensive, disillusionment over Vietnam temporarily broke the national security consensus for strategic activism.

In 1969 the Nixon (or Guam) Doctrine refocused U.S. security commitments in the Third World to assist local allies and rely on them to supply the manpower for peripheral wars.[27] In the central arena, the policy of détente aimed to cool military competition and stabilize relations with a Soviet Union seen as ascendant. The most significant result was the pair of nuclear arms control agreements signed in Moscow in 1972, especially the Anti-Ballistic Missile (ABM) Treaty. This represented acceptance of a condition of "mutual assured destruction," and codified publicly the abandonment of the long-standing strategy of maintaining meaningful nuclear superiority.[28] Détente was deceptive from the beginning, however, as the two sides failed to make clear a mutual understanding of the meaning of the Helsinki Agreement or the acceptable limits of political competition in the Third World. Within a decade détente was repudiated and the Cold War reenergized.

The most significant departure in grand strategy between the formation of NATO and the end of the Cold War was the rapprochement with China symbolized in the 1972 Shanghai Communiqué. It is hard to remember forty years later how bold this move was, hard to remember that in the 1960s Americans thought of Communist China as every bit as wild and crazy as they later thought of Saddam Hussein's Iraq, Iran, or North Korea. This reversal made "triangular diplomacy" a potent strategy for constraining Moscow. Overnight the tables turned militarily for the superpowers. In contrast to the 1950s and 1960s, it was no longer Washington that had to plan for a two-front war, but Moscow. In the 1970s and 1980s a full one-fourth of Soviet army divisions were deployed on the Sino–Soviet border. This rebalancing of the strategic equation rationalized the change in notional requirements for American conventional forces that budget pressures made necessary anyway, scaling down from the overambitious Kennedy administration standard of capabilities to fight "2½ Wars" simultaneously (meaning major wars against the Soviet Union and China and a minor war someplace like Cuba) to "1½ Wars."[29]

The Carter administration was the first to turn military planning toward the Persian Gulf. In 1977 a Presidential Review Memorandum (PRM 10) and subsequent Presidential Directive (PD 18) directed development of capabilities for rapid deployment to the region, although the Pentagon did little to implement the directive until after the Iranian Revolution.[30] The other major departure under Carter was the promotion of human rights abroad (mandated in PD 30 in 1978), consistent with the broad conception of national security.

Ronald Reagan accentuated the return to vigorous anti-Soviet policy that congealed in the last year of the Carter administration. Rhetoric was more strident, defense budgets were higher, and some actions (as in Central America) would not have been taken by a different administration, but the change was one of degree rather than of kind. In specific military strategy, however, the Strategic Defense Initiative (SDI) did constitute serious change. Research on active defense against missile attack (which had continued since the ABM Treaty and was funded before SDI) had been for Nixon, Ford, and Carter a hedge against uncertainty. For Reagan, antimissile defense became a high priority to be achieved as soon as possible. Beginning the process that culminated twenty years later in abrogation of the ABM Treaty, SDI moved away from the reliance on arms control that had taken hold in the early 1970s.

## From Bumper Sticker to Driver's Manual: The Case of NATO's Flexible Response Doctrine

When layers of rhetoric are peeled away and attention shifts from declarations to implementation, even the most important strategic plans can prove to be inconsistent, inadequate, or incredible. Yet even then they may not fail. Consider the forty-year effort to develop NATO military strategies and plans for war and, thereby, to prevent war via deterrence.

With the exception of counterinsurgency doctrine in the 1960s, almost all major controversies about Cold War military strategy, including nuclear deterrence and arms control, were rooted in dilemmas about war plans for defense of Western Europe. If Soviet capabilities for conventional war in Europe were overwhelmingly superior, as prevailing opinion in the West always assumed, could NATO build conventional military power to match the threat? If doing so was too expensive to bear, how could the United States devise options for escalation—the threat to retaliate by initiating nuclear strikes deliberately in the face of successful Soviet conventional attack—that would substitute for confidence in conventional defense? These questions underlay most debates about American military spending because more than half of the defense budget could be attributed at least indirectly to the NATO mission.

These questions about conventional defense options also drove most debates about nuclear strategy as a whole and underlay all the anxieties and controversies about the danger of apocalyptic destruction. Requirements for simply deterring an unprovoked Soviet first strike against the continental United States by the threat of devastating retaliation against the USSR were not terribly demanding. In the face of Soviet retaliatory capability, however, it was far harder to make credible the American promises to escalate to attacks on the Soviet interior as the "seamless web" of NATO doctrine envisioned. As long as the Cold War lasted the strategic dilemma— whether to derange Western economies by mobilizing on the same scale as the Soviet Union or to risk suicide by turning a conventional war into a nuclear war—was never resolved by any of the adjustments of strategy that were episodically proclaimed. All solutions devised were temporary because they proved conceptually frightening, diplomatically divisive, militarily awkward, or economically insupportable. At its center, the grand strategy of containment rested for decades on a terribly wobbly foundation of specific military strategy. Conservatives erred by exaggerating the Soviets' conventional military superiority in Europe. Liberals erred by wanting to substitute conventional deterrence for nuclear escalation, while still keeping defense budgets low. And throughout, the polite fiction of transnational solidarity overlay a quite divisive reality—the difference between

American and European strategic preferences, reflecting the geographically determined difference in their military vulnerabilities.

At the 1952 Lisbon Conference NATO resolved to build conventional forces—nearly ninety divisions and ten thousand aircraft—that could hold a line against the Soviet Army.[31] This plan immediately dissolved in the face of its budgetary requirements. Coming to office soon after the Lisbon Conference, the Eisenhower administration moved to rely on cheaper nuclear firepower. In the famous words of NSC 162/2 in 1953, "in the event of hostilities, the United States will consider nuclear weapons to be as available for use as other munitions."[32]

For the next thirty-five years NATO and American strategic decisions were bedeviled by ambivalence about how much the alliance should rely on nuclear weapons to deter Moscow from invading. Those who wanted to maximize deterrence and minimize military budgets favored resting NATO doctrine on deliberate escalation. Those who worried about what to do if deterrence failed sought to rely on conventional defenses in order to avoid mutual annihilation. Those who saw the merit in both concerns sought a range of options that would ratchet up the odds of successful defense with conventional forces alone but allow controlled and limited uses of nuclear weapons if conventional defense faltered. The compromise approach was known as "flexible response."[33]

According to folklore, the Eisenhower administration held stubbornly to the strategy of "massive retaliation"—the intent to vaporize the whole Warsaw Pact as soon as Soviet tanks poured into West Germany. Folklore also holds that Kennedy moved decisively to promote flexible response and stronger conventional defense options. In reality there was less difference than commonly assumed. Eisenhower supported the impression of staunch commitment to nuclear escalation in his rhetoric and decisions, but the commitment originally enshrined in NATO's 1954 document MC 48 was modified in official development of strategy three years later in MC 14/2.[34] Leaders of the Kennedy administration promoted improvement in conventional forces and revision of strategy, but action in these directions was inconsistent and changes in war plans were small and delayed. In Kennedy's first year Secretary of Defense Robert McNamara actually budgeted a reduction of conventional forces, and Kennedy later threatened withdrawals of U.S. forces from Europe to cope with the balance-of-payments deficit. The official adoption of flexible response as NATO doctrine in MC 14/3 occurred ironically just when capacity for conventional defense was falling, as France withdrew from the integrated command, London moved to withdraw forces from the British Army of the Rhine, and the war in Vietnam hollowed out U.S. units in Europe. MC 14/3 was a compromise in principle between conventional and nuclear emphasis in war plans but produced little change in practice.[35]

For more than two decades after 1960 the most strenuous efforts to develop new ideas and plans for limited war occurred within the arena of nuclear strategy. The logic of flexible response required the willingness to initiate "controlled" escalation in the event of a Soviet attack on West Berlin or a breakthrough on the Central Front. At one level—the hypothetical use of tactical nuclear weapons within the theater of combat—planning involved NATO as a whole. The multinational mechanism for doing this was the Nuclear Planning Group (NPG). For decades, however, the NPG never reached much agreement on which specific options would be implemented in what circumstances.[36]

The biggest controversies were about how much control the European allies would have either to prevent or to compel use of U.S. nuclear forces in the event of war. In the end, efforts to fortify multilateralism did nothing to constrain American operational independence. In principle, multinational cooperation and allied options to prevent American use of tactical nuclear weapons were assured by the official requirement for Washington to consult its allies at the appointed time, but few had confidence that the consultative system would work in practice.[37] Officially the United States insisted that capacity to compel escalation was not a problem. Most prominently in McNamara's 1962 speech to the NATO ministerial meeting in Athens, Washington promised firmly to bring all its nuclear forces into play to retaliate against invasion and used this assurance to dissuade allies from developing nuclear forces of their own.[38] Europeans were naturally suspicious—for good reason as it turned out, since McNamara later confessed that his assurances had been false: "in long private conversations with successive presidents . . . I recommended without qualification, that they never initiate, under any circumstances, the use of nuclear weapons. I believe they accepted my recommendation."[39]

The most multilateral solution to NATO's strategic dilemmas—the proposed nuclear Multilateral Force (MLF)—was a failure. This plan in the mid-1960s to man NATO ships carrying nuclear weapons with multinational crews aborted because honoring the political norm of collaboration was not important enough to override the practical fact that the arrangement would be militarily nonsensical and would not solve the credibility problem anyway. Apart from operational awkwardness, joint crews would do nothing to increase the credibility of NATO's nuclear doctrine because they might prevent release of the weapons but could not guarantee the reverse—that they would be launched—which was the whole point for credible deterrence.

Such schemes could not get around the reality that when the chips were down, the United States would control whether and how it would use its nuclear forces to defend Europe. Periodically anxieties in allied governments led to American initiatives to deploy new types of theater nuclear weapons in order to reassure the Europeans that they could rely on American nuclear deterrence: Thor and Jupiter missiles in the late 1950s, Polaris submarine-launched ballistic missiles assigned to the Supreme Allied Commander, Atlantic (SACLANT) in the 1960s, and Pershing II and ground-launched cruise missiles in the late 1970s and early 1980s. When these responses to European government fears of "decoupling" were undertaken, they ignited fears among mass publics of the reverse danger—being sucked into an American nuclear war—and produced political backlash. The strategy of deliberate escalation could be maintained as long as it remained a principle discussed abstractly among diplomatic elites but created as many problems as it solved when it had to be translated into concrete programs to revive confidence among those elites. Then it shocked public opinion because the suicidal idea of starting nuclear war defied common sense.

Conventional forces and theater nuclear forces were two parts of the flexible response strategy. The third part was the adaptation of targeting options for U.S. strategic forces—the intercontinental missiles and bombers aimed at the Soviet homeland. The political need to link long-range systems to the defense of NATO prompted most of the anxieties about the state of the nuclear balance of forces, and episodic attempts to provide options for counterforce attacks that could stop short of mutual annihilation.

When John Kennedy faced contingency planning for war over Berlin, he gave serious attention to the option of a disarming first strike on Soviet nuclear forces in order to blunt Moscow's capacity to retaliate for U.S. escalation if war broke out over the city. The harrowing experience of this planning led civilian leaders to ask for a wider menu of options in the Single Integrated Operational Plan (SIOP), the main nuclear war plan.[40] Change in the SIOP was modest and slow, however, and preoccupation with Vietnam diverted McNamara from following up on the demand for options. Nixon and Secretary of Defense James Schlesinger tried again to develop limited options, producing much controversy among arms controllers who mistakenly believed that counterforce targeting had been abandoned when McNamara's rhetoric started emphasizing "assured destruction." Their efforts again yielded less change in the SIOP than civilian strategists wanted. Professionals in the air force and Strategic Air Command resisted for fear that limited options would derange the main war plan. Jimmy Carter became the one president to take a detailed and sustained interest in nuclear war plans and finally forced substantial revision to enable protracted nuclear war, more effective targeting of the Soviet political control structure, and other options. Revised doctrine was codified in the controversial PD 59 in 1980.

All these initiatives were controversial because of the dilemma between weakening deterrence of a Soviet invasion of Western Europe and risking national suicide if deterrence were to fail. For decades, the bedrock of NATO military strategy made no good sense, but no alternative could be found that would not divide the alliance. The key to the apparent success of NATO strategy (winning the Cold War without firing a shot) was obfuscation of the strategy's incoherence.

## GRAND STRATEGY AFTER THE COLD WAR: CONTROLLING MULTILATERALISM

U.S. grand strategy moved effortlessly from managing bipolarity to exploiting primacy. Although presidents since 1989 have differed rhetorically about strategy and have honored the norm of cooperation with allies to different degrees, there has been scant disagreement on objectives. From Bush I to Obama, U.S. policy has aimed to shape a world in which all countries cooperate—on American terms. The Clinton strategy was in effect "multilaterally if we can, unilaterally if we must," while Bush II's was the reverse. Although this implies a radical difference in one sense, it implies substantial similarity in another.

For those who see multilateral cooperation as an end in itself, the difference is crucial. For those who focus on the ends rather than the means, the difference is one of style more than substance. Thus many of Bush II's Democratic critics faulted him not for attacking Iraq, but for "going it alone."

After all, unlike Bush, who invaded Iraq without UN authorization, Clinton had gained the endorsement of an international institution, NATO, for his war against Serbia. Aha! one might say: this made all the difference and reflected Clinton's respect for international law. Not really. Clinton ignored the recently prevalent notion that UN Security Council authorization is required for initiation of any war that is not direct self-defense. He dispensed with UN authorization because he knew he would not get it and used the more controllable NATO as a symbolic institutional substitute. In terms of diplomatic strategy, Bush II represented a sharp shift from Clinton's approach, but in terms of security outcomes sought from strategy, he was hardly more than Clinton's Evil Twin. After all, the main problem with the invasion of Iraq was not that it was done unilaterally but that it was done at all; it was unwise and would have been just as much a mistake if it had been done with more multilateral cover.[41]

No American leaders have blatantly invoked the value of primacy, empire, or hegemony after the Cold War, nor is it probable that many even think of national security objectives in those terms. But the conflation of supply and demand for primacy was implicit in rhetoric about the United States as the "indispensable nation"—an idea Bush II initially rejected because the Clinton crew had coined it, then embraced when September 11th triggered his missionary impulse. Activist internationalists in both parties see multilateralism not as an alternative to American control, but as a vehicle for it, a practice in a world order where the United States is first above equals, not among them. The value of primacy is covered, unconsciously as well as in rhetoric, by euphemisms, such as "*shaping* the international environment"—the Pentagon's official description of the Clinton defense strategy.[42] No euphemism is more overworked than "leadership," which allows simultaneous denial and affirmation of dominance. Thus John Kerry, who regularly excoriated Bush for unilateralism, declared, "America wasn't put here to dominate the world. . . . We have a higher calling: to lead it."[43] But the point, of course, is to get the world to where Americans want it to go, not to wherever some plebiscite of other countries might take it. And as Kerry was at pains to affirm during the 2004 campaign, he categorically rejected the possibility of giving allies a veto over American action. Confidence in responsibility is buttressed by the often asserted but seldom demonstrated notion that other countries ask the United States to order the international environment, as when Secretary of State Hillary Clinton declared, "The world is counting on us."[44]

Some see the diplomatic process that ended the Cold War in the late 1980s as one of cooperation and reciprocity since it was marked by comparative calm and amity in superpower negotiations. For example, John Ikenberry claims that the Reagan administration "embraced arms control goals that it had previously spurned," and that later Bush I decided to encourage Mikhail Gorbachev by "tangible signs of reciprocation."[45] The problem is that there is no significant evidence of reciprocity. Reagan made no substantive concessions at all on the arms control issues that dominated East–West relations in the 1980s, SDI and intermediate-range nuclear forces (INF). Instead he finally secured Gorbachev's acceptance of the U.S.-proposed "zero option" in the INF Treaty. Moscow had originally and quite reasonably cited the zero option as a completely one-sided demand for Soviet concessions and had dismissed it out of hand for years because it required the USSR to give up hundreds of missiles that it had arrayed against Western Europe for decades, while not requiring any limits on Europe-based Western forces that had been targeted on the Soviets—U.S. "forward-based systems" and British and French strategic forces. The United States only gave up deployment of *new and additional* theater forces—Pershing II and ground-launched cruise missiles. The first George Bush also gave Gorbachev virtually nothing of substance. Contrary to the myth of give-and-take in the end of the Cold War, the giving went all one way. Gorbachev gave and the West took, simply pocketing a series of concessions, watching contentedly as first the Soviets' East European empire and then the inner empire of the Soviet Union itself collapsed. The Cold War ended not with a compromise peace, but with surrender by Moscow.

The United States accomplished this despite some opposition from allies as well as from Moscow; Washington virtually dictated the reunification of Germany despite resistance from both Britain and France. This and other incidents bring back the question of how different the results of multilateral and unilateral styles in U.S. policy really are. One argument is that Europeans influenced U.S. policy along the way via institutionalization of the norm of consultation.[46] But how often did consultation compel Washington to change any important aims? The main recurring issues of consultation were about adjustments of strategic declarations and weapon deployments to bolster the credibility of extended deterrence, the U.S. commitment to use nuclear weapons first to avert defeat in a European war. The rhetorical aspects of these adjustments were not always convincing.

After the Berlin Wall opened, American grand strategy evolved with surprisingly little debate. The exception to this drift was the Pentagon exercise in the last year of the administration of Bush I to inform military planning for the post–Cold War world. Under direction of Under Secretary of Defense Paul Wolfowitz, the Draft Defense Planning Guidance outlined strategy to prevent the rise of "potential competitors," to discourage advanced countries "from challenging our leadership," and to extend security commitments to countries that had been Soviet allies only a short time before.[47] When the draft was leaked, controversy produced a toned-down version.[48] The earlier draft nevertheless revealed the real thinking of the strategic leading lights in the two Bush administrations and was consistent with U.S. behavior under Clinton and Obama too.

The broad conception of national security came into its own after victory in the Cold War mission eliminated the main military threat. Military instruments remained popular, however, as the threat vacuum left by communism's collapse sucked "rogue states," which had been minor threats, into U.S. gun sights. Small-scale military actions also increased, as humanitarian interventions and peacekeeping tasks associated with world order became temporarily popular, and policing missions in the Balkans grew into war over Kosovo. The strategic rationale for these operations, other than as charity, was dubious, so commitment faltered when operations became costly without being conclusive, as in Somalia. Bill Clinton's Presidential Decision Directive on peacekeeping simultaneously endorsed the function and undercut it, stipulating conditions that amounted to backing away.[49] This was no institutionalization of globalist ambition but a prescription for living down from rhetoric. The United States would not contract with the international community to pound the globocop beat, would not bind itself more than rhetorically, and would show up where and when it felt like doing so.

The big exception to this inconsistency was the spread of contractual defense guarantees in Europe. The initiative that most demonstrated the ascendancy of the objective of world order was the expansion of NATO, and its transformation from a military alliance to a political club, in line with Clinton's bumper-sticker strategy of "engagement and enlargement." NATO moved into the power vacuum created by the USSR's implosion even before the European Union (EU). The militarization of containment that began in the late 1940s was replaced by the militarization of enlargement.[50] As ever, official rhetoric did not distinguish between national security and international security, and none but intellectuals would call the new approach liberal imperialism.

## NATO Expansion: Staying First Above Equals

The NATO alliance was unprecedented in its peacetime institutionalization of military integration and joint planning. Did it thus embody the cosmopolitan ideal of multilateral cooperation as opposed to nationalist autonomy? In principle, yes; in practice, no. In the actual history of strategy development the United States just about always called the tune, no matter how much it bobbed and weaved to cope diplomatically with allies' anxieties. During the Cold War the United States did have to take serious account of allies' preferences because bipolarity made it imperative to add as much power as possible to the anticommunist coalition. But this meant cajoling and finessing, not submitting to allies' preferences when they conflicted with American aims. With frequent differences of opinion between Washington and allied capitals, the American position on what NATO's strategy should be always won out. When diplomacy required reassuring Europeans who disagreed, diplomacy dissembled, as in McNamara's Athens speech. The United States used alliance integration for its own purposes, and its sovereignty was not substantially compromised by the integration.

For Eisenhower, the main purpose was to reduce the financial and military burden on the United States. As Marc Trachtenberg recounts, Eisenhower supported European unity so that Western Europe could become "what he called 'a third great power bloc.' . . . America, he said, could then 'sit back and relax somewhat.'" This would require that Europeans control their own nuclear weapons, and Eisenhower pushed in this direction, endorsing EURATOM as well as the European Defense Community. He looked forward to limiting U.S. military commitment to NATO to naval and air forces, returning ground forces to the United States.[51]

To that end, Eisenhower contemplated a prospective command arrangement that today would seem bizarre or frightening. He envisioned a more or less independent SACEUR, a European but implicitly supranational figure who would have authority to initiate war, including nuclear operations, on his own authority, in response to strategic warning that a Soviet attack was imminent. (If one looks at statements that Eisenhower made under conditions of secrecy in NSC meetings, if the logic of MC 48 is traced out, and if one takes account of the studied American obfuscation of the question of when and how NATO's decision to go to war would be made, it becomes clear that the strategy of massive retaliation was really one of anticipatory retaliation—that is, preemption).[52]

After Eisenhower, however, as permanent American commitment of ground forces on the continent became accepted, American leaders honored a veneer of multilateralism while keeping control of essential war plans and options. They could rely on control of SACEUR because Eisenhower's vision of putting a European in that position evaporated. While SACEUR would always be an American general, that meant that SACEUR's second hat would be commander-in-chief of U.S. forces in Europe (CINCEUR). The precise responsibility of this individual to collective demands of the North Atlantic Council, as distinct from the American president, is formally ambiguous. But whatever the principle of multinational involvement in military decisions, CINCEUR would always be bound by the U.S. Constitution to obey orders from the American president.[53] Clear-eyed focus on the main substantive business of the alliance—operational plans for deterrence and war—makes it evident that the United States will coordinate but still command, consulting allies but still controlling the resulting actions.

This reality, overlooked or wished away by most diplomats and enthusiasts for international institutions, underlies the special estrangement between Washington and Paris that grew in the 1960s and persisted long after. The problem was that France insisted on no less independence than the United States within the alliance. Charles De Gaulle made many mistakes, but he saw through the polite fiction of automatic solidarity and recognized that Washington would not sacrifice its own national interest for the sake of its continental allies' interests when the two diverged. He explicitly exposed the unwillingness of the American president or SACEUR to be pinned down to specific plans for escalation.[54] Since military integration was on American terms, and more clearly so after 1960, De Gaulle ended France's integration in the NATO command while maintaining its membership in the Atlantic alliance on traditional terms.

The British were able to live with Washington as the boss of the alliance because of the special relationship, and because their independent nuclear deterrent gave them a hole card for hypothetical situations in which American control might prove unacceptable. During the Cold War the FRG had little choice since the division of Germany, the political legacy of World War II, and the conditions of German admission to NATO had limited its sovereignty. This was all scarcely an issue for the other members of the alliance since they did not have pretensions to great-power status. So only France fully confronted the reality of American control of the essence of NATO—its military strategy—and France remained the one important European ally with a consistently tense relationship with the United States. It is precisely because the French have dared to take their sovereignty as seriously as the United States has taken its own that Americans have found them so galling.

NATO has always been both a political and a military organization, but the priorities were reversed after 1989. NATO became a political club more than the military alliance it was originally designed to be. As a club it is inward-looking, oriented to enjoying association and common bonds, a security community emphasizing "shared values more than common threats."[55] As an alliance it is outward-looking, subordinating internal relationships to the business of confronting common threats and generating combat power. Although the organization retains significant military functions—indeed, it has engaged in two small hot wars since the Cold War ended—these are minor compared with the original missions of preventing or fighting World War III.

Leaving aside the four wars since 1989, NATO expansion was the most significant American strategic initiative of the post–Cold War era. It contradicts conservative doves' preference for a balance-of-power strategy, but it unites liberal multilateralists and anti-Russian conservatives in scooping everyone in Russia's front yard into the Western community. Expansion could proceed with practically no objections in the United States, apart from a coterie of grumpy realists who took Russia's concerns with the balance of power seriously, because proponents did not believe that the commitment at the heart of the alliance's purpose would ever have to be met.

NATO's ostensible purpose, collective defense, appears to have been barely in the minds of the sponsors of the organization's enlargement. Clinton recoiled from involvement in Somalia, and left Rwanda to its fate, because the costs of American military action were real, even if they were trivial compared with fulfilling the guarantee to a NATO member. Clinton embraced new members in NATO despite the high costs that defending them in war would impose because the possibility of facing those costs no longer seemed real. Consider the incorporation of Estonia—a country that not only lies deep within any conceivable Russian sphere of influence, but that was recently even part of the USSR itself. How many who celebrated that new admission to the Atlantic alliance really saw it as a guarantee to go to war to protect the country's sovereignty? The foolhardiness of overlooking this simple point became more apparent with the brief war between Russia and Georgia in 2008.

If military functions were beside the point, and the real point was to create a new political club, celebrating and consolidating the liberation and democratization of the former Soviet empire, why should NATO be the vehicle rather than the European Union? Because the EU did not include the United States. For Washington, whose domination of NATO's command structure has never been in doubt, expansion of the alliance was an extension of American power into Eastern Europe. This is particularly evident in the greater affinity that many new members have for Washington as compared to their Western European neighbors, and Secretary of Defense Donald Rumsfeld's celebration of "the new Europe" as opposed to America's older allies.

The evaporation of NATO's founding purpose is reflected in the Bush administration plan announced in 2004 to redeploy U.S. forces from Europe to areas closer to unstable regions in which the United States may intervene. What military purpose remained in NATO shifted completely from self-defense toward managing world order or undercutting terrorism by fighting in Afghanistan. Never officially promulgated, this new mission falls in line with the wisecrack, "Out of area or out of business." In practice, this mission has included humanitarian aggression, as reflected in the alliance's assault on Serbian Yugoslavia in 1999 on behalf of an oppressed population group within one of that country's provinces, Kosovo. In Bosnia as well, the objectives of regional order and protection of threatened groups were clear while strategy was not. The United States aimed to constitute stable governments where secession, communal violence, and civil war had destroyed the local political order, yet at the same time American leaders foreswore involvement in "nation building." Given the contradiction, military intervention sucked Washington into nation building anyway, but in a half-hearted manner that left the viability of states after the end of occupation in doubt.

NATO is the institution that bridged the Cold War and the hiatus that followed. A dozen years after the collapse of communism, American security priorities changed precipitously. Before September 11, 2001, arguments were about military charity: how often and how much to commit American power to settle ethnic conflicts, protect foreign populations from local enemies, and build stable states. Those with the broad view of national security saw such charity as self-interest in the long run since political as well as economic globalization would make the world safer—and more profitable—for the United States. After the hiatus that gave national security a holiday, September 11th highlighted the downside of globalization: the backlash against Westernization and American primacy.

In the first decade of the twenty-first century, counterterrorism became the top national security priority. As in the Cold War, both cosmopolitan and nationalist conceptions of security converged on similar strategies—aggressive collection of intelligence and the use of force to eliminate terrorists who can be located. Until September 11th there was debate about whether counterterrorism should be conceived primarily in terms of law enforcement or of war. The broad view, emphasizing law, held the edge then because terrorism was not yet perceived as a major threat. The FBI subordinated intelligence collection to the primary mission of apprehending and prosecuting terrorists as criminals.[56] September 11th settled the debate in the other direction, and law enforcement took a back seat to national security. As had happened a half-century earlier with the shock of war in Korea, objectives of world order and American power converged on strategies emphasizing force.

## Always Leaning Forward

For most of the time since Pearl Harbor, faith in the American mission and fear of enemies' power have united liberals and conservatives in a consensus for activism abroad and muscular military strategies, even when they argued about whether economic or military programs should be the focus of that activism. Only a bloody nose suppresses the impulse to military activism, and then not for long. Retreats from Beirut in 1983 and Somalia ten years later made policymakers hesitate for a time but were soon followed by other uses of force. The earlier disaster in Vietnam produced a longer period of caution, but still only for a decade.

Opponents of the consensus for forward strategy have rarely been influential since World War II. The only challenges at the highest level were failed presidential candidacies of Republican Robert Taft in 1952 and Democrat George McGovern twenty years later. Taft could not get his party's nomination and McGovern was buried by Nixon in a landslide, despite public frustration with the Vietnam War. Most of the time critics are stuck on the fringes and tarred as isolationists. At the dawn of the Cold War critics of forward strategy were strange bedfellows. The Truman Doctrine was resisted by both the extreme Left, which opposed aid to allegedly reactionary governments, and extreme Right, which feared that it would lead to war. Leftist Henry Wallace said at one point that rightist Robert Taft was more likely to keep the peace than was Truman.[57]

Despite the radical change in context, the same bedfellows could be found after the Cold War as well. Anti-interventionist arguments from the Left and Right, by Ralph Nader and Dennis Kucinich or Pat Buchanan and Ron Paul, and pundits in the *Nation* and the *American Conservative*, sounded eerily similar. These critics from the two ends of the spectrum have generally been impotent, with the partial exception of the period of reaction against failure in Vietnam; although Nixon was elected twice, his foreign policy was marked by retrenchment. Buchanan and Nader together received no more than 4 percent of the vote in 2000—enough to defeat Al Gore, but not to advance the anti-interventionist agenda. Anti-interventionist views could grow again if the American ventures in Iraq and Afghanistan fail and the ambition to make the world safe for democracy is seen as the cause. The only reason to bet that such sobering up might last longer than the decade of retrenchment after the Tet Offensive is the lack of a global threat comparable to the old Soviet Union to revivify fear—although revolutionary Islamism may continue to fill that role in many eyes.

The post–Cold War world is no longer new, but it has not yet lasted half as long as the Cold War, the long struggle that capped a century of vicious ideological competition, catastrophic global war, and decades of vulnerability to the potential annihilation of modern civilization. In light of the scope and intensity of those problems, U.S. national security strategy has to be judged as quite effective from World War II through the end of the Cold War. After all, it is hard to find fault with total victory in an epochal global conflict. The one glaring exception was the catastrophe of the long war in Vietnam. With that exception, the discipline of bipolarity made the United States active and steadfast but also kept it from overreaching strategically. The United States valued its primacy *within* the Western world but recognized that this did not mean control of the world as a whole. The shift from bipolarity to unipolarity unbound the United States and opened the road to moral ambitions.

# 3 | CONFUSED INTERVENTIONS
## PUTTERING WITH PRIMACY

The end of the Cold War freed the United States to use its power not just to prevent the spread of communism, but on behalf of the so-called international community, to set the world right where bad or ineffectual regimes were hurting their own people. But the United States, the United Nations, and the North Atlantic Treaty Organization had rocky experiences trying to do this in civil conflicts after 1990. Since U.S. aims in these cases stressed the importance of a multilateral imprimatur for action, the fate of UN and NATO missions reflects directly on U.S. policy. As it was, mistakes and shaky successes rivaled jobs solidly well done. Many peacekeeping operations (PKOs) designed to monitor situations after wars stopped were reasonably effective.[1] Many other interventions, especially the more consequential ones designed to make peace, were not.[2] In Africa, efforts to pacify Sierra Leone and Liberia were messy but eventually good enough, but attempts in bigger cases like Somalia, Congo, and Sudan proved hesitant, weak, and inconclusive, and in Rwanda in 1994, catastrophically impotent. One reasonable success in a major case—Cambodia—came with a huge price tag that cannot be paid very often.

After the turn of the century there was some learning from earlier errors, but not enough. The biggest intervention until then—the 1999 war over Kosovo—remained controversial. First, although NATO clearly came out on top in the war, there was disagreement about whether it should be counted a success or a failure.[3] NATO induced Serbia's surrender in a deal that gave up two major elements of the Rambouillet ultimatum (the set of demands that Belgrade rejected before NATO attacked), and that recognized Kosovo's continuing status as part of Yugoslavia, an agreement that was forgotten years later when Kosovo declared independence. Intervention in Kosovo did not make one of the two mistakes emphasized in this chapter (it was not impartial), but it did make the other (it was limited).

Second, after Western occupation dragged on for many years, the United States and some allies moved to settle the question by recognizing Kosovo's independence, but most other countries did not sign on. (As of early 2011 little more than one-third of the United Nations' members—75 out of 192—had recognized Kosovo.) Independence posed a disturbing prosecession precedent for how to deal with internal cleavages in other countries. In another big case—Bosnia—NATO intervention produced a provisional peace settlement in 1995 after a UN effort proved bankrupt. This was only achieved by stipulating contradictory terms in the Dayton Peace Accords: in principle, reunification of three parts of the country, but in practice, partition. In all these cases—even Kosovo—Washington and its partners were reluctant to face the fact that bringing an end to bitter civil wars meant not just sending police but waging war to settle the question of who rules.

Despite some learning, many humanitarian interventionists still did not get it a decade into the twenty-first century. Some were sobered, but earlier misconceptions still infected thinking among many who seek to use military instruments to relieve suffering and injustice in benighted countries. Peacemakers would do well to pay more attention to the physicians' motto: "First, do no harm." Neither the United States nor the United Nations quite grasped this for most of the 1990s. True, many peacekeeping operations promoted stability or at least did not work against it.[4] In too many cases, however, intervenors unwittingly prolonged suffering where they meant to relieve it.

How did they do this? By following a principle that sounds like common sense: intervention should be both limited and impartial because weighing in on one side of a struggle undermines the legitimacy and effectiveness of outside involvement, and when violence is necessary it should be used only abstemiously because it hurts people. These Olympian presumptions resonate with respect for law, international cooperation, and humane values. They have the ring of prudence, fairness, and restraint. They make sense in old-fashioned UN peacekeeping operations, where the outsiders' role is not to make peace, but to bless and monitor a cease-fire that all parties have decided to accept. But they become destructive misconceptions when carried over to the messier realm of "peace enforcement," where the belligerents have yet to decide that they have nothing more to gain by fighting.

Limited intervention may end a war if the intervenor takes sides, tilts the local balance of power, and helps one of the rivals to win—that is, if it is not impartial. Impartial intervention may end a war if the outsiders take complete command of the situation, overawe all the local competitors, and impose a peace settlement—that is, if it is not limited. Trying to have it both ways (limited *and* impartial) usually blocks peace by doing enough to keep one side from defeating the other, but not enough to make them stop trying.

## WHO RULES?

Wars have many causes, and each war is unique and complicated, but the root issue is always the same: Who rules when the fighting stops? In wars between countries the issue may be sovereignty over disputed territory, or suzerainty over third parties, or influence over international transactions. In wars within countries the issue may be which group will control the government or how the country should be divided so that adversaries can have separate governments. When political groups resort to war, it is because they cannot agree on who gets to call the tune in peace.

A war will not begin unless both sides in a dispute would rather fight than concede. After all, it is not hard to avert war if either party cares only about peace—all it has to do is let the other side have what it claims it is due. A war will not end until both sides agree who will control whatever is in dispute.

Is all this utterly obvious? Not to enthusiasts for international peace enforcement who are imbued with hope for global governance, unsympathetic to thinking of security in terms of sovereignty, or viscerally sure that war is not a rational political act. They cannot bring themselves to deal forthrightly in the currency of war. Even in the extreme case, when bombing Serbia for seventy-eight days on behalf of Albanian Kosovars, killing hundreds of Serbs, NATO's commander recounts, "We were never allowed to call it a war."[5] Interventionists in the 1990s assumed instead that outsiders' good offices could pull the scales from the eyes of fighting factions, make them realize that resorting to violence was a blunder, and substitute peaceful negotiation for force. But wars are rarely accidents, and it is no accident that belligerents often continue to kill each other while they negotiate or that the terms of diplomatic settlements usually reflect results on the battlefield.

Others sometimes proceed from muddled assumptions about what force should be expected to accomplish. For instance, in a bizarre set of statements in 1993, President Clinton threatened air strikes against Bosnian Serbs but then said, "The United States is not, and should not, become involved as a partisan in a war." At another point he declared that the United States should lead other Western nations in ending ethnic cleansing in Bosnia, only to say a moment later, "That does not mean that the United States or the United Nations can enter a war, in effect, to redraw the lines . . . within what was Yugoslavia."[6]

This profoundly confused policy, promulgated with the best of lawyerly intentions, cost lives on all sides in Bosnia. For what legitimate purpose can military forces be directed to kill people and break things, if not to take the side of their opponents? If the use of deadly force is to be legitimate killing rather than senseless killing, it must serve the purpose of settling the war—which means determining who rules, which means leaving someone in power at the end of the day.

How is this done without taking someone's side? How can outside powers pretend to stop ethnic cleansing without allocating territory—that is, drawing lines? Yet for several years Clinton and UN secretary-general Boutros Boutros-Ghali made threats not in order to protect recognized or viable borders, but to enforce naturally unstable truce lines that made no sense as a permanent territorial arrangement. In the early 1990s such confusion made intervention an accessory to stalemate, punishing either side for advancing too far, but not settling the issue that fueled the war.

Some saw method in the madness. There are two ways to stop a war: either one side imposes its will after defeating the other on the battlefield or both sides accept a negotiated compromise. The hope for a compromise solution accounts for misconceived impartiality. This is not to say that compromise never works. Indeed, after the turning point of 1995 in Bosnia, the Dayton Accords emerged as a compromise, but one that embedded instability in the settlement, by proclaiming political integration while accepting the reality of ethnic segregation. To work, compromise first must be possible and then must prove durable.

When is compromise possible? When both sides believe that they have more to lose than to gain from fighting. Because leaders are often sensible, this usually happens before a war starts, which is why most crises are resolved by diplomacy rather than combat. But peaceful compromise has to seem impossible to the opponents for a war to start, and once it begins, compromise becomes even harder. Emotions intensify, sunk costs grow, demands for recompense escalate. If compromise was not tolerable enough to avert war in the first place, it becomes even less attractive once large amounts of blood and treasure have been invested in the cause.

If neither side manages to pound the other into submission and a stalemate emerges, does a compromise peace become more practical? Not for a long time, and not until many more lives have been invested in the contending quests for victory. Stalemates rarely seem solid to those with a strong stake in overcoming them. Belligerents conjure up one set of military stratagems and schemes after another to gain the upper hand, or they hope for shifts in alliances or outside assistance to tilt the balance of power, or they gamble that their adversary will be the first to lose heart and crack. Such developments often do break stalemates. In World War I, for example, trench warfare in France ebbed and flowed inconclusively for four years until the Russian capitulation. This allowed the Germans to move armies from the East and achieve a breakthrough that unglued the Western Front and almost brought them victory in the spring of 1918. Then the Allies rebounded, turned the tables with newly arrived American armies, and won the war six months later.

Stalemate is likely to yield to negotiated compromise only after it lasts so long that a military solution appears hopeless to both sides. In the Iran–Iraq War, where UN mediation was useful, the two sides had fought ferociously but inconclusively for eight years. The United Nations smoothed the way for both sides to lay down their arms, but it is hard to credit that diplomatic intervention with as much effect in bringing peace as the simple exhaustion and despair of war makers in Tehran and Baghdad. Mediation is useful, but it helps peacemaking most where it needs help least.

## COMPROMISES THAT KILL

If there is any place where peacemaking needed help most, and failed most abjectly, it was Bosnia in the early 1990s. There, the West's attempt at limited but impartial involvement abetted slow-motion savagery. The effort wound up doing things that helped one side but then counterbalanced them with actions that helped the other. This alienated both sides and enabled them to keep up the business of killing each other.

The United Nations tried to prevent the Serbs from consolidating their early victory, but without going all the way to provide consistent military support for the Muslims and Croats. The main UN mission was human-itarian delivery of food and medicine to besieged communities, but this amounted to breaking the sieges—a military and political effect. It is hardly surprising that the Serbs interfered when they could get away with it. In line with the humanitarian rationale, the United Nations supported "safe areas"—pockets of Muslims and Croats hanging on in areas conquered by the Serbs. Apart from such limited action to frustrate the last phase of ter-ritorial rearrangement by force, UN and U.S. attempts to settle the war were limited to diplomatic mediation, an arms embargo, a "no-fly zone," and economic sanctions on Belgrade.

For over a year, the UN presence inhibited forceful reaction to Bosnian Serb provocations because French, British, and other units on the ground were hostage to retaliation. In November 1994 Bosnian Serbs took about 250 UN peacekeepers hostage in retaliation for NATO air strikes (which had only been symbolic "pinprick" raids). In May 1995 the Serbs took nearly 400 UN personnel and tied them to poles as human shields. Presi-dent Clinton stopped the air strikes.

U.S. and UN threats were not just weak and hesitant; by trying to be both forceful and neutral, they worked at cross-purposes. First, after much danc-ing around and wringing of hands, the United Nations and NATO used force on behalf of the Bosnian government. The outside powers did this, however, while refusing to let those they were defending buy arms to defend themselves. Given the awkward multilateral politics of the arms embargo, this may have been understandable; but as strategy, it was irrational, plain and simple. The embargo was impartial in the sense that the law impartially prevents both the rich and the poor from sleeping under bridges—it fa-vored the Serbs, who had access to arms from Belgrade. Since Washington favored the Muslims, this pseudo-impartiality was actually quite partial, but on behalf of the wrong side. (The Clinton administration recognized this and tried to convince its multilateral partners to lift the embargo but shrank from doing the right thing—overriding it unilaterally—when they would not.)

Impartiality compounded the absurdity in August 1994, when the UN military commander also threatened the Bosnian government with at-tack if it violated the weapons exclusion zone around Sarajevo.[7] UN strat-egy thus bounced between unwillingness to undertake any combat at all and a commitment to fight on two fronts against both belligerents. Such lofty evenhandedness might make sense for a judge in a court that can enforce its writ, but hardly for a general wielding a small stick in a bitter war.

UN pressures maintained a teetering balance of power between the belligerents; the intervenors refused to let either side win. Economic sanctions worked against the Serbs, while the arms embargo worked against the Muslims. The rationale was that evenhandedness would encourage a negotiated settlement. The result, however, was not peace or an end to the killing, but years of military stalemate, slow bleeding, and delusionary diplomatic haggling. War among the Serb, Croat, and Muslim populations went on for nearly four years until the catastrophe at Srebrenica in 1995 laid bare the bankruptcy of UN efforts. With no regard for its inability to enforce its fiat, the UN blithely declared the city a "safe area," encouraging fearful refugees to go there, then watched the one Dutch battalion on the scene stand by impotently as Serb forces overran the town, rounded up five to seven thousand Bosniac men and boys of military age, and murdered them. After this disgrace NATO finally entered the fray in a less frivolous way, tilted decisively against the Serbs, bombed heavily in the "Deliberate Force" campaign, and stood by as the Croatian ground offensive cleansed the Krajina region of Serbs. Thus external intervention became more effective when it switched to being much less impartial and much less limited. But why did it take outside powers so long to get to that point?

The desire for impartiality and fairness had led outside diplomats to promote territorial compromises that made no strategic sense. The Vance-Owen Plan of 1993 mimicked the unrealistic 1947 UN partition plan for Palestine: a geographic patchwork of noncontiguous territories, isolated enclaves, vulnerable corridors and supply lines, exposed communities, and indefensible borders. Implementing such a plan would have created a territorial tinderbox and a perpetual temptation to renew the conflict. Yet Clinton was initially willing to thrust tens of thousands of American troops into the Bosnian tangle to enforce such an accord and avoided doing so because the Dayton Accords did not rest on the Vance-Owen patchwork. It accepted a de facto three-way partition, where most of the territory controlled by each of the three factions was connected.

In Somalia in 1992–93 the United States succeeded laudably in relieving starvation. Then, fearful that food supply would fall apart again after withdrawal, Washington took on the mission of restoring civil order. This was less limited and more ambitious than the outside powers' action in Bosnia, but it stopped short of taking charge and imposing a settlement on the warring factions.

Incongruously, the international operation in Somalia worked at throwing together a local court and police organization before establishing the other essential elements of government, an executive and a legislature. Then U.S. forces set out to arrest General Mohammed Farah Aideed—who was not just a troublemaker but one of the prime claimants to governing authority—without championing any other contender. The U.S. attempts failed but killed a large number of Somalis and further roiled the political waters in Mogadishu. Stung by casualties to U.S. forces, Washington pulled out and left UN troops from other countries holding the bag, maintaining an indecisive presence, and taking casualties of their own.

It may have been wise to avoid embroilment in the chaos of conflict among Somali clans. But then it was naïve to think that intervention could help to end the local anarchy. As Michael Maren asked, "If the peacekeepers aren't keeping the peace, what are they doing?"—especially after the cost of the intervention topped $1.5 billion (in 1993 dollars). Not only was the UN operation indecisive, but it fueled the fighting by letting the feuding factions compete for UN jobs, contracts, and cash. In areas where UN forces were absent, the parties reached accommodation in order to reestablish commerce rather than jockey for UN resources.[8]

Elsewhere in Africa the record was no better. The United States executed a reasonably effective intervention in Liberia in 2003; U.S. participation was limited, but in support of a larger effort by African forces under a Nigerian commander. Before and after, however, Washington intervened but refrained from decisive action, or refrained from intervention altogether. Eighteen dead American soldiers on a bad day in Somalia in 1993 led President Clinton to pull back from the attempt to impose political order in that country. Months later this experience led him to forbid intervention in the Rwandan genocide—a case that cried out for it. Otherwise, Washington left intervention in the multiple disasters in Africa to the United Nations and African Union, with painful results. In Congo and Sudan the multilateral forces were spread thin over huge areas (UN peacekeepers in Congo, a country as large as several in Western Europe combined, numbered about eighteen thousand in 2010). The "peacekeepers" allowed massacres to occur unimpeded within their areas of operation, provoked violent protests from local populations frustrated with their inaction, even let some of their convoys submit passively to raids, robbery, and kidnapping, and, as in the early years in the Balkans, did not take sides in local combat.[9]

Not all problems have been due to impartiality. In Haiti in 1994, the United States and the United Nations clearly did choose sides, supporting the exiled president Jean-Bertrand Aristide; eventually the incipient American invasion forced the junta in Port-au-Prince to back down. Even there, however, suffering had been prolonged by the initially limited character of the intervention. For over a year after the junta reneged on the July 1993 Governors Island Agreement (which provided for Aristide's return), Washington relied on economic sanctions, a "trickle-up" strategy of coercion that was bound to hurt the innocent long before it touched the guilty. The blockade gradually damaged the health and welfare of the country's masses, who were powerless to make the policy changes demanded by Washington and on whose behalf the sanctions were supposedly being applied. Yet sanctions offered no incentive to Haiti's kleptocratic elites to cut their own throats, and sanctions were not what made the generals sign the accord brokered by former president Jimmy Carter. The U.S. invasion force did that. Instead, the junta used the many months during which sanctions were left to work to track down and murder Aristide supporters at a steady pace.

The September 1994 agreement that accompanied the entry of U.S. forces hinted that—for the first time in the crisis—Washington might err on the side of impartiality. American leaders spoke of the generals' "military honor," U.S. troops were ordered to cooperate with the usurpers' security forces, and many of the anti-Aristide gangsters were left free. The agreement did not disband the Haitian military or even completely purge its officer corps, whose corruption and terror tactics had long been most of the problem. Within these limits meddling in the tragic saga of Haitian misgovernment was a dubious gamble for the United States, considering the island's predatory political culture. Deciding whether to intervene in Haiti was agonizing. Once that was done, however, picking a side was certainly wise. But that choice was weakened by dithering too long with sanctions and then appearing to waver in support for the chosen side when U.S. military force was finally applied. Fortunately in succeeding years Haiti's politics did not degenerate to a level worse than the historic norm, but the result was not much better either, and no advertisement for interventionist nation building.

Impartiality is a tenacious norm. It worked in cases that lie beyond traditional peacekeeping, such as the cease-fire mediation between Iran and

Iraq in the 1980s or the political receivership of the United Nations Transitional Authority in Cambodia (UNTAC). When looking at the reasons for these successes, however, it becomes apparent that impartiality works best where intervention is needed least, where wars have played themselves out and the fighting factions need only the good offices of mediators to lay down their arms. Impartiality is likely to work against peace in the more challenging cases—where intervention must make the peace, rather than just preside over it—because it reflects deeper confusion over what war is about.

## IMPERIAL IMPARTIALITY

If outsiders such as the United States, the United Nations, or NATO are faced with demands for peace in wars where passions have not burned out, they can avoid the costs and risks that go with entanglement by refusing the mandate—staying aloof and letting the locals fight it out. Or they can jump in and help one of the contenders defeat the other. But can they bring peace sooner than exhaustion from prolonged carnage would, if they remain impartial? Yes, but not with a gentle, restrained impartiality, only with an active, harsh neutrality that overpowers both sides—an imperial impartiality. This is a tall order, seldom with many supporters, and it is hard to think of many cases where it has worked.

The closest thing to a good example of imperial impartiality was the UN operation in Cambodia in the early 1990s—a grand-scale takeover of much of the administrative authority in the country and a program for establishing a new government through supervised elections and a constituent assembly. Despite great obstacles, tenuous results, and eventual unraveling, UNTAC fulfilled most of its mandate; the final unraveling also left the country better off than it had been before the UNTAC operation. This success should be given its due. As a model to rescue the ideal of limited and impartial intervention, however, it falls short.

First, the United Nations did not nip a horrible war in the bud; as was the case with Iran and Iraq, it capitalized on fifteen years of exhaustion and bloody stalemate. The outside powers recognized that the main order of business was to determine who rules, but they did not act before the local factions were weary enough to agree on a procedure for doing so.

Second, UN intervention was limited only in one sense: it avoided direct enforcement of the transition agreement when local contenders proved recalcitrant. Luckily, such incidents were manageable, or the whole experiment would have been a fiasco. In other respects, the scale of involvement was too huge to provide a model. Apart from the wars in Korea and Kuwait, UNTAC was the most massive intervention in UN history. It involved thousands of personnel from a host of countries and billions of dollars in expenditures. The Cambodia operation proved so expensive, at a time when other demands on the United Nations were escalating dramatically, that it could not be repeated more than once in a blue moon.

Third, although UNTAC should count as a success—especially after the election it conducted against all odds in 1993—the results were unstable for quite some time. Despite a tremendous UN presence, the terms of the transition agreement were never faithfully followed by all the local combatants and continued to erode after UNTAC's departure. For example, because the Khmer Rouge reneged, none of the Cambodian factions disarmed to the degree stipulated in the agreement; after the election, the constituent assembly did not seriously debate a constitution but more or less rubber-stamped King Norodom Sihanouk's demands; and sporadic fighting between the Khmer Rouge and other parties continued before and after UNTAC left. Yet years later it was true that the Cambodian government was rickety but better than what it was before UNTAC.

Fourth, the UN success in Cambodia was linked with impartiality only in principle, not in effect. The real success of the transition overseen by UNTAC was not in fostering a final peaceful compromise among the parties in Cambodia, but in altering the balance of power among them and marginalizing the worst one. The transition did not compel an end to violent strife, but it did facilitate the realignment of parties and military forces that might bring it about. The old Cold War alignment of Sihanouk, Son Sann, and the Khmer Rouge against the Vietnamese-installed government in Phnom Penh was transformed into a new coalition of everyone against the Khmer Rouge. Any peace Cambodia could achieve had to come from a new distribution of power. Ultimately the revised balance that facilitated the peace accord shifted altogether, as the Khmer Rouge was eliminated completely, and then the Hun Sen forces suppressed moderate opposition and took firm control of the country.

The least impartial and most imperial example of post–Cold War intervention was NATO's war against Serbian Yugoslavia for the purpose of protecting the Albanians of Kosovo. One may question that intervention on many grounds: whether starting the war was justified (greater crimes against humanity were being perpetrated elsewhere, in places such as Sudan, without prompting such forceful intervention); whether NATO's insistence on limiting the military effort to aerial attack delayed resolution of the conflict and increased Albanian suffering (invasion might have saved more sooner); whether the result represented a huge net improvement on the prewar situation (Kosovo's Serbs suffered in the end as its Albanians had in the beginning); whether the humanitarian benefits were outweighed by the strategic costs (damage to relations with great powers—Russia and China); or whether Washington's way out of entanglement in occupation was either legal or honorable (it reneged on the 1999 agreement to recognize Belgrade's sovereignty over the province in exchange for the Serb surrender). The last question was ultimately the biggest, although few in the West paid much attention to it. The UN resolution that Belgrade accepted for ending the war endorsed "substantial autonomy and meaningful self-administration for Kosovo," but in the context of "*reaffirming* the commitment of all Member States to the sovereignty and territorial integrity of the Federal Republic of Yugoslavia." More specific clauses authorized Kosovo's "substantial autonomy *within* the Federal Republic of Yugoslavia, *to be decided by the Security Council* of the United Nations."[10] The Security Council never authorized the independence of Kosovo recognized by the United States in 2008. Yet the fact remains that the intervention did succeed in its primary purpose: removing Kosovo's Albanians from the oppression of the Serb central government. NATO did so by unambiguously supporting one side in the civil war and by executing military operations that, while not unlimited, were impressively destructive.

## MEDDLING WITHOUT MUDDLING

The peacekeeping operations that have been the United Nations' forte can help fortify peace, but they do not create peace as "peace enforcement" is supposed to do. During the decade after the Cold War, the United States and the United Nations stumbled into several imbroglios where it was not clear which of the two missions they were pursuing, and there was much head scratching about the gray area between operations under chapters 6 and 7 of the UN Charter. The United States and United Nations responded to rough experiences by remaining mired in indecision and hamstrung by half-measures (Bosnia to 1995), facing failure and bailing out (Somalia), acting only after a long period of limited and misdirected pressure (Haiti), or holding back from action where more awesome disaster than anywhere else called for it (Rwanda). UN performance was so frequently disappointing that American leaders turned to another multilateral organization—NATO—when they wanted to use force effectively in Bosnia and Kosovo. In Kosovo NATO almost avoided the delusion of impartiality. Indeed, it launched a war against Belgrade explicitly on behalf of the Kosovar Albanians. At the time, however, NATO could not bring itself to own up to the logic of what it was doing, because it refused to endorse independence for the group for which it was fighting. This illogic may have eased the way for Slobodan Milosevic to capitulate, but it left the intervenors with no straightforward legal way out of indefinite occupation of Kosovo.

If intervention is not to be foresworn and is not to be undertaken arbitrarily, what is the alternative? To do better in picking and choosing, it would help to be clearer about how military means should be marshaled for political ends. The following points should be kept in mind.

*Recognize that to make peace is to decide who rules.* Making peace means determining how the war ends. If U.S. or UN forces are going to intervene to make peace, they will often have to kill people and break things in the process. If they choose to do this, they should do so only after they have decided who will rule afterward.

If claims or capabilities in the local conflict are not clear enough to make this judgment, then they are not clear enough for intervention to bring peace. By the same token, international forces should not mix in the dangerous business of determining who governs without expecting deadly opposition. An intervention that can be stopped in its tracks by a few dozen casualties, as the U.S. operation in Somalia was in 1993, is one that should never begin.

*Avoid half-measures.* If the United States or the United Nations wishes to bring peace to violent places before tragedy unfolds in full, gruesome detail, they should act decisively by either lending their military weight to one side or forcing both sides to compromise. In either case, leaders or outside powers should avoid what the natural instincts of successful politicians and bureaucrats tell them is sensible: a middle course.

Half-measures often make sense in domestic politics, but that is precisely because peace already exists. Contending interests accept compromises negotiated in legislatures, adjudicated in courts, and enforced by executives because the state has a monopoly on organized force; the question of who rules is settled. That is the premise of politics in peace; in war, that premise is what the fighting is all about. A middle course in intervention—especially a gradual and symbolic use of force—is likely to do little but muddy both sides' calculations, fuel their hopes of victory, or kill people for principles only indirectly related to the purpose of the war. If deadly force is to make a direct contribution to peace, it must engage the purposes most directly related to war—the determination of borders and the distribution of political power. NATO used force less hesitantly and abstemiously in Bosnia in 1995 and Kosovo and Serbia in 1999. In neither of these cases, however, did NATO go all the way to settling the terms of local government. It embraced the ideal of re-creating integral multiethnic states, rather than reinforcing permanent partitions, yet did not act to prevent the locals from proceeding with partition and, in Kosovo, secession.

*Do not confuse peace with justice.* If outside powers want to do the right thing but do not want to do it in a big way, they should recognize that they are placing a higher premium on legitimacy than on peace. Most international interventions in the post–Cold War hiatus were not driven by the material interests of the outside powers but by their moral interests: securing peace and justice. Peace and justice, however, are not natural allies, unless right just happens to coincide with might.

Outside intervention in a civil war usually becomes an issue when the sides are closely enough matched that neither can defeat the other quickly. When material interests are not directly involved, it is impractical to expect great powers or the United Nations to expend the resources for an overwhelming and decisive military action. So if peace should take precedence, and intervention is to be limited, it should support the mightiest of the rivals, irrespective of their legitimacy. If the United Nations had weighed in on the side of the Serbs when they were dominant in Bosnia in the early 1990s or had helped Aideed take control in Mogadishu rather than trying to jail him, there might well have been peace in Bosnia and Somalia much earlier—just not the kind of peace the intervenors wanted. If justice takes precedence, however, limited intervention may well lengthen a conflict. Perhaps putting an end to killing should not be the first priority in peacemaking, but interventionists must admit that any intervention involves such a choice. If the United States does not want to support the stronger side because it is the wrong side, yet also does not want to pay a high price to bring peace, it should stay out of the conflict.

Tension between peace and justice also arises in assessing territorial divisions like those proposed for Bosnia in the earliest years, such as the misconceived Vance-Owen Plan. If the aim is to reduce violent eruptions, borders should be drawn not to minimize the transfer of populations and property, but to make the borders coherent, congruent with political solidarity, and defensible. This, unfortunately, makes ethnic cleansing the solution to ethnic cleansing. Also, it will not guarantee against later outbreaks of revanchism. All it can do is make war less constant.

*Do not confuse balance with peace or justice.* Preventing either side from gaining a military advantage prevents ending the war by military means, but it does not end the war. Countries that are not losing are likely to keep fighting until prolonged indecision makes winning seem hopeless—that is, after much additional bloodshed. Outsiders who want to make peace but do not want to take sides or take control themselves try to avoid favoritism by keeping either side from overturning an indecisive balance on the battlefield. This supports the military stalemate, lengthens the war, and costs more lives.

*Make humanitarian intervention militarily rational.* Sometimes the imperative to stop the slaughter or save the starving should be too much even for the most hard-boiled realists, and intervention may be warranted even if it does not aim to secure peace. This was a motive in Bosnia and Somalia in the early 1990s, but intervention there involved presence in battle areas, friction with combatants or local political factions, and skirmishes that escalated without any sensible strategic plan.

Operation Provide Comfort, the U.S. humanitarian intervention in northern Iraq after the 1991 Persian Gulf War, provides a better model. In this case the intervening force carved out lines within which it could take command without fighting, but which it could defend if challenged—an area within which the intervenors themselves would rule temporarily. Then they got on with ministering to the needy populations and protecting them from assault. Such action is a stopgap, not a solution, but it is less likely to make the war worse. As it turned out, U.S. forces soon withdrew as Kurdish forces took control of the zone. In Bosnia, by contrast, the "safe areas," weapons exclusion zones, and towns supplied by American airdrops in the early 1990s were islands surrounded by hostile forces and represented messy territorial anomalies in what was effectively, at that point, a Serb conquest. It was no surprise that the Serbs would hover, waiting to pounce whenever they thought they might get away with it, probing and testing the resolve of the outsiders to fight, waiting for the international community to tire of the effort to keep the enclaves on life support. The nadir of this disregard for military reality was the 1995 conquest of Srebrenica.

Calling attention to mistakes, confusion, and uncomfortable choices is not intended to discredit intervention altogether. It is meant to argue for caution because confusion about what is at issue can make such undertakings cause conflict rather than cure it. Doing it right is not impossible. The United States and the United Nations have collaborated successfully in peacemaking in the past, most notably in the wars over Korea and Kuwait. Enthusiasm for widespread involvement in local conflicts in the early 1990s was based on expectations that it would require a small proportion of the effort of those two huge enterprises. Unfortunately, this was probably true in some cases where the United Nations held back, as in Rwanda, and untrue in some cases where it jumped in, as in Bosnia. Peacemaking will not always cost as much as it did in Korea and Kuwait. The underlying issues, however, are much the same—who is in charge, and in what pieces of territory, after a war ends. Intervention that proceeds as if the issues are different—and can be settled by action toward the belligerents that is both evenhanded in intent and weak in capability—will more likely prevent peace than promote it.

Scarcely better are interventions that learn this lesson halfway and use ample force and diplomatic legerdemain to secure peace agreements that do not really settle the question of who rules. This is what happened in Bosnia in 1995 and in Kosovo in 1999. Such interventions step up to the delusion of impartiality when they apply force but then back away in the diplomatic aftermath. By pretending not to side decisively with one side against the other in a peace settlement, and pretending to support the reintegration of hopelessly riven polities, such interventions purchase peace at the price of an indefinite, multilateral imperium. To put the question of final judgment in focus, consider in detail the record of postintervention results in the Balkans that most officials count as successes, and consider some thought experiments about how sensible strategy should have defined and assessed the choices years ago.

## AFTER INTERVENTION

Washington half-learned some of the lessons just mentioned. After years of violence, peace did come to Bosnia and Kosovo. But the peace was uneasy because it rested on a conspiracy to prop up contradictions. Inhabitants and intervenors conspired to live with political practices that contradicted constitutional principles, and to prolong foreign occupation while genuflecting to the aim of democratic self-government. The American foreign policy elite on both sides of the political spectrum was complicit. Clintonites promoted the conspiracy in order to do the right thing without overstepping the bounds of domestic support. The Bush II team came to office disapproving of entanglement in peacekeeping, yet relishing American primacy on the world stage—a contradiction of its own that blocked a graceful way out. Then after a decade of temporizing, Washington moved to closure on Kosovo by recognizing it as an independent country, but its situation and Bosnia's remained politically tense. The overloaded Obama administration left the Balkans on the back burner, simmering but at risk of boiling over when all external control of the countries ends.

With the Dayton Accords in 1995 President Clinton justified sending American troops to Bosnia with the assurance that they would be out within a year. He mistook an exit date for an exit strategy, and U.S. forces stayed on for many years. Unlike the occupations of Germany and Japan after 1945, NATO and the United Nations settled into operations in the Balkans best understood as institutionalized temporizing. There were good efforts at economic reconstruction, but political reconstruction was confused and weak.

In fact, confusion of the political status of these areas was a vital necessity. It let occupiers and inhabitants pursue separate agendas. Western presence was sustainable because it rested on unresolved contradictions between the de jure and de facto settlements of the two wars: Bosnia was a single state in principle but a partitioned one in practice, and for nine years Kosovo continued to be a province of Yugoslavia in principle although not in practice. The contradictions allowed the inhabitants of Bosnia and Kosovo to avoid organizing their societies in the ways that the occupiers wanted, while allowing the occupiers to pretend that they were supervising a transition to the type of social organization that the West approves. For almost a decade in Kosovo, and longer in Bosnia, resolving the contradictions was too daunting, so temporizing was the result. Rather than face up to an unpalatable choice between much stronger efforts that might have better chances of cultivating political stability and a withdrawal that might reignite war, the United States, NATO, and the United Nations drifted in open-ended occupation. This was the path of least resistance only because the costs were modest—little treasure and no blood.

During the Cold War the United States was often accused of neoimperialism. At the time this was wrong. U.S. interventions often found the client's tail wagging the patron's dog, as Washington became mired in support of problematic Third World governments, but without direct governing authority. By the turn of the century, though, Washington was engaged in *real* neoimperialism, although a quite peculiar multilateral and humanitarian form of it.[11] Under the aegis of international organizations, the United States collaborated with other governments in the direct control of Bosnia and Kosovo, a return of the Western great powers to tutelary administration of backward nations. There was certainly no economic benefit to the imperial metropoles. Rather the Western presence was a sort of *mission civilisatrice.*

Despite rhetorical backing and filling, the Clinton administration embraced the idea of imperial administration. Indeed, it was the implicit rationale for maintaining U.S. primacy that animated Holbrooke, Berger, and Albright's view of the United States as "the indispensable nation." And although intervention in Bosnia was a Clinton project, the U.S. commitment to protect Kosovo went back to the Bush I administration.

As a thought experiment, consider how choices could have been conceived once Washington was entangled. To get out of the Balkans the United States could have aimed for six main objectives:

*Establish self-government to allow terminating the occupation.* The United States should not be an imperial power and should not accept indefinite responsibility to administer foreign countries. Ironically this objective was achieved where it was least legitimate, in Kosovo, but as of 2011 incompletely in Bosnia, where Belgrade has no claim to sovereignty.

*Stabilize security and peace for local states.* The prime motive of intervention in the Balkans was to end the violence there. Withdrawal that allowed war to erupt again would represent failure.

*Withdraw U.S. forces.* Aside from the moral interest in ending occupation, there was a material interest in reducing the strains on American military forces—particularly the personnel rotation system and training in the army—that were imposed by prolonged peacekeeping expeditions.[12] This was accomplished gradually, barely in time to meet the demands of occupation in Iraq.

*Minimize damage to relations with other great powers.* The main reasons for intervention were humanitarian, but good deeds should be done without paying significant costs in the aspects of international politics that count the most.

*Honor moral obligations.* At least as long as the cost is low, there is no reason not to do this.

*Honor legal obligations.* Other considerations being equal, it is in the interest of the United States to observe the terms of its international agreements if it wishes such agreements to be useful instruments in the future. But other considerations in the Balkans were not equal. To realist critics, "legalism and moralism" are often lumped together as impediments to the wise pursuit of material interests. In Kosovo, however, legal obligations to Belgrade conflicted with moral obligations to the Albanian population. The latter eventually won out.

Some would add preservation of NATO's credibility and America's leadership to the list of objectives. Indeed, some cited these as the most important, and they headlined many statements by officials and pundits. Mortgaging the mission to these buzzwords, however, put the cart before the horse. It reflected a penchant for self-entrapment that is not unique to involvement in the Balkans but is a problem of U.S. foreign policy in general.

Credibility is not served by reinforcing failure or by stubborn persistence in doing the wrong thing. Just because the costs were on a greater scale does not mean that Vietnam's lessons on this score are irrelevant. Credibility should serve the pursuit of substantive objectives, not dictate what those objectives should be. Leadership means convincing others to want what we want, not changing what we want in order to keep followers faithful. If the United States could succeed in meeting the six objectives listed above, leadership would be evident and credibility would follow. The problems with the list are that each objective was hard to achieve in itself and that it was impossible to achieve some without undercutting others.

A glaring part of the problem is the inconsistency of principles on which principled intervention proceeded. The United States has made it utterly unclear whether it wants multinational states to remain unitary and to strive for social integration or will forcibly support secession by aggrieved ethnic populations. It has officially supported integration in Cyprus and Bosnia but secession in Kosovo and tacitly in southern Sudan; it opposes independence for Taiwan in principle but supports it in practice; it avoids saying anything about Tibet but implicitly accepts its integration in China.

Perhaps American leaders should fall back on Emerson's line that foolish consistency is the hobgoblin of small minds, but it is dubious that on a matter of this importance consistency is foolish.

## SOVEREIGNTY AND STABILITY

The hinge of a solution in the Balkans is the connection between sovereign self-government and interstate stability (meshing the first three objectives above). Self-government was established but for many years was stable because it was limited—self-government of a kind reminiscent of colonies in the more enlightened of the old European empires. Well into the twenty-first century self-government in Bosnia and Kosovo remained subject to the higher authority of the occupying forces. The benefit in this was that it prevented self-government from reenergizing local conflict; the cost was that it deferred resolution of the essential issue. *Genuine* self-government requires termination of the controlling role of occupying powers.

Self-government and stability threatened each other because the conflict was over the conditions of self-government. The lack of congruence of cultural and political communities had caused the explosions in the first place. The essential issue was what the number, form, and boundaries of independent governments would be—which units should constitute the "selves" of self-government—when sovereignty ceased to be limited by outside occupation. Would the solution be self-government of a genuinely unified Bosnia and of a Yugoslavia that included the province of Kosovo, as multiethnic states (a model for idealists, but a nonstarter)? Or autonomy arrangements for ethnically defined territorial areas within a Bosnia and Yugoslavia that were organized as loose confederations (the continuing situation in Bosnia, the official aim of the outside powers for Kosovo until some accepted its independence)? Or self-government of smaller ethnically defined states in formal partitions of the larger units that were until then the juridically legitimate ones (the solution Washington ultimately accepted for Kosovo, but not for Bosnia's subdivisions)? Peace in Bosnia and Kosovo depended on the contradiction between principle and practice. As long as outside powers continued to run the region, the contradictions could be finessed and were even quite functional.

Bosnia remained at peace because of the dualistic political structure established by the Dayton Accords: legally a single Bosnian state, but really three separate ones. Officially the single state was composed of two "entities," the Muslim-Croat Federation and the Republika Srpska, but each had veto rights over actions of the central government. In effect there were three entities, as the federation broke down into Croat and Muslim areas that cooperated only minimally. What is the real function of the unified state, if any, when the fundamental divisions behind the war remain in place in the peace? As Ivo Daalder put it, "By incorporating rather than resolving the fundamental disagreement among the parties about Bosnia's future, Dayton assured that its implementation would become little more than the continuation of conflict by other means."[13]

What made this situation preferable to formal partition, other than a belief that a hypocritical liberal fiction is better than legitimizing a reactionary reality? What made this peace more than a glorified armistice? The occupying powers could not grant Kosovo independence without violating the agreement that ended the 1999 war. Nor could NATO decide to ignore that provision of the agreement without also disregarding UN jurisdiction. As Barry Posen pointed out, the Security Council had the authoritative role in the occupation, to continue " 'until the Security Council decides otherwise.' Thus, if either the Chinese or Russians choose not to decide otherwise, insofar as both have veto power, Security Council control over Kosovo will last forever."[14] The United States elected to ignore that provision and resolved the occupation question by recognizing Kosovo's independence.


## FIXING WHO RULES: EXAMPLES TO EMULATE OR AVOID?

If policymakers had aimed to resolve sovereignty issues rather than temporize, where should they have looked for a basis on which to predict how ethnic conflicts in the Balkans could be settled? Liberal optimists tend to rely on logic: secure domestic peace and international aid, both provided by peacekeeping missions, should foster civil cooperation and tolerance because they make more rational sense than destructive parochialism. But logic depends entirely on assumptions, which in politics are often unexamined. Conservative pessimists look more for precedents to confirm assumptions. If the aim is to make viable multinational states out of the riven polities in the region, what examples offer encouragement?

Few spring to mind. Switzerland or the United States may seem to be models. But really? Neither has suffered a bitter and horrific war among its constituent groups that still lives in their citizens' personal memories. Political integration in the American South took more than a hundred years after the Civil War, and social integration is elusive to this day. Singapore? It is peaceful and orderly, but not very democratic. Southern Africa? The settlement in Zimbabwe crumbled as the Mugabe government expropriated land from white farmers, descended into corruption, and wrecked the economy. South Africa so far offers the best example of hope, but even if reconciliation there proves durable, is it more similar to the Balkans than other examples of failure?

Those who want to bank on joining contending ethnic groups in functioning polities need more relevant examples of successful connection. Other ethnically divided states and regions of the twentieth century encourage skepticism about secular integration after bitter civil wars. This is especially true if the states emerging from the resolution are to be democratic and genuinely self-governing. Compared to its previous decades of civil strife binational Lebanon is ostensibly stable and democratic, but that comparison sets a low bar. For many years the stability lasted in great part because Syria kept the country under its thumb, as NATO did for so long in the Balkans. Internal cleavages continued and made Lebanon a victim of external attack as Israel smashed up the country to retaliate against Hezbollah in 2006. Before and since then the UN pretended to keep the peace with a token force of a few thousand, a force that is heftier than the old one deployed on the country's border and brushed aside by Israel in its 1982 invasion, yet still a force that exerts no force, has no authority to take meaningful independent action, was not even empowered to enforce the UN-mandated disarmament of militias, does not police traffic in military contraband, and does nothing to control Hezbollah actions.[15] Lebanon's temporary and tenuous stability soon eroded. Democracy, especially the rickety illiberal democracy emergent in many postauthoritarian countries, is no cure-all. Authoritarianism can suppress divisive identity politics and democracy can release it. Yugoslavia before the 1990s was united and stable in great part because it was not democratic; secular communism overrode ethnic particularism.

Legal issues aside, is formal division of a country the lesser evil? The history of ethnically based partitions in the twentieth century was mostly a sorry one.[16] The 1947 partitions in Palestine and the Indian subcontinent were each followed by several wars, and Northern Ireland remained violently unsettled for eighty years after its separation. Cyprus has experienced no war since Turkey imposed partition in 1974, but other countries have not accepted the solution. The relevant question, however, is the counterfactual one: would history in the sorry cases have been better or worse if the states had *not* been partitioned? The arguments for partition are not that it is good, but that it may be less constantly horrendous than keeping the warring communities in the same state, or that it is preferable to indefinite foreign occupation of an uneasy confederation.[17]

Some relevant lessons might be sought among wars ended by partition along ethnic lines, for example, Palestine, Kashmir, and Cyprus. The mention of these unhappy and unsettled places suggests rejecting formal separation as a model for Bosnia or Yugoslavia and Kosovo, but a closer look suggests a more equivocal conclusion. The partition of Palestine in 1947 was immediately revised by the war of 1948 and was altered again by the Six-Day War, the Camp David Accords, and the Oslo Agreement—and it remains in question. Kashmir too has remained a dangerous cauldron of conflict. In this case either a more careful plan for partition of India in 1947 that allocated the area to Pakistan (on grounds of ethnic affiliation) or a more decisive war that left it fully within India (as Israel's gains in the 1948 war overcame the unviable noncontiguity of the partition plan's territorial divisions in Palestine) might have yielded more stability. An independent Kashmir or an accepted division of the area between India and Pakistan would be additional hypothetical alternatives. The analogous hypothetical choices in Kosovo would be union with Albania, reincorporation in Yugoslavia, or what Washington ultimately accepted: independence. There is no good analogy in Bosnia since the Muslims—who have no supporting external state comparable to Croatia or Serbia—create an unbalanced tripolar situation more complicated than Kashmir or Kosovo.

If one takes the UN role in Cyprus seriously, that case presents the model of indefinite and indecisive peacekeeping; the UN force has been in the country for almost fifty years, and there is still not a final peace agreement accepted locally or internationally. During that time the mission has been eased by its irrelevance to the main security issues on Cyprus—it has not had the powerful controlling role of the West in the Balkans, was often ignored by local contestants, and when it did take forceful action did not always have a good effect.[18] It did not stop either the Greek coup on the island nor the Turkish invasion in 1974. More relevant is the unilateral Turkish partition imposed then. Unacceptable as that partition may be on legal grounds (it remains unrecognized by virtually the entire world outside Turkey), it has meant peace on the island for almost forty years, a peace underwritten by the presence of Turkish and Greek deterrent forces on opposite sides of the partition line, rather than by the UN force that failed to prevent escalation of conflict several times before. If justice is to take precedence over peace, what is the solution for Cyprus—return to the unitary state that preceded the Greek coup? If so, what mechanism would protect the Turkish minority more satisfactorily than Ankara's intervention did? If peace is to take precedence over justice, there is a strong case for international recognition of the partition and the legitimacy of the Turkish Republic on Cyprus. If justice and peace are to rank equally, a solution is nowhere in sight—after a half-century of impotent UN presence.

Do these examples suggest that Bosnia would do better to insist on an integrated multinational state? Could anything have been much worse than the past half-century of tension and periodic wars in the Middle East and South Asia? Well, yes. It is unlikely that internationally enforced creation of an integrated Arab-Jewish state in the 1940s (no harder to imagine then than the integration of Serbs and Albanians in Kosovo today) would have been less violent or more viable than what developed. Would a never-born Pakistan, a never-partitioned India, populated by a more even balance of Hindus and Muslims, have avoided constant or cataclysmic internal turmoil? We cannot know, but we do know that Cyprus experienced both alternatives since World War II, and proved to be more peaceful in the four decades since its partition than it was in the preceding years.

A different illustration by analogy of choices for Kosovo is the untidy periphery of contemporary China. Should intervenors have wanted to model Kosovo's future on Tibet, Hong Kong, or Taiwan? Since 1950 Tibet has suffered the fate that NATO went to war to prevent in Kosovo. Hong Kong represents the hope of the original temporizers in the Balkans, the way out of the choice between betraying the Kosovar Albanians or violating the agreement that ended the war with Belgrade—the promise of indefinite actual autonomy under nominal Chinese (in this case, Yugoslav) sovereignty. Taiwan represents independence de facto but not de jure—autonomy with a claim to sovereignty recognized by some but not most other countries in the world and guarded by force rather than, as in Hong Kong, by Beijing's sufferance. The analogy is a Kosovo recognized by some as a sovereign state but by others as a province of Yugoslavia, but armed and able to prevent Belgrade from imposing its writ. Unlike Taiwan, Kosovo lacks the geographic conditions (no water buffer) to make self-defense without foreign forces feasible. By 2008 Kosovo came closest to the last of these, the Taiwan model, but can compensate for its geographic vulnerability with the backing of the United States—and because Serbia is weaker than the People's Republic of China (PRC).

## U.S. National Security

Moral interests were the prime reason for outside intervention in the Balkans—the humanitarian imperative to suppress atrocities (although why this imperative should be irresistible in Europe, but not in Rwanda, Sudan, or other places plagued by worse atrocities, was not clear). Some also believed that intervention in the Balkans was warranted as well by material interests, traditional security concerns about the international balance of power and the need to keep local chaos from expanding and bringing on conflict among major states. This argument, however, has it backwards. Intervention worsened conflict with other great powers instead of dampening it. It would be nice if moral and material interests reinforced each other, but in reality they have been in tension. Moral interests have prevailed mainly because material interests have not been seriously threatened.

If the objective had been to prevent escalation of the local conflict to confrontation with a major adversary, there is no reason to assume that Western intervention would accomplish this, or would do so more effectively than diplomatic collusion to insulate the conflict by foreswearing intervention by *any* of the great powers, from West or East. It is disingenuous to think that intervention from the West alone would not aggravate already disagreeable relations between NATO and Russia. Luckily, worsened relations with Russia did not seem a crucial problem in the 1990s, and some considered them a price worth paying for the moral benefit of stopping the locals from killing each other. Russia was weak and had few options for responding to its alienation in a way that would threaten NATO. The West did not have to worry about maintaining a balance of power, reassuring Russia about its security, or pandering to Moscow's wounded *amour propre*. In short, NATO could simply take advantage of its hegemonic position and leave the Russians to lump it. Moscow had no choice but to accept the Dayton Accords and participate in both occupation missions. Although the Kosovo War infuriated the Russians, there was little they could do to counter NATO there. The Russian *coup de main* in seizing the Pristina airport at the end of the war, however, and British General Jackson's refusal of American General Clark's order to have NATO forces block them, raised the specter of unintended military confrontation. (Backed by his government in London, Jackson replied to Clark, "Sir, I'm not starting World War III for you.")[19] Most important, however, was the short-sightedness of counting on indefinite Russian weakness, rather than looking ahead toward stabilizing relations on a more equitable and cooperative basis before an aggrieved and resurgent Russia regained options of its own.

The Kosovo War brought an unanticipated cost to U.S. relations with another potential great power adversary: China. The accidental bombing of the Chinese Embassy (which the Chinese did not believe was really an accident) had a gratuitously damaging impact not only on diplomatic relations, but on Chinese public opinion. Moreover, the entire rationale for Western intervention in Kosovo represents a threat in principle to Chinese sovereignty. The rationale could just as easily be applied to justify humanitarian intervention on behalf of the oppressed populations of Tibet or Xinjiang, or Taiwan's claim to autonomy, in the same way that it impugned Russia's sovereign right to pacify Chechnya.

## WAYS OUT

More than a decade after intervention, Washington had managed more or less to extricate American forces from the Balkans, but by leaving the basic cleavages in Bosnia and Kosovo unresolved, suppressed by a wobbly peace that still depended on imperial management by foreigners. A majority of countries in the world had not recognized Kosovo's U.S.-backed declaration of independence. Despite outsiders' investment of more than $18 billion in aid since 1995, Bosnia was still overseen by a UN high representative with ultimate administrative authority, had made negligible progress toward integration of political or even educational institutions, and experienced continuing internal migration that increased ethnic segregation.[20] Could Washington and its allies in multilateral imperialism have done better?

Recognizing a reality that admitted of no good strategy right after the war over Kosovo, two supporters of the venture were reduced to recommending that Americans avoid the question: "Kosovo may now have shattered the exit strategy concept. . . . Not only is it impossible to say when NATO troops will leave Kosovo, it is also impossible to specify under what circumstances they will do so. . . . One cannot say; it would be unwise at this point even to try."[21] But it was necessary to try unless Americans or their collaborators in international institutions were to occupy the region forever. There was to be no way out of the Balkans for the United States that did not entail high cost in either effort or honor. There was no support for a much stronger effort, so the price was paid in honor—withdrawal without resolution of the problem, and violation of the agreement that ended the war over Kosovo. To decide whether intervention could have done better, consider another thought experiment.

By the end of the war in 1999 there were three general options: worst, bad, and not quite so bad:

*Inertia: open-ended occupation.* This seemed the path of least-resistance, but it put Washington at the mercy of events. It was foolish to assume that either the locals or American voters would want U.S. forces in place forever, or that the costs of responsibility on the ground would remain low. Albanian insurgencies in southern Serbia and northern Macedonia suggested the dangers that could arise to complicate the peace that was to be kept.

If there was a rationale for this option other than mindless inertia, it would have been a long-term tutelage designed to transform the local societies and allow eventual disengagement and durable peace. If a long period of neoimperial tutelage had high odds of civilizing the locals and making the next generation willing practitioners of secular liberalism, it might have been worthwhile to gamble on it, to view the institutionalized temporizing as gradual behavior modification. To give such a gamble a chance, however, suggested a bigger effort—a more muscular tutelage, forcing the locals to be free as the Allies forced Germans and Japanese after 1945—rather than the dwindling effort that actually occurred. A stronger attempt would have meant forcing the locals to be free on Western terms of liberal, secular democracy; cracking the heads of the few but crucial nationalist fanatics in all areas; intervening inventively in civics education; imposing the equivalent of denazification ruthlessly on all the local communities rather than leaving them to shelter indicted war criminals; decisively crushing subversive activism by the Albanians for whom NATO fought in 1999; and changing political culture to root protections for minorities in custom rather than foreign fiat.

These ambitions would have been a very tall order even under better circumstances. Contrary to the implicit logic of enthusiasts for limited intervention, there is no evidence that a liberal, tolerant, deethnicized political order is the natural default option once a peaceful truce is attained, no evidence that it is what the societies will necessarily fall into if given the chance by temporary international policing and reconstruction. This conclusion does not rely on the common exaggeration of the historic depth of animosity among ethnic groups in the Balkans; indeed, the assumption that intense centuries-old group hatreds there are irrepressible may be in some respects a myth.[22] For whatever tragic reasons, however, members of these groups have killed each other in large enough numbers in very recent times to prevent easy reestablishment of civic trust. To create secular liberalism in the Balkans amounts to remaking the societies—nation building and state building—the ambitious, hubris-laden mission that Vietnam made anathema for awhile, was reborn in Iraq and Afghanistan, and is not easily elected after rough experiences.

While state building is not impossible, even a long and strenuous effort cannot guarantee success. Unlike the Balkans, neither Germany nor Japan, the success stories usually invoked, was an ethnically divided society. Nor does duration of occupation necessarily correspond to durability of reform. A dozen years of Reconstruction in the American South did not consolidate emancipation and prevent the replacement of slavery by serfdom. Nearly twenty years of American occupation in the interwar period left Haiti hardly more just or more stable than at the start, and the same may be said for the U.S. effort in the country after 1994. The Philippines may be a more promising example, but such success as there was there occurred after nearly a half-century of direct American rule—and the country's internal stability since then has still been rocky.

There was no reason to believe that the responsible powers would permit the more ambitious form and degree of nation building in the Balkans. Inertia was all toward thinning out the occupation efforts rather than fortifying them. The path of least resistance at the time seemed to be a permanent presence only because it was an attenuating one. Indeed, the occupation withered gradually with only two thousand peacekeepers (none American) left in Bosnia fifteen years after the Dayton Accords.

*Formal partition*. This was a fallback, in theory at least, if the chance of creating integrated liberal societies within the actually segregated ones was too low—and if the occupiers would not make a strenuous effort to raise the odds. Phony multinational states are not harmless. They fool few and make no one happy but the lawyers, diplomats, or foreign moralists who prefer a shameless fiction of decency to a shameful stability. Partition would make de jure political lines congruent with de facto social lines; political separation would reduce the exaggerated expectations of day-to-day cooperation among the communities whose antagonism was the source of the wars of the 1990s.

Partition, however, was still a bad option.[23] To make states both ethnically homogeneous and territorially defensible (that is, geographically coherent rather than a checkerboard collection of noncontiguous or strategically vulnerable swatches of land) would require revised borders and forced population transfers. This would contravene international law and Western moral sensibilities to a degree that makes it a fanciful option. The kind of partition that might be salable diplomatically for Bosnia would likely be one etched along the lines that existed after Dayton. This would have made for an awkwardly shaped Muslim Bosniac state, lacking access to the sea, difficult to defend. It would have required a Western military guarantee to that state, regardless of whether the Croat sections and Republika Srpska joined Croatia and Serbia.

In one sense partition of Kosovo would be easier, if only because ethnic cleansing was more extensive there. The 1999 war and its aftermath concentrated the majority and minority in relatively distinct zones and more or less exchanged cleansing of the province's Albanians by the Serbs for the reverse. A negotiated partition would have carved off a northern slice for Serbia and given independence to the remaining Albanian bulk of Kosovo. If Belgrade accepted this deal it would have avoided the violation of the 1999 peace agreement that ultimately occurred with recognition of Kosovo's independence. Formally blessed partitions of Bosnia and Kosovo, however, would undermine the shaky foundation of Macedonian statehood and could energize a crack-up there as nasty as what happened elsewhere in Yugoslavia in the 1990s. The rationale for propping up that multinational amalgam would be hard to sustain after giving up on the other two.

*Handoff to the European Union.* This too was a bad solution, only less bad than the others—and it is what happened in Bosnia, though the UN Security Council retained jurisdiction in principle over Kosovo. Policing the periphery of Europe is a perfect mission for a European Union groping toward an independent "defense identity." To some, though, this is a shameful escape for the United States, which led the charges to the Rambouillet ultimatum and the Dayton Accords. In material terms, however, there is no reason that Europeans whose unity is worth anything, and whose collective resources are greater than those of the United States, should not be expected to handle the problem in their neighborhood without us, as we intervene in our neighborhood (Central America and the Caribbean) without them. The mission was finally handed to the European Union.

The Balkans are just one reminder of the uncertain strength provided by primacy. There is only one global superpower, involved strategically everywhere in the world, but global reach spreads American strength thin, and the variety of such involvements limits the effort possible in any one and makes the United States one of a coalition of great powers in each region of importance outside the Western Hemisphere. The post–Cold War world is unipolar globally, but multipolar regionally.[24] Or as Shin'ichi Ogawa has said, since the Cold War economy has been globalized but security has been regionalized. Clintonites lurched prematurely toward the mirage of political globalization, conflating U.S. leadership with multilateralism, committing the United States to humanitarian activism ambitious in aims but limited in action. Half-measures left Washington bogged down in the Balkans until extrication proceeded without resolution.

Unless the projection of moral force is backed by material force that is decisive rather than hesitant, intervention risks ineffectiveness and embarrassment. By the same token, American primacy means less if it is not exercised when challenges to American preferences arise. The first post–Cold War administration did not have to face this issue. Bush I left office before the Somalia mission went bad and before his commitment in principle to Kosovo came home to roost. The Clinton administration never fully faced the issue and did not escape the consequences. Bush II embraced muscular primacy with a vengeance and ignited the disaster in Iraq, which simply eclipsed concern with the Balkans. By the time Obama came to office, the Balkans had slipped off the overloaded American list of priorities.

Even for those willing to intervene forcefully, the puzzle for interventionists in the post–Cold War world has been how to decide the standard for selection. There are too many disastrous political disorders around the world to deal with decisively. Their prevalence would offer the death by a thousand slices to any consistent American policy aimed at imposing peace and justice where they are in demand. Politicians' natural and normal answer is that just because we cannot do everything does not mean that we should do nothing. But then how to choose? If Bosnia, why not Burundi— or any number of other divided societies on the brink of violence?

The only prudent and politically sustainable answer is that the United States should intervene where probable benefits exceed probable costs by a hefty margin. Estimating those probabilities in advance is hard. Keeping the costs low, in turn, may often require compromising moral principles to privilege peace over justice in the hierarchy of objectives. For example, intervention that separates antagonistic communities and allows them independence may face fewer obstacles to success than intervention that tries to impose Western standards of civic decency and reintegration of communities that have recently soaked each other in blood.

To reject humanitarian intervention altogether, even under this cautious standard, is unnecessarily callous. To demand more is to raise the question of how to marshal the international will and resources to make frequent and decisive intervention feasible rather than spotty, limited, and ineffective. Those focused on material interests must deal with the former point, and those focused on moral interests must deal with the latter. Neither material nor moral interests alone can make a foreign policy that works, yet remains truly American.

# 4

## NEW THREATS OF MASS DESTRUCTION
### CAPABILITIES DOWN, INTENTIONS UP

During the Cold War weapons of mass destruction (WMD) were the centerpiece of foreign policy.[1] Chemical and biological weapons were developed and fielded in large numbers with little notice, but nuclear arms above all hovered in the background of every major issue in East–West competition and alliance relations. The highest priorities of U.S. policy could almost all be linked in some way to the danger of World War III and the fear of millions of casualties in the American homeland.

In the hiatus after the Cold War other issues displaced strategic concerns on the foreign policy agenda, and that agenda itself was barely on the public's radar screen. After September 11 national security bounded back to the fore, but the focus was on terrorism, rogue states, and irregular warfare. WMD figured in George W. Bush's rationale for attacking Iraq, but fear of these weapons remained in the background of public consciousness compared with their high profile in the twentieth century. Apart from defense policy professionals, few Americans still lose sleep over WMD. After all, what did normal people feel was the main relief provided by the end of the Cold War? It was that the danger of nuclear war was off their backs.

While the lower anxiety about WMD after the Cold War was understandable, it was hardly sensible. North Korea's entry into the nuclear club and Iran's movement toward it revived concern and turned attention to what Fred Iklé, in a particularly gripping way, characterized as "the heart of the matter":

Two overarching and profoundly serious problems that dominate the nuclear age, casting a dark shadow far into the future. The first of these is that we have become habituated to—indeed, utterly dependent on—a world predicated on the non-use of nuclear weapons. This order might end abruptly. It would be a unique revolution in military affairs if the most powerful weapons in the arsenals of many nations were never used. Yet this uniqueness has become the norm on which trade, economic growth, international relations, as well as the domestic functioning of democratic governments now depend. Not only is the fact of continued non-use vital for our political order, but also the frame of mind that evolved with it. For it allows us to go about our business and plan our lives without the imagery of mushroom clouds superimposed on our hometown.[2]

In the second decade after the Cold War national security policy elites returned some attention to managing the inherited nuclear weapons establishment, but these efforts remained less than page-one news, and their results were dominated by inertia. Controversy developed over whether and how to maintain and modernize the aging weapon stockpile and supporting infrastructure, without creating officially "new" weapons or testing them. The Congressional Commission on the Strategic Posture of the United States (the Perry-Schlesinger Commission) reported in May 2009 but presented no dramatic recommendations (being politically balanced, it could not even reach an agreed position on ratification of the Comprehensive Test Ban). The Defense Department's Nuclear Posture Review was released in April 2010, but it too avoided any sharp change of course.

The one major break with Cold War inertia was the 2008 launching of the Global Zero movement to eliminate nuclear weapons worldwide in a phased project by 2030. Among the sponsors were not only predictable doves, but a roster of hard-headed veterans of high office, including several former assistants to the president for national security affairs, secretaries of state and defense, four-star generals, subcabinet officials from administrations of both parties, and others whose hawkish credentials could not be doubted. This effort represented consciousness of the danger of living indefinitely with nuclear weapons, but its traction in international politics remains to be seen. Half of the twenty-first-century problem of WMD is about managing the big residue of a Cold War in which the adversary had tremendous capability, but little intention to use it (and now, most assume even much less intention). The other half is about new adversaries with the reverse combination—tremendous desire to harm Americans, but so far little capability.

Today WMD present more and different things to worry about than during the Cold War. For one, nuclear arms are no longer the only concern, as chemical and especially biological weapons came to the fore. For another, there is less danger of complete annihilation, but more danger of mass destruction. Since the Cold War is over and American and Russian nuclear inventories are much smaller, there is less chance of an apocalyptic exchange of many thousands of weapons. But while the scale of vulnerability is lower, the probability that some smaller number of WMD will actually be used in other quarters is growing. And the potential vulnerability to economic devastation from cyberwarfare has added a new dimension to the concept of mass destruction. In all this, many of the standard ideas for coping with threats from WMD are no longer as relevant as they were when Moscow was the main adversary and nuclear strategy was the main currency of defense policy. But more than two decades since the Cold War, new thinking has still not congealed in as clear a form as the old Cold War concepts of nuclear deterrence theory.

The new dangers have not been ignored inside the Washington Beltway. "Counterproliferation" became a cottage industry in the Pentagon and intelligence community in the 1990s and an even greater preoccupation since, and many worthwhile initiatives to cope with threats have been taken. Some of the most important implications of the new era, however, have not yet registered on the public agenda. This in turn limits the inclination of politicians to push some appropriate programs. In the post–Cold War hiatus the defense establishment focused mainly on countering threats WMD pose to U.S. military forces operating abroad, rather than on the more worrisome danger that mass destruction would occur in the United States itself, killing large numbers of civilians. September 11th then riveted attention on the vulnerability of the American homeland, but WMD were still not the center of that attention.

There are five main points to keep in mind about the new world of mass destruction:

First, in contrast to the Cold War, the main danger comes from enemies whose capability to inflict mass destruction is low (so far), but whose intention to do all they can to harm us is high. The old Soviet Union had the capability to annihilate the United States, but no incentive to use it. Al Qaeda would use any capability for mass destruction that it could get.

Second, the roles WMD play in international conflict have changed radically in a way little appreciated even by many experts. These weapons no longer represent the technological frontier of warfare. They are increasingly weapons attractive to the weak states or groups that are militarily third or fourth class and desperately need an equalizer.

Third, the importance of different types of WMD has shifted. Biological weapons should now be as serious a concern as nuclear weapons, while chemical weapons should be trailing far behind.

Fourth, the mainstays of Cold War security policy—deterrence and arms control—are not what they used to be. Some new threats may not be deterrable, nor will arms control treaties do much to contain them. In a few instances, continuing devotion to deterrence and arms control poses side effects that may hurt as much as they help.

Fifth, some of the responses most likely to cope with the threats in novel ways do not find a warm welcome. The category of responses that should now be the highest priority is one long ignored, opposed, or ridiculed in the past: serious civil defense programs to blunt the effects of WMD if they are unleashed within the United States. Some of the most effective measures to prevent attacks within the United States may also challenge traditional civil liberties if pursued to the maximum. And the most troubling conclusion for foreign policy as a whole is that reducing the odds of WMD attacks within the United States might require pulling back from involvement in some foreign conflicts. American activism to guarantee international stability is actually the prime source of American vulnerability to WMD.

This was partly true in the Cold War, when the main danger that nuclear weapons might detonate on U.S. soil sprang from strategic engagement in Europe, Asia, and the Middle East to deter attacks on U.S. allies. But engagement back then assumed a direct link between regional stability and U.S. survival. This is less evident today, when there is no globally threatening superpower or transnational ideology to be contained—only an array of serious but entirely local disruptions. Today, as the only nation using military muscle outside its own region, the United States makes itself a target for states or groups whose aspirations are frustrated by U.S. power. For those who take an activist American mission for granted, September 11th may just make such entanglements inevitable. If so, Americans need to accept some greater risk of mass destruction at home as a cost of doing business.

## FROM MODERN TO PRIMITIVE

When nuclear weapons were born, they represented the most advanced military applications of science, technology, and engineering. None but the great powers could hope to have them. By now, however, nuclear arms are very old military technology; they have been around for almost seven decades. Chemical and biological weapons, of course, are even older, indeed ancient. WMD are not just old. Despite the fact that they are hard to obtain, in the strategic terms most relevant to American security they have become primitive. Once the military cutting-edge of the strong, they have become the only hope for so-called rogue states or terrorists who want to contest American power. Why? Because the United States developed overwhelming superiority in conventional military force against any conceivable adversary—something Americans never thought they had against the old Soviet Union.

The Persian Gulf War of 1991 was the first dramatic demonstration of this supremacy, stunning many abroad. Despite anxieties in the defense establishment, that advantage in conventional power is not yet threatened. Although U.S. defense budgets went down after the Cold War, other countries did not close the gap. U.S. military spending remained more than triple that of any potentially hostile power, and higher than the combined defense budgets of Russia, China, Saddam Hussein's Iraq, Iran, North Korea, Syria, and Cuba—the biggest conceivable array of adversaries at any one time. With September 11th and the wars in Iraq and Afghanistan, U.S. military spending climbed again.

More to the point, there is no evidence that potentially hostile countries' level of military professionalism is developing at a rate that would make them competitive even if they were to spend far more on their forces. Although the concept of a "revolution in military affairs" was shaken in recent years, American forces continue to make unmatched use of state-of-the-art weapons, surveillance and information systems, and the organizational and doctrinal flexibility for managing the integration of these complex innovations into "systems of systems" that is the key to modern military effectiveness. Embroilment in unconventional combat in Iraq and Afghanistan reminded Americans that some aspects of warfare are timelessly simple and challenging, but the greater danger is still the risk of eventual conflict with a major power. For that, more than ever in military history, brains are brawn. Even if hostile countries do somehow catch up in an arms race, their military organizations and cultures are unlikely to catch up in professionalism or the "competence race"—the developed skills for management, technology assimilation, and combat command.[3] In any case, few lessons from the Gulf War have been more widely repeated than Indian general K. Sundarji's: "Don't fight the United States unless you have nuclear weapons."[4]

If it is infeasible for hostile states to counter the United States in conventional combat, this is even truer for smaller groups such as terrorists. If we are lucky, the various violent groups with grievances against American government and society will continue to think of schemes with conventional explosives as the means of choice for smiting Americans. For some reason few terrorist groups to date have concentrated their efforts on inflicting true mass destruction. Al Qaeda, which we worry most about, has indicated strong interest in WMD, but there is no evidence yet that it has made obtaining them top priority. With the huge exception of September 11th, bombings or hostage seizures have generally killed or threatened no more than a few hundred lives.

There is no sure reason, however, to bet on restraint. Indeed, some have tried to use WMD, only to see them fizzle. The Japanese Aum Shinrikyo released sarin in Tokyo but killed only a few people. Eventually such a group will prove less incompetent. If terrorists decide that they want to stun American policymakers by inflicting massive damage, WMD become more attractive at the same time that they are becoming more accessible.

Unchallenged military superiority shifted the attention of the regular U.S. military establishment away from WMD. In the Cold War, nuclear weapons were the bedrock of American capabilities for war. They were the linchpins of defense debate, procurement programs, and arms control ideas because the United States faced another superpower, one that conventional wisdom feared could prevail at the conventional level of warfare. Today no one but professionals in the bowels of the Pentagon cares about modernizing intercontinental delivery systems or replacing aging warheads in the U.S. nuclear inventory, few care very deeply about maintaining arms control agreements with Russia, and hardly anyone lobbies for undertaking formal arms negotiations with China. In a manner that could only have seemed ludicrous during the Cold War, proponents came to rationalize the astronomically expensive B-2 bomber as a weapon for conventional war. Hardly anyone in the armed services is still interested in how the United States could use WMD for its own strategic purposes.

What strategic planners *are* interested in is how to keep adversaries from using WMD as asymmetric means to counter U.S. conventional power. In the decade after the Cold War this concern focused on how to protect U.S. ground and naval forces abroad from WMD attacks. This concern was all well and good, but it abetted a drift of attention away from the main danger, one that September 11th brought back to the fore. The primary risk is not that enemies might lob some nuclear or chemical weapons at American battalions, fleets, or airbases, awful as that would be. Rather it is that they might attempt to punish the United States by triggering catastrophes in American cities.

## WHICH WMD?

Until the 1990s the issue was nuclear arms—period. Chemical weapons received some attention from specialists but never got onto the list of priority problems that presidents and cabinets worried about. Biological weapons were almost entirely forgotten after they were banned by treaty during the Nixon administration. Chemical and biological weapons got more attention in the 1990s. The issues posed by the trio lumped under the umbrella of "mass destruction," however, differ. Most significantly, biological weapons received less attention than the other two types but may represent a greater danger than either of them.

Chemical weapons have always been noticed, especially since Iraq used them against Iranian troops in the 1980–88 war and against Kurdish civilians. Deadly chemicals are also far more widely available than nuclear weapons because the technology required to produce them is far simpler, and large numbers of countries have undertaken chemical weapons programs. But chemical weapons are not really in the same class as other weapons of truly *mass* destruction, in the sense of capacity to inflict a huge number of civilian casualties in a single strike. If this means tens of thousands of fatalities, as in, say, the biggest strategic bombing raids of World War II, chemical weapons have to be used in huge numbers with extraordinary preparation and skill to qualify. It is logistically and operationally very difficult to deliver them in the quantities necessary over wide areas.[5]

Nevertheless, much attention and effort were lavished on a campaign to eradicate chemical weapons. This may be a good thing, but the side effects are not entirely benign. For one, banning chemicals means that for deterrence, nuclear weapons became even more important than they used to be. That is because a treaty cannot assuredly prevent hostile nations from deploying chemical weapons but does prevent the United States from keeping the capacity to retaliate in kind against them.

In the past the United States had a no-first-use policy for chemical weapons but reserved the right to strike back with them if an enemy used them first. The 1993 Chemical Warfare Convention (CWC) required the United

States to destroy its stockpile, thus ending this option. Washington did the same with biological arms long ago, in the Nixon administration. If deterrent options were to be maximized while eliminating our own chemical and biological weapons, a no-first-use policy for nuclear weapons would be precluded since they provide the only WMD available for retaliation. There are reasonable arguments for resting on the threat of retaliation with conventional force, but that is still a weaker deterrent.[6]

Would the United States follow through and use nuclear weapons against a country or group that had killed "only" a couple thousand Americans with deadly chemicals? It is hard to imagine breaking the post-Nagasaki taboo in that situation. Are there schemes for conventional military retaliation that would suffice without detracting from the credibility of American deterrent threats? There would be a risk in setting a precedent that someone could use WMD against Americans without suffering similar destruction in return. Limiting the range of deterrent alternatives available to U.S. strategy will not necessarily cause deterrence to fail, but it does not strengthen it. Nevertheless, the Obama administration moved in that direction by promising not to use nuclear weapons against nonnuclear countries in compliance with their obligations to the nonproliferation treaty.

The ostensible benefit of the CWC is that it makes chemical arms harder to acquire and every bit as illegal and stigmatized as biological weapons have been. If so, what effect will the ban have on the choices of countries or groups who want *some* kind of WMD in any case, whether for purposes of deterrence, aggression, or revenge? At the margin, the ban reduces the disincentives to seek biological weapons since they are no less illegal, no harder to conceal, and far more damaging than chemical weapons. If major reductions in the chemical threat were to produce even minor increases in the biological threat, it would be a bad trade. The benefits of banning chemical weapons, even without verifiability, may well be worth the cost, but they are not cost-free. There is no certainty that making chemical weapons harder to get will push the strategies of American adversaries down the escalation ladder rather than up.

One simple fact should make Americans worry more about biological than about nuclear or chemical arms: biological weapons are more lethal than chemical and more available than nuclear. It is fortunately difficult to develop, deploy, and disseminate effectively weaponized biological agents. While biological weapons that are imperfectly produced and deployed would not have the killing capacity of the high-yield nuclear weapons in

## TABLE 4.1 Biological Weapons' Deadly Combination

|              | LETHALITY | |
| --- | --- | --- |
|              | HIGH | LOW |
| AVAILABILITY  HIGH | biological | chemical |
| AVAILABILITY  LOW | nuclear | 0 |

great powers' inventories, they may come close to that of the crude first-generation fission weapons available to rogue states. (North Korea's nuclear tests have been in the low kiloton range.) And although it is likely to remain beyond the means of terrorists to refine and employ biological weapons with optimal effectiveness, it may not be impossible forever. A famous study by the Office of Technology Assessment (OTA) in the 1990s concluded that a single airplane delivering one hundred kilograms of anthrax spores by aerosol on a clear, calm night over the Washington, D.C., area could kill *between one and three million people* —three hundred times as many fatalities as if the plane delivered sarin nerve gas in amounts ten times larger.[7] Assuming for the sake of argument that such an estimate was wildly exaggerated, discounting it by 90 percent would still mean casualties greater than at Hiroshima or Nagasaki, and discounting by 99 percent would mean more than three times as many dead as on September 11th. If prudence suggests that it would be reckless to discount an official scientific study by a government agency by 90 percent, the OTA document remains frightening.

Efficient biological weapons are not as easy to make as chemical weapons—they cannot be whipped up in a bathtub by a few graduate students—but they are much easier to make than nuclear weapons. Innovations in biotechnology have obviated many of the old problems in handling and preserving biological agents, and in the past many were freely available to buyers doing scientific research.[8] Nuclear weapons are not likely to be the WMD of choice for nonstate terrorist groups unless they can get them prefabricated from rogue-state suppliers. Actual production of nuclear weapons requires huge investments and infrastructures that are easier to target than small laboratories or commercial facilities in which biologicals can be generated and hidden. Those who want WMD without accountability or vulnerability to retaliation will logically be more interested in biological weapons. An aggrieved group that decides it wants to kill huge numbers of

Americans will find the mission easier to attempt with anthrax than with a nuclear explosion.

Inside the Pentagon concern with biological weapons picked up tremendously in the 1990s, and the delivery of anthrax-laced letters that killed several people in 2001 raised attention in the outside world. That attention soon flagged, however, perhaps because the actual casualties were not shockingly high or because the possibility of effective treatment with antibiotics and programs to prepare for their distribution in a crisis made the threat seem manageable. Nevertheless, it is unrealistic to have confidence that multiple strikes executed with no more nor less competence than the attacks of September 11th would not overwhelm the preparations.

## DIMINISHED DETERRENCE AND MARGINALIZED ARMS CONTROL

Old vocabulary still peppers policy discussion of WMD. Rhetoric in the defense establishment often falls back on the all-purpose strategic buzzword of the Cold War: deterrence. Since the Cold War, however, deterrence covers fewer of the threats facing the United States.

The logic of deterrence is clearest when the issue is preventing unprovoked and unambiguous aggression, when the aggressor recognizes that it is the aggressor rather than the defender. Deterrence is less reliable when both sides in a conflict see each other as the aggressor. This is often the case when the United States intervenes in messy Third World conflicts; the side that we want to deter may see itself as trying to deter us. These situations are ripe for miscalculation.

For the country that used to be the object of U.S. deterrence—Russia—the strategic burden has been reversed. During the Cold War NATO assumed that the Soviet Union and its Warsaw Pact allies had conventional military superiority in Europe. As a result, U.S. strategy relied on the threat to escalate, to be the first to use nuclear weapons during a war, to deter attack by the Soviet Army. Today the tables are turned. There is no Warsaw Pact, Russia has half the military potential of the old Soviet Union, and NATO has grown and camped at Russia's doorstep. It is now Moscow that has the incentive to compensate for conventional weakness by placing heavier reliance on nuclear capabilities. So although the Russians adopted a nuclear no-first-use policy in the early 1980s, they backpedaled after their precipitous post–Cold War decline.

Today Moscow needs to be reassured more than deterred. Russia's regime took a disappointing turn after hopes for liberalization following the Cold War, but Western distaste for the country's internal political order should not poison foreign relations. The main danger from Russian WMD after the Cold War was leakage from vast stockpiles to anti-American groups elsewhere—the "loose nukes" problem. As long as the West has no intention of attacking the Russians, their greater reliance on nuclear forces for their own deterrent purposes is no problem. If we have an interest in reducing nuclear stockpiles dramatically, however, it is. The traditional American approach—thinking in terms of our own deterrence strategies—provides no help on this. Indeed, noises some Americans still make about deterring the Russians compound the problem by reinforcing Moscow's suspicion.

Similarly, U.S. conventional military superiority gives China an incentive to consider more reliance on an escalation strategy. The Chinese have a long-standing no-first-use policy, but it was adopted when their strategic doctrine was "People's War." That doctrine was severely shaken by American performance in the Persian Gulf War of 1991. Again, we might assume that there is no problem as long as Beijing only wants to deter and we do not want to attack. But how does all this relate to the prospect of a war over Taiwan? This is a conflict that no one wants but that can hardly be ruled out. If the United States decides forthrightly to deter Beijing from attacking Taiwan, the old lore from the Cold War is relevant. But if Washington leaves policy ambiguous, who will know who is deterring whom? Ambiguity is a recipe for confusion and miscalculation in a time of crisis. For all the upsurge of attention in the national security establishment to the prospect of conflict with China, there has been remarkably little discussion of the role of nuclear weapons—on either side—in a Sino-American collision.

The main problem for deterrence today is that it relies primarily on a threat of retaliation, but this is hard to make credible against a threat of anonymous attack, hard to make effective against attackers who do not fear death, and hard to implement against large numbers of individual independent perpetrators rather than the few leaders who control governments. Retaliation requires a return address—knowledge of who has launched the attack and exactly where the retaliation can be delivered. This is no issue when the threat comes from a government, but it is a problem if the enemy is anonymous or a clandestine transnational group like Al Qaeda. Today some groups may wish to punish the United States without taking credit for the action. This is particularly true when it comes to cyberwarfare, where pinning definite responsibility for an attack can prove impossible.

Terrorists who must be deterred may also be indifferent to suffering retaliation. Suicide terrorists by definition are immune to such threats. In the realm of cyberwar, deterrence may need to engage thousands of independent decision makers—the alienated or fanatical individuals motivated to damage or destroy the computer capabilities of governments or vital economic and social institutions. Traditional interstate deterrence involves strategies and threats against a limited number of people in authority in a few governments and institutions. Even credible threats may not be effective against thousands of independent individuals, even if they would be against a few leaders of a few governments.

If we do know terrorists' addresses, deterrence can still apply. Nevertheless, the options of choice favored in planning within the defense establishment shifted completely from deterrence to preemption, and for some, preventive attack. The old corpus of deterrence theory that undergirded Cold War policy was dominated by reliance on the threat of second-strike retaliation, and a majority of those who dealt with nuclear weapons policy adamantly opposed developing options for first-strike counterforce. Today scarcely anyone looks to that old logic when thinking about rogues or terrorists, and most hope to be able to mount a disarming action against any private group with WMD.

Finally, eliminating chemical weapons trims some options for deterrence. Arms control restrictions on the instruments that can be used for deterrent threats are not wrong (there is more to national security than deterrence) but do work against maximizing reliance on deterrence. Overall, however, the problem with arms control is not that it does too much, but that it now does relatively little.

From the Limited Test Ban in the 1960s, through the Strategic Arms Limitation Talks (SALT), Strategic Arms Reduction Talks (START), and Intermediate-Range Nuclear Forces (INF) negotiations in the 1980s, arms control treaties were central to managing threats posed by WMD. Debates about whether particular agreements with Moscow were in the U.S. interest were so bitter because everyone believed that the results mattered. Today there is no consensus that treaties regulating armaments matter much, and stories about arms control are usually buried in inside pages. After the Chemical Warfare Convention, efforts to control WMD by treaty became small business. The biggest news in arms control in the decade after the

Cold War was not any negotiation to regulate WMD, but a campaign to ban land mines! More recently, signing of the new START treaty by presidents Obama and Medvedev in April 2010 was close to a one-day story, despite the partisan drama about ratification in the U.S. Senate. Among national security experts the corps that pays close attention to START and the Conventional Forces in Europe (CFE) Treaty has shrunk.

Our Cold War partner in arms control, Russia, has disarmed a great deal voluntarily. But despite standard rhetoric, the United States has not placed a high priority on convincing Moscow to divest more of its nuclear weapons; the Clinton administration put a higher priority on NATO expansion, which pushed the Russians in the opposite direction, and abrogation of the ABM Treaty by Bush II aggravated Moscow's incentives to buttress its forces. Inertia has led the national security establishment to continue effectively assuming a mutual deterrence relationship between the United States and Russia despite the end of the Cold War. Yet the potential emergence of great imbalance in capability—even the possibility of an effective American first-strike option—generates no significant controversy.[9] This combination of excessive and insufficient concern reflects the shift of first-order threat assessment from the concentration of destructive capabilities (still in the forces of the United States and Russia) to the concentration of malign intentions (in the new enemies emerging since the Cold War).

The Nuclear Non-Proliferation Treaty (NPT) remains a hallowed institution, but it has nowhere new to go. It will not convert the problem countries who want to obtain nuclear arms—unless, like Iraq, North Korea, and Libya, they choose to accept the legal obligation and then simply cheat on it. (It was not the NPT, but sanctions related to terrorism, that led Libya to give up its program.) The NPT regime will continue to impede access to fissile materials from the open market, but it will not do so in novel or more effective ways, nor will it address the problem of "loose nukes" any better than the Russian and American governments do on their own.

Formal agreements are also unpromising for constraining small WMD programs because it is impractical to devise reliable verification arrangements. In the golden age of superpower arms control, technical means of monitoring were quite adequate. Why worry about the Soviets hiding a dozen weapons in some warehouse when they had thousands of observable missiles deployed? For an Iran or North Korea, however, the issue of concern is precisely that handful of weapons that might be concealed somewhere, immune to detection by satellites or even on-site inspectors.

Not even the most intrusive on-site inspection rights could assure anyone that these governments had not stashed weapons, fissionable material, or nuclear contraband in a cave or basement. For outlaw states, proving the negative about possession of WMD is impossible, so as a practical matter definitive verification of disarmament is impossible.

## REAL DEFENSE

Despite all the new limitations, deterrence remains an important aspect of strategy, if only for dealing with enemies that are identified and targetable. There is not much the United States needs to do to keep up its capability for deterrence, however, given the many nuclear weapons and conventional military superiority it still has. Where capabilities are underdeveloped is in the responses for coping if deterrence fails.

Old thinking still prevails among those who promote strategic defense. Until September 11th, enthusiasts for defensive capability, mostly veterans of the factions promoting the Strategic Defense Initiative in debates of the Reagan years, remained fixated on the least relevant form of it: high-tech active defenses to intercept intercontinental ballistic missiles (ICBMs). There was scant interest in what should be the first priority: civil-defense preparations to cope with actual uses of WMD within the United States. (Nearly a decade after the Cold War, only half a billion dollars—less than two-tenths of 1 percent of the defense budget—went to chemical and biological defense, while nearly $4 billion was spent annually on ballistic missile defense. Two decades after the Cold War, the defense budget allocated more money to missile defense than to the whole Coast Guard.)[10] Active defenses against missiles are expensive investments that might or might not work against a threat the American homeland does not yet face, but that would do nothing against the threat that it already faces. Civil-defense measures are comparatively cheap and could prove far more effective than they would have against a large-scale Soviet attack.

During the Cold War, debate about antimissile defense was about whether it was technologically feasible or cost-effective, and whether it would threaten the Soviets and ignite a spiraling race between offensive and defensive weapon deployments. One need not refight the old battles over SDI to see that the priority for current threats posed by WMD is premature. As of 2011 neither Iran nor North Korea had deployed reliable ICBMs with the technically sophisticated small warheads they require. Nor, if they are strategically cunning, should they want to. For the limited number of nuclear weapons they are likely to have, and especially for biological weapons, easier means of delivery than ballistic missiles are available. Alternatives include simpler machines and unconventional means at which the intelligence agencies of these countries have excelled, such as smuggling. Nonstate perpetrators will choose clandestine means by necessity.

For state adversaries rather than nonnational terrorists, active defenses against technical means of delivery other than ballistic missiles deserve as much concern. There is no reason to assume that comparatively poor or technologically underdeveloped countries looking for an overt means will choose the most expensive and technically challenging means of delivery for a handful of WMD. Air-breathing systems—ship-to-shore cruise missiles hidden on merchant vessels, or wide-body aircraft diverted from or masked by national airlines—are choices at least as plausible as ballistic missiles. Yet there has been nowhere near as much attention to optimizing air-defense systems as there has been to inaugurating ballistic missile defense. Many even in official positions wrongly assume that existing air defenses have a high probability of intercepting the air-breathing vehicles just mentioned.

A ballistic missile defense system may be warranted before long, but not to counter these modes of attack. Indeed, if a larger part of our worry about WMD these days concerns their use by terrorist states or groups, we have to worry that the odds are growing that sometime, somewhere in the United States, some of these weapons will go off, despite the best efforts to stop them. If this happens, we should have in place whatever measures can mitigate the consequences.

By the later phases of the Cold War it was hard to get people interested in civil defense against an all-out Soviet attack that could detonate thousands of high-yield nuclear weapons in U.S. population centers. To many, the lives that would be saved seemed less salient than the many millions that would still be lost. It should be easier to see the value of civil defense, however, if we are thinking about more limited attacks, perhaps with only a few low-yield nuclear or biological weapons. There are a host of minor measures that can increase protection or recovery from biological, nuclear, or chemical effects. Examples are stockpiling or distribution of protective masks; equipment and training for decontamination; standby programs for mass vaccinations and emergency treatment with antibiotics; wider and deeper planning of emergency response procedures; and public education about hasty sheltering and emergency actions to take to reduce individual vulnerability. Efforts in this direction, especially toward preparing responses to biological attacks, got a boost after September 11th. They still have not engaged the public much, however, and lack of such preparation is bound to hobble efficient response in the alarm and confusion of an actual crisis.

Indeed, there is powerful psychological resistance: recall the prevalent ridicule of "duct tape" countermeasures in the wake of the October 2001 anthrax letter attacks. Resistance may be rooted in recognition that defenses against WMD are inevitably limited in protective power; promoting imperfect defenses alarms people by reminding them of vulnerability that cannot be eliminated. The disproportionate official focus on ballistic missile defense may follow from the fact that it is a way of promoting defense without requiring public attention, effort, and engagement with potential threats.

Better civil-defense programs and more public education would not make the prospect of absorbing an attack by WMD tolerable. Inadequacy, however, is no excuse for neglecting actions that could reduce death and suffering, even if the difference in casualties is limited. This is especially true since such passive defenses are cheap compared with regular military programs or active defense systems. (An exception to this point would be maximal defenses against catastrophic cyberattacks.) Public education need not be as unsettling as the fallout-shelter campaign of the early 1960s, but a level closer to that than has so far been attempted would make sense. Extreme forms of the priority may come to seem advisable only after a successful attack shocks government and public opinion into radical adjustments. A hypothetical extreme example would be major changes in urban planning and building codes to reduce vulnerability to explosion or chemical dissemination—building down (below ground) more than up, or changing air-circulation systems in large structures.

Mobilizing defensive efforts is hobbled by conceptual inertia. The Cold War accustomed strategists to worrying about an enemy with thousands of WMD, rather than ones with a handful. For decades the question of strategic defense was also posed as a debate between those who saw no viable alternative to relying on deterrence and those who hoped that an astrodome over the United States could replace deterrence with invulnerability. None of these hoary fixations addresses the most probable threats by WMD in the post–Cold War world.

Old opposition to Cold War civil-defense programs underwrites psychological aversion to them since. Opponents used to argue that civil defense was a dangerous illusion because it could do nothing significant to reduce the horror of an attack that would obliterate hundreds of cities, it would promote a false sense of security, and it could even be destabilizing and provoke attack in a crisis. Whether or not such arguments were valid then, they are not now, most certainly not in regard to terrorist threats. But both then and now, there is a powerful reason that civil-defense efforts are unpopular: they frighten people. They remind them that their vulnerability to mass destruction is not a bad dream, not something that strategic schemes for deterrence, preemption, or interception can be sure to solve. It admits the possibility that the disaster could happen.

Civil defense can limit damage but not minimize it. Opponents may be able to develop biological agents that circumvent available vaccines and antibiotics. (Those actors with marginal technical capabilities, however, might be stopped by blocking the easier options). But which is worse—such limitations or having to answer for failure to try? The moment that WMD are used somewhere in a manner that produces tens of thousands of fatalities, there will be hysterical outbursts of all sorts. One of them will surely be, why didn't the government prepare us for this? It is not in the long-term interest of political leaders to indulge popular aversion. Energetic civil-defense initiatives would put the public on notice and soften recriminations when the time comes. If public resistance prevents widespread distribution, stockpiling, vaccination, and instruction for use of defensive equipment or medical services, the least that should be done is to optimize plans to surge such activities quickly when the first crisis ignites demand.

As threats of terrorism using WMD were taken more seriously, interest grew in preemptive defense measures, the most obvious of which is intensified intelligence collection. Where this involves targeting groups within the United States, controversies arise about constitutional limits on invasion of privacy or search and seizure. As long as the danger of WMD remains hypothetical, such controversies will not be easily resolved. They have not come to the fore so far because U.S. law enforcement has been lucky in apprehending terrorists. In the 1990s the group planning to bomb the Lincoln Tunnel between New York and New Jersey happened to be infiltrated by an informer, and Timothy McVeigh happened to be picked up for driving with a faulty license plate. Since September 11th several plotters have been arrested before they could do anything. Those people who fear compromising civil liberties by allowing permissive standards for government snooping should consider what is likely to happen once such luck runs out and it proves impossible to identify perpetrators easily and openly. Suppose a radical Islamist group executes a biological attack that kills a hundred thousand people and announces that it will do it again unless its terms are met. (Such a scenario may be improbable but cannot be consigned to science fiction.) In that case it is hardly unthinkable that a panicked legal system would roll over and treat Arab Americans as it did the Japanese Americans who were herded into concentration camps after Pearl Harbor. Stretching limits on domestic surveillance, to reduce chances of facing such choices, could be the lesser evil.[11]

## Mass Destruction of Information

There is one grave danger that has provoked attempts to invent new modes of deterrence or negotiated restraints in the twenty-first century: cyberwarfare that could cripple modern society by fracturing the computerized communication and control systems on which it has come to depend in the Internet age. A preview of dire possibilities was seen in the chaos Estonia suffered when coordinated cyberattacks, apparently from sources in Russia, overwhelmed the country in 2007. Some fear this prospect as "only" mass disruption rather than destruction, but the potential threat includes large-scale physical destruction if sophisticated cyberattacks were to destroy control systems for nuclear power plants, water supplies, air traffic, and so on. This possibility is no longer just hypothetical—hackers have already breached Defense Department information systems and, in an example of the potential for civilian damage, the Federal Aviation Administration's air traffic computer networks.[12]

Here too, however, deterrence offers less than in the Cold War. As with terrorists, the problem is inability to know for sure the return address of the perpetrator. The fundamental problem is imperfect attribution—the fact that there is yet no foolproof way to detect the precise origin of an attack. Careful investigation can trace the source back to a particular country but cannot prove that the government rather than private hackers was responsible, or that the "guilty" computer had not been innocently commandeered by an unidentified malign third party. Because of the attribution problem, cyberwar gives governments options for anonymous attack that are otherwise associated only with terrorists or subnational groups, but governments have deeper pockets from which to mount campaigns.

Cyberwar is a threat potentially posed by hostile governments that can conceal their responsibility for the damage they inflict, aggrieved groups without government sponsorship, or just plain terrorists. It is an awesome potential because very small groups, or even talented individuals, may wreak havoc if they can circumvent defenses. Given the limitations of deterrence in this realm, priority has to go to investment in constantly improved and adapted cyberdefenses against penetration by hostile computer jockeys.

The new consciousness of vulnerability to cyberwarfare raises the possibility that the most expensive defensive investments could be warranted in the area where they have been least discussed in public: security of the national information technology infrastructure. The first line of defense and its importance are well recognized: firewalls, safeguards, and countermeasures of various sorts within particular information systems themselves. The Defense Department does not need reminding to focus on these, with one proviso: that an absolute priority is to make the command, control, and communication system for U.S. nuclear forces invulnerable to corruption or some form of takeover by a cyberattack *of type and quality that may not be foreseen*. If this requires adjustments in system design and operation that seem primitive or cumbersome by technical standards to which we have become accustomed, it is a price worth paying.

The second line of defense—constructing a system of resilience for society at large in the face of catastrophic attack—is less recognized and in its most ambitious forms potentially controversial. The information revolution has a dark side: technical and economic progress produced by increasing globalization and integration of communication and control systems means dependence on the invulnerability of a limited set of interdependent systems. It is in the nature of evolving information technology that ability to anticipate particular innovative forms of attack, let alone capacity to neutralize them, cannot be assumed. Prudence dictates that defenses must plan not just on blocking attacks, but also on coping with recovery from a successful and impressive enemy assault.

Serious resilience means deploying backup systems within institutions that can reestablish control, communication, and integrity of records if primary information systems are corrupted or crippled and cannot be safely reconstituted on short notice. This could potentially mean various things from retaining up-to-date paper records to keeping in reserve parallel communication systems that may be inferior but can operate disconnected from external channels. Certain institutions—for example, critical elements of the financial system, such as the Federal Reserve or major banks, nuclear power plants, or electrical-grid control networks—need to make this a higher priority than others. Promoting this priority faces resistance from organizations, especially in the private sector, that fear publicizing the problem because alarm will drive away customers, but which ignore the risk that cybercrime or cyberwarfare could escalate from tolerably limited to catastrophic levels.

More generally, radical improvement of resilience could mean something increasingly unthinkable: reducing society's dependence on the integrity of the Internet. Emphasis here is on the qualifier "radical" since this would be an exceptionally tall order. If technical experts judge the possibility of a catastrophic compromise of the Internet to be negligible, robust hedges against it may not be worth the price. If we cannot know for sure, however, the risks in economizing on options for coping are not small. More and more economic and administrative functions rely completely, and without reflection, on utilization of the Internet. This creates a potential mega vulnerability if malign forces were to find a way to bring down or commandeer action on the Internet.

Institutionalizing buffers and safeguards on a large scale will be extremely expensive, and many people will refuse to admit the need for such sacrifices as long as a catastrophic attack has not happened. The argument for investing heavily against a threat that is only hypothetical is akin to the argument for spending on strict building codes to limit damage from earthquakes, or arguments for spending on revitalization of regular infrastructure (such as roads, bridges, and power-generation facilities), but as if all the old roads and bridges have the potential to collapse at once. In a climate of frustration about uncontrolled debt, the argument for big investments against so far hypothetical dangers may not fare well. Justifying them might depend on resuscitating the respectability of economic stimulus programs.

## Is Retreat the Best Defense?

No programs aimed at controlling adversaries' capabilities can eliminate the dangers. One risk is that in the fluid politics of the twenty-first century, the United States could stumble into unanticipated crisis with Russia or China. There are no well-established rules of the game to brake a spiraling conflict over the Baltic states or Taiwan, as there were in the old superpower competition after the Cuban Missile Crisis. The second danger is that some angry group that blames the United States for its problems may decide to coerce Americans, or simply exact vengeance, by inflicting devastation on them where they live.

If steps to deal with the problem in terms of capabilities are limited in what they offer, can anything be done to address intentions—the incentives of any foreign power or group to lash out at the United States? There are few answers to this question that do not compromise the fundamental strategic activism and internationalist thrust of U.S. foreign policy over the past half century. That is because the best way to keep people from believing that we are responsible for their problems is to stay out of their faces. Sometimes that would abdicate proper responsibility for engaging problems; at other times it would make sense but contradict the enduring impulse to seek control of world events.

Ever since the Munich Agreement and Pearl Harbor, with only a brief interruption during the decade after the Tet Offensive, there has been a consensus that if Americans did not draw their defense perimeter far forward and confront foreign troubles in their early stages, those troubles would come to them at home. Thinking about the changing sources of danger from WMD, however, raises the possibility that American intervention in troubled areas is not so much a way to fend off such threats as it is what stirs them up.

Will U.S. involvement in instabilities around the former USSR head off conflict with Moscow or generate it? Will making NATO bigger and moving it to Russia's doorstep deter Russian pressure on Ukraine and the Baltics or provoke it? For Russia and China, there is less chance that either will set out to conquer Europe or Asia than that they will try to restore old sovereignties and security zones by reincorporating new states of the former Soviet Union or the province of Taiwan. None of this means that NATO expansion or support for Taiwan's autonomy will cause nuclear war. It does mean that to whatever extent American activism has an effect on those countries' incentives to rely more on WMD, at the same time that it intensifies political friction between them and Washington, it works in the wrong direction.

The other main danger is the ire of smaller states or religious and cultural groups that see the United States as an evil force blocking their legitimate aspirations. One does not have to sympathize with Al Qaeda to empathize with it. It is hardly likely that Islamist radicals would be hatching hostile schemes if the United States had not been identified for so long as the mainstay of Israel, the shah, and conservative Arab regimes; the killer of Muslims in Iraq, Afghanistan, and Pakistan; and the source of a cultural assault on Islam. Cold War triumph magnified the problem. U.S. military and cultural hegemony—the basic threats to radicals seeking to challenge the status quo—are directly linked to the imputation of American responsibility for maintaining world order. September 11th simply illustrated the alienating effects of American hegemony that have existed before and since. Playing globocop feeds the urge of aggrieved groups to strike back.

Is this a brief for isolationism? No. First, it is too late to turn off foreign resentments by retreating, even if that were an acceptable course. Alienated groups or governments would not stop blaming Washington for their problems. Second, there is more to foreign policy than dampening incentives to hurt the United States. It is not automatically sensible to stop pursuing other interests for the sake of uncertain reductions in a threat of uncertain probability. Security is not all of a piece, and survival is only part of security. For some purposes, provoking terrorists may just have to be a cost of doing business. But there is still a difference between energetically pursuing influence via diplomacy and economic aid and doing so with force.

It is imprudent to assume that important security interests complement each other as they did during the Cold War. The interest at the very core—protecting the American homeland from attack—is now often in tension with security more broadly conceived and the interests that mandate promoting American political values, economic interdependence, social Westernization, and stability in regions beyond Western Europe and the Americas. The United States should not give up all its broader political interests, but it should tread cautiously in areas—especially the Middle East—where broader interests grate against the core imperative of preventing mass destruction within our own borders. The growing potential for hostile governments or groups to seek and use WMD to deter, coerce, or punish Americans simply reinforces the other reasons for a less adventurous national security policy.

# PART II. HISTORY STRIKES BACK

# 5

## TERRORISM
## THE SOFT UNDERBELLY OF PRIMACY

What made countering terrorism the first priority of U.S. foreign policy after September 11, 2001, was the shock, rage, and fear the attacks triggered in Americans. Intense emotional reactions obscured the limits of the threat, the difficulties in confronting some of its causes, and the full range of costs and benefits in counterterrorism strategies. Sober strategy requires sharper understanding of the connections among three things: the imbalance of power between terrorist groups and counterterrorist governments; the reasons that groups choose terror tactics; and the operational advantage of attack over defense in the interactions of terrorists and their opponents. It also requires confronting a paradox: that American power was a source of vulnerability. September 11th reminded Americans that the overweening global primacy they had taken for granted in the dozen years after the Cold War was not the same as omnipotence. Less obvious was that the power itself is much of the cause of terrorist enmity, and thus what provokes attempts to hurt us. This notion does not come easily to American minds, whose common sense tends to assume that our benign and generous intentions are obvious to foreigners, but it needs to be grasped if counterterrorism is to pick its battles effectively. The first questions, though, are to what extent terrorism should really count as a national security problem, and what most distinguishes it from other hostile uses of force.

### Is Terrorism Really Important?

The psychological impact of terror attacks outweighs the material damage they cause. Cold, economistic logic should discredit the visceral consensus

on the dire nature of the terrorist threat. The new priority of terrorism after September 11th came from the shock of nearly three thousand dead in
one day, the worst casualty toll for Americans since the Battle of Antietam,
and a toll inflicted mostly on civilians. Terrorism also became the priority by default: Americans faced no other significant security threat at the
beginning of the century. With the Cold War over and the China challenge
only on the horizon, there was nothing else of significance on the agenda to
compete with what had previously been considered a minor and manageable problem.

When compared with many other forms of political violence, *typical* terrorism has always inflicted little damage. The occasional incidents to which
the world became accustomed in the late twentieth century (hijacking of
aircraft for hostage taking; assassination of individuals or groups like the
Israeli athletes at the Munich Olympics; planting of bombs in cities as the
Irish Republican Army, Basque separatists, and other groups have done in
Europe; or suicide bombings in the Middle East) seldom produced more
than a few dozen casualties, and next to none inside the United States apart
from the homegrown 1995 attack in Oklahoma City. As John Mueller points
out, except for 2001, "far fewer Americans were killed in any grouping of
years by all forms of international terrorism than were killed by lightning.
And . . . fewer people have been killed in America by international terrorism than have drowned in toilets or have died from bee stings."[1]

Nevertheless, while the number of incidents shrank after the Cold War,
their average lethality grew, and even typical terrorism had a political impact out of line with the damage actually done.[2] This imperfect correlation
of psychological and material effects can be found in conventional warfare
as well. For example, fear of ballistic missiles armed with conventional high-
explosive warheads outstripped the actual damage they did in the 1944 V-1
and V-2 strikes on London and the 1988 "war of the cities" between Iran
and Iraq.[3] September 11th was on a whole different level from typical terrorism, and it literally stunned both popular and official opinion despite the
fact that specialists in national security had been warning for a long time
that mass-casualty terror attacks could happen anytime.

If repeated frequently, strikes on the scale of September 11th would pose
a radically greater threat than typical terrorism. The lack of follow-up attacks inside the United States in the years after 2001, however, showed the
inability of terrorists to do this regularly. If a September 11th happened once
every decade, or even at twice that rate, the damage would be far less than

that from a number of other dangers that Americans willingly accept as the cost of doing business—for example, driving, which kills several hundred thousand people in this country in every decade. Public psychology, however, does not see terror attacks in that light.

John Mueller's argument that overreaction costs far more in wasted resources and harm to other interests than does the damage absorbed from terrorism is, in part, compelling—but only in part, and the exceptions discredit his dismissal of the threat.[4] Three problems make his argument internally inconsistent, complacent, and untenable.

First, the argument mistakes low probability for insignificant probability. Mueller argues for relaxing obsessive efforts to deploy antiterrorist safeguards and countermeasures by claiming that another attack like those of September 11th "is *virtually impossible*." With greater vigilance, and the knowledge now that a hijacking could be a suicide mission rather than hostage taking, Mueller maintains that passengers and crews would act to prevent any takeover of an aircraft.[5] True, but not the point. It is easy to imagine reading a Mueller essay before 2001 arguing that a repetition of the December 1993 bombing of the World Trade Center, which killed six people, "is virtually impossible." The main risk is not that Al Qaeda will make another attempt tactically identical to the last one, but that it will find a way to bring off some other spectacular initiative. Mueller dismisses various concerns with potential complicated schemes for inflicting mass casualties on grounds that they are beyond terrorists' practical operational capacities. On this too one can easily imagine him in the 1990s dismissing a scenario like what came to happen on September 11th as fanciful, and ridiculing suggestions to investigate enrollments in flight schools as silly alarmism. Indeed, what Mohamed Atta and his colleagues managed to do was extremely improbable—and thus the FBI agent who wrote the "Phoenix memo" two months before the attacks, recommending such an investigation of flight schools, did not make an impression on his colleagues, and no investigation was carried out.

Second, Mueller uses the positive result of obsessive precautions to discredit the obsession. The main reason he gives to explain the lack of terror attacks inside the United States since 2001 is the possibility that there simply are no major international terrorists in the country.[6] If so, this hardly validates a recommendation to relax. It is likely that the paucity of foreign terrorists on American soil these days, or their inability to execute devastating operations, flows directly from the energetic actions taken after

September 11th—deportations of suspects rounded up and caught in viola-tion of immigration laws, tightened visa requirements screening out risky visitors, beefed-up monitoring of cargoes and ports of entry, and scrutiny of participants in activities analogous to flight training that could enable catastrophic action (for example, trucking, crop dusting, and handling of biological pathogens). If all this had been done before September 2001, the odds that Mohamed Atta and company would have gotten into the country, or stayed under the radar in flight schools, or succeeded in smuggling box cutters through airport security screening—and that the hijackings would ultimately have gone off—would have been far lower.

Third, dismissing the risk that terrorists might detonate weapons of mass destruction is complacent. The main concerns are nuclear and bio-logical weapons. Chemical and radiological weapons are officially catego-rized as WMD but would seldom be capable of killing many thousands except in the most extreme scenarios. They remain important because their psychological and economic impact could be devastating even if they kill few people.

Some of the most prominent terrorism experts—for example, Paul Pil-lar, David Rapoport, and Bruce Hoffman—have also criticized preoccupa-tion with the threat of terrorist WMD. They believe it distracts attention from the regular and probable activities of terrorists, and like Mueller they believe that furtive groups will be unable to master the difficulties of get-ting and deploying nuclear weapons. (Al Qaeda's desire to get WMD is not at issue, only its capability. According to the U.S. government, "In 1998, Usama bin Laden proclaimed the acquisition of WMD a 'religious duty,' and evidence collected in Afghanistan proves al-Qaida sought to fulfill this 'duty.'")[7] Mueller also sees biological weapons, which would be easier for subnational groups to get, as far less dangerous than nuclear. Aversion to focusing on WMD is deeply wrong.

First, events of low probability but high consequence should usually be of more concern than the reverse. An economist's logic would suggest that a few dozen minor attacks could be as damaging as a single big one, but the psychological and political effects of the latter are bound to be greater. Before the fact, the coordinated attacks by radical Islamists piloting wide-bodied jets on September 11th would have been judged to be as remote a possibility as Al Qaeda's access to biological weapons or its ability to get usable nuclear weapons from Russian loose nukes or Pakistani renegades seems today.

Second, radiological "dirty bombs" would yield only mild contamination of small areas, which Mueller believes should not then be considered uninhabitable. He makes this case by cavalier claims that the Environmental Protection Agency's standards for unacceptable levels of radiation are too low, and that contamination of the Chernobyl area was exaggerated.[8] Few citizens would be so nonchalant about buying, working, or living in Manhattan real estate where radiological weapons had gone off. Since it is easier for terrorists to acquire radiological than nuclear or biological weapons, the potential for economic disaster from detonating several in high value areas is hardly negligible.

Third, in contrast to other examples of logical inconsistency, the psychological impact of a prospective biological attack is less than its potential material effect. Ineptly deployed pathogens would not cause tens or hundreds of thousands of casualties, but ones that are efficiently used could. Compared with the low-yield first-generation nuclear weapons in the stockpiles of Pakistan, India, or North Korea, which instill ample respect in the West, the potential killing power of effectively aerosolized anthrax is impressive. (Since anthrax is not contagious, and the main form of it can be cured by antibiotics, a limited attack might be neutralized. If efficient attacks were made over several cities at once, however, friction in response procedures, maldistribution or shortages of antibiotics, and the lack of practice in handling the situation could easily leave many victims untreated, and dead, despite technological capacity to cure in principle.) Optimists are confident that Al Qaeda could never master the extremely challenging technological requirements of effective deployment and coordination of mass attacks with biological agents, and they cite the experience of Aum Shinri-kyu's bungled attempts, which were able to kill only a handful of people in Japan. Even if the probability of more proficient performance in another case is lower than the probability of coordinated kamikaze hijackings was before September 11th—a dubious assumption—it would be reckless to write it off.

So terrorism is a limited but significant threat—only modestly damaging in most cases, only potentially catastrophic on a grand scale, but psychologically quite powerful. Why do enemies resort to terrorism, and why did it come to the fore after the Cold War?

For all but the rare nihilistic psychopath, terror is a means, not an end in itself. Terror tactics are usually meant to serve a strategy of coercion, a use of force designed to further some political purpose.[9] This is not always evident in the heat of rage felt by the victims. Normal people find it hard to see instrumental reasoning behind an atrocity, especially when recognizing that the political motives behind terrorism might seem to make its illegitimacy less extreme. This is especially true for Americans, who tend to assume that foreigners must naturally see our benign motives and appreciate our good deeds. Stripped of illusions and rhetoric, however, a war against terror must mean a war against political groups who happen to choose terror as a tactic.

American global primacy is a prime cause of the war against terrorists.[10] It has animated both the terrorists' purposes and their choice of tactics. To groups like Al Qaeda, the United States is the enemy because American military power dominates their world, supports corrupt governments in their countries, and backs Israelis against Arabs; American armed forces attempt to subjugate Muslims in Iraq and Afghanistan; American cultural power insults their religion and pollutes their societies; and American economic power makes all these intrusions and desecrations possible. Japan, in contrast, is not high on Al Qaeda's list of targets because Japan's economic power does not make it a political, military, and cultural behemoth that penetrates their societies. Or as Osama bin Laden put it in his speech to the American people, "Bush's claim that we hate freedom" is false because if true, "then let him explain to us why we don't strike for example—Sweden?"[11]

Political and cultural power make the United States a target for those who blame it for their problems. At the same time, American economic and military power prevents them from resisting or retaliating against the United States on its own terms. To smite the only superpower requires unconventional modes of force and tactics that make the combat cost-exchange ratio favorable to the attacker. This offers hope to the weak that they can work their will despite their overall deficit in power.

## PRIMACY ON THE CHEAP

The novelty of complete primacy may account for the thoughtless, innocently arrogant way in which many Americans took its benefits for granted in the 1990s. Most who gave any thought to foreign policy came to regard the entire world after 1989 as they had Western Europe and Japan during the past half-century: partners in principle but vassals in practice. Many also confused primacy with invulnerability. American experts warned regularly of the danger of catastrophic terrorism—and Osama bin Laden explicitly declared war on the United States in his fatwa of February 1998[12]—but the warnings did not register forcefully in the public consciousness. Even some national security experts felt stunned when the attacks occurred on September 11th. Before then, the American military wanted nothing to do with the mission of "homeland defense," cited the 1878 Posse Comitatus Act to suggest that military operations within U.S. borders would be improper, and argued that homeland defense should be the responsibility of civilian agencies or the National Guard. The services preferred to define the active forces' mission as fighting and winning the nation's wars—as if wars were naturally something that happened abroad, and homeland defense involved no more than law enforcement, managing relief operations in natural disasters, or intercepting ballistic missiles outside U.S. airspace.

Being number one seemed cheap. The United States could cut the military burden on the economy after the Cold War and still be able to plan, organize, and fight a major war in 1991 at negligible cost in blood or treasure. In the one case where costs in casualties exceeded the apparent interests at stake—Somalia in 1993—Washington quickly stood down from the fight. This became the reference point for vulnerability: the failure of an operation that was small, far from home, and elective. Where material interests required strategic engagement, as in the oil-rich Persian Gulf, U.S. strategy could avoid costs by exploiting a huge advantage in conventional capability. Where conventional dominance proved less exploitable, as in Somalia, material interests did not require strategic engagement. Where Americans could not operate militarily with impunity, they could choose not to operate.

Power made it possible to let moral interests override material interests where some Americans felt an intense moral concern, even if in doing so they claimed, dubiously, that the moral and material stakes coincided. This happened in Kosovo but most of all in the Arab-Israeli conflict. After the Six-Day War the United States supported Israel diplomatically, economically, and militarily against the Arabs, despite the fact that doing so put it on the side of a tiny country of a few million people with no oil, against more than ten times as many Arabs who controlled nearly half the world's oil reserves.

This policy was not just an effect of primacy, since the U.S.–Israel alignment began in the Cold War era of bipolarity. Indeed, the salience of the moral motive was indicated when U.S. policy proceeded despite the fact that it helped give Moscow a purchase in Cairo, Damascus, Baghdad, and other Arab capitals. Luckily, the largest amounts of oil remained under the control of the conservative Arab states of the Gulf. The hegemony of the United States *within* the anticommunist world helped account for the policy. That margin of power also relieved Washington of the need to make hard choices about disciplining its client. For decades the United States opposed Israeli settlement of the conquered territories, indeed termed the settlements illegal, yet in all that time Washington never demanded that Israel refrain from colonizing the West Bank as a condition for receiving U.S. economic and military aid.[13] Washington continued to bankroll Israel at a higher per capita rate than any other country in the world, a level that has been indispensable to Israel, providing aid over the years that now totals more than $200 billion in today's dollars.[14] Although this policy enraged Arabs, U.S. power was great enough that such international political costs did not outweigh the domestic political costs of insisting on Israeli compliance with U.S. policy.

Far more than subsidizing Israeli occupation of Palestinian land was involved in the enmity of Islamist terrorists toward the United States. Many of the other explanations, however, presuppose U.S. global primacy. When American power becomes the arbiter of conflicts around the world, it makes itself the target for groups who come out on the short end of those conflicts.

## PRIMACY AND ASYMMETRIC WARFARE

The irrational evil of terrorism seems most obvious to the powerful. They are accustomed to getting their way with conventional applications of force and are not as accustomed as the powerless to thinking of terror as the only form of force that might work for them. This is why terrorism is the premier form of "asymmetric warfare," the Pentagon buzzword for the type of threats likely to confront the United States in the post–Cold War world.[15] Murderous tactics become appealing by default—when one party in a conflict lacks other military options. Terror is especially appealing because small investments can produce exponential returns. A character in Eric Frank Russell's *Wasp*, a 1957 work of science fiction, pithily explains the ideal instrumental efficiency of terrorism:

> In given conditions, action and reaction can be ridiculously out of proportion. . . . One can obtain results monstrously in excess of the effort. . . .

Let's consider this auto smash-up . . . the driver lost control at high speed while swiping at a wasp which had flown in through a window and was buzzing around his face. . . . The weight of a wasp is under half an ounce. Compared with a human being, the wasp's size is minute, its strength negligible. Its sole armament is a tiny syringe holding a drop of irritant, formic acid. . . . Nevertheless, that wasp killed four big men and converted a large, powerful car into a heap of scrap.[16]

Resort to terror is not necessarily limited to those facing far more powerful enemies. It can happen in a conventional war between great powers that becomes a total war, when the process of escalation pits whole societies against each other and shears away civilized restraints. That is something not seen since the 1940s. One need not accept that Allied strategic bombing in World War II was terrorism to recognize that the British and Americans did systematically assault the urban population centers of Germany and Japan. They did so in large part because precision bombing of industrial facilities proved ineffective.[17] During the early phase of the Cold War, in turn, U.S. nuclear strategy relied on plans to counter Soviet conventional attack on Western Europe with a comprehensive nuclear attack on communist countries that would have killed hundreds of millions. (In the 1950s Strategic Air Command targeteers even went out of their way to plan "bonus" damage by moving aim points for military targets so that blasts would destroy adjacent towns at the same time.)[18] In both World War II and planning for World War III, the rationale was less to kill civilians per se than to wreck the enemy economies. In short, the instrumental appeal of strategic attacks on noncombatants may be easier to understand when one considers that states with legitimate purposes have sometimes resorted to such a strategy.

Osama bin Laden's rationale for striking the World Trade Center was utterly consistent with the logic behind World War II strategic bombing: economic warfare intended to collapse the basis of enemy power. He overestimated the effectiveness of the strategy even more than Allied planners in World War II did, but in a videotape a few months after the attacks bin Laden said: "These blessed strikes showed clearly that this arrogant power, America, rests on a powerful but precarious economy, which rapidly crumbled. . . . Hit the economy, which is the basis of military might. If their economy is finished, they will become too busy to enslave oppressed people. . . . America is in decline; the economic drain is continuing but more strikes are required and the youths must strike the key sectors of the American economy."[19]

A double standard—relaxing prohibitions against targeting noncombatants for the side with legitimate purposes (one's own side)—occurs most readily when the enemy is an equal power. When one's own primacy is taken for granted and the threats confronted are limited, it is easier to revert to a single standard that puts all deliberate attacks against civilians beyond the pale.

In contrast to World War II, most wars are limited—or at least limited for the stronger side. In such cases, using terror to coerce is likely to seem the only potentially effective use of force for the weaker side, which faces a choice between surrender and savagery. Radical Muslim zealots cannot expel American power with conventional military means, so they substitute clandestine means of delivery against military targets (such as the Khobar Towers barracks in Saudi Arabia or the Pentagon) or targets that are outposts of government (embassies in Kenya and Tanzania). To liken their strikes that kill civilians to tactics that their Western enemies have used, terrorists have been said to suggest, "If you will let us lease one of your B-52s, we will use that instead of a car bomb."

Kamikaze hijacking of American airliners on September 11th was an instance of strategic judo, the turning of the West's strength against itself. The flip side of a primacy that diffuses its power throughout the world is that advanced elements of that power become more accessible to its enemies. Nineteen men from technologically backward societies did not have to rely on home-grown instruments to devastate the Pentagon and World Trade Center. They used computers and modern financial procedures with facility, and they forcibly appropriated the aviation technology of the West and used it as a weapon. They not only rebelled against the "soft power" of the United States, they trumped it by hijacking the country's hard power.[20] They also exploited the characteristics of U.S. society associated with soft power—the liberalism, openness, and respect for privacy that allowed them to go freely about the business of preparing the attacks without observation by the state security apparatus. When soft power met the clash of civilizations, it proved too soft.

Strategic judo is also evident when U.S. retaliation compromises its own purpose. When the Taliban regime in Kabul refused to surrender Osama bin Laden after September 11th, the counteroffensive was necessary to destroy Al Qaeda's base of operations and to demonstrate to terrorists that they could not hope to strike the United States for free. But even the initially successful war in Afghanistan increased polarization in the Muslim world and mobilization of terrorist recruits. U.S. leaders could say that they were not waging a war against Islam until they were blue in the face, but this would not convince Muslims who already distrust the United States. The longer-term result of that necessary retaliation became the worsening war in Afghanistan, which then posed more costs and risks than Al Qaeda.

## ADVANTAGE OF ATTACK

The academic field of security studies had reason to be embarrassed after September 11th. Having focused primarily on great powers and interstate conflict, scholars had produced sparse literature on terrorism; most of the good books were by policy analysts rather than theorists.[21] Indeed, even science fiction had etched out the operational logic of terrorism as well as had political science. Russell's novel vividly illustrates the strategic aspirations of terrorists, but especially the offense-dominant character of their tactics. It describes the dispatch of a single agent to one of many planets in the Sirian enemy's empire to stir up fear, confusion, and panic through a series of small, covert activities with tremendous ripple effects. Matched with deceptions to make the disruptions appear to be part of a campaign by a big phantom rebel organization, the agent's modest actions divert large numbers of enemy police and military personnel, cause economic dislocations and social unrest, and soften the planet up for invasion. Wasp agents are infiltrated into numerous planets, multiplying the effects. As the agent's handlers tell him, "The pot is coming slowly but surely to the boil. Their fleets are being widely dispersed, there are vast troop movements from their over-crowded home-system to the outer planets of their empire. They're gradually being chivvied into a fix. They can't hold what they've got without spreading all over it. The wider they spread the thinner they get. The thinner they get, the easier it is to bite lumps out of them."[22]

Fortunately Al Qaeda and its ilk are not as fantastically effective as Russell's wasp. By degree, however, the phenomenon is quite similar. Comparatively limited initiatives prompt tremendous and costly defensive reactions. On September 11th a small number of men killed almost three thousand people and destroyed a huge portion of prime commercial real estate, part of the military's national nerve center, and four expensive aircraft. The ripple effects multiplied those costs. A major part of the U.S. economy—air travel—shut down completely for days after September 11th. Increased security measures dramatically increased the overall costs of the air travel system thereafter. Normal law enforcement activities of the Federal Bureau of Investigation were radically curtailed as legions of agents were transferred to counterterror tasks. Anxiety about the vulnerability of nuclear power plants, major bridges and tunnels, embassies abroad, and other high-value targets prompted plans for big investments in fortification of a wide array of facilities. A retaliatory war in Afghanistan ran at a cost of a couple billion dollars a month. (This was in the initial phase of the war, when only a few hundred American military personnel operated in the country. If the full cost of the later years of bigger war in Afghanistan are attributed to the September 11th attacks, the payoff for Al Qaeda was disproportionate beyond measure.) In one study just months afterward, the attacks were estimated to have cost the U.S. economy 1.8 million jobs.[23]

Or consider the results of a handful of letters containing anthrax, posted with 34-cent stamps, probably sent by a single person. Besides killing several people, they contaminated a large portion of the postal system, paralyzed some mail delivery for long periods, provoked plans for huge expenditures on prophylactic irradiation equipment, shut down much of Capitol Hill for weeks, put thousands of people on a sixty-day regimen of strong antibiotics (potentially eroding the medical effectiveness of such antibiotics in future emergencies), and overloaded police and public health inspectors with false alarms. The September 11th attacks and the October anthrax attacks together probably cost the perpetrators less than a million dollars. If the cost of rebuilding and of defensive investments in reaction came to no more than $100 billion, the cost-exchange ratio would still be astronomically in favor of the attack over the defense. Even if the disproportionate effects of terror attacks are not decisively damaging, perpetrators take heart from the belief that they are. Three years after the Twin Towers went down, bin Laden continued to brag about Al Qaeda's "bleed-until-bankruptcy plan," claiming a hugely favorable cost-exchange ratio by which every dollar Al Qaeda invested in attacks caused the United States to spend a million dollars in various reactions and defenses.[24]

Two old bodies of work help to illuminate the problem. One is the literature on guerrilla warfare and counterinsurgency, particularly prominent in the 1960s, and the other is the offense-defense theory that burgeoned in the 1980s. Revolutionary or resistance movements in the preconventional phase of military operations usually mix small-unit raids on isolated outposts of the government or occupying force with detonations and assassinations in urban areas to instill fear and discredit government power. As in terror attacks, in guerrilla operations the weaker rebels use stealth and the cover of civilian society to concentrate their striking power against one among many of the stronger enemy's dispersed assets; they strike quickly and eliminate the target before the defender can move forces from other areas to respond; then they melt back into civilian society to avoid detection and reconcentrate against another target. The government or occupier has far superior strength, in terms of conventional military power, but cannot counterconcentrate in time because it has to defend all points, while the insurgent attacker can pick its targets at will.[25] The contest between insurgents and counterinsurgents is "tripartite," polarizing political alignments and gaining the support of *attentistes*, those on the fence. (In today's principal counterterror campaign, one might say that the yet-unmobilized Muslim elites and masses of the Third World—those who were not already actively committed either to supporting Islamist radicalism or to combating it—are the target group in the middle.) As Samuel Huntington noted, "a revolutionary war is a war of attrition."[26] Or as others have said, insurgents win as long as they do not lose, and governments lose as long as they do not win.

Offense-defense theory applied nuclear deterrence concepts to assessing the stability of conventional military confrontations and focused on what conditions tended to give the attack or the defense the advantage in war.[27] There were many problems in the theory, having to do with unsettled conceptualization of the offense-defense balance, problematic standards for measuring it, and inconsistent applications to different levels of warfare and diplomacy.[28] Proponents of offense-defense theory, who flourished when driven by the urge to find ways to stabilize the NATO–Warsaw Pact balance in Europe, have said little directly about unconventional war or terrorism. The theory actually applies more aptly, however, to this lower level of strategic competition (as well as to the higher level of nuclear war) than to the middle level of conventional military power. This is because the cost-exchange ratio between opposing conventional forces of roughly similar size is very difficult to estimate, given the complex composition of modern military forces and uncertainty about their qualitative comparisons, but the exchange ratio in both nuclear and guerrilla combat is quite lopsided in favor of the attacker. Counterinsurgency folklore held that the government defenders needed something on the order of a 10-to-1 advantage over the guerrillas if they were to drive them from the field (see chapter 7).

There has been much confusion about exactly how to define the offense-defense balance, but the essential idea is that some combinations of military technology, organization, and doctrine are proportionally more advantageous to the attack or to the defense when the two clash. "Proportionally" means that available instruments and circumstances of engagement give either the attack or the defense more bang for the buck, more efficient power out of the same level of resources. The notion of an offense-defense balance as something conceptually distinct from the balance of power means, however, that it cannot be identified with which side wins a battle or a war. Indeed, the offense-defense balance can favor the defense, while the attacker still wins because its overall margin of superiority in power was too great, despite the defense's more efficient use of power. (I have been told that the Finns had a saying in the Winter War of 1939–40: "One Finn is worth ten Russians, but what happens when the eleventh Russian comes?") Thus to say that the offense-defense balance favors the offensive terrorists today against the defensive counterterrorists does not mean that the terrorists will prevail. It does mean that terrorists can fight far above their weight, that in most instances each competent terrorist will have much greater individual impact than each good counterterrorist, that each dollar invested in a terrorist plot will have a bigger payoff than each dollar expended on counterterrorism, and that only small numbers of competent terrorists need survive and operate to keep the threat to American society uncomfortably high.

In the competition between terrorists on the attack and Americans on the defense, the disadvantage of the defense is evident in the number of high-value potential targets that need protection. By the beginning of the twenty-first century the United States had "almost 600,000 bridges, 170,000 water systems, more than 2,800 power plants (104 of them nuclear), 190,000 miles of interstate pipelines for natural gas, 463 skyscrapers . . . nearly 20,000 miles of border, airports, stadiums, train tracks."[29] All these usually represented American strength; after September 11th they also represent vulnerability:

> Suddenly guards were being placed at water reservoirs, outside power plants, and at bridges and tunnels. Maps of oil and gas lines were removed from the Internet. In Boston, a ship carrying liquefied natural gas, an important source of fuel for heating New England homes, was forbidden from entering the harbor because local fire officials feared that if it were targeted by a terrorist the resulting explosion could lay low much of the city's densely populated waterfront. An attack by a knife-wielding lunatic on the driver of a Florida-bound Greyhound bus led to the immediate cessation of that national bus service. . . . Agricultural crop-dusting

planes were grounded out of a concern that they could be used to spread chemical or biological agents.[30]

Truly energetic defense measures do not only cost money in personnel and equipment for fortification, inspection, and enforcement; if maximized, they would repeal some of the very underpinnings of civilian economic efficiency associated with globalization. "The competitiveness of the U.S. economy and the quality of life of the American people rest on critical infrastructure that has become increasingly more concentrated, and more sophisticated. Almost entirely privately owned and operated, there is very little redundancy in this system."[31] This concentration increases the potential price of vulnerability to single attacks. Tighter inspection of cargoes coming across the Canadian border, for example, would wreck the "just-in-time" spare-parts supply system of Michigan auto manufacturers. Companies that have invested in technology and infrastructure premised on unimpeded movement could "see their expected savings and efficiencies go up in smoke. Outsourcing contracts will have to be revisited and inventories will have to be rebuilt."[32] How many safety measures would suffice in optimizing airline security without making flying so inconvenient that the air travel industry never recovers as a profit-making enterprise? A few more shoe-bomb or underwear-bomb incidents—especially if they succeed rather than fizzle—and Thomas Friedman's proposal to start an airline called "Naked Air, where the only thing you wear is a seat belt," becomes as plausible as it is ridiculous.[33]

The offense-dominant character of terrorism is implicit in mass detentions of Arab young men after September 11th, and in military tribunals that compromise normal due process and weaken standard criminal justice presumptions in favor of the accused. The traditional axiom that it is better to let a hundred guilty people go free than to convict one innocent reflects confidence in the strength of society's defenses—confidence that whatever additional crimes may be committed by the guilty who go free will not grossly outweigh the injustice done to innocents convicted, that one criminal who slips through the net will not go on to kill hundreds or thousands of innocents. Fear of terrorists plotting mass murder reverses that presumption and makes unjust incarceration of some innocents appear like unintended but expected collateral damage in wartime combat.

Offense-defense theory helps to visualize the problem. It does not help to provide attractive solutions, as its proponents believed it did during the Cold War. Then offense-defense theory was popular because it seemed to offer a way to stabilize the East-West military confrontation. Mutual deterrence from the superpowers' confidence in their counteroffensive capability could substitute for defense at the nuclear level, and both sides' confidence in their conventional defenses could dampen either one's incentives to attack at that level. Little of this applies to counterterrorism. Both deterrence and defense are weaker strategies against terrorists than they were against communists.

Deterrence is still relevant for dealing with state terrorism; hostile governments may hold back from striking the United States for fear of retaliation. Deterrence offers less confidence for preventing state *sponsorship* of terrorism (it did not stop the Taliban from hosting Osama bin Laden). It offers much less for holding at bay transnational groups like Al Qaeda, which lack a return address against which retaliation can be visited, or whose millennialist aims, religious convictions, or interest in suicide make them unafraid of retaliation. Defense, in turn, is better than a losing game only because the inadequacy of deterrence leaves no alternative.[34] Large investments in defense will produce appreciable reductions in vulnerability but will not minimize vulnerability.

Major investments in passive defenses (airline security, border inspections, surveillance and searches for better intelligence, fortification of embassies, and so forth) are necessary, but they reduce vulnerability at a cost disproportionate to the costs competent terrorist organizations have to bear to probe or circumvent them. The cost-exchange ratio for direct defense is probably worse than the legendary 10-to-1 ratio for successful counterinsurgency, and certainly worse than the more than the 3-to-1 ratio that Robert McNamara's analysts calculated for the advantage of offensive missile investments over anti-ballistic missile systems.[35] Nevertheless, major investments in defenses make sense for lack of a better alternative.[36] At least the resource base from which the United States can draw is vastly larger than that available to transnational terrorists. Al Qaeda is well funded but does not have the treasury of a great power. Primacy has a soft underbelly, but it is far better to have primacy than to face it.

Given the offense-dominant nature of terrorist operations, a serious war plan means emphasis on counteroffensive operations. When terrorists or their support structures can be found, preemptive and preventive attacks will accomplish more against them, dollar for dollar, than the investment in passive defenses. Which is the more efficient use of resources: to kill or capture a cell of terrorists who might otherwise choose at any time to strike whichever set of targets on our side is unguarded, or to try to guard all potential targets? The big danger to avoid is strategic judo, or counterproductive counteroffensive operations. This happens if they degenerate into brutalities and breaches of laws of war that make counterterrorism appear morally equivalent to its target, sapping political support at home, and driving the uncommitted abroad to the other side in the process of polarization that is inherent in war. Whether counteroffensive operations gain more in eliminating perpetrators than they lose in alienating and mobilizing "swing voters" in the world of Muslim opinion depends on getting beyond the "crossover point" where attrition eliminates terrorists faster than new ones are recruited.

## PRIMACY AND POLICY

September 11th reminded those Americans with a rosy view that not all the world sees U.S. primacy as benign, that primacy does not guarantee security, and that security may entail some retreats from the globalization that some had identified with American leadership. Primacy has two edges—dominance and provocation. For terrorists who want to bring the United States down, U.S. strategic primacy represented a formidable challenge, but one that can be overcome. Terrorists underestimated the benefits primacy gives the United States, but Americans overestimated them. Americans have been reluctant to make compromises of comfort or principle that would take the edge off the vulnerability fostered by primacy. Most Americans have so far preferred the complacent and gluttonous form of primacy to the ascetic, blithely accepting the dependence on Persian Gulf oil that could be limited by compromises in lifestyle and a serious energy policy. There have been no groundswells to get rid of SUVs, support the Palestinians, or refrain from promoting Western standards of democracy and human rights in societies where both traditionalists and radicals see them as aggression.

Most Americans react to terrorists' choice of tactics, and few reflect very deeply on their motives or strategic calculations. Even the top figures in the Bush II administration seemed to regard Al Qaeda as mindlessly murderous nihilists. An adversary is likely to resort to terrorism, however, only when two conditions coincide: intense political grievance and gross imbalance of power. The first without the second is likely to produce conventional war, and the second without the first, peace. Conventional war is probable if grievance is intense but power is roughly balanced since successful use of respectable forms of force appears possible. If power is imbalanced but grievance is modest, the weaker party is likely to live with the grievance; use of regular military force offers no hope of victory, while indignation is not intense enough to overcome normal inhibitions against murderous tactics. Under American primacy, candidates for terrorism suffer from grossly inferior power by definition. This should focus attention on the political causes of their grievance.

Few Americans yet see primacy as provoking terrorism. Rather, most see it as a condition that can be exploited or not, at will. So U.S. foreign policy exercised muscular primacy in byways of the post–Cold War world when intervention seemed cheap, but not when doing good would clearly be costly. Power has allowed Washington to play simultaneously the roles of mediator and partisan supporter in the Arab–Israeli conflict. In the dozen-year hiatus after the Berlin Wall opened nothing, with the near exception of the Kosovo War, suggested that primacy could not get Americans out of whatever problems it generated.

How far the United States goes to adapt to the second edge of primacy depends on outcomes in Iraq, Afghanistan, and Pakistan, and whether stunning damage is inflicted by terrorists again. If the two wars do not end in disaster, September 11th gradually fades into history, and Al Qaeda and its ilk fail to execute more catastrophic attacks on U.S. home territory, scar tissue will harden on the soft underbelly and the positive view of primacy will survive. If the campaign against terror falters, however, and the exercise of power fails to prevent more big incidents, the consensus will crack. Then more extreme policy options will get more attention. Retrenchment and retreat will look more appealing to some, who may believe the words of Sheik Salman al-Awdah, a dissident Saudi religious scholar, who said soon after September 11th, "If America just let well enough alone, and got out of their obligations overseas . . . no one would bother them."[37]

More likely, however, would be a more violent reaction. There is no reason to believe that terrorist enemies would let Americans off the hook if they retreated and would not remain as implacable as ever. Facing inability to suppress the threat through normal combat, covert action, and diplomatic pressure, and shocked by a catastrophic event such as an attack by WMD, many Americans would consider escalation to more ferocious action. In recent decades the march of liberal legalism has delegitimized tactics and brutalities that once were accepted, but this delegitimation occurred only in the context of fundamental security and dominance of the Western powers, not in a situation of truly dire threat, or the "supreme emergency" that even ethicist Michael Walzer believed justified terror bombing of Germany.[38] In a situation of that sort it is foolhardy to assume that American strategy would never turn to tactics like those used against Japanese and German civilians, or by the civilized French in the *sale guerre* in Algeria, or by the Russians in Chechnya, in hopes of effectively eradicating terrorists despite massive damage to the civilian societies within which they lurk.

This dark eventuality would reveal how terrorists underestimate American primacy. There is much evidence that even in the age of unipolarity opponents have mistakenly seen the United States as a paper tiger. For some reason—perhaps wishfully selective perception—they tend to see retreats from Vietnam, Beirut, and Somalia as typical weakness of American will,[39] instead of considering decisive exercises of power in Panama, Kuwait, and Kosovo, or the long persistence in Vietnam, Iraq, and Afghanistan. As Osama bin Laden said in 1997, the United States left Somalia "after claiming that they were the largest power on earth. They left after some resistance from powerless, poor, unarmed people whose only weapon is the belief in Allah. . . . The Americans ran away."[40]

This apparently common view among those with an interest in pinning America's ears back ignores the difference between elective uses of force and desperate ones. The United States retreated where it ran into trouble helping others, not where it was saving itself. Unlike interventions of the 1990s in Africa, the Balkans, or Haiti, counterterrorism is not charity. With vital material interests involved, primacy unleashed may prove fearsomely potent.

The most general strategies of counterterrorism are attrition and demobilization. The former requires killing or capturing terrorists at a faster rate than new ones can be recruited. The latter depends on undercutting motives for terrorism by sapping grievances or providing incentives not to cooperate with terrorists. In most ambitious form, demobilization means "winning hearts and minds" and striking at "root causes." The main problems with attrition are finding and fixing perpetrators so they can be fought, and taking them out of action without the collateral damage that evokes strategic judo—formidable challenges of intelligence collection in alien environments and tactical finesse with blunt military instruments. Root causes pose formidable challenges for social science analysis, economic sacrifice, and political and organizational skill on a grand scale.

The two big questions about root causes are: (1) What are they? and (2) Can they be fixed? Unless there are general answers that cut across various cases, dealing with them will require complex judgments about particular circumstances and options in every case confronted. Says one of the prime experts on terrorism, "A rather disturbing implication is that the United States needs ... as many counterterrorist policies as there are terrorist groups."[41] Washington would not have a counterterrorism policy, but instead a counter–Al Qaeda policy, a counter-Hezbollah policy, a counter–Jemmah Islamiyya policy, and so on. The odds that the American government will do a good job of careful ad hoc assessment and judgment in a variety of circumstances across a long span of time are not good. On the other hand, there is no consensus on general causes of terrorism, and investigating root causes requires a challenging array of expertise and analytical skills: "because terrorism is an epiphenomenon of broader political and social developments, to forecast terrorism requires the forecasting of many of those other developments."[42]

Which categories of potential causes are most relevant? Consider common arguments from economics, politics, education, and psychology. Poverty, lack of democracy, ignorance of American values, or psychopathology are often cited as prevalent causes, but I am aware of no data that are both systematic and dense to support focusing primarily on any these. Where elements in these categories are persuasive as partial explanations, they do not seem to be ones that are readily fixable.

Economics? Poverty can be a contributing cause, but it is neither a necessary nor a sufficient condition. Fundamentalist madrassas might not be full to overflowing if young Muslims had ample opportunities to make money, but the fifteen Saudis who hijacked the flights on September 11th were from one of the most affluent of Muslim countries. Poverty is pervasive in the less developed world, but terrorism is not. Yet if poverty were the cause, the solution would not be obvious. Globalization generates stratification, creating winners and losers, as efficient societies with capitalist cultures move ahead and others fall behind, or as elite enclaves in some societies prosper while the masses stagnate. And what are the odds that U.S. intervention with economic aid would significantly reduce poverty? Successes in prompting dramatic economic development by outside assistance have occurred, but they are the exception more than the rule. In any case, very few poor people become terrorists, and organized terror is planned and produced by the privileged, not the poor: "Terrorism is essentially the result of elite disaffection."[43] Two of the countries that are among the biggest sources of recruits, financing, or government support for terrorists are Saudi Arabia and Iran, with high per capita GDPs.

Politics? One problem is that Americans do not want to eliminate one big political cause of terrorism: American primacy. Another is that American ideological values are often considered a weapon in the fight for hearts and minds, but they cut both ways in confronting terrorists' grievances. Western liberals want to complete the End of History, and remaking the world in the Western image is what most Americans assume to be just, natural, desirable, and only a matter of time. But that presumption is precisely what energizes anti-Western zealots' hatred. Secular Western liberalism is not their salvation, but their scourge.

Nevertheless, democratization is usually assumed to help demobilization by providing nonviolent mechanisms for resolving grievances. Angry Muslims do not oppose American democratic theory as much as American policy practice. Yet terrorism occurs more in democratic than in authoritarian societies, and more democracy may sometimes spur rather than dampen it. Rohan Gunaratna argues that "until democracy returned, the political environment in Indonesia was not conducive for Al Qaeda to establish a base in that country," and according to Pillar, terrorism has generally "been more prevalent in free than in unfree societies."[44] This does not mean that the United States should oppose democratization—indeed, promoting it is an ideological cornerstone of both major American political parties and recent presidents' programs. U.S. support for repressive governments is clearly among the grievances Al Qaeda cites, and terminating that source of incitement would not hurt the effort to demobilize populations sympathetic to Al Qaeda. It might also impair attrition campaigns in the short run, however, if the governments providing bases, intelligence support, and police establishments are thrown out, and it would hurt even more if democracy produces radical anti-American regimes.

Education or advertising? There is no more evidence that potential recruits are attracted to terrorism out of ignorance of American values than that familiarity breeds contempt. Often-cited examples of the latter problem include Sayyid Qutb, the Egyptian Islamist executed in Cairo in 1966, and Hasan al-Turabi, the Sudanese facilitator for Al Qaeda. Their extensive travel and studies in the United States and England in the late 1940s and early 1960s, respectively, had confirmed their convictions that secularism, capitalism, and Western society are ungodly and evil.[45] For some, as Michael Mousseau puts it, "Anti-American rage is the result of people knowing Americans too well. The problem is that they just do not like what they see."[46] Indeed, one of the root causes of terrorism, if we are to believe the perpetrators themselves, is what the United States does in the world.[47] Intervention in support of Western political values, support of unpopular regimes, and backing of Israel provoke bitter Islamist opposition. At the same time, overwhelming American military power leaves terrorism as the only effective weapon in response. Washington is not about to abandon its larger foreign policies because they provoke, but neither will a thousand speeches convince enemies that these policies and objectives are good for them. None of this means that Washington should prefer foreigners to remain ignorant of the United States, and it is peculiarly unfortunate that Senator Jesse Helms succeeded in getting the U.S. Information Agency abolished just before it was most needed. The mistake would be in ignoring the two edges of more communication, and seeing ideal public diplomacy as a major tool of counterterrorism.

Psychology? There are two contending images of the mental state of terrorists. One sees terrorists as instrumentally rational strategists who choose the tactic for its efficacy in pursuing their political aims.[48] That image channels counterterrorism toward political and operational matters. The other common image, more nihilistic, is drawn from psychoanalysis: terrorists are disturbed people seeking subconscious goals, not really the political ones they profess. They are narcissistic and aggressive and "need an outside enemy to blame" for psychological damage suffered in childhood (such as loss of the father or failure in school), projecting "onto others all the hated and devalued weakness within." For them, "political violence is driven by psychological forces. . . . *The cause is not the cause.*" It only "becomes the rationale for acts the terrorists are driven to commit. . . . *individuals become terrorists in order to join terrorist organizations and commit acts of terrorism.*"[49] Others have argued that Islamist terrorists often have psychosexual disorders, perhaps a result of separation from the company of women enforced by Islamic custom and the arithmetic of polygamy, which denies marriage opportunities to many men. If any of these explanations are correct, they offer little help for counterterrorism strategy because psychological causes are among the deepest and least malleable, and attacking the sexual norms of Islamic culture will generate opposition rather than defuse it.

Without attacking causes, counterterrorism is a holding action. As long as motives exist, recruits will keep coming. But it is hard to identify general causes confidently, and hard to attack them effectively even when high costs are acceptable, especially when some of the causes are values or policies most Americans do not want to change, or changing them would interfere with attrition. For example, withdrawing the visible American presence (especially ground-based military forces) from Muslim countries is a demand of militant Islamists that could be met, but it would compromise more general political aims of American activists and would also compromise tactical options for striking at terrorist organizations.

Americans must hope that some revolutions in the Muslim world can be democratic, remain democratic, develop democracy in a liberal rather than illiberal form, and produce foreign policies that are not drastically more hostile to American interests than those of the regimes they replace. This is hoping for a lot, and a Las Vegas odds-maker would not bet money on those outcomes in many cases. But the United States should support such revolutions as long as they are not captured outright by malign forces. The reasons make as much sense for realists as for idealists. Clinging to the "wrong side of history" will not advance U.S. power or interests in the long run but will increase and energize the coalition arrayed against them. That result would outweigh the short-run side effects that give a boost to terrorists from the fall of friendly authoritarian regimes. Whatever can be done to make American support of democratic reform seem credible rather than disingenuous, and to distance the United States from policies that Muslims see as oppressive or insulting, cannot guarantee that new regimes will be friendly, but cannot hurt in efforts to demobilize the social base for terrorism.

One initiative that would make solid strategic sense would be to push U.S. policy on the Arab–Israeli conflict as far as it could go toward supporting Palestinian interests. This certainly does not imply compromising solid support for Israeli security within the borders of Israel proper, nor would it demobilize Islamist terrorists, but it would help. It is also the right thing to do on the merits of the territorial dispute and to reduce the unpopularity of pro-American Arab governments. The obstacle to this is the absence of any potent constituency in the American political system for such a change, and the existence of strong constituencies opposing it.

# 6 | STRIKING FIRST
## WELL-LOST OPPORTUNITIES

When the United States sends forces into combat it usually does so as an intervention, where a war is already under way between an American client and its adversary. Indeed, commentary on the use of force in the age of American global activism often carelessly uses the terms war and intervention interchangeably. *Starting* a war against a country that is still at peace does not come naturally and is something that the United States has rarely done. Nevertheless, the specter of weapons of mass destruction held by an aggressive tyrant provoked George W. Bush to launch a war against Iraq in 2003. That venture proved disastrous, yet in subsequent years the specter of nuclear weapons held by a fanatical regime led hawks in the United States and Israel to recommend launching another attack—this time against Iran.

For strategists, the most important issues for judging the wisdom of preemptive or preventive war are effectiveness (whether it will achieve political objectives at acceptable cost) and efficiency (whether it will do so at less cost than other options). Most debate about the question, however, has revolved around the issue of legality. Whether or when international law permits war initiation is a question that deserves attention by political theorists, politicians, and jurists.[1] To some, the question is the main basis for discrediting the option, since these days combat action other than direct self-defense is widely considered a breach of international law. For national security strategists, however, the legal focus is misplaced, for two reasons. First, in foreign policy, legal arguments rationalize actions but do not determine them. Indeed, in recent times liberal lawyers have been amenable to rationalizing offensive force in the service of humanitarian aims, while realists who look to the past for practical guidance on what works strategically find a record that does not provide good grounds for striking first. With few exceptions, that record turns out to be one of opportunities thankfully lost, or ones tragically taken. Second, decisions for or against starting a war are not necessarily struggles between strategic incentive and legal constraint. This is because legal arguments about war initiation have ranged across the whole spectrum from forbidding it to requiring it, and many become contorted in the attempt to square imperatives for action with traditional prohibitions. For example, one thoughtful approach presents a permissive standard yet eight pages later suggests a more restrictive one.[2] Others stretch or muddle concepts in order to let preferred options conform to stipulated conditions.[3] Such tensions reflect the simple fact legalists find uncomfortable: international law is usually deemed to forbid initiating war except in direct self-defense, while modern circumstances are widely recognized to make it necessary under other conditions.

Strategists' lack of attention to the legal issues about initiating war is not due to disdain for moral concerns, but to the fact that councils of war seldom yoke moral concerns to legal ones. Every decision for war rests on moral judgment, even if it is the morality of *raison d'état*.[4] What the state *should* do in the external realm for the safety of its citizens is the moral judgment governments make. This may or may not correspond with what leaders truly believe the relevant international law to be.

International law rarely if ever constrains governments from initiating war. Legal conclusions figure as public justifications for decisions made on other grounds. It is hard to think of a case in which international law, or whatever it was alleged to be, blocked a decision to wage war—that is, a case in which a government decided that it should wage war yet refrained because international law was deemed to forbid it. Moreover, since some assert that the sanctity of sovereignty has been overtaken by an alleged "responsibility to protect" in the evolution of international law, law may not constrain decisions to go to war but compel them.[5] Before entering government the director of Secretary of State Hilary Clinton's Policy Planning Staff, lawyer Anne Marie Slaughter, even joined in arguing the obligation to initiate preventive force.[6]

"Good" initiations of formally prohibited force have led even those who pay attention to international law to overlook or excuse admitted illegality. As a former legal adviser to the U.S. State Department put it, "Preventive force, in other words, has been used widely even though it is generally regarded as illegal. This discrepancy poses a challenge for international law, whose strength and credibility depend partly on consistency and objectivity." He points out that the 2004 report of the UN Secretary General's High-Level Panel on Threats, Challenges, and Change "proposed that the Security Council adopt 'a set of agreed guidelines, going directly not to whether force can be legally used but whether as matter of good conscience and good sense it should be.' The Panel, in other words, rightly acknowledged that the legitimacy of an action can differ from its legality."[7]

All this underlines the misplaced emphasis on legal concerns for explaining, predicting, or deciding on the government's resort to force. But there is a profound difference, in stable constitutional systems like the United States, between the applicability of international law, which figures as a normative symbol, and of domestic law, which must be obeyed. American presidents normally adhere to domestic legal constraints, if only because they can be removed from office if Congress decides that they have broken the law. What gives law causal, as distinct from normative, effect is the existence of effective mechanisms for its adjudication and enforcement apart from the relative physical power of the parties to the legal dispute. These mechanisms do not exist in the international system, where the parties (states) are themselves the effective adjudicators and enforcers. Crises managed by negotiation are the analog to settling out of court in domestic law, and war is the analog to litigation. Yet in the twenty-first century simple *raison d'état* no longer justifies action admitted to be extralegal. So in real life, government leaders decide what they believe is right to do, and (in countries like the United States) what domestic law allows. Then they have a lawyer devise a rationale by which to tell the world that international law allows it. So as a practical matter assessment of the wisdom of war initiation is left in the realm of strategy, where judgment rests on what option achieves political objectives at least acceptable cost.

## To Strike or to Wait

Strategy selects military plans and operations best designed to achieve policy objectives. Both objectives and military strategies can be either defensive or offensive, but the characteristics at both levels do not always go together. Aggressive objectives can only be pursued militarily with offensive operations. Defensive objectives, however, may appear to require offensive operations, depending on technical conditions and other circumstances.

This is the root of the problem. If defensive motives required only defensive strategies there would be no problem, but if benign motives require a strategy that initiates war, war becomes harder to avoid.

At one end of a continuum on which political objectives and strategic choices are combined is the dual offensive: the policy of predatory, unprovoked aggression, and the military plan to accomplish it by conquest. This has been universally delegitimized ever since the eradication of fascism. At the opposite end is the purely defensive combination: the policy of keeping the status quo by defensive military operations—waiting behind one's own borders to block and repel enemy forces when they strike the first blow. This purely defensive option is considered legitimate by all but pacifists, and if it is strategically reliable, most of the dilemma disappears. Those who want to minimize reasons to strike first, therefore, try to promote doctrines and configurations of military capabilities that make defensive operations more efficient and thus militarily preferable to attack, so that countries who want peace will not feel compelled to initiate war. But the purely defensive combination of political motives and military strategy does not always seem technically feasible.

Between the extremes of pure aggression and pure defense lie two mixed options, where motives are defensive but military strategy is operationally offensive. The option closer to aggression is *preventive* war: resort to force in order to cripple potential enemies before they grow in power, become harder to fight, and eventually decide to start the war themselves. The one closer to pure defense is preemptive attack: striking first to beat the enemy to the draw when that enemy has decided for war and is preparing an imminent attack.

Victims always cite enemy attacks as aggressive; perpetrators always cite them as preventive or preemptive. This has a lot to do with the irrelevance of international law to decisions on making war. With few exceptions, governments making war *believe* that they are acting defensively and legitimately, and with practically no exceptions they *say* they are doing so. (Even Hitler claimed that Poland struck first in September 1939.)

Preventive war is almost always a bad choice, strategically as well as morally. Preemption is another matter—legitimate in principle and sometimes, if not often, advisable in practice. The rationale for preventive war is that conflict with the adversary is so deep and unremitting that war is ultimately inevitable, on worse terms than at present, as the enemy grows stronger over time. Thus it is better to face the music sooner, when chances

TABLE 6.1 Military Strategy and Political Legitimacy

| UNPROVOKED AGGRESSION | PREVENTIVE WAR | PREEMPTIVE ATTACK | PURE DEFENSE |
|---|---|---|---|

least ----------⋮----------------------------⋮----------------------------------------⋮------------------------------------------------⋮----------most
legitimate                                                                                                                              legitimate

of military success are greater. It is never possible, however, to know that war is inevitable. The most bitter conflicts sometimes cool with time, even turning enemies into allies.

If the term is used accurately, rather than in the sloppy or disingenuous manner in which the Bush II administration used it to justify preventive war against Iraq, and if perfect information is assumed, preemption is unobjectionable in principle. In the strict sense it is only an act of anticipatory self-defense in a war about to be initiated by the enemy. Preemption assumes intelligence on the enemy's decision to strike, or detection of enemy forces actually mobilizing for attack, which represents the start of the war.[8] Beating the enemy to the draw is reactive, even if it means firing the first shot. If offensive operations are stronger than defensive, striking first is the only way to avoid deadly consequences, or at least relatively greater losses, from holding back until the other moves.

In practice, however, it is rarely possible to be sure that an enemy mobilization is aggressively motivated, rather than a precautionary reaction to rising tension and fear, or that enemy deployment of forces in readiness for combat is preparation to attack rather than to stand and defend. These uncertainties reflect the concepts of "security dilemma," "crisis instability," and "reciprocal fear of surprise attack" that made Cold War strategists focus on conditions that could trigger mistaken preemption. Nevertheless, it would be risky to foreswear preemption. Although it is rarely possible to be sure that enemy attack is imminent, immediate evidence is more solid ground on which to make such a judgment than is an estimate of the more distant future that could prompt preventive war. Preemption is more legitimate than preventive war not because of a moral difference between the two, but because of a difference in the weight of evidence that the adversary is bound to attack.

Precisely because adversaries are rarely certain whether each other's preparations for war are aggressive or defensive, *preemption is extremely rare*. Dan Reiter counts only three preemptive cases in the past century: World War I, Chinese intervention in Korea, and the Six-Day War of 1967.[9] Preventive wars, however, are common, if we count according to the rationales of those who start wars, since most countries that launch an attack without an immediate provocation believe their actions are preventive.

## STANDARDS FOR STRIKING

Are there good examples of preemptive or preventive war—that is, ones that were strategically effective (meaning only that the action served the initiator's objectives, irrespective of whether those objectives were legitimate)? Taking the most promising of the two categories—preemption—only one actual case qualifies well: the Israeli attack on Egypt and Syria in June 1967. This judgment rests on separating the short- and long-term issues. Israel's colonization of the conquered territories in later years was both illegitimate and counterproductive, but the risks to its survival at the time were real if it waited for the Arabs to strike first. Nasser's closure of the Strait of Tiran, eviction of the UN peacekeeping force from the Sinai, and political rhetoric made the circumstantial evidence that the Arabs were preparing to attack Israel as good as such evidence ever gets. Even if Israel's political objectives were perfectly defensive, and even if it could not be absolutely certain that the Arabs would strike, it could not rely on a defensive military strategy. First, within the narrow 1967 borders the country was vulnerable to being dismembered by an Arab offensive. Second, Israel had to fully mobilize reservists, denuding the civilian labor force, in order to match Arab military manpower and could not maintain that level of mobilization for long without inviting economic collapse. Mounting a surprise attack on June 5 enabled numerically inferior Israeli forces to eliminate the Arab military threat.

Reiter's other examples are not easy to approve. U.S. forces would not have moved into China if they had successfully completed the advance to the Yalu. If China intervened in Korea to preempt such an invasion, therefore, it started an unnecessary war that lasted for two more years. (In reality, national defense was not the only Chinese motive. Mao wanted to intervene to save the communist regime in North Korea.) World War I makes the negative case most starkly. It is the best example of the danger in preemption—a catastrophe brought on by mistaken hopes for a short, successful war and mistaken fear of the military consequences of relying on pure defense. Given the military technologies of the time and the density of forces on fronts, purely defensive military strategies would have been a better choice all around in 1914—as demonstrated by the four years of stalemate that followed.[10]

There are cases of preemptive actions that *would have* been justifiable but were not undertaken—cases where countries fell victim to surprise attack. For example, if American forces in December 1941 had been able to detect and strike the Japanese carriers while they were still out to sea, before they could launch against Pearl Harbor, it would have been right to do so. But measured against other cases that could have turned out like World War I or worse (for example, the Cuban Missile Crisis), these missed opportunities do not support a presumption in favor of preemption.

There are many examples of preventive wars that proved blunders. The most recent one was Bush II's assault on Saddam Hussein's Iraq, a momentary stunning success followed by years of chaos, casualties, destruction, and disorder in the country. Are there good past examples of preventive war? Perhaps, but it is hard to think of many. In contrast to the preemptive Israeli attack in 1967, the preventive Sinai Campaign in 1956 lost more than it gained. Israel struck to cut Egypt down to size before it assimilated the weaponry from a big arms deal with Czechoslovakia. But then the Israelis, along with the British and French, evacuated the peninsula soon after conquering it, which did nothing to suppress the long-term threat from the Arabs. If anything, the short-lived military success aggravated Egyptian bitterness and spurred the actions a decade later that produced the Six-Day War.

Are there preventive wars that were not fought but should have been? The one obvious case was the French decision not to fight Germany when Hitler remilitarized the Rhineland in 1936. If the Nazis had been stopped then, when they were weaker than they were three years later, Europe might have been spared the apocalypse of World War II and the projection of communism into the heart of the continent for forty years of the Cold War. But this counterfactual benefit was not certain. Even if the Nazi regime had been overthrown in 1936, the problem of disproportionate German power and unresolved German grievances would not have been settled, and the potential for conflict and eventual wider war would have remained. Nevertheless, this is the best example imaginable to justify preventive war.

The problem in 1936 was underestimation of the long-term threat. The issue was not blocking immediate aggression; the Rhineland was German territory. Rather the issue was whether the legal restrictions imposed on German military presence in their own territory—restrictions imposed by force in the victors' Versailles Treaty—should be maintained by force. No one then foresaw the full horror of 1939–45 or considered another world war inevitable, and all felt the imperative to avoid repeating the mistake that had led to the awesome carnage twenty years earlier.

In the Cold War many in the West did believe that a third world war was probable, and they saw Stalin in 1950 as comparable to Hitler in 1936. Some argued in favor of preventive war against the Soviet Union, and later against China. Secretary of the Navy Francis Matthews, Senator John Mc-Clellan, Major General Orvil Anderson, and others promoted war against the USSR in the early 1950s, and it was considered in studies early in the Eisenhower administration.[11] Destruction of developing Chinese nuclear facilities was also considered in the national security community in the 1960s.[12] With benefit of hindsight, such proposals appear reckless, based on overestimates of the communist powers' intention to undertake direct military aggression. At the time, however, Stalin and Mao were widely viewed in the same light as Saddam Hussein or Mahmoud Ahmadinejad were seen later—as aggressive fanatics whose lust for conquest could not assuredly be deterred. Even serious philosophers and intellectual statesmen wrung their hands over the apparent dilemma. Consider Harold Nicolson's diary entry from November 1948:

> Vita and I discuss after dinner whether Bertie Russell was right in stating that we should make war on Russia while we have the atomic bomb and they have not.... I think it is probably true that Russia is preparing for the final battle for world mastery and that once she has enough bombs she will destroy Western Europe, occupy Asia and have a final death struggle with the Americas. If that happens and we are wiped out over here, the survivors in New Zealand may say that we were mad not to have prevented this while there was still time. Yet, if the decision rested with me, I think I should argue as follows: "It may be true that we shall be wiped out, and that we could prevent this by provoking a war with Russia at this stage. It may be true that such a war would be successful and that we should then establish some centuries of Pax Americana—an admirable thing to establish. But there remains a doubt about all this. There is a chance that the danger may pass and peace can be secured by peace. I admit it is a frail chance—not one in ninety. To make war in defiance of

that one chance is to commit a crime. Better to be wiped out by the crime of others than to preserve ourselves by committing a deliberate crime of our own. A preventive war is always evil. Let us rather die." And the New Zealanders would say, "The man was mad—or cowardly, or stupid, or just weak."[13]

Within a few short years of recommendations for preventive war against Stalin, however, the threat that he posed had changed—he was dead. His successors, in turn, were not megalomaniacs. Before long the case for preventive war against China in the 1960s was washed away when Richard Nixon's secret diplomacy produced the rapprochement of the early 1970s. Overnight, Mao went from being a dire threat to a tacit ally against the Soviet Union. The ultimate evidence against preventive war was the surprisingly peaceful end of the Cold War, which clearly demonstrated the wisdom of waiting the adversary out and relying on containment and deterrence rather than precipitating a showdown that turned out to be unnecessary.

## THE OSIRAK FALLACY

America's most recent venture in preventive war does nothing to recommend the option. Invasion of Iraq did guarantee that the country would not deploy WMD—at least as long as U.S. forces remain in the country.[14] This assault was unnecessary for the declared purpose—to eliminate Iraqi biological and chemical weapon stocks and stop rebuilding of a nuclear arms program—since Saddam Hussein turned out to have destroyed the stocks he had, and to have made only a negligible effort to redevelop the nuclear program. It was also a reckless venture even if the WMD had existed as U.S. estimates assumed.[15] Even if the other humanitarian reasons for invasion later touted after the WMD were revealed to be missing were legitimate grounds, and even if they are ultimately achieved, the awesome costs in blood and treasure of achieving them can hardly be justified. Nevertheless, fear of another rogue state's nuclear potential spurred calls for preventive war in the last years of the Bush II administration.

As pressure mounted in Bush II's last years to reckon with Iran's nascent nuclear program, attention was drawn to Israel's 1981 strike on Iraq's Osirak reactor as a model for action. Most saw this as a bold stroke flying in the face of international opinion, nipping Iraq's nuclear capability in the bud or at least postponing a day of reckoning. This widely held view overestimates what that strike accomplished. Contrary to prevalent mythology, there is no evidence that Israel's destruction of Osirak delayed Iraq's nuclear weapons program. In fact evidence about decisions and actions inside Saddam Hussein's government uncovered since demonstrates that the attack accelerated it.[16] (The apparent Israeli attack on a Syrian reactor under construction in 2007 resembles the 1981 case. Because much less is known about this event, and Syria is a much smaller and weaker country than Iraq or Iran, less capable of ratcheting a nuclear weapons program back up, analysis here focuses on the Osirak case.)

The appeal of the Osirak experience is that it was done by air attack alone, in contrast to the bigger, prolonged war that Bush undertook to eliminate WMD Iraq was thought to have two decades after the Israeli strike. In contrast to war on the ground, air power has the allure of quick, clean, and decisive action without messy entanglement. Smash today, gone tomorrow. Iraq's nuclear program before the first Persian Gulf War, though, demonstrates how unsuccessful air strikes can be even when undertaken on a massive scale. Consider the surprising discoveries after that war, which occurred less than ten years after the Osirak attack. In 1991 coalition air forces destroyed the known nuclear installations in Iraq, but when inspectors of the United Nations Special Commission (UNSCOM) went into the country after the war, they unearthed a huge infrastructure for nuclear-weapons development that had been mostly unknown to Western intelligence before the war.

Obliterating the Osirak reactor did not necessarily put the brakes on Saddam's nuclear weapons program; the attack did both more and less than was necessary. First, the reactor that was destroyed could not have produced a bomb on its own. Second, the reactor was not even necessary for producing a bomb by a different technological method. The Iraqis simply used that second method. Nine years after Israel's attack on Osirak, Iraq was very close to producing a nuclear weapon. Had Saddam been smart enough in 1990 to wait a year longer, he might have had a nuclear weapon in his holster when he invaded Kuwait.

There are two methods for developing fissionable material for a nuclear weapon. One is to reprocess spent fuel from a nuclear reactor like Osirak into fissionable plutonium. To reprocess the fuel from Osirak on a significant scale, the Iraqis would have needed a separate plutonium-reprocessing plant. Many lay observers commonly assume that the Israeli strike was effective because they mistakenly believe that a nuclear reactor alone can produce explosive material for a bomb. Iraq had bought a "hot cell" from Italy that could have been used to extract limited amounts of plutonium, but it had not moved to build a larger reprocessing facility at the time the Israelis struck the reactor.

Iraq pursued the method for which a reactor in itself is not required. The destruction of Osirak did nothing to impede the separate development project that brought Iraq to the brink of weapons capability less than a decade later. Iraq went on to a fast-paced weapon-development effort by choosing the second route to fissionable material, enrichment of natural uranium. This is also the route that Iran took years later. Western and Israeli intelligence did not detect Iraq's enrichment facilities when Saddam Hussein was actively developing a nuclear capability during the 1980s.

If anything, the destruction of the reactor probably inflamed Saddam's incentive to rush the program via the second route and to hide the facilities. It is not clear that Saddam would have been able to develop nuclear weapons much faster through Osirak than via enrichment, given the need for separate plutonium reprocessing and the limited output of the reactor. There is only a supposition, no clear evidence, that Israel's preventive strike was an example of effective delay.

The Israelis' thinking was certainly not mindless. They had every reason to assume that Iraq's building of a reprocessing plant was just a matter of time, that Saddam wanted a nuclear weapon, and that he intended to use Osirak's output to build one. Nevertheless, Israel's strike did not preempt an imminent threat. The Israelis understood in 1981 that Osirak's threat lay in the future. If the reactor was ever to be bombed, however, it made sense to do so before its construction was complete, since once it was in operation its destruction would have spread radioactivity to the surrounding area. But this required a provocative action before it was certain that full-scale plutonium reprocessing was in fact going to be developed. After the strike, Prime Minister Menachem Begin made a gaffe, for which he later had to apologize, when he claimed the Israeli planes had destroyed a secret underground laboratory in the reactor, forty meters beneath the Earth's surface.[17] Had the Iraqis actually constructed such an underground chamber, its existence would have made a case for the attack because it might have facilitated concealed reprocessing. Some analysts speculated that Begin had suffered a "senior moment," confusing Osirak with Israel's own secret underground facility, which it had constructed long before at the Dimona reactor site to conceal its nuclear weapons program.

Iraq's Osirak-era capabilities were not comparable to Iran's nuclear program, which was far more advanced by the twenty-first century. Iran was put on notice long ago, however, that it was being targeted by American and Israeli military planners. Any strategist in those countries would have been foolish to assume that Tehran was leaving its entire nuclear establishment vulnerable and had failed to disperse and conceal some important assets in order to frustrate hostile intelligence collection. Indeed, the revelation of a major facility at Qom in 2009 underlined the obvious point that other such units could exist, still undetected. A thorough air campaign could easily destroy all of Iran's identified or suspected nuclear facilities—at least any not located in very deeply buried bunkers—but attack planners could not be sure that all crucial facilities had been hit because they could not be confident that all had been identified.[18] As Amrom Katz famously put the problem, "We have never found anything that the Soviets have successfully hidden."[19] Inspections after the 1991 Gulf War uncovered unknown installations, and before 2003 Western intelligence agencies could only guess where Iraq's supposed WMD were kept. Either of these opposite experiences is a caution against assuming adequate knowledge. How could American or Israeli intelligence have confidence in years afterward that they knew all the necessary aim points for an air attack on Iran?

Desperation or bravado led some hawks to downplay this problem. While they recognized that an air campaign would not guarantee full destruction of Iran's nuclear capability or even prevent Iran from rebuilding, they reasoned that it could at least delay the program. The question remains, then, would a strike that was successful in wiping out a big chunk of Iran's capacity be more effective than Israel's venture in 1981?

With more to destroy than there was in Iraq back then, the evolving Iranian program might be more disrupted, but by the same token more hidden capabilities might survive. Although most of Iran's nuclear infrastructure has probably been detected, when it comes to nuclear weapons, *the key is not how much capability a preventive attack eliminates, but how much it does not.* Unless Iran's leaders are surprisingly stupid or negligent, they cannot be assumed to have left all capacity for developing fissionable material in locations accessible to intelligence collectors and targeting staffs.

Advocates of an air assault took comfort in the proposition that the destruction of a major portion of Iran's nuclear establishment would set back acquisition of weapons by some years. When asked what to do when Iran picks up the pieces and starts over again, they echo the argument of General Curtis LeMay, who advocated the preventive destruction of China's industry in the early 1960s. When Assistant Secretary of State Averell Harriman asked LeMay what the United States should do when China rebuilt its capability, he said, "Hit 'em again."[20] This approach blithely assumes that American or Israeli policymakers would have the stomach for "maintenance bombing," and that Iran would continually fail to adjust and curb its vulnerability. And the China example underlines the danger in dismissing the potential for détente with a bitter enemy, however radical and hostile it seems to be at present.

Political, diplomatic, and military obstacles to taking action in Iran have been well recognized. Hawks who think of themselves as stalwart, steely-eyed and far-seeing have regarded these obstacles as challenges to be overcome or disregarded in order to do what is necessary, even if it is less than a perfect solution. But if bombing known nuclear sites were to mean that Tehran could only produce, say, a dozen weapons in fifteen years rather than two dozen in ten years, would the value of the delay outweigh the costs? The costs would not be just political and diplomatic, but strategic as well. Intensifying alienation of non-Western governments and Islamic populations around the world would undermine the worldwide American campaign against terrorism. Inflaming Iranian nationalism would turn a populace that has been divided in its attitudes toward the West into a united front against the United States. Rage within Tehran's government would probably trigger retaliation, via more state-sponsored terrorist actions by Hezbollah or other Iranian agents. Trading a short-term reduction in a country's nuclear capacity for a long-term intensification of its incentives to retaliate when it eventually has a nuclear weapon is not obviously a net gain.

The military option that is possible would be ineffective, while the one that would be effective is not possible. The military action that would guarantee elimination of a nuclear weapons program—invasion and occupation of Iran—cannot be done. Overwhelming political obstacles aside, America's volunteer army already neared the breaking point in handling missions less challenging than subduing Iran, a country with nearly three times as many people as Iraq or Afghanistan. Yet the only means of definitively preventing Iran from acquiring nuclear weapons would be to occupy the country indefinitely, to ensure that the installed regime remained compliant with

American judgments about what the country does not need for its own security in a dangerous neighborhood.

Conventional military options are not the only means of preventive attack. If it is feasible, covert action poses fewer costs and risks. It is less violent, less public and provocative, more discriminating, more deniable, and traditionally more accepted as a mode of hardball competition short of war. If facilities could be destroyed from within, the aim of retarding the Iranian program might be accomplished with less danger of military backlash and nationalist mobilization. The main problem with this secret alternative is the difficulty of getting agents and deploying them effectively inside hostile territory. The reported use of the Stuxnet computer worm in a suspected Israeli or American covert operation to wreck some important Iranian nuclear equipment may have accomplished the same purpose and is the type of preventive action that cautious American strategists could welcome. Killing of Iranian nuclear scientists by unknown assassins, which also occurred around the same time as the Stuxnet cyberattack, is a step up of more dubious appeal, but still less destructive and dangerous than outright war.

What else should Washington do? This is simply one of the tragic problems in international politics for which there is no good answer. The crusade to keep all second-rate powers from acquiring a nuclear weapon can succeed in some cases for some time, and in fact the record of nonproliferation has been surprisingly good. Who in 1945 would have estimated that nearly seventy years later there would be no more than nine countries in the world with nuclear weapons? Ultimately, however, the effort is a rearguard action. The approach taken to both North Korea and Iran to induce them to come back into compliance with the Nuclear Non-Proliferation Treaty—offering diplomatic and economic carrots and sticks—is unsatisfactory if the aim is confidence in achieving the result. It is just less unsatisfactory than launching wars to compel compliance.

## BALANCE OF RISKS

What should be the benchmark for how to deal with the threats posed by the dangerous regimes in Pyongyang and Tehran: Hitler in 1936 or Stalin and Mao during the Cold War? If Hitler, there are two crucial differences between the recent situation and the 1930s that support restraint. First, even if intentions in Pyongyang and Tehran are as bad as they could be, neither of the regimes has power comparable to what Germany's was. They are me-dium powers, not great powers in the normal sense. Second, neither has allies willing to join in military adventurism. Indeed, almost all the great powers are arrayed against them. If Hitler had been faced at Munich, or in September 1939, by a united front of other great powers—with the United States and Soviet Union joined with the French and British against Ger-many, rather than the second two standing alone—indefinite containment of Germany until the passing of the Nazi regime would have been quite a plausible policy.

The difference of nuclear capability points in the other direction. Devi-ant states with weapons of mass destruction that are growing more potent with time pose a threat disproportionate to their standing in the traditional calculus of balance of power. This is a difference that may weaken com-parison to the 1930s, but not to the Cold War. Antagonistic great powers survived more than four decades of confrontation in the shadow of nuclear war. Bertrand Russell turned out to be wrong, and Harold Nicolson right. Deterrence and containment are the fallback policy from failure to induce denuclearization. It is not comfortable to rely on deterrence to prevent ag-gression, it is just better than precipitating precisely the clash that is feared. Many today forget that Stalin's Soviet Union and Mao Zedong's China were seen in their time as more dire threats than the mullahs in Tehran. Despite common fears in the early Cold War that the threat of nuclear retaliation would not suffice to prevent Soviet or Chinese attack, it did. With benefit of hindsight, it is clear that giving in to the arguments for preventive war in the 1950s would have been an epochal disaster.

Is the Cold War record irrelevant? Despite common assertions that rogue state leaders like Saddam Hussein, Kim Jong-Il, and Mahmoud Ahmadine-jad are crazy and undeterrable, evidence has yet to demonstrate this. Yes, rogue state leaders have been risk-prone and have frequently miscalculated. But North Korea and Iraq attacked their neighbors in 1950, 1980, and 1990 *only when the United States failed to deter them.* Indeed, Washington gave them a green light in all three cases. In 1950 Secretary of State Dean Ache-son's speech to the National Press Club excluded South Korea from the U.S. defense perimeter in Asia six months before North Korea struck. In 1980 the United States was engaged in a bitter struggle with Iran and did nothing to discourage Saddam Hussein from invading. In 1990 Ambassador April Glaspie told Saddam Hussein that the United States had no position on Iraq's dispute with Kuwait.

When the United States did pose deterrent threats against Iraq and North Korea, they worked. Going to war in 1991, the Bush I administration warned Saddam of dire consequences if he used WMD during the war. Despite humiliating defeat, Saddam held back the chemical and biological weapons he did have at the time. Nor did he attack any of Iraq's neighbors after American deterrence was made clear in the years following the 1991 war. North Korea, in turn, mounted many reckless and murderous provocations, but still limited ones, and has not repeated the big mistake of 1950 since the Korean War ended and U.S. deterrence was institutionalized in peacetime. If there is reason to worry about a rogue regime gambling on attack, though, North Korea provides better reason than Iran. Pyongyang has a longer record than Tehran of unleashing violence externally. Yet the drumbeating in Washington for preventive war has all been directed at Iran.

Reliance on containment, deterrence, and pressure short of force remains unsettling to Americans who seek closure in conflict and see restraint as fecklessness. Force has the allure of apparent decisiveness. But Clausewitz warned, "In war the result is never final."[21] Unless victor and vanquished come to agreement on a peacetime order, peace will not endure. Military action might at best suppress nuclear ambitions temporarily; no less probably, an attack could make incentives more intense and more dangerous.

If a government could ever know for sure what the future would bring, decisions would be easy. Uncertainty forces choices that pose risks either way. In the war against Al Qaeda, the question of striking first is not at issue. Having already been attacked, it is logical for the United States and other victims to strike against Al Qaeda and similar groups whenever possible. The issue of striking first does not arise in regard to groups or states who have already struck.

If fully reliable intelligence is ever obtained that an adversary is preparing an imminent attack, and if striking first can reduce the damage that will otherwise be absorbed as a result of waiting to defend against the blow, preemption is the strategically logical decision—and the moral one in consequentialist terms. But those are two very big ifs. Neither of the conditions is often met. The conditions for legitimate preventive war are even more rarely met, if ever. As long as the costs of initiating a war are certain, while the probability that the enemy will eventually strike is less than 100 percent, the burden of proof is on the case for striking first.

This burden should be especially heavy for the United States, which is not a small power beset by populous enemies all around its borders, as Israel was facing in 1967, nor a great power facing another that was rebounding and potentially superior, as France was facing in 1936. For a superpower, "the military power that gives it unrivaled ability to launch anticipatory attacks also reduces the need for them. The more powerful a state is, the more likely it is to be able to deal effectively with most of the threats it faces through deterrence or defense."[22]

# 7

## BIG SMALL WARS
### IRAQ, AFGHANISTAN, AND VIETNAM

American force comes in doses from light to large. First and preferred, if it works, is latent force: military capability unused but held at the ready, a threat that may constrain or compel adversaries without being called to the test. Second, and the mildest application of force, is covert action: secret manipulation of foreign politics that usually amounts to a shove short of violence. A step up is direct support for paramilitary operations of foreign clients such as rebels backed by the United States during the Cold War in Laos, Cuba, Tibet, Nicaragua, and elsewhere, or hands-on advice and direction by U.S. military personnel to client governments battling revolutionaries, as in Greece in the 1940s, Vietnam before 1965, or El Salvador in the 1980s. Next are the numerous policing or punitive actions where U.S. military units themselves deploy for minor combat or raids in places such as Lebanon, the Dominican Republic, Libya, Grenada, Somalia, Haiti, and Bosnia. All these ventures add up to a large total of forcible actions, but they are of small significance compared with the six outright wars the United States has fought since 1945 in Korea, Vietnam, Kuwait, Kosovo, Afghanistan, and Iraq.

War is the biggest venture in national security policy. It may not always be the last resort, but it should be close to it. If conciliatory diplomacy does not work, a government's aim should still be to get what it wants without having to implement the threat of force. Prevailing through preparation for combat rather than execution—via deterrence or active coercion—is the best measure of success in peacetime military policy. In a unipolar world, succeeding without combat should be easier than in the traditional world of international politics, where unclear imbalances of power and shifting alliances made miscalculation of relative capability harder to avoid. Yet within just fifteen years of becoming the sole superpower, the United States got into twice as many wars (although smaller ones) as it did in a full forty-five years of bipolarity. Indeed, American forces were in major combat during less than one-fourth of the years of the Cold War (1950–53 and 1965–72) but have been during more than half the years since the Cold War ended (1991, 1999, and ever since 2001). This contrast is quite ironic, given how the size of military threats to American security plummeted after the collapse of communism.

In a unipolar world any resort to force is necessarily a failure of sorts. Even if the sole superpower wins a war it gets into, its deterrent strategy must have failed (by not making clear why it would be folly for the enemy to attack), or its coercive strategy must have failed (by not making clear why the enemy should give in without a fight). On the other hand, if a superpower gets into a war that it loses—which can only happen where its interests and resolution prove less than those of the enemy—it must recognize that the war should not have been undertaken.

If the rational aim of winning without fighting fails, success in wartime is measured first by effectiveness and then by efficiency. Effectiveness simply means winning: achieving policy objectives. This is the necessary condition, but not sufficient for full success. Perfect strategy requires efficiency: winning at the lowest possible cost in blood and treasure. By the same logic failure is measured by defeat, or by victory gained at a price higher than the value of the stakes. So how have American arms done by these measures?

In the age of multipolarity, the first 175 years of the republic, the United States never lost a war (at least by Americans' own accounting—Canadians remember the War of 1812 differently). Not all these were necessary or thoroughly admirable (for example, the Mexican and Spanish-American Wars), but the United States did come out on top. The costliest—the Civil War, with by far the highest per capita casualty rate of any American conflict—preserved the nation against the greatest challenge to its survival. The next greatest success was World War II: the United States entered late, after the other contestants had already mangled each other, but it picked up all the marbles at the end, dominating the noncommunist world. The effort also revived the depressed U.S. economy in the bargain. This was all accomplished at a blood price terrible in absolute terms: just over 400,000 dead soldiers, marines, sailors, and airmen. This was a very low price, however, in relative terms; *fewer than 1 percent* of the total casualties in World War II were American.

America's greatest strategic achievement since 1945 was peaceful victory in the Cold War. This success came at a tremendous price in prolonged mobilization and defense spending for capabilities kept constantly at the ready but largely unused, yet a trivial price compared with what would have been paid in the unlimited World War III that was avoided. In resorts to actual war on a smaller scale during the Cold War and since, however, the results have been mixed. In the age of bipolarity the two U.S. hot wars ended in one tie and one defeat. In the age of unipolarity the scorecard is incomplete: one strong win against Iraq in 1991, one weak win against Serbia in 1999, and two cases with the verdict still out (or with the verdict in the second war in Iraq stacking up as a pyrrhic victory). Looking forward, the United States seems best equipped to win the conventional type of war it should not have to fight for quite some time, and least likely to prevail at acceptable cost in the unconventional type of war in which it has more than once become embroiled against its will.

## Six Limited Wars

None of the six wars since 1945 has been an unqualified success or failure. The most successful was the 1991 Persian Gulf War. This was an unprecedented stunning performance on the battlefield, achieving the objectives of liberating Kuwait and crippling Iraq's military power at minimal cost to the United States: fewer than two hundred American battle deaths and hardly any dollar expenditure, since allies provided most of the funds. Bush I did not take a chance of jumping halfway across the ditch but applied overwhelming force to the mission, making the war an execution rather than a fair fight.

The strategic and operational success, however, was not a policy success. The war might have been avoided entirely if not for botched crisis management, a complete failure to apply deterrence. In the summer of 1990 Washington gave Saddam Hussein a green light to invade Kuwait, then changed course when faced with the result.[1] This reversal was due to an absence of forethought; an Iraqi annexation of Kuwait was a surprise that had not figured in U.S. contingency planning. The American reversal after the invasion eerily resembled what had happened forty years earlier, when

Secretary of State Acheson, thinking of what priorities would be in a global war with the Soviet Union, had left South Korea outside the U.S. defense perimeter in Asia.

If the 1991 Persian Gulf War was a military success following diplomatic failure, the Indochina War was the reverse. It was certainly the biggest disaster of all six wars, with the stakes lost entirely after twenty years of deep American involvement, seven years of heavy combat by U.S. forces, more than 58,000 U.S. dead, and huge expenditures. Yet that catastrophic defeat was followed by a political situation as good as Americans could have hoped for at the outset: exceptional international stability in Southeast Asia and strategic cooperation between the United States and China, the enemy whose containment had been a prime purpose of the war! In Korea and Kosovo the results were more compromised than they were for Vietnam or Kuwait. The outcomes were acceptable, but the aims originally envisioned were only partly achieved, and at a price higher than would have been considered acceptable at the outset.

If the outcomes in Afghanistan and Iraq ultimately prove acceptable, the question will be whether they were worth the cost. In 2011 it is unclear what the answer will be for Afghanistan, which at least began as a necessary war, in contrast to the elective assault on Iraq in 2003. Afghanistan is the only one of the six wars that began as direct self-defense by the United States; the Taliban's refusal to extradite Al Qaeda after September 11th made them accessories to strikes on U.S. territory and justified the American counterattack. If Afghanistan is eventually counted a modest success, a high price may be considered worth it.

For Iraq there is no way that a modest success will prove worth the price: thousands of American casualties, dozens of times more Iraqi casualties, prolonged economic dislocation in the country, hordes of refugees, increased Iranian influence in the region, expanded and inflamed anti-American Islamist movements throughout the world, and an astronomical bill to fund the direct, indirect, and delayed financial costs: up to three trillion dollars, by the accounting of a Nobel Prize–winning economist and former chairman of the Council of Economic Advisers.[2] Even if Saddam Hussein's regime had possessed weapons of mass destruction as then assumed, attacking it was strategically nonsensical. (Future WMD could only be intolerable if Iraq would be likely to launch them without provocation and despite U.S. deterrence. By that logic, initiating a war against Iraq would make it all the more likely that the regime, provoked and desperate, would use the biological weapons it was thought to have already. Thus by the administration's assumptions, preventive war would precipitate exactly what it was meant to prevent.)[3] Although Saddam Hussein's regime was evil and dangerous, it was not more so than others Bush left unstruck, and in any case it was quite effectively contained and deterred in 2003.

The Bush II administration leapt into war for many reasons, but on the assumption that victory would be quick and easy. If a crystal ball could have revealed what would happen in the following several years, none but fanatics would have gone ahead with the venture. Because starting the war was a terrible mistake, however, does not mean that perseverance in the mission was unwarranted after the "surge" of 2007. By that time the issue was not the sunk costs of years of disaster, but whether the marginal cost of success was reasonable. Since the United States broke Iraq it also had a moral obligation to fix it. Together these considerations mean that persistence and gradual withdrawal after 2007 do not redeem the mistake but were a reasonable gamble for limiting the damage.

Of the six American wars since 1945, three would be considered "conventional" (the ones over Korea, Kuwait, and Kosovo) and three have been combinations of conventional war and counterinsurgency (Vietnam, Afghanistan since 2001, and Iraq after 2003). In actual cases the distinctions between these types of warfare become complicated. For purposes here, conventional war refers to combat between states by regular military forces, usually fought on linear fronts and from the air, while insurgency (or guerrilla, irregular, or asymmetric war) refers to combat between groups within states, with some aided by external patrons, to determine which group will constitute the government. Insurgencies are not waged on fronts, but in raids throughout the contested country.

After the 2003 invasion failed to pacify Iraq, the main issue for military strategists became whether U.S. defense planning should concentrate on conventional war or counterinsurgency. Enthusiasts for the "revolution in military affairs" (RMA) focused on the former and were ascendant for a dozen years after the first war against Iraq. The RMA revolves around the radical improvements in technology and information systems that enable regular forces to apply combat power more quickly, neatly, and decisively than in the past. This capital-intensive approach relies on the natural comparative advantage of the richest and most technically advanced power in the world, and it allows military forces to practice their craft without becoming entangled in long political imbroglios.

Counterinsurgency, in contrast, must work on terms set by the enemy, benefits little from technological superiority, is labor-intensive, and demands extraordinary effort and skill in integrating military and political instruments in strategy over long periods of time. In situations where American conventional military superiority proves ineffective, such as Iraq after 2003, counterinsurgency requires a "counterrevolution in military affairs."[4] If strategy is to be dictated by the strategist rather than by circumstances or by politicians, a focus on conventional warfare is the natural choice. If strategy depends instead on the contingencies and enemies that tend to arise despite the best-laid plans, that choice may not be available.

Where conventional war is at issue, in a unipolar world there is little for the United States to worry about. Imbalance of power in general and technical military prowess in particular almost assure the United States of victory in any conventional contingency where it is willing to make a maximum effort. Washington did settle for less than it wanted in Korea and Kosovo, but only because it did not want to make a maximum effort. In 1953 Eisenhower's NSC considered but rejected the option of a push back up the peninsula in the following year. To pay the military price of a more decisive victory in Kosovo would have required the use of ground forces against Serbia, an option NATO rejected from the beginning.

When unipolarity wanes, strategy for conventional warfare will become a challenge once again. This may happen before long, but one decade into the twenty-first century, facing messy conflicts in Afghanistan and Iraq, the main concern for military strategy lay in the circumstances where conventional warfare is not an appropriate instrument. In these cases there is great uncertainty about whether the alternative of counterinsurgency strategy can succeed. In the last quarter of the twentieth century, by one accounting, counterinsurgents won in only about one-fourth of cases. Lyall and Wilson believe this was due in part to dogged attachment to conventional modes of operation.[5] Even when tactical practice is more enlightened, however, the obstacles to counterinsurgency are tremendous, and decisions to undertake wars that require unconventional strategies are the riskiest.

An external intervening force like the United States faces choices in counterinsurgency that have double edges, choices that can work toward both success and failure. One choice is between a strategy of brutality and coercion to frighten the population into submission, or one aimed to win the people's willing loyalty by wooing their "hearts and minds." Another is between combat on a large scale to inflict maximum attrition on guerrilla forces, or restraint aimed to avoid alienating people. A third is between intervention designed to control outcomes by imposing the policies and solutions Americans think best, or intervention designed to promote devolution and democratic reform in the host country—which takes many means of control out of American hands.

A decade into the twenty-first century Americans found themselves stuck inconclusively in two of these messy irregular wars at once. These two could turn out better than the disaster in Vietnam. Even if not, Vietnam is not a template for understanding Afghanistan and Iraq; the differences among the wars are greater than the similarities. Similarities there are, nonetheless, and just the duration and frustration of the current cases inevitably invite consideration of what the old disaster might teach.

## COERCE OR CONVINCE

Decent Americans assume that if the United States is to intervene against a rebel movement, the key to success is winning the allegiance of the population, and that this is done by providing positive inducements: security, services, and good government. This strategy may work best, but not necessarily, and the principle does not always drive practice. In the past, many in the American military resisted responsibility for providing such nonmilitary benefits and remained fixated on the professional mission of combat to eliminate enemy forces. In Vietnam American soldiers and Marines were known to point out that the acronym for "winning hearts and minds" was WHAM, or to quip that "if you grab 'em by the balls the hearts and minds will follow." Such attitudes reflected professional ethos, not considered strategic calculation. There is, however, a strategic rationale for coercive brutality rather than military social work—a strategy that is morally untenable yet sometimes effective.

By one accounting of past cases, the efficacy of the hearts-and-minds approach is a myth, and the most successful counterinsurgency campaigns have been the brutally coercive ones.[6] Historically, irregular warfare was considered illegitimate by great powers whose conventional armies confronted it, and harsh countermeasures were applied. Captured guerrillas were often subject to summary execution, and their civilian supporters to collective punishment.[7] Brutal repression, either premeditated or episodic, was the practice not only of odious governments but of supposedly enlightened ones like Britain in its empire and the United States in the Philippines.[8]

Colonialist campaigns often followed the logic of Colonel C. E. Callwell, an astute if inhumane theorist a century ago: When there is "no capital to seize, no organized army to overthrow, and when there are no celebrated strongholds to capture, and no great centres of population to occupy, the objective is not so easy to select. It is then that the regular troops are forced to resort to cattle lifting and village burning and that war assumes an aspect that may shock the humanitarian." The purpose of such brutality, according to Callwell, is "the overawing and not the exasperation of the enemy."[9] As to effectiveness, Martin van Creveld invokes the example of Syrian Hafez Asad's 1982 assault on his own rebellious city of Hama. The town was leveled by artillery, its famous great mosque was literally turned into a parking lot, at least ten thousand and perhaps as many as thirty thousand people were killed, and Asad later *exaggerated* the civilian death toll in order to terrorize potential dissidents into submission.[10] Thereafter he faced not a whiff of armed resistance. When his son tried more hesitant repression three decades later, resistance spread and continued.

To convince the targets that opposition is hopeless, the brutal approach must be consistently murderous and unrelenting, not just episodically callous. But deliberate and sustained terror is not an option for the United States even if it works. Americans are capable of premeditated slaughter of civilians under extraordinary circumstances like the strategic bombing campaigns of World War II, but not in idealistic interventions assumed to be for the benefit of the contested populations. In these cases the danger is not systematic savagery, but accidental collateral damage that enrages locals without being consistent or extreme enough to cow them into compliance.[11] So the practical question is, if intervention is to be undertaken—a very important "if"—how can military forces make a hearts-and-minds approach work?

## How Few Are Enough? Are Enough Too Many?

At the top of the list of dilemmas in unconventional warfare is whether an outside power intervening in the conflict should do so in a big way, to overwhelm the insurgents with the weight of numbers and resources, or in a minimal way, to avoid provoking popular resentment and resistance. At different times either answer has seemed correct. The riskiest course is the middle option: a medium-scale foreign intervention too thin to pacify most of the territory, but big and clumsy enough to alienate the people it wants to woo. Most strategists would prefer the minimal approach, but it depends on having a competent host government that can apply the resources and advice it gets from a light-handed intervention. That is just what is missing in the most challenging cases. If direct action by the foreign forces to undercut the insurgents is the solution and not the problem, it should logically be done as widely and intensely as possible.

The quality of doctrine and performance—what counterinsurgency forces do, and how well—is the hardest thing for an intervening power to get right. Yet professional debates about counterinsurgency have usually begun with numbers of forces needed. Technological substitution for manpower gives the modern American military its edge, but it cannot be applied very well in unconventional warfare. To defuse rebellion via persuasion and reassurance rather than repression, forces need to interact with the population and serve it, not fire from a distance at fleeting targets intermingled with it. Doing this requires personnel on the ground, in quantity. Apart from the quality of forces' training and skill, the need for high numbers poses a big constraint for an American volunteer military with a limited supply of troops to go around for missions throughout the world. Moreover, a population-centric strategy is in tension with the aim of keeping a small American footprint to minimize nationalist reaction against foreign forces.

Official notions about requirements have most often focused on the ratios of friendly forces to (1) enemy forces, (2) territorial space, or (3) civilian population. Force-to-force ratios were the metric most cited in Cold War campaigns, and the need for a ten-to-one superiority of counterinsurgent forces became a cliché. This axiomatic figure was suspiciously round if not picked out of the air, and the leading practitioners of guerrilla warfare rhetorically discounted it, arguing that their will to persist would overcome even that high a ratio. Ho Chi Minh told French representatives in 1946, "You will kill ten of our men and we will kill one of yours, and in the end it will be you who tire of it."[12]

Force-to-force ratios have little significance apart from force-to-space ratios because the key problem for counterinsurgency is the guerrillas' option to concentrate forces in secret against a single point, while the government has to garrison the entire country, spreading its forces thin. As Sun Tzu put it, "If I am able to determine the enemy's dispositions while at the same time I conceal my own, then I can concentrate and he must divide. And if I concentrate while he divides, I can use my entire strength to attack a fraction of his."[13] Lawrence of Arabia described the dynamic in practice in World War I:

> The Arab army . . . must develop a highly mobile, highly equipped type of force, of the smallest size, and use it successively at distributed points of the Turkish line, to make the Turks reinforce their occupying posts beyond the economic minimum of 20 men. The power of this striking force would not be reckoned merely by its strength. The ratio between the number and area determined the character of the war, and by having five times the mobility of the Turks the Arabs could be on terms with them with one-fifth their number.[14]

Thus even when vastly outnumbered in the country as a whole, insurgents can inflict tactical defeats piecemeal on the occupying force or the government and make their offense dominate the government's defense. In Mao's words, "Our strategy is to 'pit one against ten' and our tactics to 'pit ten against one.'"[15] If the government's position is defensive and reactive, its countrywide margin of superiority must be overwhelming to provide forces to cover all points. Thus the British gained the upper hand in the Malayan Emergency as the ratio of government forces to armed communist rebels grew over time from about 5:1 to 12:1 in the early 1950s and better than 25:1 later. Conversely, the government's position in South Vietnam deteriorated as the ratio fell from an initial 50:1 advantage to about 10:1 in 1965.[16]

In Iraq it was impossible to estimate real force-to-force ratios for years because information was unreliable about not only the number but even the identity of insurgents. Mobility made force-to-space ratios telling anyway. For years after the invasion the number of U.S. troops in the country was kept too low by either standard because Secretary of Defense Donald Rumsfeld, an enthusiast for the RMA, fixated on demonstrating that American wars could be waged and wrapped up frugally. More to his credit, Rumsfeld hoped that a small American footprint and quick handoff of governing responsibility to Iraqis would avert involvement in counterinsurgency altogether. His assumption that an effective occupation could be brief and lean, however, was quickly discredited as low force-to-space ratios left most of the country untouched and uncontrolled by the American invaders, and defeated Iraqis were left free to regroup, recover, and rebound. Iraq is two-and-a-half times the size of South Vietnam and has more than half again as many people as South Vietnam at the peak of U.S. combat action, 1968.

Yet for years after 2003 Iraq had only one-tenth the density per square mile of military forces—American, allied, and Iraqi—as in South Vietnam in 1968. Even in Baghdad, a city of nearly seven million people, the initial U.S. occupation force had no more than 10,000 soldiers available to patrol (only about 1,200 of them dismounted infantry). An occupation force with the same ratio of troops to local population as in Bosnia would have been 450,000, more than triple the number of U.S. forces in Iraq until the surge of 2007.[17] Although Rumsfeld always claimed that his generals never asked for more troops, commanders at all levels made clear at various times that they lacked the numbers to get their jobs done. When Ambassador L. Paul Bremer asked the top U.S. general in Iraq what he would do if he could get two more divisions, Ricardo Sanchez answered, "I'd control Baghdad."[18] Eventually both U.S. and Iraqi security forces increased, but the damage from initial limits was long lasting.

Adequacy of a combat force of any size within a given area depends on what it has to do inside that area. After the Cold War, force-to-population ratios became the popular metric for both peacekeeping and counterinsurgency. This is certainly more appropriate when dealing with urban insurgencies, where control of large numbers of people is a challenge even within a small space, and it also accords with emphasis on the nonmilitary aspects of the mission. In earlier times great powers could intervene effectively in countries with small populations by securing entry ports and moving out to confront insurgents in rural areas. Today, capitals and ports are densely populated, "and rather than being centers of stability on the fringe of disordered interiors, such cities are now likely to be the center of disorder."[19] Emphasis on force-to-population ratios also recognizes that mobility for government forces is not the answer to mobility of guerrillas. David Galula, the greatest Cold War counterinsurgency theorist, noted that a government can always control a hostile area by concentrating its own forces in it, but this simply prompts the guerrillas to move and operate somewhere else.[20] If the government forces withdraw from the pacified area to move against another one, the insurgents return and wash away the government's gains. Americans relearned this at a high price in Iraq in the early years after invasion; bloody campaigns to oust insurgents from Fallujah and elsewhere produced gains that evaporated when the U.S. forces left the conquered areas.

Maximizing the force-to-population ratio also accords with a more passive or defensive tactical orientation that deemphasizes attrition of enemy forces and reduces the odds of strategic judo. Energetic attrition campaigns increase collateral damage. As a British Army field manual concludes, "Having deployed conventionally trained troops and large amounts of firepower, the attritionalist commander generally feels compelled to use them," and the results "will often be an upward spiral of civilian alienation."[21] Thompson warned that "most search and clear operations, by creating more communists than they kill, become in effect communist recruiting drives."[22] A standard line used by the Viet Cong was that the government army brought violence to the village, while the communists only wanted peaceful struggle.[23] If hearts and minds are the prize, government forces do better to provide security by mingling with the people to be secured than by hurling firepower after nimble guerrillas.

So what is the right force-to-population ratio for successful counterinsurgency? The figure most often cited in recent years has been 20-to-1,000 (although a figure as low as 2-to-1,000 has also been cited, perhaps plausible for peacekeeping operations in benign environments). James Quinlivan points to two implications of the 20-to-1,000 figure: "First, very few states have populations so small that they could be stabilized by modest-sized forces. Second, a number of states have populations so large that they are simply not candidates for stabilization by external forces. Between the two extremes are countries large enough that only substantial efforts on the part of great powers or substantial contributions from many states could generate forces large enough to overcome serious disorder in such populations."[24]

If the 20-to-1,000 norm is valid, American strategy in both Afghanistan and Iraq faced long odds for years. If the entire area of each country is counted, both fell in Quinlivan's hopeless category for a long time. The World Bank estimated both countries' populations in 2010 at about thirty million, so the 20-to-1,000 norm would require a counterinsurgency force of 600,000 for each—higher than the combined total of foreign and local soldiers and police fielded in Iraq until very late in the game, and not yet in Afghanistan as of 2011. The figures look more promising when civilian contractors are counted. Otherwise the only way to square the figures is if large areas of the countries are uncontested and thus out of the equation, or the level of violence in contested areas is low. Thus in Afghanistan the plan was not to reach the 20-to-1,000 ratio everywhere, but in selected important areas.

There is in fact no consistent evidence for what force ratio of any type is the key to success. An examination of 171 cases since World War I found that "neither aggregate forces nor troops per square kilometer are statistically correlated with counterinsurgency outcomes." Data on troop density did not show a basis for the canonical 20-to-1,000 force-to-population ratio. Calculations in this study combining measures of numerous variables indicated that probabilities of success in counterinsurgency will rise with troop density, but under pessimistic assumptions only modestly, even at very high levels of density; with optimistic assumptions the increase in probability is higher, yet still below 50 percent at the highest level of density.[25]

Results vary depending on unique conditions. After World War II the United States supported successful campaigns against insurgents both in Greece, where the force-to-population ratio was almost 30-to-1,000, and the Philippines, where it was less than 3-to-1,000. The amount of violence was much higher in Greece. *In both of these successful cases, however, a key fact is that all the government security forces were local personnel*, not foreign interveners.[26]

All else equal, one would expect less nationalist opposition to counterinsurgency by fellow countrymen than by foreigners who can all too readily seem to be invaders, so it seems obvious that foreign troops should try to transfer responsibilities as fast as possible to indigenous security forces. But this is far easier said than done in poor countries where the pool of competent human capital on which to draw for soldiers, police, and administrators is small, and it does not always turn out to improve the quest for hearts and minds when it is done. The process was painfully slow in Afghanistan, and sometimes counterproductive. Nearly five years after the United States began training it, the Afghan National Army (ANA) still numbered less than 20,000.[27] The quantity increased thereafter, but by then the Taliban had gained momentum, and the quality of the government personnel did not keep pace with the quantity. Performance of many ANA personnel after U.S. forces cleared Marja in 2010 was incompetent, abusive, or corrupt.[28] This was especially worrisome since Marja was a highest priority operation that presumably had first call on the best of what the government had.

Optimistic advocates of counterinsurgency respond to such disappointing results by citing the necessarily long duration of campaigns and admitting the risk that they may never end decisively. One British expert titled his study of the famously successful Malayan campaign *The Long, Long War*.[29]

Seth Jones estimates that after 1945 it took counterinsurgents an average of fourteen years to win, a quarter of the cases took more than twenty years, and many contests remained inconclusive.[30] Some insurgencies persist for generations, going dormant and reemerging episodically—for example, in the Philippines or Northern Ireland throughout the twentieth century.

Duration presents a huge obstacle. Long-term commitment to embroilment in unconventional war is risky for strategists to count on, given the vagaries of American democracy. In the fourteen-year span Jones cites as the average required to win in the field, three to four presidential elections could take place in the United States. Even if a president is willing to bear the costs of long commitment, he or she cannot guarantee that any successor will follow through on that faith. True, public opinion has been permissive in all these cases. Despite vocal and visible protests from the Left, the public did not become a strong force for withdrawal from Vietnam until extremely late in the game. On Iraq and Afghanistan opinion became heavily skeptical of the enterprises, yet without exerting much political pressure to liquidate them (in no small part because without conscription, and with a small military force involved in either country, few American families have any personal stake in ending combat). Eventually, however, patience or indifference erodes if the situation seems to be stalemate rather than progress. The foreign policy elite can take the United States into a morass, but it cannot mobilize support for staying in it forever. This is a risky basis for repeated Wilsonian projects.

The United States did persevere in Vietnam for a long span of time, in large part because no president wanted to have to answer for losing on his watch.[31] The awful effects of that case, however, dampened subsequent support for indefinite combat, even without immediate or irresistible public opposition. Presidents do not live in the long term and normally have little interest in strategies that promise no payoff during their time in office. They wind up in inconclusive unconventional wars such as Iraq and Afghanistan not by willing strategic calculation, but because plans for quicker victory go awry. All this means that the United States is unlikely to undertake an unconventional war deliberately. Reorienting military planning completely to counterinsurgency, therefore, would amount to mortgaging doctrine to the probability that mistaken commitments will be made and will have to be redeemed—a tragically realistic assumption, perhaps, but not a politically realistic basis for strategic planning.

## THE POLITICAL-MILITARY NEXUS

If suppressing insurgency requires high force-to-force and force-to-space ratios in order to cover territory, if legitimate local government is essential, and if indigenous personnel work better than foreign forces in countering the political appeal of insurgents, the military key should be formation of local self-defense forces or village militias of part-time soldiers guarding their home turf. As Samuel Huntington recognized long ago, the relative weakness of the defense in revolutionary warfare means that "the security of the target group can be protected only by the mobilization of the group itself."[32]

Mobilization of local forces is also a key to the practicability of the "oil spot" or "inkblot" strategy of pacification: concentrating counterinsurgency projects and forces in a few areas until government control is firm, and expanding gradually outward. Given the limits of force ratios, expansion relies on moving government forces from solidly secured zones to contested ones that can be occupied and won over, and then moving government forces further again. To do this without backsliding in the earlier pacified areas requires measures of civic action, administrative activism, and effective police performance, but it especially requires replacing central government military units for the task of day-to-day local defense in areas that are currently but not irrevocably secure.

The importance of these measures is fundamental and is not a new idea, but they are hard to institutionalize. In South Vietnam there were efforts to develop territorial forces from the beginning. The Diem regime promoted armed village Self-Defense Corps (SDC) units in the 1950s. Although they were initially popular, interference by the Can Lao Party lowered the groups' morale, and then the focus on developing the conventional Army of the Republic of Viet Nam (ARVN) led to neglect of the SDC despite its greater relevance for combating guerrillas. In later years province-level Regional Forces and district-level Popular Forces were developed on a large scale; by 1968 their personnel numbered about 90 percent of the strength of the ARVN, and they took more casualties than the ARVN.[33] They were also very cost-effective, inflicting 12–30 percent of communist casualties while absorbing only 2–4 percent of South Vietnamese war costs.[34]

The big role of territorial forces did coincide with military progress in pacifying South Vietnam, but trying to increase rural security without concentrating on political reform robbed the progress of durability. After the Tet Offensive the Viet Cong were decimated and driven further underground, but not eliminated. Although set back militarily, they persisted in political organizing activity, increasing "the number of liberation committees in government-controlled areas."[35] To the extent that Viet Cong influence in the countryside was replaced, it was not with effective political organization from Saigon, but with remote government and peasant neutralism. The Viet Cong National Liberation Front was built on a raft of mass-based social and political "functional liberation associations" and 350,000–500,000 members of the Communist Party, while by 1970 only 1 percent of adult South Vietnamese belonged to a government-sponsored political organization of any kind. Government officials remained insensitive to peasant interests, and instead of South Vietnamese military and paramilitary forces becoming independent, they became more reliant on U.S. support and supplies.[36] With economic aid and the Chieu Hoi and Phoenix programs to encourage defections and root out the Viet Cong infrastructure, the Saigon government and American forces won the counterinsurgency war in a superficial and temporary sense, but without establishing the basis for resilience on the government side that might have been able to withstand the eventual conventional assault from the North.[37]

In Afghanistan, creation of strong territorial forces has been limited by villagers' fear of confronting the Taliban or has been accomplished at the price of complicating the national governing project. The Afghan interior minister in 2010 worried about the success of the Local Defense Initiative because militia commanders became the local powers, warlords levying taxes and supplanting the central government.[38] Subsequent U.S. pressure to develop such units depended on making them paid and controlled by the central government in Kabul and overseen by the Afghan police[39]— who had a reputation for incompetence and corruption.

Some formulas for winning hearts and minds simply emphasize competent and honest government administration. Sir Robert Thompson, a guru of this approach, even opposed the inclusion of elected politicians in administrative structures. This antipolitical rationale might conceivably work if the capital can provide effective services and clean government without actively politicizing the rural population. It is a tall order, however, for distant authorities to compete effectively with rebels who practice "bureaucratic asceticism," the style of communist cadres in South Vietnam that contrasted with the Saigon government's prevalent image of corruption.[40] It is especially hard to do when the insurgent infrastructure is well organized and disciplined and *does* act politically to mobilize people in villages, as the Viet Cong did, or simply to control them with a combination of judicial fairness and terror against resisters, as the Taliban have done.

## DOMINATE OR DEMOCRATIZE?

Cooptation by administration is hard to do in any case. For old colonial powers, it was impractical to mobilize local populations without giving them a stake in the political order that insurgents opposed. In Indochina the French failed to prepare the Vietnamese for self-government and relied on a Westernized but weak ruling class that had little connection to village life other than as landlords, and which had an unrealistic "restricted concept of politics."[41] The problem is that administration does not override politics. In Afghanistan attempts to extend effective government from Kabul have been weak. The Karzai administration purposely used minority outsiders as provincial governors to prevent them from building independent tribal power bases. This disempowered the tribes in the majority and enabled the Taliban to claim the role of defenders of local self-rule.[42]

Americans can disapprove of this sort of host government action and can apply ample leverage of various sorts to push the government toward desirable political action, but in the end Americans cannot be sure of control without undercutting their own client regime. A measure of success against Al Qaeda in Iraq was due to just that sort of double dealing. In the Anbar Awakening American forces supported local tribes and Sunni militia, some of whom had even been insurgents themselves, independently of the Baghdad government. As Austin Long pointed out in 2008, the United States sought not only to make Iraq stable and democratic but to defeat Al Qaeda in the country. "If the Iraqi government ceases to support the tribal strategy, these two goals would become mutually exclusive, at least in the short run. Already, the strengthening of unelected sheiks in Anbar means an end to democracy in that province, at least for the present."[43]

The tension between military efficiency and political sovereignty is an old problem, inherent in the purpose of American intervention.[44] When failure to find weapons of mass destruction discredited the main reason given for attacking Iraq, the Bush II administration shifted to another rationale: replacing dictatorship with democracy. The candidate for president who had campaigned against Bill Clinton's ventures in nation building decided as president that the biggest nation-building project since Vietnam was a vital mission. The Bush team believed that Iraq's democratization would get the United States off the hook after it liberated the country. But if a liberation is genuine, it makes the locals independent. Democracy of any sort creates a process but guarantees no particular result. There was no reason to expect that self-determination for Iraqis would yield behavior, alignment, or objectives consistent with American aims. Iraqi democracy, if it takes root, enables Iraqis to do what *they* want to do—or, more problematically, what a plurality or rickety coalition of Iraqis want—not what Americans want. As it is, setting elections in Iraq for December 2005 proved premature because the weakness of secular political organizations strengthened sectarian identity as a basis of appeal, and the aims of democratization and stability were in conflict.[45] Afghanistan's elections in 2009, in turn, were grossly compromised by fraud, but Washington was stuck with the unsavory result. Yet another problem is that democracy may unfold in paralytic fashion: Iraq held elections in 2010 but could not form a government and remained without one all the way through termination of American combat operations.

The United States does not often get what it wants from democratization, even in terms of the process. In practice, the change of regime usually proves incomplete and illiberal. Iraq, for example, quickly developed a raucous electoral pluralism but did not curb its damaging effects by imposing respect for liberal norms of tolerance and loyal opposition. Democratization of any sort usually increases instability anyway, as political participation, aspirations, and unleashed antagonisms outpace institutionalization.[46]

Few Americans think of the old host government in Saigon as a model of democracy, but its independence from Washington was no small part of the problem for American policy in Vietnam. Robert Komer, the legendary hard-charging head of the pacification program and relentless promoter of "the other war" (and known as "Blowtorch Bob" because of the heat he generated in getting things done), bitterly complained that recognizing the sovereignty of the incompetent host government clashed with efficient pursuit of American strategy, depriving American personnel of the authority to make programs work better.[47] He regretted particularly that Washington never established unity of command, which would have subordinated South Vietnamese forces and organizations to American leadership, providing coordinated action and effective direction of all effort. He cited the integration of British and local forces in the Malayan Emergency as a model. But in Malaya the British were still sovereign as the colonial government. In Vietnam the American intervention was supposed to be aiding an independent local government.

Komer's frustration with South Vietnamese waywardness reflects his focus on efficient management. He often cites Thompson—a British general, veteran of Malaya, and adviser in Saigon—with approval. Thompson had proposed a Joint Operations Center for South Vietnam, on the Malayan model, and the idea had been rejected. Similar proposals were always shot down. Komer complains that "whenever combined command was considered, the chief argument was essentially political—that it would smack of colonialism."[48]

Well, that argument was exactly right. The underpinning of the U.S. position in Vietnam was that Americans had not simply replaced the French colonialists in manipulating a puppet government, as the communists charged. If the South Vietnamese government was to have any chance of competing with the communists for Vietnamese nationalism, this principle was an absolute necessity. Komer's main criticism was that the U.S. effort in Vietnam was overmilitarized, yet he seems to have had a tin ear for the importance of political symbols and decorum. The Thompson model of counterinsurgency that he admired so much, in fact, was a completely administrative and politically sterile conception of the task, when a core issue in Vietnam was which side could claim the mantle of nationalism.

In either Iraq or Afghanistan the United States could best prevent abuses of minorities and women, atrocities carried out by the state security organs of the host governments, corruption and shakedowns, nepotism, malingering, and other bad behavior if it had direct command authority over the new Iraqi and Afghan police, army, and militia units—what Komer wanted in Vietnam. But this would make a mockery of the principle that the new governments are truly sovereign, that the U.S.-sponsored elections represented genuine democracy, and that the American intervention is temporary. In a sad example of the dilemma, in 2010 General David Petraeus "said an American anticorruption campaign should not 'be seen to threaten the sovereignty of the Afghan government.'"[49]

Administrative efficiency and democracy do not easily go together in Afghanistan or Iraq any more than they did in South Vietnam. Rather, there is every reason to expect that a genuinely functioning democracy in either country can easily dissolve any unity of purpose between the American liberators and the locals. Iraqi and Afghan constituencies are not children waiting to be schooled to political maturity. They have their own agendas and priorities, and they have no more reason to bow to American sensibilities about interethnic civility, humane behavior, or honest stewardship of resources than American Republicans or Democrats have to bow to each other's demands on Capitol Hill.

U.S. strategy in unconventional war is inevitably inhibited. It had to promote democracy in Iraq and Afghanistan and has to cope with its two edges. Of course American power is by no means helpless. It can provide hefty inducements and sanctions to affect clients' behavior—but it cannot execute a counterinsurgency strategy completely on its own terms, and it cannot change its larger political approach to shed the inhibition. This far into the postcolonial age, policymakers could not answer to American voters or look anyone else in the world in the eye if they imposed long-lasting direct rule or real puppet governments. What is known of the record of covert action projects to channel political developments in the right direction—a record in which successes have been less obvious than failures—does not inspire confidence in that means of control. Nor can American tutelage create an ideological, nationalist, or religious movement as a basis for mobilization against insurgents, a movement of political solidarity apart from patrimonial or criminal ties that are otherwise the alternative to an insurgent movement's idealism or organizational discipline.

Enemy ideological advantage does not appear to be a problem in Iraq, where the minority status of Sunnis left the Baathist part of the resistance without much chance of taking over the country. In Afghanistan, however, an asymmetry of idealism does challenge the American side. The Taliban evolved into a motley collection of interests, but much of it has been animated by religious fervor melded with xenophobic nationalism—a powerful combination by default if its opposition is parochial, patrimonial, and criminal, or simply staffed with personnel just out for themselves.

The difference between the mobilizing power of communist ideology and that of the Saigon regime's stagnant conservatism was certainly much of the story in Vietnam. Idealism and organization did not bring the Viet Cong insurgency to power in the face of huge investment of American resources and manpower in direct combat and in building up and nurturing the forces of the Saigon government. It did, however, account for the basic structural problem in the contest that ultimately determined the outcome once American intervention receded: the restriction of the struggle to half of the country (South Vietnam) and the complete political immunity and security of the regime in the other half (North Vietnam), from which the

communist side in the South could receive support, reinforcements, and ultimately deliverance by conventional invasion. If the conflict in South Vietnam had played out with the territory isolated and the contestants limited
to the Saigon government and the Viet Cong, and with the United States
pouring in as much manpower and matériel as it did in the actual war, the
noncommunist regime would have won.

This difference is the biggest limitation of the relevance of the Vietnam
analogy to America's recent unconventional wars. There is no equivalent
of North Vietnam facing Iraq or Afghanistan, although Iran and Pakistan
play a stripped-down version of that role. They do provide sanctuaries and
some support for rebels in Afghanistan. The Al Qaeda and Taliban forces
in Pakistan, however, are a far cry from the North Vietnamese Army, and
Iran's army would be a foreign invader in Iraq. If the wars in the two countries could play out according to the Vietnam analogy, with this difference,
the outcomes could well be acceptable—although at high cost.

All this could be, assuming adeptness in American strategy, if the question of success in wars like those in Iraq or Afghanistan hinged on the level
and durability of American commitment, and a if high level and long duration were possible. Neither of those questions has a clear answer. American
patience wore thin on Iraq and Afghanistan, but both elite and mass opinion still allowed persistence. Even if long effort is possible, however, success
may be frustrated if the obstacles prove insurmountable. Robert Komer's
old retrospective on Vietnam captures the problem in his uncharacteris-
tic ambivalence about whether the war could have been won if the United
States had done its part better.

Komer's main theme was that U.S. strategy in Vietnam was not adept
for a long time: bureaucratic pig-headedness and inadequate leadership
spoiled the chance for good ideas and appropriate programs to succeed.
Rhetoric about the importance of "the other war" was not followed up with
action. There was a "yawning gap" between "policy and its execution in the
field." Parochial services defined tasks to suit their own repertoires rather
than adjusting repertoires to perform needed tasks. Failure did not spawn
new thinking; "if obstacles are encountered, the natural tendency is to do
more of the same—to pour on more coal—rather than to rethink the problem." Most of all, the client government in Saigon was incompetent and
unresponsive to American advice and pressure to reform.[50]

Yet much as he harps on it, Komer hesitates to rest a verdict on this
theme. In telling asides he quotes Barbara Tuchman approvingly on how
General Joseph Stilwell's World War II mission in China "failed in its

ultimate purpose because the goal was unachievable," and then he says of Vietnam, "it is difficult to evaluate how much our failure to move the GVN [Saigon government] was owing to the intractable nature of the problem and how much to the way we went about it." Near the end of the book he repeats the same line.[51] This question is not incidental. Efficiency in application of means is irrelevant if the objective cannot ultimately be reached at acceptable cost. Nowhere in his laments about failures of execution does Komer claim that if the United States had implemented everything just right, South Vietnam would not ultimately have succumbed.

Can U.S. objectives be achieved in such cases if we learn from mistakes, continue the effort, and do things as well as they can be done by a foreign force? If so, the issue comes down to calculating the probable marginal cost of persisting long and hard enough to get the job done; then it is up to Americans to decide if they want to pay that cost. Where the United States has already jumped into a mess, most would endorse persistence if success could be achieved within a few years. Moral obligation aside, if Iraq is not stabilized under a friendly regime, the result could turn out worse for material U.S. interests than was Saddam's dictatorship. If the stakes in either Iraq or Afghanistan should not have justified getting into these wars, the involvements raised them.

By the time U.S. combat forces were withdrawn in 2010, the situation in Iraq was tenuous—potentially satisfactory, but uncertain, as Iraqi politicians stayed gridlocked without a government, insurgent violence continued, and the possibility of degeneration into civil war remained. In Afghanistan at the same time U.S. efforts to clear, hold, and build against the Taliban proceeded haltingly and far behind schedule while corruption scandals in the Kabul government and diverging efforts among American, Afghan, and Pakistani players blocked coherent strategy.

Too many enthusiasts for persistence in long counterrevolutionary wars forget one simple point: just because failure is unthinkable does not mean that success is possible. By the same token, we cannot know whether success is possible in necessarily long wars unless we keep trying—at the risk of simply throwing good money, and lives, after bad. This has been the dilemma in the decade-long efforts in Afghanistan and Iraq, and it was the same dilemma during the two-decade-long attempt to keep South Vietnam noncommunist. The allure of identifying bad management of the American nation-building project as the main problem, as Komer did at most points in his retrospective, is that it implies we can succeed if we pull our socks up, crack some heads, and apply a blowtorch to the administrative impediments. But if the obstacles to success are more deeply rooted, as Komer wondered at other points in his postmortem, then all the best managers in the world will not do the trick. Indeed, the deep-rooted obstacles must have been the greater problem in Vietnam because Blowtorch Bob himself overcame much of the managerial mess and succeeded in whipping the pacification program into shape. But his effort still did not produce the politically motivated and mobilized South Vietnam necessary in the end to contest the communists.

If a final fix at acceptable cost for either Iraq or Afghanistan is beyond American capability, both material and moral interests mandate capping the ultimate costs of failure. As Clausewitz says of war termination, "Once the expenditure of effort exceeds the value of the political object, the object must be renounced."[52] What if we simply cannot control the violent political development of these countries in some cases, no matter how adeptly we go about it? Giving up when the price exceeds the value of the object is a policy that makes perfect sense to an economist, but not one that is psychologically easy for many normal people to accept. And it is never an absolutely clear choice anyway since it is never absolutely certain that persistence would not succeed, and there is never a consensus on the value of the stakes.

American strategy in both the second war against Iraq and the war in Afghanistan jumped halfway across the ditch. In 2003 Bush II conquered Iraq with a lean American force but mistook initial operational success for political success. Rather than replacing Saddam Hussein's regime, the conquest unleashed anarchy, which the lean force was too small to suppress. Then until 2007, four years into the war, Bush tried to pacify the country with that small force. By 2010 the United States had managed to terminate its combat role in Iraq, but at a cumulative price beyond reckoning, and without assurance of an ultimately acceptable outcome.

The missteps in Iraq had been initiated and underwritten by premature trimming of the military effort in Afghanistan. After the situation in Afghanistan then deteriorated to the point of crisis, Obama authorized a large increment of U.S. forces to turn it around in 2009. That increment, however, was still quite limited, and its effect was vitiated by simultaneous announcement that U.S. forces would begin to withdraw in less than two years. The compromise between big and small footprint strategies left Washington with a program still subject to strategic judo if large presence alienates the population, but a presence still too small to apply counterinsurgency tactics widely and intensely at one time. If foreign forces are the problem, the U.S. presence is too large, but if they are the key, it is too small.

If an oil-spot strategy of gradual expansion of government control is the key, progress will be slow, which requires steadfast commitment of very long duration, but American domestic politics precludes a plan to fight in the country for twenty years. If pacification is to succeed in a short time, in contrast, it must be undertaken nearly everywhere at once, but limits on the U.S. presence preclude doing that.

By 2010 Washington had found a way to back out of Iraq. The obstacles to success in the continuing combat commitment in Afghanistan, however, appeared tremendous, if not overdetermined: a Taliban whose growth outpaced its attrition; a mercurial and completely undependable Afghan client, in the person of Hamid Karzai; a debile and corrupt political culture on the government side, with resulting increase in its unpopularity; slow increases in production of trained native Afghan security forces; severe limits on the quality of those forces because of illiteracy, reluctance to perform, and high desertion rates; uncertain but probably high rates of infiltration of government security forces by Taliban personnel; inability to prevent regular incidents of collateral damage that are publicized and incite rage and opposition among the population whose hearts and minds are the stakes of the conflict; an opium-dependent economy that must be suppressed if U.S. narcotics policy is to have any credibility but could not be suppressed without alienating the local population that profits from it; and a surreal situation of inescapable dependence on Pakistan for logistical support, while Pakistan played a double game supporting the Afghan Taliban.

Against such odds, how could an American gamble on continuing the war seem sensible? Yet deciding to cut losses in this case is hard for any president to contemplate. As Stephen Biddle notes, if in the event of an American withdrawal "the Karzai government falls, the Taliban establishes an Afghan state haven, Pakistan collapses and a Pakistani nuclear weapon falls into bin Laden's hands, then a decision to walk away from Afghanistan would be seen as one of the greatest foreign policy blunders of the modern era."[53]

## PLANNING FOR THE NEXT WAR

If the next war the United States fights is a conventional one like the wars over Korea, Kuwait, and Kosovo, the odds of success at acceptable cost are high. No other country, even rich American allies, will soon field a military that matches the combat power of the American armed forces. Confidence wavers if the next conventional war is against a major power such as China, or if it begins conventionally with the expectation of ending at the same level but degenerates into counterinsurgency, as in Iraq.

In recent times the only potential contingencies officially identified for conventional war have been against North Korea or Iran. Either case risks combat that would not end as decisively or safely as planners hope. The last Korean War turned into a war with China. Even if that were not to happen in a second run, the new factor of North Korean nuclear weapons in the equation is nearly as frightening. As for a war Washington might launch against Iran, chapter 6 showed the improbability of achieving objectives with limited operations, and the unacceptable cost of decisive operations, which would require invasion. Leaving aside the implausibility of that option in light of recent experience and limits on available U.S. ground forces, Iran has far more than twice the population of Iraq and a regime that is repugnant to Americans but less unpopular at home than Saddam Hussein's was. Invasion could produce chaos and insurgency that would make the American experience in Iraq, Afghanistan, or even Vietnam look mild.

It is possible that the next American war will be like those in 1950 and 1991—against an utterly unanticipated adversary who must then be countered with capabilities that were not developed with it in mind. If only for that reason, it is important for the United States to keep a minimum critical mass of capabilities in more than one dimension. The debate within the U.S. Army and Marine Corps over whether to emphasize conventional capabilities or counterinsurgency should remain a debate about emphasis, not about which should displace the other. One clear lesson of the seven decades since World War II is that the armed services do not get to decide what wars they will fight and cannot predict the type of wars to which civilian authorities will dispatch them. The U.S. Army especially did not understand this lesson for a long time. Its professional leadership thought they could decide what wars to avoid, and after the fall of Saigon they decided vehemently to avoid entanglement in unconventional conflicts. The service made a corporate project of deliberately forgetting what it had learned about counterinsurgency in the 1960s, so no thought was given to the subject when assaulting Iraq. The service was dragged kicking and screaming into relearning, and new learning, after the burgeoning of insurgency in the country.

If the wars in Iraq or Afghanistan were somehow to come out as acclaimed great successes, the opposite danger might emerge—too great a reorientation of doctrine and planning to unconventional warfare, and the atrophy of conventional military supremacy and the promise of an RMA. This might not matter in the short run since there are few plausible contingencies that would call the United States to conventional war. In the long run, however, the most important mission of the American armed forces is to be prepared for a contingency to be avoided if at all possible, but which might not be: conflict with China.

# 8 THE MAIN EVENTS
## CHINA'S RISE AND RUSSIA'S RESURGENCE

Since the end of the Cold War U.S. defense policy has been absorbed in second-order problems of deterring or defeating medium powers such as Iraq, Iran, North Korea, and Serbia, and waging counterinsurgency and counterterror campaigns in Afghanistan, Iraq, and Pakistan, and third-order problems of peacekeeping and humanitarian intervention. The first priority of national security policy, however, is to handle discontented, nuclear-armed, major powers. The only risk of utter destruction of the United States is the risk of war with a great power. After the Cold War that risk appeared to evaporate, but it is likely to grow in the long run as unipolarity wanes. The risk may be manageable, if policymakers have enough skill and luck, but peace will not be the natural default option.

The two major powers of concern are Russia and the People's Republic of China (PRC). American foreign policy has been too concerned about Russia and too complacent about China. The risk with Russia is its interest in reasserting influence over areas it traditionally ruled but lost in the Soviet collapse, areas whose populations include Russian minorities. Blunders and miscalculations about Georgia, Ukraine, or the Baltic countries could cause a confrontation neither Moscow nor the West wants. On a global scale, however, Russia is less of a potential challenge than China given the lopsided distribution of power in Europe since the Cold War, the fragility of Russia's economic recovery, and the lack of a casus belli as insoluble as the Taiwan problem could prove to be. China's economic trajectory raises the question of whether a "hegemonic transition" is coming in Asia if uneven growth eventually makes China the number one power. In Robert Gilpin's interpretation such transitions historically have usually led to major war.[1]

Optimists believe that there is no reason for this to happen, that the main danger is talking ourselves into a self-fulfilling prophecy of conflict, energizing military competition and tension. Instead, peace and prosperity can be consolidated if governments focus on shared interests and the positive-sum character of international relations in a world order of law, reciprocity, and institutionalized problem solving. This logic can easily pan out if moral demands and political processes do not follow a course independent of material interests and do not put a higher priority on concerns about identity, honor, and status—a very big if.

The chances for the economically oriented optimistic prognosis also vary with how committed the United States is to keeping its preeminent position in international politics. Americans have been accustomed to identifying their country's primacy with international stability, justice, and progress. Russia and China do not accept that notion and are less likely to submit to the writ of international institutions if the institutions are a vehicle for American political and strategic interests. If the institutional approach to preserve peace is to be used effectively, it might require ceding the prerogatives that Washington has taken for granted in the era of unipolarity, but such a tradeoff is not admitted by American political leaders.

China is the main potential problem because it poses a choice Americans are reluctant to face. Washington can strive to control the strategic equation in Asia, or it can reduce the odds of conflict with China, but it will be a historically unusual achievement if it manages to do both. It is not inevitable that China will threaten American interests—depending on how Americans define those interests. But in any case the United States is more likely to go to war with China than with any other major power. Other current or emerging great powers of the world are aligned with the United States (NATO countries and Japan), or have less power potential than China (Russia), or have a sometimes abrasive diplomatic relationship with Washington but no plausible occasion for war (India). China, in contrast, is a rising power with high expectations, unresolved grievances, and an undemocratic form of government. Taiwan, Korea, and disputes with half a dozen countries over islands in what Beijing calls the South China Sea are all potential occasions for conflict.

Debate about whether, where, when, and how China might threaten U.S. security interests has often been simplistically polarized. Views range from alarm to complacency: from those who see China emerging as a hefty and dangerous superpower, to those who believe the country's prospects are vastly overrated; and from those who see economic growth as a welcome force for political liberalization and international cooperation, to those who see it as an engine for building threatening military capabilities.

Most strategic debate about China fastens on a few simple questions. In regard to capabilities, most observers want to know above all whether the Chinese armed forces will develop to the point that they rival American military power, and whether the economic surge that can provide resources for military transformation will continue indefinitely or stall. In regard to intentions, most want to know how thoroughly and how soon the country will be integrated in a globalized economy that allegedly constrains conflict, whether Beijing will adopt aggressive aims as its power grows, or whether political liberalization will occur to change the government and make its policies benign. In any discussion, concern with capabilities and intentions ultimately zeroes in on the question of whether the PRC can take Taiwan by force.

The more likely possibilities to worry about, however, lie between the answers to these questions, and between the alarmist and complacent diagnoses. The PRC can turn out to be a big problem even if it does not become a military power on the American model, even if it does not intend to commit aggression, even if it becomes integrated in a globalized economy, and even if it liberalizes politically. The United States could face intense danger in a conflict over Taiwan even if Beijing lacks the capacity to conquer the island.

## WILL CHINA'S MILITARY POWER RIVAL AMERICA'S?

For many years after China's economic development took off in the 1980s, the People's Liberation Army (PLA—a generic designation for all the armed services) remained a threadbare force, well below Western standards. Pockets of excellence notwithstanding, most personnel were poorly educated and sparsely trained; weapon systems were old, and those acquired last were still less advanced than those in Western militaries; many units spent much time in nonmilitary activities; staffs did not practice complex, large-scale operations; exercises and training regimens were limited; much equipment was not well maintained; and defense spending even by the highest estimates was very low per soldier, indicating the dominance of quantity over quality in the Chinese force. Some of these deficiencies remain very significant, but Chinese capabilities have been improving as more is invested in technology and training and the size of the force has been compressed. The PLA's interest in moving into a new era of modernity, efficiency, and competitiveness as economic reform and growth translate into commensurate military reform and growth has long been indicated by a large number of PLA writings about a prospective Chinese revolution in military affairs.[2] The backwardness of the PLA up to the turn of the century reflected its low priority in the country's modernization efforts and the diversion of professional energy into business activities within the military (which have been curtailed).

For China to develop a twenty-first-century military on the model of the United States, however, is still a stretch. The main question is not whether Beijing will have high defense budgets or access to cutting-edge technology. A rich China might well be able to acquire most types of advanced weapons. Deeply ingrained habits of threat assessment in the U.S. defense community focus attention on these terms of reference. Basic "bean counts" of the quantity of manpower and units and the quality of weapon platforms, however, are poor measures of truly modern military capability. A bigger question is whether the PLA establishment can use its increasing resources to build the complex supporting infrastructure necessary to make Chinese forces competitive in combat effectiveness. The PLA's recent mediocrity—like that of most armed forces in the world—may be rooted in history, ideology, and culture that are incompatible with the patterns of organization and social interaction necessary to rival the few highly proficient First World militaries. This does not mean that the PLA can never break out of this box, but it will take more than money to do so.

Modern conventional military effectiveness has become clearly more a matter of quality than of quantity of forces, and less a matter of pure firepower than of the capacity to coordinate complex systems. The essence of American military superiority is not advanced weapon technology per se. Rather it lies in the interweaving of capacities in organization, doctrine, training, maintenance, support systems, integration of surveillance, targeting, and weaponry, and the overall level of professionalism. These factors are harder to measure, but they are what make it feasible to assimilate, apply, and sustain state-of-the-art weapons effectively. Those capacities require conditions that are exceedingly rare: high levels of education throughout a military force, a culture of initiative and innovation, and an orientation to operating through skill networks as much as traditional command and obedience hierarchies. In the twentieth century few militaries besides the German, American, Israeli, and British developed these capabilities. Indeed, experience in the Persian Gulf in 1991, over Kosovo in 1999, and against Iraq in the conventional phase of the war in 2003 indicated that the United States is in a class by itself in these respects. If the PLA has the potential resources in organization, culture, education, and willingness to delegate authority to approach such a standard, it is a well-kept secret. Before reaching for an American-style RMA, the PLA will probably need revolution in organizational affairs.

If the PLA remains in the second tier of professionalism as it improves, should Washington breathe a sigh of relief? No. First, American military power is not the only relevant standard of comparison. Other armed forces in the region that the PLA could come up against are much closer to the Chinese level than to the American. (This is true even of Taiwan's technologically sophisticated military, whose long isolation has eroded its quality.) Second, the United States has global interests and often finds itself distracted or pinned down elsewhere. Third, the Chinese do not need to match American capabilities to cope with them. Rather than trying to mimic an American RMA, they may do better to develop a "counterrevolution in military affairs"—offsetting or asymmetrical strategic options on various parts of the technological spectrum (for example, information warfare) that can circumvent U.S. advantages.

Pundits on defense policy commonly observe that China lacks power projection capability—the ability to send and sustain combat forces far from home. By U.S. standards this is quite true. China's interest in obtaining aircraft carriers has proceeded slowly, the navy and air force do not have many assets for "lift" (to transport and supply large units for operation abroad), and Chinese forces have little logistical capacity as American military professionals know it. For those worried about facing a Chinese force on the American model, these are all good grounds for optimism. But must China match American standards to achieve capabilities for using force effectively to reshape the Asian strategic environment? A different set of questions makes one less dismissive of Chinese capabilities.

*Where* is projection of power an issue? Taiwan is the most dangerous and most likely case, but it is not the only one. The Middle Kingdom is literally in the middle of everything and has land borders with a dozen countries. China has dormant claims or conceivable points of conflict in several places that would not require forces to cross large bodies of water, and where it would not be facing opposition as potent as Taiwan's military. Although less likely, scarcely less dangerous than conflict over Taiwan would be an imbroglio in Korea if the Pyongyang regime collapses and South Korean or American forces move into the vacuum without Beijing's agreement. Far too little attention has been focused on the odds of miscalculation in a confused situation of that sort. The PLA does not have the American army's logistical capacity, but it did manage to project a force of hundreds of thousands of men deep into Korea more than half a century ago. The Chinese Navy is also weak compared to the American, but is growing impressively, and some of its neighbors' navies are much weaker still. Two of these neighbors—Vietnam and the Philippines—have outstanding sovereignty disputes with China and did not fare well in naval skirmishes in past decades. One can also not rule out the possibility of a land attack on its neighbors over the long term. The PLA did poorly in its invasion of Vietnam in 1978, but the Vietnamese Army is now less than half the size it was then, and the Vietnamese economic base is now far more inferior to China's than it used to be. Logistical limitations would hamper but not preclude PRC action against Mongolia or against the Russian Far East should that region fall out of Moscow's effective control. Granted, conflict over these places is quite improbable. The problem is that the same could be said of most wars until they happened.

## Will China Become the World's Leading Economy?

Military potential grows out of economic capacity. In recent times China's has been the fastest-growing major economy in the world. It has been common for analysts to project high growth rates straight into the future and see China surpassing the American GDP before long. Reality has been rockier: China has had numerous problems in managing economic development, and some may get worse; official PRC data on growth may be exaggerated; growth rates naturally decline as economies mature; environmental degradation is extreme; demographic imbalances will pose progressively bigger social and economic constraints.[3] If internal discontent grows, the regime's capacity to control events is uncertain.

Nevertheless, power is relative, and uneven economic growth eventually tells. Even if exaggerated, Chinese growth has been consistently stronger than America's for decades, and the United States faces big economic dilemmas itself. There is also no reason to believe that the regime in Beijing will be less successful in applying the political discipline necessary to resolve hard choices than the regime in Washington, which has long been deadlocked in inability to balance revenues and expenditures. As it is, China propped up the U.S. economy for years by funding a significant portion of the profligate budget deficit. Moreover, China does not have to surpass the United States to challenge it, if not for global hegemony, for regional dominance in Asia. China can cause a great deal of trouble without fully catching up to the United States.[4]

If Chinese development were to reach the level of South Korea or Taiwan—about one-third of U.S. GDP per capita in 2008—China would have a total GDP significantly greater than the American. The lower per capita amount would limit disposable income that could be reallocated to the military, so the United States and its allies should remain ahead by a wide margin, for a long time, in capacity to fund military expenditures. Then the question is the relative will to exploit that capacity, rather than fund domestic programs, pay down debt, or limit taxes. In the first decade of the twenty-first century China's defense budget soared, while the much larger U.S. military capability was expended disproportionately in wars and deployments outside East Asia. If these trends are not reversed, Chinese economic growth will steadily narrow the gap in military capabilities the two countries deploy in East Asia.

So should Americans want China to prosper or not? For optimists, the answer is yes, since a large fraction of the world's people would be relieved from poverty, and because economic growth should make democratization more likely, which in turn should prevent war between Beijing and other democracies. For realists, the answer should be no, since a rich China would overturn the regional balance of power. But what can the United States do about it anyway? Americans do not have a clear advantage in the balance of leverage, especially since they became more dependent on China to buy the nation's spiraling debt. In any case, active U.S. efforts to keep China poor or to break it up are hard to imagine, would probably fail, and if tried would be counterproductive by aggravating antagonism. Coldhearted realists at best can passively hope for Chinese economic misfortune. Otherwise, they had better hope that liberal theory about the causes of peace pans out, so that what is good for China turns out to be good for everyone. As Harry Harding once pointed out, policy may begin with a realist diagnosis but be forced into banking on liberal solutions because the costs of controlling the balance of power may be too high. The liberal solutions most widely seen as stabilizing are the spread of Western political, economic, and social values and the elaboration of international institutions for organizing cooperation among nations—the complex of developments known as globalization.

## WILL CHINA BE PACIFIED BY GLOBALIZATION?

To pessimists steeped in realpolitik, a rich China will necessarily be a threat because economic power can be translated into military power, and power generates ambition. To others who are impressed with the revolutionary implications of globalization, a more powerful China will not be a threat because it will have too much to lose from disrupting international trade and investment. The latter view is more common in the West than the former, which seems to many to reek of old thinking. As President Obama said in a speech about China, "In an interconnected world, power does not need to be a zero-sum game, and nations need not fear the success of another."[5] The notion that a web of commercial ties discourages resort to war, however, is itself quite old, if not venerable. It was popularized by Henry Thomas Buckle in the 1850s, by Norman Angell just a year before World War I erupted, and in the 1970s when interdependence was said to have reduced the utility of force. The argument this time around is that the proposition is finally true, for two reasons.

First, the nature of interdependence has changed in a crucial way. A century ago interdependence was characterized by vertical trade between imperial centers and colonies, trade in final products between wealthier nations, and portfolio investment. Now there is much more direct investment and transnational production of goods that fosters "a growing interpenetration of economies, in the sense that one economy owns part of another."[6] With the PRC, Taiwan, Japan, and the United States all owning pieces of one another, how can they fight without destroying their own property? As the Chinese elite make more and more money from investments in and by Taiwan, simple greed will prevent political huffing and puffing from crossing the line to war. If development thoroughly enmeshes the PRC in the globalized economy, peace should follow.

Second, cooperation is now the clearly rational choice for governments because an institutionalized international order has evolved that stabilizes interdependence by organizing rules of the game, mechanisms for interaction, and regularized opportunities for profitable exchange. China may surpass the United States in a power transition as in previous epochs, but this time it does not have to matter. The cooperative international order in which China can be integrated is not dominated by a single country and therefore does not challenge Chinese interests, so participation in the system can make the transition benign.[7] The web of interdependence, vested interests, and peace-inducing institutions will defang China because the country will have too much to lose from conflict and too much to gain from cooperation. It will be weaned from mercantilist approaches to securing energy and raw materials, and nationalism will remain under control. Creeping democratization will eventually make China a partner in the worldwide "democratic peace." Optimism is underwritten by the strategically risk-averse character of Chinese policy to date.

Perhaps the Chinese government will see the wisdom of this theory and continue to suppress the ambitions that historically have gone with being a great power. But much of that hope rests on a universalism that is actually ethnocentric. The international norms and institutions crucial to this vision of taming China are nominally global, but they are essentially those developed by the rich and previously dominant states of the West. Americans thinking in this vein tend to assume that China will be domesticated, that the process will proceed according to norms and behavior that now seem the natural order of things to cosmopolitan elites, that Western preferences for world order are universal and will limit the future importance of military power relationships. Security interests and options will be shaped by economic interests. In this complex of liberal assumptions the West, in effect if not intent, manages China's rise. Washington does not need to resist the rise in power, but only to enlighten China about its natural self-interest.

The grimmer view is that China will not behave differently from most other rising powers in the past. It will not be managed politically and militarily but will chart its own course, bending to other powers as long as it is weaker, but only that long. As the country grows it will become less and less patient with what it considers simmering injustices or unfair constraints and double standards and will grow more insistent on getting what it sees as its rights. The country is not yet powerful enough to indulge this natural urge, but it is getting there fast. Potential losses from conflict are no more a constraint on Beijing than on Washington, since both sides have the stake in not overturning profitable economic integration. The PRC might not want to kill the golden goose, but neither would the United States. Mutual dependence makes a potential crisis a game of chicken in which each side refuses to back down because it expects the other to bow to the stakes, making concession no more likely than collision.

This collision can happen even if China becomes a conforming partner in open-market globalization, forswearing mercantilist approaches to trade and development. But there is no assurance that China will avoid economic nationalism or play by all the West's diplomatic rules. The PRC has already pursued bilateral arrangements for assured supply of natural resources in Africa and elsewhere, rather than relying on the international market; it has interfered with other countries' market access to its own resources (for example, cutting Japan off from purchases of rare earths in the midst of controversy over disputed islands); and it has asserted political jurisdiction over its extended maritime economic zone in a manner not legally recognized by other countries. If these habits are not curbed they could produce growing international friction.

Nevertheless, assume the best scenario for China's acquiescence to Western norms about economic interaction. There is still little reason to assume that sober economic interest will necessarily override national honor in determining the outcome of a political and military crisis. In an imbroglio over Taiwan, which capitals will feel the biggest emotional inhibitions against conceding? Beijing and Taipei both have much more material and moral interest and more history invested in the outcome than does the United States. Even if Washington cares enough to fight, there is no reason for leaders in Beijing to assume that they must naturally cave in before the Americans, who are so far away and have less at stake. Many Chinese writings on strategy emphasize that the asymmetry of stakes in the Taiwan Straits will make Washington retreat first.[8]

The globalized economy does change logical incentives to compromise in political conflict, but not in a way that makes Beijing likely to be more reasonable than anyone else. Economic globalization does not wash away the high value that nations place on their political identity and territorial integrity. Drawing China into the web of global interdependence may do more to encourage peace than war, but it offers no reason to assume that pursuit of emotionally potent political interests will be blocked by fear of consequences for crass economic interests, or that China will muffle its urge to define the regional order more than the United States will.

## WILL CHINA BECOME AGGRESSIVE?

Whether China has aggressive motives, and is simply waiting to amass the power necessary to do something about them, is what most policymakers want to know about Beijing's strategic intentions. Optimists say the answer is no because the PRC is ideologically anti-imperialist and only wants respect as a status quo great power. Pessimists say the answer is yes because Chinese leaders have only suppressed a seething set of grudges and territorial ambitions until they are confident of their ability to act on them, or simply because all great powers tend to expand when they get the chance.

Focusing on the odds of deliberate aggression—which would be dangerous but is unlikely—diverts attention from the possibilities that are much more likely and almost as dangerous. Most countries viewed as aggressors by their adversaries view their own behavior as defensive, legitimate, and rightful. Whether Beijing is a tiger in waiting, about to set out purposefully on a predatory rampage, is not the most relevant question. No evidence suggests that Chinese leaders will have an interest in naked conquest of the sort practiced by Genghis Khan, Napoleon Bonaparte, Adolf Hitler, or Saddam Hussein. The most likely danger lies in the situation in which action China sees as defensive and legitimate appears aggressive to Washington.

The model more often invoked by pessimists is the structural theory of the German Problem: even without evil designs, the country's search for security will abrade the security of surrounding countries. Geographically the Middle Kingdom is close to virtually everyone in East Asia. It is also the strategic pivot between the otherwise distinct subregions of Northeast and Southeast Asia. Individually, countries on the mainland cannot hope to deter or defeat China in any bilateral test of strength; collectively, they cannot help but worry China if they were to seem united in hostility. Like Germany a century ago, China is a late-blooming great power emerging into a world already ordered strategically by earlier arrivals; a continental power surrounded by other powers who are collectively stronger but individually weaker (with the exception of the regional outsider, the United States); a bustling country with great expectations, dissatisfied with its place in the international pecking order. The quest for a rightful "place in the sun," in this view, will inevitably foster growing friction with Japan, Russia, India, or the United States.

Optimists can reasonably brush off this analogy to competition among states of different culture on a different continent at a different time, a long-gone era when imperialism was the norm for civilized international behavior. The most benign view, that economic development and trade will inevitably make China fat and happy, uninterested in throwing its weight around, strikes many as common sense. It could turn out to be true. It is more an article of faith, however, than a prediction grounded in experience. The United States, for example, has been quite interested in gaining the goodies from globalization, yet on the world stage it has also thrown its weight around with righteous zeal.

Indeed, the most disturbing analogy for China's future behavior is not Germany, but the United States. If China acts no more cautiously and responsibly in its region in the twenty-first century than the United States has in its neighborhood, Asia is in for big trouble. Washington has intervened frequently in Mexico, Central America, and the Caribbean for reasons most Americans consider obviously legitimate, defensive, altruistic, and humane. Not everyone else has seen such regional policing in the same way, and the United States and its allies in Asia would not see comparable Chinese actions as anything less than a mortal threat. The United States is the eight-hundred-pound gorilla in North America, where there are no other hefty primates to keep it from sitting wherever it wants. China is the six-hundred-pound gorilla in Asia, with a potentially comparable sense of entitlement, but without the same assurance that it can move with impunity. China faces actual alliances involving the United States, Japan, Australia, and South Korea and potential alliances in Southeast Asia or with India. The fact that there are others who can respond to the growth of Chinese power sets up the possibility of a classic spiral of conflictual actions and reactions between China and the others, even if all view their security policies as defensive.

## WOULD CHINA'S POLITICAL LIBERALIZATION GUARANTEE PEACE?

Many assume that as long as political progress accompanies China's growth, China will not pose a security challenge. If China becomes a democracy, there will be nothing to fear from added Chinese power. This logic—the theory of the democratic peace—has traditionally been the most popular theory in one form or another among American foreign policy elites. Developed democracies virtually never fight one another.[9] Since the United States is an advanced democracy, Chinese democratization should solve the China problem for us. On balance it is in American interest to promote democratization of China, even holding moral concerns aside. For one thing, establishment of democracy on the mainland would remove much of the reason to support Taiwan's autonomy, since the dispute between Taipei and Beijing would no longer be between a democracy and autocracy. But even if we accept the democratic peace theory on its face, there are several problems with applying it to China.[10]

First, the PRC has not been rushing to make itself a democracy. Economic liberalization has only loosened authoritarianism, not put it into terminal decline. The regime's brand of Leninist capitalism could persist indefinitely. Second, the democratic peace theory really applies only to liberal democracies on the Western model, ones with restraints on government action and guarantees of minority rights. Democratization in China could just as conceivably turn in a simple majoritarian, illiberal direction, on the model of post-Tito Yugoslavia, Iran, or other unpleasant examples of virulent nationalism or violent activism.[11] Third, the democratic peace theory explains an absence of international wars between democracies, but it does not apply clearly to civil war. Democracies have to see each other as democracies for the theory to apply.[12] They also have to view each other as legitimate, independent, sovereign states. No matter how many Americans and Taiwanese believe that Taiwan is or should be a sovereign state, this view is widely and emotionally rejected on the mainland—nor does official U.S. policy accept it. A fourth problem is that a community of mature liberal democracies is pacific but democratization is not. The process of becoming a democracy can be quite violent and destabilizing. This is particularly true in those democratizing states with poorly developed civil societies and news media. They lack healthy outlets for popular grievances. They also lack a marketplace for ideas where views can be debated and counterarguments brought to bear. This gives elites incentives to manipulate populist, nationalist themes and to adopt tough international policies as an electoral strategy.[13] Nationalism can also erupt beyond the government's control. The ruling Communist Party is intensely aware that in a future international dispute, especially over Taiwan, it is potentially vulnerable to mass demands for strong action.

## CASUS BELLI

American strategy in Asia is built on a hub-and-spokes pattern of bilateral security connections, an approach that has stood for over half a century in stark contrast to arrangements in Europe that hinge on multilateral political and military institutions, especially NATO. This difference is a spanner in the works of the institutional model of strategic management. There is no

"NEATO" (a hypothetical Northeast Asia Treaty Organization) in the works to replicate the functions of NATO in securing the long peace in Europe. The pretensions of other multilateral organs in Asia such as the ASEAN Regional Forum to deal with security concerns have proved weak.[14] Yet the optimistic argument rests on the benefits to be derived from the wonderful web of Western institutions, even though the multilateral mechanisms that apply in Asia do not address military security. In one of the most prominent promotions of the institutional model, John Ikenberry says nothing about what U.S. military policy should be in the region, brushes off the whole dimension of analysis with the assumption that nuclear deterrence precludes major war, and asserts with breath-taking confidence that "war-driven change has been abolished as a historical process."[15] He does not discuss how disputes over territory, sovereignty, and rebellion will be handled by the institutional system, primarily a set of economic arrangements. And above all there is one word that does not appear anywhere in his whole article about coping with the rise of Chinese power, a word whose absence is thunderous: *Taiwan*.

The island of Taiwan is the main potential flashpoint for the United States in East Asia. China can complete its rise without tangling militarily with the United States if Americans do not challenge China's core national security interests. Intervening in the final resolution of China's civil war, however, by defending Taiwan would do just that. Americans downplay the importance of Taiwan to the PRC because Beijing has regularly subordinated reunification to other interests. China has made quite clear, however, that reunification is a question of when, not whether.

For many years after normalization of relations with Beijing, Washington maintained a stance of strategic ambiguity, keeping unclear its commitment to military protection of Taiwan. After 1996 the ambiguity declined, most evidently in the second President Bush's rash statement that the United States would do "whatever it takes" for the island's defense. In the interest of longer-term flexibility on how to handle a China that has become a superpower, there would be some benefit in reestablishing more ambiguity.

The danger in ambiguity, however, is the risk that in a pinch Beijing might think it could get away with an attack, while Washington would decide to fight when the attack thrust the question in the president's face. The United States has a record of innocently misleading other countries about whether it would counter them militarily, as before the wars that eventuated over Korea and Kuwait. Were this to happen over Taiwan, the risks would be much higher than in the previous cases because China has nuclear weapons.

While flexibility has advantages, ambiguity by definition abets miscalculation. The danger just mentioned recommends more clarity about the extent and limits of U.S. commitment. Clarification, however, would prove awkward. Although not stated so baldly, in practical terms U.S. policy in recent years has been that it would defend Taiwan as long as it remains a rebellious province, but not if it claims to be an independent country. This makes good strategic sense to reinforce dual deterrence—against moves toward independence by Taiwan, and against military action by the mainland. It makes clever sense to foreign policy elites. But it is not common sense. If this idea ever becomes a subject of broad public discussion, it is likely to strike normal Americans as bizarre. Support for such a policy might falter just when it was needed most.

Unless the president is willing to declare that the United States will *not* defend Taiwan (a reasonable position in terms of realpolitik, but politically unwise in the American domestic arena), the risk in clarifying exactly whether and when the United States would fight for Taiwan is worth taking. If Washington *would* in fact fight, Beijing should know that for sure, so that deterrence can be fully applied, and the chances of miscalculation reduced. If Washington would *not* fight, Americans should know that for sure, lest they step into a confrontation and then retreat in humiliation. Failing to decide limits in advance poses the biggest danger of war from a game of chicken where neither side swerves in time. Backing down from war with the PRC would be damaging to U.S. credibility and honor, but it would be better than stepping into combat where escalation may be the price of avoiding defeat for either side. Being sure in advance of what either side would do, however, is more than policymakers can realistically expect. There is no reason for confidence that in a crisis, even when neither side wants war, the Chinese would swerve before the Americans do, and thus no reason for confidence that a U.S.–PRC war in the Taiwan Strait would be avoided, or that if it broke out it would be kept to the conventional level.

The natural course of politics and diplomacy is to leave the Taiwan question on the back burner. As time passes there will still be no incentive to focus attention on it as long as nothing happens. The path of least resistance is to hope that the issue will remain quiescent until economic ties, rising stakes in cooperation, political softening in Beijing, and skillful diplomacy eventually converge to engineer a peaceful modus vivendi. The optimistic institutional model of coping with China's rise favors this scenario. The problem is that exactly how China and Taiwan agree to unite is left quite vague, and optimists implicitly plan as though the current situation of de facto independence for the island can endure indefinitely. The pessimistic power politics model, in contrast, expects Beijing's patience with the status quo to diminish with time, eventually forcing either peaceful capitulation by Taipei or military confrontation to bring de facto and de jure status into alignment.

The possibility of war over Taiwan could be the biggest danger that American security policy faces. No other flashpoint is more likely to bring the United States into combat with a major power, and no other contingency compels Washington to respond with such ambiguous commitment. Americans and Chinese see the issues at stake in the dispute over Taiwan in different terms; U.S. policy on the defense of Taiwan is uncertain, and thus so is the understanding in Beijing, Taipei, and Washington over how far the United States might go under different circumstances; and because Taiwan is more independent than either Washington or Beijing might prefer, neither great power can fully control developments that might ignite a crisis. This is a classic recipe for surprise, miscalculation, and uncontrolled escalation.

Can the mainland conquer Taiwan? The PLA's ability to mount a Normandy-style assault on the island is not the toughest question. Geography (the water barrier), together with U.S. supplies and intelligence support, would provide powerful means to Taiwan for blocking invasion, even without direct American combat involvement. A greater challenge would be a blockade or limited commerce warfare by the PRC. Taiwan's proximity to the mainland and its dependence on international trade and investment enhance the potential effect of blockades—or limited terror campaigns involving missiles—even if the military impact of these missions is modest. Moreover, to break a blockade by sweeping the seas would require direct attack on PRC vessels. If Chinese submarines had not already struck at U.S. ships by that point, it would be up to Washington to decide to fire the first shots against a nuclear-armed country that was attempting to regain limited control of what it believes is its own territory. Who backs off then?

If it comes to war to save a Taiwan that has already declared independence against a resolute China, it is hard to imagine how the United States could win decisively. Too many assessments inside the Washington Beltway stop at the operational level of analysis and assume that tactical victories answer the American strategic question. Sinking the Chinese Navy and defeating an invasion attempt against the island, however, would not likely be the end of the story. Unless the U.S. Air Force and Navy were to mount a massive and sustained assault against mainland targets—the requirements of such a campaign would make the air operations against Serbia or Iraq look puny—the PRC would maintain the capability to disrupt commerce, squeeze Taiwan, and threaten American forces in the region.

Moreover, strikes against the mainland evoke huge risks. Recall that for three years while the PLA was killing American soldiers in Korea, the Truman administration refrained from carrying the war to the mainland from fear of a wider war—and that was at a time when China had no nuclear weapons and even its Soviet ally had fewer deliverable weapons than China currently does. The more decisively the fortunes of conventional war turned in American favor, the more Chinese incentives to escalate would grow. Several times in the mid 1990s Chinese officials called attention to this possibility. Xiong Guangkai, deputy chief of the PLA General Staff, told Ambassador Chas. Freeman that the United States would not trade Los Angeles for Taipei; Disarmament Ambassador Sha Zukang said, "As far as Taiwan is concerned it is a province of China. . . . So the policy of no-first-use does not apply"; and Major General Zhu Chenghu said that if U.S. forces attacked Chinese territory, "I think we will have to respond with nuclear weapons."[16] These statements were not blessed as official government positions, but they indicate that Washington can hardly be confident that China is irrevocably committed to no-first-use of nuclear weapons as Americans understand the concept.

If a conventional engagement leaves U.S. naval forces in control of the strait, can anyone be confident that Beijing would not dream of using a nuclear weapon against the Seventh Fleet? Thinking about such a nuclear engagement seems alarmist to many in the post–Cold War era. But it is no more so than such concerns ever were when Cold War defense planning focused on crises with the Soviet Union. In any case, is this an experiment an American commander in chief should run?

Even if there is no nuclear danger whatever, there are still considerable problems for the United States. If Chinese conventional capabilities do not deter American escalation, and Chinese forces prove relatively ineffective against American weapons, a broader question remains: how long is the United States willing to continue a war of attrition against a country of more than a billion people, or even just to camp multiple aircraft carrier battle groups and minesweepers off the Chinese coast? What would American allies such as Japan—where crucial U.S. bases are located—do? What is the endgame? Taiwan will always be just one hundred miles from mainland China, and Chinese nationalism is extremely unlikely to wither under American bombardment. Indeed, it would probably harden.[17]

China's growing power causes so many headaches in part because its strategic implications are not clear. But before lamenting the rise of Chinese power, consider one even more uncertain and possibly more frightening alternative: Chinese weakness and collapse. Nothing ordains that the country's march to superpower status cannot be derailed. Severe economic dislocation and political fragmentation could throw the country into disorder, and the central government could prove too crippled to use external adventures to rally support. A venerable theory of revolution sees it as most likely when progress and rising expectations are dashed by a downturn.[18] China has a revolutionary tradition as well as a formal ideology that, though now dormant, is available for reactivation to legitimize rebellion. Hard-bitten realists should hesitate before hoping for the country to founder. The last time China was weak and disunited—in the era of revolution, warlordism, and civil war in the first half of the twentieth century—it proved a disaster for international peace and stability.

A decade into the twenty-first century there are no indications that China is headed for a crackup rather than continued ascent. As the country has risen, friction with Washington (and Tokyo) has grown. The classic security dilemma is emerging. Liberals are correct to worry about preparations for the worst case making for a self-fulfilling prophecy; a new cold war would be tragic if China's ambitions are strong but limited and satiable. Few liberals, however, are willing to do what is necessary to prevent eventual confrontation: scale back American claims to leadership in China's neighborhood and cede that role to Beijing. Too many want us to have our cake and eat it too, to mount a dovish military policy without ratcheting down hawkish political demands. This combination would invite disaster.

## RUSSIA COMES BACK

Unlike Asia, Europe has been well endowed with multilateral institutions focused on security: NATO, the old Western European Union (WEU), the Organization for Security Cooperation in Europe (OSCE), and the European Security and Defense Policy (ESDP) initiative of the European Union. Of these, NATO is by far the most substantive and significant.

NATO's evolution over the past twenty years is a paradox. On one level the institution became a more muscular and combative military alliance just when it least needed to be: after accomplishing its strategic purpose by winning the Cold War. It did this, ironically, outside its own environs, since the potential for war with Russia had evaporated, although the alliance retained a residual deterrent orientation toward Moscow. This was unfortunate because it prejudiced the chances of pulling Russia into the Western political order, even though no plausible potential for war remained after the collapse of communism. At the same time, on another level, as it ventured into combat abroad and kept Moscow at arm's length, NATO came to take its main military purpose less seriously. The alliance was created to prevent World War III, and it did this for forty years by preparing to defend its members and retaliate if the Soviet Union attacked any of them. It won the Cold War without once engaging in combat as an organization, yet within a dozen years afterward it engaged in two hot wars, over Kosovo and in Afghanistan—or three, if the brief 1995 campaign against the Bosnian Serbs counts.

The paradoxical inattention to the organization's original main purpose is less obvious but may ultimately matter more. That original main purpose was to prevent conquest of member countries by a hostile great power. From the beginning NATO had a secondary purpose of serving as a diplomatic vehicle for transatlantic political unity. By the 1990s, after disposing of the threat that had generated the alliance, that secondary purpose became primary, and the function of direct defense was all but forgotten. In the years after the Berlin Wall fell, NATO's main function within its original ambit became to serve as a political club, to celebrate and consolidate the democratization of the continent, by bringing the liberated countries of the Warsaw Pact into the Western fold. The organization not only declined to disband, it did not even stand down after victory. Instead it nearly doubled in size, incorporating not just former Eastern European allies of the USSR but former Soviet republics, and rolled itself up to Russia's front door.

One need not be an apologist for the regime in Moscow to empathize with its resentment of this revolutionary overturning of the balance of power. In traditional strategic terms NATO expansion was a threat to Russia, but the West's leaders considered traditional strategic terms passé, antiquated concerns of outmoded realpolitik. Americans tend to assume that their benign intentions are obvious to all and that their right to shape world order in a virtuous direction should be unobjectionable.

Why was the function of unifying the continent performed by NATO rather than by the European Union, whose inclusion of countries from the old Soviet empire proceeded much less expeditiously? For the United States the reason was that it is not a member of the EU. Making NATO the vehicle kept Washington in the driver's seat and extended its reach in Europe. This was especially true regarding the new entrants to the organization in the east, what Secretary of Defense Rumsfeld called "the New Europe."

For Europeans the EU was not to be the vehicle for political consolidation because the EU was serious business. To most politicians after the Cold War, willingness to wage hot war to defend new members—the core of the Atlantic Treaty, embodied in its article 5—was an irrelevant abstraction because the sort of war that NATO had been developed to handle had become utterly implausible. EU membership, on the other hand, involved money! For a long time it was politically more difficult to let Poland sell tomatoes in France than to give Warsaw a pledge to fight and die for it.

Russia's violent disciplining of Georgia in 2008 was a rude reminder that article 5 is the essence of the alliance, that NATO's longest-standing function is readiness for major war, and that despite the end of the Cold War, Russia remained a potential adversary in the eyes of some within the alliance and especially those clambering to join. In preceding years NATO had blithely taken in most of the old Soviet empire, but without ever seriously considering inviting Moscow itself in. While NATO's original members assumed that the end of the Cold War was the end of deterrence, containment, and opposition to Russia, new entrants like Poland or would-be members like Georgia certainly did not.

The administration of Bush II and most of the foreign policy establishment in both American political parties envisioned that Ukraine and Georgia would eventually follow the Baltics into NATO, even though Russian support for secession of Abkhazia and South Ossetia was well established long before the 2008 engagements. *What were they thinking?* That the breakaway regions would voluntarily reintegrate with Georgia before the country was admitted to NATO? That Georgia would regain the territories by force without Russian intervention? That Georgia would be admitted without the two separatist regions and NATO would add a codicil to admission that its defense guarantee excluded them? Were any such options plausible? Are they in the future? Yet many continued to endorse Georgia's eventual admission as well as Ukraine's—and Ukraine, which involves much bigger stakes, has potentially explosive internal cleavages as well. Somehow the idea that a country's membership in NATO obliges the United States to go to war with Russia for it escaped much of the American political elite.

For years Washington and Western governments pushed Russia with no concern about provocation. They were blinded by post–Cold War triumphalism and also because they were spoiled by the shocking ease with which the victory over communism had been accomplished. Beginning in the late 1980s with Soviet acceptance of the "zero option" Intermediate-Range Nuclear Forces (INF) Treaty—which Soviet leaders had reasonably insisted for years was absurdly inequitable—Gorbachev began steadily giving away everything the West could ask for and gave most of it away for free. The INF Treaty did oblige the United States to withdraw Pershing II and ground-launched cruise missiles, but these were just being deployed after a quarter-century in which U.S. missiles capable of hitting Soviet territory had been taken out of Europe following the Cuban Missile Crisis. In exchange for the new American missiles, Moscow had to withdraw not only its recently deployed SS-20s, but hundreds of older missiles that had been targeted on Europe since the 1950s. At the same time, the INF Treaty put no constraints whatever on American nuclear-capable tactical aircraft based in Europe or on British and French missiles aimed at the USSR.

After this breakthrough Gorbachev's concessions got next to nothing in return. Reagan and Bush I would make offers or demands that the Soviets would huffily dismiss as absolutely unacceptable and awhile later would accept without a murmur. In a two-year whirlwind, one revolution after another strengthened NATO: the Berlin Wall fell, the Warsaw Pact collapsed, Germany unified, the Soviet Communist Party was deposed, and the Soviet Union itself ceased to exist. Stunned and crippled, Russia tumbled into decline.

Washington, and under its prodding other NATO governments, succumbed to victory disease and kept kicking Russia while it was down. American political leadership took U.S. global primacy and perquisites for granted. The price of intervention in the Balkans turned out heavier than expected, but extending American dominance in Europe by moving NATO eastward was accomplished at low cost. For twenty years Americans became accustomed to having Moscow roll over belly-up for whatever they insisted on doing. For years Russia got no respect.

Then the country had the temerity to start acting like a great power again. Russia manipulated gas supplies to Ukraine and the West, demonstrating its leverage over European economies; was the prime suspect when crippling cyber attacks were mounted against Estonia in 2007; flirted with military basing arrangements in Venezuela; gave Russian passports to Ukrainian citizens in Crimea; and defeated Georgia handily in military action. Shortly after the miniwar in Georgia President Medvedev denounced American global hegemony and declared Russia's right to a sphere of influence.[19]

The combat with Georgia was the wake-up call that registered in Washington and Europe. Little notice had been taken over the years that Moscow supported separatists in Abkhazia and South Ossetia, so direct intervention against Georgian attempts to reclaim the territories provoked naïve surprise and chagrin in the West. How could the Russians still act like they had a sphere of influence, a right to impose discipline in unstable border areas? How dare they assert the same protective prerogative toward secessionists in South Ossetia that NATO had toward Albanians in Kosovo (an analogy that Western officials denied but is essentially correct)? The chickens had come home to roost. After years of poking Moscow in the eye at the price of only feeble protests, the West had to notice that Russia was back and NATO's wave had crested. After having taken Russian impotence for granted for so long, the United States and its allies had to meet Moscow's claim to a sphere by rejecting it in principle but accepting it in practice. While poking Moscow again by undertaking military exercises with Georgia in 2009, Washington did nothing concrete to challenge Russia's protection of the secessionist areas in the country and cooled the movement to admit the country to NATO.

## GREAT POWER OR NOT?

Was there a better alternative to this evolution? Probably, but give the case for the choices that were made their due. Exploiting American primacy and NATO expansion to encircle Russia might make clear that the former superpower simply has to accept that it cannot play in the big leagues anymore and must accept its status as a lesser power indefinitely. There is no consensus among realists in favor of balance of power. Some consider hierarchy or unipolarity more stable because an unambiguous pecking order precludes miscalculation and adventurism. Leaving Russia a sphere of influence could be dangerous because the buffer zone would be a power vacuum, and continuing to respect Russia's status as a great power would leave its strategic prerogatives uncertain—all in all, an invitation to inadvertent conflict. Keeping Russia permanently debased and isolated might be strategically sensible. The problem with that rationale is that it is difficult to sustain against a recovered Russia. Then the humiliation imposed during the triumphal period gives the country's reentry to power politics a harder edge.

To optimists this whole framework is simply the wrong way to look at the question. To those who reject putting the first priority on the distribution of power rather than on economic and ideological enlightenment, reduction to military weakness should not have been a problem for Moscow because liberalization and the democratic peace should make military balances irrelevant. The problem with that rationale is that its credibility depends on universalizing the Western political club—that is, bringing in not just Russia's former allies, but Russia too. Otherwise, nothing would negate the perception that NATO remains an anti-Russian alliance.

Russian membership in the organization, however, has never been a serious option, even in the period just after the Cold War when the country seemed to be on the road to democracy. A few Western leaders genuflected to the principle that Russian membership was a theoretical possibility in the distant future, but the idea had no traction at all. It was also anathema to NATO's newest members in the East, who eagerly grasped the alliance's deterrent mission as liberals to the west forgot it. And of course there is no reason to believe that Moscow would have leaped at the chance to join even if it had been offered.

So, friendly rhetoric notwithstanding, and despite consensus that the Cold War was over, NATO remained implicitly an anti-Russian alliance. This was not a conscious choice by most of the original members' governments. Indeed, most still believe that it is not true, that Moscow is being thin-skinned or obstreperous for no good reason. But the residual anti-Russian quality is the inevitable result of including all of Europe except Russia, and the more forthright unfriendliness toward Russia of the newer eastern members of the organization. This reality was illuminated by the little war in Georgia. Moscow's attack or counterattack, depending on whose version of the story is believed, set tongues to clucking about a dark new chapter in European security, if not the rebirth of the Cold War. Russia's resurgence, however, should have been expected, should not be alarming, and may not last.

Resurgence should have been expected because in their own eyes the Russians after the Cold War were down but not out. With the economic recovery under Putin it was natural to get back in the game, and to demand respect once again. Defeated great powers usually become competitive again as soon as they can. Two decades of humiliation were a potent incentive for Russian pushback. Indeed, this is why many realists opposed NATO expansion in the first place.

Resurgence should not be alarming because there is yet no evidence that Russia's use of force points toward dangerous aggression, any more than NATO's actions in the Balkans did. Support for separation of two regions from Georgia is objectionable, but no more an indicator of Napoleonic ambitions than was American support for Kosovo's independence. Even if Russian motives are malign and tension with the West rises, the imbalance of power in NATO's favor is overwhelming, a radical difference from Cold War bipolarity. For forty years NATO doubted its capacity to defend against Soviet attack without resorting to nuclear strikes because it faced more than 175 Soviet divisions, their vanguard ensconced in the middle of Germany, and a third of Europe in the Soviet camp. Today the tables are turned. Russia has at best half the heft of the old Soviet Union and faces a far more potent West than in the Cold War—a united Europe, its old allies of the Warsaw Pact and nearly half of the old Soviet Union itself on the other side of the fence.

Resurgence may not last because the fragile economic recovery depended on high oil prices, and the country faces demographic implosion even if the economy holds up. Renewed internal turmoil could once more divert Russian government efforts to shoring up the domestic social and political order.

The gross imbalance of power makes NATO's military capacity to prevent Moscow from conquering Western Europe, the concern that animated it throughout the Cold War, a nonproblem. That does not mean, however, that political conflict between Russia and the West poses no risks. What should NATO do to keep Europe stable?

If we could go back in time it might have been worth trying to apply either collective-security or balance-of-power solutions, either of which would have required restraint and respect rather than isolation of Russia. The regional collective-security option would have transmuted NATO from the alliance it was originally designed to be by bringing Russia in. (To do so, and overcome Russian opposition to joining, the organization might have had to be cosmetically renamed.) Including Russia would have made the organization a primarily symbolic and toothless institution, first because there is now no plausible scenario in which a state outside Europe will attack one inside, and second because the lofty concept of collective security is really an unworkable concept in practice.[20] Such a new form might only have been a glorified OSCE, an institution built for talk rather than action. In a peaceful Europe, however, that might be quite enough. Over the long run it might have been a better solution for the United States, facing a rising China with Russia on its side rather than Beijing's. The collective-security option would have been a long shot, but there was a window in the early 1990s when diplomatic magnanimity just might have buttressed Russian liberalization and cooperation, helping make the country a fit partner.

The balance-of-power option, in contrast, would have kept the old NATO intact but more or less on ice, unexpanded—an alliance effectively in reserve in case things went bad again. Newly liberated Eastern Europe would be left without the military embrace of the West, but separated from Russia by a buffer zone of new, formerly Soviet states fallen away from the old union's carcass. That buffer zone, in turn would have been considered a Russian sphere of influence, in which the newly independent states would abuse the Near Abroad or Russian economic interests at their peril.

The collective-security alternative may have been too idealistic, and the balance-of-power option too cynical, for twenty-first-century democratic sensibilities. In any case, deterioration of Russia's foreign relations and domestic political development makes it too late for the first alternative, and NATO's expansion over the past dozen years makes it too late for the second. Unless conditions improve enough to revive the possibility of something like changing NATO into a collective-security organization, a truncated version of the balance-of-power alternative presents a better option than continuing the course NATO was on to admit more former Soviet republics. Thus Georgia and Ukraine should understand that they will not be getting into NATO, will not be protected militarily by the West, and in their own interest should avoid provoking Moscow. They would be, to use a Cold War term, "Finlandized." That status was considered awful back then, but compared with the fate of Hungary, Czechoslovakia, and other Warsaw Pact members at the time, Finland did not have a bad deal.

There would be no small risk in this. Having all countries except Russia inside the NATO perimeter might prevent inadvertent conflict by making clear that Russian military action would mean war. NATO could let Moscow fume and accept its alienation from the West and bad political relations as the price of military stability. Leaving potential flashpoints outside the perimeter risks repetition of miscalculations like those of 1950 and

1990, when the United States excluded South Korea and Kuwait from its promise of protection, encouraging their enemies to pounce, but then reversed itself and wound up in combat with the invaders to whom it had given the green light.

Admitting the two controversial candidates to NATO, however, would be extraordinarily messy and provocative, given the secession of two regions in Georgia and, in Ukraine, severe internal disagreements about being in NATO and the constraint of a sizable Russian population in the country. Debates about the implications of article 5 would grow in volume, as current members were forcibly reminded that the organization remains more than an ideological club or fighter of humanitarian wars against small enemies far from home territory. Membership in NATO could also embolden opportunistic leaders in the eastern regions most at odds with Moscow to ratchet up anti-Russian behavior. It is not in the interest of most of the countries of the alliance to be dragged into confrontation with Moscow, even a relatively weak Moscow, over disputes between a country and former parts of itself.

The sad irony is that the urge to broaden the political community of old and new democracies undermined the peace that broke out in the early 1990s. It is unlikely that NATO can resolve this paradox well enough to make the future like that brief euphoric period of amity from the Atlantic to the Urals right after the Cold War. It is not impossible, however, if Russia were to democratize and be invited to join the NATO fraternity. Either change is very unlikely. But if very unlikely things never happened, the Cold War would not have ended.

## The Power of Order or the Order of Power

There are three approaches to promoting peace among great powers: rely on multilateral institutions and accepted rules to settle disputes; rely on a stable hierarchy of power, a clear pecking order that forces the weaker to accept the rules of the hegemonic power; or rely on a balance of power to deter resort to force. None of the three is a sure bet for dealing with the two great powers that the United States has the most to worry about.

The institutional solution has not even gotten a start in Asia. The fans of this solution focus on economic relations and have almost nothing of substance to say about how military power should be handled or regulated in this region or how disputes over territory can be settled reliably. Peace may endure if economic interests trump nationalist grievances or ambitions indefinitely, but that is a big if; the experiment is continuing. In Europe, the most significant multilateral institution has so far acted in effect as the vehicle for the second approach, asserting Western dominance over Russia. To be a real solution truly independent of the distribution of military power, NATO would have to include Russia rather than surround it.

The second approach, assertion of Western hegemony, might work in regard to Russia. As long as NATO remains united its economic and military power dwarf Russia's. If Moscow's leaders are cautious they will bow to their fate, accept subordination, and avoid testing NATO's resolve in Georgia, Ukraine, or the Baltics. Even an economically vibrant Russia would not be able to counterbalance the might of the West. But what a price for Western rule—from Cold War to icy peace.

In Asia, however, China is already too strong for American hegemony to apply, and its relative strength is still growing. The United States will remain the sole global superpower much longer than it will dominate Asia. The United States presides globally but operates regionally. Although the world is unipolar, American power is fractionated, stretched across many regions of the world. Thus particular regions are multipolar, requiring the United States to collaborate with other states to work its will. In Asia this collaboration is more fragmented and limited than in Europe. The main U.S. ally in the region, Japan, has a constrained military policy and cannot be assumed to fight alongside the United States in a war with China. This is actually all to the good since Japan still frightens and angers many Asians, and especially the Chinese, more than Germany still unsettles Europeans. A stronger Japanese role that reduced the burden on the United States would be strategically shortsighted, losing more in diplomatic and political costs than it would gain in military benefits.

In terms of balance of power, the Asian scene is still quite favorable to American interests. China's rise may preclude U.S. hegemony in the region, but China has no firm allies among the great or medium powers in Asia. Its closest allies, North Korea and Myanmar/Burma, are embarrassments, not assets. In contrast, Japan, South Korea, and Australia are huge assets to the United States. Nevertheless, Washington has no assurance that any other countries would follow it into a war over Taiwan.

The worst outcome for U.S. interests would be a solid anti-Western alliance between Russia and China. This would not create an equal weight against the West, but it would be a more potent opposition than if the two were alone and not cooperating. The two have ample reasons for mutual distrust and could return to the days of the late Cold War when they both had better relations with Washington than with each other, but this is unlikely. They have moved closer since the Cold War. After communism's collapse liberals in Russia hoped to orient the country in an "Atlanticist" direction, but lost ground to "Eurasianism" as these hopes were frustrated and disputes with Japan over the Kurile/Northern Islands limited options for alignment with the West. Meanwhile, Russia and China resolved most of their border disputes, undertook significant trade in arms, and entered into a friendship pact.[21] Both have also become more vulnerable to American nuclear striking power and have a common interest in opposing U.S. deployment of ballistic missile defenses.[22] Most to the point, Washington has been stoking their incentives to collaborate strategically. With unbridled NATO expansion, criticism of Moscow's backsliding on democratization, abrogation of the ABM Treaty, and frictions with Beijing over human rights, economic policies, and Taiwan, the United States has increased Russia's and China's reasons to subordinate mutual conflicts of interest to their common interest in resisting Western domination.

# PART III. DECISION AND IMPLEMENTATION

# 9 | CIVIL-MILITARY RELATIONS
## A SPECIAL PROBLEM?

Democracy and powerful professional military organizations do not rest easily with each other. This is the premise of Samuel Huntington's *The Soldier and the State*, the book that has set the terms of debate for more than half a century about proper norms of civil-military relations in the United States.[1] These norms have concerned political leaders since the earliest days of the republic, when many who shaped the institutions of American politics feared the potential influence of a standing army. Because the armed forces would have the physical power to intervene decisively in politics if not restrained by loyalty to principle, the Constitution was potentially hostage to the good will of those forces. For most of U.S. history keeping the regular military in its place was the priority, and Americans idealized the Cincinnatus model of military leadership and the tradition of the citizen soldier. These ideals had to be abandoned when the Cold War mandated indefinite mobilization in peacetime, and the priority of ensuring military effectiveness grew. The need to combine expert military professionalism and hefty military forces with firm civilian control of those forces brought the old concerns back.

Huntington offered two alternative models for civilian mastery. One was *objective control*, which aimed to maximize military professionalism and minimize military involvement in politics by recognizing the military's claim to the primary role in decisions and implementation on operational matters, at the price of instilling the ironclad norm that the military would not be involved in making policy or taking sides in high-level policy disputes, which would remain the purview of civilian politicians and executives. Objective control would involve a rough division of professional and

political labor. Military leaders would abjure political influence, whatever
their own opinions might be, in exchange for autonomy on purely military
matters. The contrasting model was *subjective control*, which would resolve
the problem of potential military insubordination by relying on military
loyalty to the particular politicians in power, fusing civilian and military
identities by choosing military leaders who shared the aims of the government in power—in short, by politicizing the military in the mold of civilian
authorities.

Many who ponder civil-military relations do not share Huntington's formulation of the problem and its solutions, but most share the premise that
the relationship between the two camps is a significant continuing problem. Some believe that the problem reached the proportions of a crisis even
in recent times.[2] Is this true? The underlying potential for serious political
conflict over the role of military professionals in foreign policy seemed apparent when Huntington wrote in the 1950s. In the half-century since, however, the potential has not been realized, despite harsh experiences in war
and sharp political divisions within American society. The state of civil-
military relations is indeed a problem worth concern, but politics and government are full of problems. Struggles for influence and control among
political and bureaucratic constituencies pervade our national life.

If political control of the military seems a bigger problem than controlling civilian bureaucracies, it is because the consequences of military policy
decisions seem greater than the consequences of other public policy decisions. Civilian officials become nervous about contradicting military advisors for fear of appearing irresolute and weak, and they fear being boxed
into open-ended commitments of blood and treasure by those advisors.
Military leaders become nervous about being sucked into combat with limits and provisos typical of political compromises in a democracy, but which
risk leaving their effort between two stools: too much to avoid embroilment, but not enough to win. They fear winding up halfway across Clausewitz's ditch. Both sets of fears are well-founded. Welcome to the gravity of
national security policy. But just because these matters are grave does not
mean that the essential political problem, or the potential solutions to it,
are different from other problems in government. Contrary to the fears of
many in the twentieth century, civil-military relations are not an outsized
problem as political and managerial conflicts in a democracy go. The special nature of the stakes would make them more worrisome than other such
frictions if there were the slightest chance that the military would use their

physical power to usurp governing authority, the danger that has generated concern with civil-military relations in so many other countries. But there is not. In the United States civil-military relations are a permanent problem, but not a crisis in any of the time since the firing of General Douglas MacArthur.

How has the problem been kept manageable? Not by clear and consistent adoption of either of Huntington's ideal types of objective or subjective civilian control: neither has ever been officially proclaimed as the norm. This is natural given the difference between an ideal type and actual practice. In practice, the balance has been kept through a dynamic equilibrium, as political players tack back and forth in tacit emphasis on the two approaches. Either emphasis revealed problems. In recent years theorists have tended to reject Huntington's preference for objective control, seeing it as too indulgent of military autonomy. But on balance, given the record since he wrote, Huntington's opposition to subjective control remains persuasive in the twenty-first century. Critics of objective control have focused on the risks that professional soldiers may make the wrong *military* choices and have neglected the risks that go with politicization of the military—which objective control is designed to avoid.

## THE TWO FACES OF MILITARY POLICY

The concern behind *The Soldier and the State* was that the Cold War posed a demand unique in American history: prolonged peacetime mobilization. No longer could the nation rely on the tradition of the citizen-soldier who would provide armed force for only as long as necessary to fight a war. In the Cold War the professional military would have to perform a major role in national life indefinitely rather than episodically. This novel challenge existed only because the United States was engaged in containment and deterrence of a superpower with staying power.

So why did the American defense establishment not return to its historic role and status after the end of the Cold War and the unprecedented prolonged mobilization of 1940–90? Why has uncertainty persisted about the proper degree of professional military involvement in policy and strategy, despite two hundred years of experience and experiments to get it right, and a half-century of concentrated concern with military affairs?

Huntington's second book, *The Common Defense*, covers the broader political canvas on which civil-military relations play out. It opens by focusing on the interaction between the external and internal realms of American policy:

> The most distinctive, the most fascinating, and the most troublesome aspect of military policy is its Janus-like quality. Indeed, military policy not only faces in two directions, it exists in two worlds. One is international politics, the world of the balance of power, wars and alliances, the subtle and the brutal uses of force and diplomacy. The principal currency of this world is actual or potential military strength: battalions, weapons, and warships. The other world is domestic politics, the world of interest groups, political parties, social classes, with their conflicting interests and goals. The currency here is the resources of society: men, money, material. Any major decision in military policy influences and is influenced by both worlds. A decision made in terms of one currency is always payable in the other. The rate of exchange, however, is usually in doubt.[3]

The Janus faces of military policy overlay the two imperatives Huntington posed at the outset of *The Soldier and the State* for understanding the more specific challenge of civil-military relations: the functional imperative (effectiveness in war-making and deterrence) and the societal imperative (conformity of the professional military with the liberal American social and ideological order). The problem motivating Huntington in *The Soldier and the State* was the concern that, on one hand, "it may be impossible to contain within society military institutions shaped by purely functional imperatives," but on the other hand, the Cold War had made the functional imperative ascendant. Historically, Americans could handle the problem of civil-military relations by suppressing military professionalism, but the threats of the mid-twentieth century made it too risky to continue to do so: "Previously the primary question was: what pattern of civil-military relations is most compatible with American liberal democratic values? Now this has been supplanted by the more important issue: what pattern of civil-military relations will best maintain the security of the American nation?"[4]

Although the priority of the two imperatives had changed, the interaction between them remained the central issue for Huntington. Neither imperative could be ignored; the model by which they could be reconciled was the issue. Critics who were unhappy with the course of civil-military relations in subsequent years, or who rejected Huntington's preferred model of objective control, did not all recognize this. Many focused entirely on the problems in one side of the equation alone. Some did not like objective control since it appeared to contribute to the social gap between the military community and the rest of society, but they did not apply equal attention to the impact of alternatives to objective control on military effectiveness, the functional imperative. Others did not like objective control since it appeared to deprive the civilians of leverage over military operations and strategy, but they did not argue forthrightly in favor of subjective control, or even directly address the question of whether or how alternatives to it would politicize military leadership.

Two recurrent sources of friction between military and civilian leaders since the middle of the twentieth century stand out. One is about strategy and operations: the tendency for military professionals to oppose undertaking combat actions without a commitment to application of "overwhelming force," in frequent contrast to politicians' interest in waging low-profile war, intervention on the cheap, or economically efficient operations. Another is about management and control: the question of where to draw the line between military expertise and political authority, and whether military leaders have too much influence or not enough.

The preference for overwhelming force is a long military tradition because it is associated with *decisive* action as opposed to ineffectual piecemeal pressure. The preference is rooted in sensitivity to the unpredictability of combat, the pervasiveness of Clausewitzian "friction," and the unanticipated resilience of many enemies. Safer to crush an opponent, it is assumed, than to poke her or him. (This does not mean that soldiers prefer total war, only that they prefer erring on the side of more force than seems necessary to compel submission to whatever American demands are at issue.)

Conservative politicians often share this disposition. What became known as the Powell Doctrine in the 1990s, after all, was little more than the Weinberger Doctrine of the previous decade.[5] Liberal and neoconservative politicians (in contrast to paleocons or leftists) often see recommendations in this vein as obstructionist, exaggerated caution, and a disingenuous attempt to put down a marker to ensure that any failure is blamed on civilian authorities.[6] Civilians are often more interested in using small doses of force to accomplish good deeds, such as peacekeeping or discipline of odious regimes abroad, or they wish to show that force can be used economically, without wasteful overkill. Soldiers tend to see these urges as naïve or feckless. Joint Chiefs of Staff (JCS) Chairman Colin Powell complained to a journalist, "As soon as they tell me it's limited, it means they do not care whether you achieve a result or not."[7] Tension over the scale on which combat power should be applied bubbled up in the 1960s, particularly in regard to deliberations about intervention in Laos, the Cuban Missile Crisis, and the air war against North Vietnam; again in the 1990s, when the military resisted pressure to use force hesitantly in the Balkans; and in the 2002 run-up to war against Iraq. (The preference for overwhelming force is a tendency, not absolute. Exceptions include the Korean War, Kosovo War, and Iraq before the 2007 "surge." In these cases service chiefs opposed escalations favored by the field commanders, in part on grounds that maintaining readiness for a potential big war elsewhere took precedence over the small war that was actually going on.)[8]

The question of where to draw the line between the legitimate spheres of authority of civilian policymakers and professional soldiers arose in the past in the context of the management of budgets and procurement programs and of interference by civilian managers in choices of tactics in combat operations. Two contrasting lines of argument have been prominent. One, in opposition to the Huntington model, was that civilians should play a much more active role, intervening deeper in the hierarchy of the military establishment than allowed by the division of labor envisioned for objective control. The other, more sympathetic to the principle of division of labor, was that precisely that sort of civilian interference produced bad functional results: irresponsible strategies and corruption of sensible military plans and operations by naïve or dishonest politicians.

Examples of the first genre are the works of Graham Allison, Barry Posen, and Eliot Cohen.[9] They represent attempts to enforce the essential Clausewitzian notion that policy and operations must be integrated rather than separated if war (or preparation for it) is to be rational. Allison's organizational model of decision making emphasized the danger that parochialism and goal displacement by complex organizations like military services could produce dysfunctional implementation of policy, unanticipated consequences, and accidental escalation.[10] To avoid bureaucratic slips between cup and lip, in this view, top policymakers needed to burrow into tactical details and interfere in the military chain of command to ensure that standard operating procedures did not refract the president's intent when force was used. Posen argued that militaries could not be counted on to adapt doctrines or to procure forces appropriate to changing strategic circumstances, and that civilian leaders should "audit" programs and cooperate with minorities in the officer corps who offered sensibly novel solutions. Cohen argued that the mark of a great civilian war leader was the inclination to question military advice on operational matters and to impose alternatives to military preferences when their judgment conflicted. Cohen's was the one work that directly attacked Huntington's model of objective control, citing it as the "normal theory" of civil-military relations.[11] (It is normal among professional officers, but not a consensus among civilian politicians.) Cohen looked to examples of civilian war leaders whose military judgment appeared better than that of the military.

The opposite critique of civil-military relations, popular among professional soldiers, is represented by H. R. McMaster's *Dereliction of Duty*.[12] The greatest sin leading to the biggest national security policy disaster of the past half-century, in this view, was the imposition by Lyndon Johnson and Robert McNamara of a no-win strategy for waging war in Vietnam, against the expert advice of military leaders. The second greatest sin—the one behind the book's title—was the willingness of the Joint Chiefs of Staff to go along with the misguided plan, keeping quiet in the face of alleged administration duplicity about it, rather than resign or speak frankly to Congress. That is, the sin of JCS Chairman Earle Wheeler and company was to do as Cohen prescribed: disagree with their superiors, and then shut up once those superiors made their decision, irresponsible as it may have seemed.[13]

## THE NEW FACE OF FOREIGN THREATS

The knowledge on which all these arguments about civil-military relations were based came from the Cold War or earlier. Huntington's arguments were about the American political system as it was organized in the 1950s. Since then, the strategic environment of American national security and the domestic environment of American politics have both changed substantially. When Huntington wrote in 1957, a reader contemplating the hypothetical end of the Cold War might well have expected that if it occurred as it ultimately did, with the virtual unconditional surrender of the adversary, the societal imperative of containing the military domestically would come to trump the functional imperative again. The change in external threats after 1989 was as profound as the changes in the 1940s that brought the United States to center stage in world politics, but in the opposite direction, bringing it far greater relative power and security. In the heady days of the early 1990s, some observers steeped in realpolitik expected that the United

States might move "forward to the past"—that is, stand down from a long but aberrant period of high peacetime preparedness and activism abroad to adopt a more relaxed foreign policy oriented primarily to economic inter-action, watchfulness about the rise of other great powers, and abstemious resort to force. This did not happen.

Despite defeating the epochal challenges of fascism and communism, American activism abroad did not wane; it accelerated. Even before Sep-tember 11th the United States was not moving forward to the past. Although forces and budgets had declined markedly during the 1990s, and reductions were huge by Cold war standards, what remained was a peacetime military establishment that was still gargantuan by pre-1940 standards.

In the hiatus between the opening of the Berlin Wall and the Al Qaeda attacks, foreign policy objectives became matters of choice rather than ne-cessity more than at any time since the 1930s. U.S. policy did not have to worry about the balance of power since there was no balance, only Ameri-can dominance. After the splendid and easy success of the 1991 war against Iraq, the main issue was how much of the responsibility for world order to take on, and how to exert American leadership and control over small con-flicts without paying much blood or treasure. These choices created mild civil-military tensions. The neo-Wilsonian impulses of presidents Clinton and, after September 11th, Bush II, reflected a civilian idea of war closer to what it had been in the early twentieth century, flowing from experience in pacifying the western frontier. As Morris Janowitz described it: "war was essentially a punitive action . . . to bring people who lived outside the rules of law and order within the orbit of civilization. . . . There was little concern with the philosophy of the use of organized violence to achieve a specific political settlement or a new balance of power. Military action was designed to facilitate total political incorporation, or merely to 'punish' the lawless."[14]

For military professionals, this way of thinking created anxiety. They had long since forgotten the frontier experience and the policing of the Ca-ribbean region and instead were oriented to modern conventional warfare against militarily worthy opponents. Their self-image was dominated by what the armed forces accomplished in Europe and the Pacific in the 1940s, and in forty years of preparation for World War III on NATO's Central Front, and not least because the Vietnam experience confirmed their dis-taste for unconventional warfare. "Rogue" states with big armies replaced the Soviet colossus as the object of the armed forces' strategic planning.

Not until after 2003 was this orientation effectively challenged, as it had been in the 1960s. September 11th and its aftermath highlighted the importance of unconventional special operations, but most military professionals still saw it as an additional important mission, not the most important one. The failure of victory in the conventional opening phase of war against Iraq to produce final victory was a deeper blow to the ethos of the professionals. The descent into inconclusive counterinsurgency aggravated tensions in civil-military relations, although not as much as the war in Vietnam had done (there the main conflicts were over the air war against North Vietnam, which has no analogue in Iraq or Afghanistan).[15]

After Vietnam, friction between the two camps was mild compared to the 1950s and 1960s. The air force resisted civilian pressures, begun under President Kennedy and Secretary of Defense Robert McNamara and revived by President Nixon and Secretary of Defense James Schlesinger, to develop a menu of options for limited nuclear war. President Carter finally made the directives stick. Otherwise, the services were content to be as recalcitrant as any large bureaucracies usually are, to lick their wounds from Vietnam, and to retreat to their preferred mission: conventional deterrence and preparation for World War III against the Soviet Union. Civilian leaders did not counter the military's desire to forget Vietnam and did not insist that they preserve counterinsurgency capability as a hedge against the future—a terrible mistake that came to bite in Iraq in 2003.

The option of falling back on a European mission does not exist in the twenty-first century. Until a worthy great-power opponent emerges, the main issues will be how to fight a global campaign against Al Qaeda and its allies, and whether to elect missions using American power for charitable purposes (humanitarian intervention) and grand ambitions (regulation of world order). The regular military is a secondary instrument for the counterterrorism mission, and the elective missions remain potential sources of contention between military realists and idealist politicians. Enthusiasts for using force to promote justice and democracy believed the mission could be accomplished cheaply. Military pessimists will continue to demand commitment to overwhelming force if they are to support the habit of empire.

## THE NEW FACE OF GOVERNMENT

Changes in political processes, institutional constraints, and partisan tendencies have accumulated over fifty years. The one most often cited as worrisome, the Republicanization of the officer corps, is actually not a terribly threatening development (I say this as a Democrat)—*unless* the principle of objective control is abandoned. The change that has had the biggest negative effect is one scarcely noted in debates about civilian control: the reorganization of the army in the 1970s to require mobilization of reserve forces for any significant contingency.

Consider some milestones in the evolution of government and politics:

• The year after *The Soldier and the State* was published, the 1958 legislative reorganization of the defense establishment codified the system of unified and specified commands (later renamed "combatant" commands by Secretary of Defense Donald Rumsfeld); these evolved into major centers of regional politico-military coordination, with unusually influential diplomatic roles for the four-star officers in charge of them.

• In subsequent years, staffs of the military services, commands, and JCS, the civilian secretariat of the Defense Department, the National Security Council, and congressional committees and agencies such as the Congressional Budget Office all expanded, creating more complex interactions and mechanisms for leverage.

• Heavy-handed civilian management of Pentagon business came and went in the 1960s, and came back again after 2000.

• Legislative oversight of foreign relations, defense, and intelligence activities increased significantly, and Congress established budget committees.

• Congress asserted its constitutional prerogatives through the 1973 War Powers Resolution but then consistently failed to enforce it in contests with the executive.

• The federal budget became top-heavy with obligations of domestic entitlement programs, and the share of national resources spent on defense declined.

• The 1986 Goldwater-Nichols legislation strengthened the Joint Chiefs of Staff but removed them from the chain of command.[16]

• Conscription ended and the portion of the American population with experience of military service steadily declined. Political elites and Congress in particular, which had traditionally overrepresented veterans, came to underrepresent them (that is, the percentage of members of Congress with military service became smaller than the percentage of the population at large that serves).[17]

- Many traditionally military support functions were privatized by shifting them to civilian firms such as Halliburton, KBR, and Dyncorp.
- The two national political parties became more polarized, and the partisan identification of military officers became more pronounced and concentrated in one party.

One change whose significance was little appreciated has been the relaxation of resource constraints. This is quite ironic, considering how stretched budgets have seemed to those inside the military, and how little the growth in military spending increased the quantity of deployable military power, compared with increases in earlier times. In the early 1960s, with a 13 percent real increase in defense spending, "the number of army combat divisions went up from eleven to sixteen and air force tactical wings from sixteen to twenty-one. Marine corps manpower increased from 175,000 to 190,000 and army manpower by 100,000."[18] The large increases in the defense budget after the late 1990s bought far smaller increases in deployable armed forces.

The recent situation would seem less anomalous if not for a post–September 11th strategy-structure mismatch. The pre–September 11th goal of "transformation" and the revolution in military affairs focused on conventional warfare and relied on maximizing the quality of forces. Imperial policing, unconventional warfare, and the need for "boots on the ground" in many places simultaneously, however, require manpower in quantity and get only a minimal boost from expensive, high-tech advantages in naval and air power. Maintaining personnel levels in the ground forces under the strain of prolonged deployments and combat, and without the cushion of conscription, costs progressively more in bonuses and other expenses that did not enter the equation in the era of mass conscript forces.

Nevertheless, money for the military in recent peacetime has been less pinched than it ever was before the era of confrontation with great powers (see chapter 11). Between the Democratic Party's urge to shed the post-Vietnam image of weakness on national security and the Republicans' gradual abandonment of genuine (as distinct from rhetorical) insistence on budget balancing, the defense budget became comparatively unbound (see chapter 11). This eased civil-military relations when political appointees managed programs with a light hand, which was most of the time apart from the tenures of McNamara and Rumsfeld. Intramural peace was purchased by a modicum of objective control, restraining the intrusive civilian monitoring endorsed by critics such as Allison, Posen, and Cohen.

Unconcealed partisanship of military professionals is one of the bigger changes since Huntington wrote. Its implications are badly misunderstood, however, if it is seen as a reason for subjective control. Ruling the armed forces by choosing military leaders from among those identified politically with the civilian administration would turn an unfortunate but manageable problem into a destructive one.

The stances of the two American parties have evolved, nearly crossing over each other, in the past fifty years. Once upon a time Republicans labeled the Democrats as "the war party." Democrats also regularly favored more defense spending than Republicans did during the first phase of the Cold War.[19] In the 1970s Democrats became identified with opposition to military spending and to the use of force. They were repeatedly burned by the electorate for the shift, and after the 1980s they tended to leave the military's priorities nearly intact. Neither party's nominee recommended cutting defense spending in any of the four presidential elections from 1996 through 2008.

The Republican Party nevertheless succeeded in capturing the banner of nationalism in the decades after the Johnson administration, and the Democrats failed to shake the image of strategic fecklessness.[20] Professional officers, however, have always been conservative in ideology. They became overtly Republican after the 1960s because realignments concentrated conservatism unambiguously in that party. (The fact that a fair number used to think of themselves as Democrats before the 1960s was due mostly to the old affiliation of southerners with the party, and the World War II cohort of other officers whose social origins were in the New Deal coalition and who did not retire until the Vietnam period.) So it is still not likely that officers' party identification will change much.

But so what? Officers' Republican affinity did not compromise civilian control when Democrats took power. Although some critics were alarmed at reported episodes of disrespect for Clinton, those incidents appeared motivated less by partisanship than by anger at Clinton's perceived personal record of antimilitary sentiment and behavior. Apart from the military resistance that forced a compromise on the plan to admit homosexuals to the armed forces, a plan that aborted because civilian political authorities were also divided, Clinton had no trouble of consequence from the military. It is true that he did not challenge many military preferences, but this was because of his vulnerability to public opinion at large on national security issues, not because he feared military insubordination.

Although officers overwhelmingly prefer the Republican Party, this is rarely a big part of their sense of identity, and it is not the biggest problem of politicization of professions. (The lopsided identification of members of the academic profession with the Democratic Party—or groups further to the left—is no less objectionable. Whereas military officers are habituated to keeping their political preferences to themselves when acting in a professional capacity, many professors are far less scrupulous when it comes to teaching impressionable students.) The weak salience of officers' party identification allows Democrats to maintain businesslike relations with their military subordinates. Paradoxically, however, that would change if real subjective control of the military became the norm. If Democratic administrations looked for officers who were Democrats, promotions and assignments would become politicized, and military careers would involve explicit choices of which party to bet on for personal advancement. Military partisanship is less problematic when the functioning concept of civil-military relations is some sort of objective control.

One change that links the functional imperative (military effectiveness) and the societal imperative (conformity with ideological values) is the de-democratization of war. The era in which American defense policy was absorbed in the challenge of fighting World War II and then preparing for World War III, both of which entailed significant mobilization of society, ended long ago. Yet many remain reluctant to lose the social effects of the mass military. Several decades of conscription and draft-induced officer accessions after 1940 replaced the long tradition of social distance between the military and society with the ethos of the nation in arms. The norm of readiness for major war allowed many Americans to believe that civilian control would be enhanced by the mass military, which ensured that the ranks represented all of society, not just a self-recruited professional elite.[21] Reemergence of a gap between the military and society in recent years has alarmed some critics.[22] In part this reflects fear that an unrepresentative military is dangerous, in part nostalgia for the Jacksonian ethos of reliance on militias and citizen-soldiers and desire for subjective control of the military establishment from the bottom up, and in part egalitarian resentment at the vanishing involvement of social elites in responsibility for national defense.[23] Whether it matters or not, there is little that can be done about the gap as long as the military is small and self-selected, but also little reason for concern that the change will damage the system of political control. Given modern communications, the gap will never become huge.

Interest in keeping social bonds between the armed forces and society at large has been almost as great in some sectors of the military itself, especially the army. In one sense this is now a forlorn hope, irrespective of whatever efforts may be made to make temporary military service appealing. It is mathematically impossible to have a society where service is the norm and where at the same time the standing military force is small. Moreover, the civilianization of the military that characterized the Cold War era has been reversed, as more support functions have been taken over by contractors, leaving a larger proportion of those in uniform remilitarized.[24] In another sense it is not hard to keep the armed forces linked with society since modern communications make the day-to-day connections of military personnel with people and institutions elsewhere easy. (Consider the revolutionary novelty of soldiers in combat able to telephone home or converse by e-mail.)

Whatever the desirability of social representativeness of military personnel might be, there is scant evidence that it matters much for civilian control. If purchased at the price of long-service professionalism, it also limits military effectiveness. The notion that conscription and mass forces are safeguards against professional military usurpation or misconduct is sentimentally satisfying and played a more central role in many other countries with a problematic tradition of civil-military relations, such as France. In reality, however, it is an unreliable restraint apart from the expectation that enlisted soldiers and junior officers would refuse to obey illegal orders by rebellious senior officers. Conscript forces did not prevent coups or military revolts in French Algeria, Greece, Turkey, Argentina, or elsewhere. If the idea is that nonprofessionals would exert a leavening effect on military politics in general, there is no reason to believe this. Participation at the policy level is always limited to career officers far above the ranks at which citizen-soldiers are found.

## A PROBLEM WITHOUT A CRISIS

Neither perfect amity between military and civilians nor obsequiously unquestioning obedience by the military is the proper measure of good civil-military relations. There is a problem if the military has excessive influence, but also if it does not have enough; that is, if civilian control is exerted irresponsibly. The former possibility is what concerns most civilians. But has it been more of a threat to good political order than the latter? The record is mixed.

Why should civil-military relations be of more concern than relations between the political leadership and other professional and bureaucratic groups within government? First, the military has the hypothetical capability to impose its political will by force. Second, mistakes in communication or in understanding between the two camps about policy objectives or operational actions risk inadvertent escalation and disaster in crises. Third, lack of integration of policy and operations can produce strategic incoherence that wastes blood and treasure in uses of force even when they prove successful. Even critics who worry mightily concede that the first of these, the risk of a coup d'état, is not an issue in the United States. The second risk was extremely important during the Cold War, when mistakes could potentially trigger World War III. The third risk is constant. It is the fact that the first risk is off the table, however, that is most important for assessing the acceptable limits of give-and-take between military advisors and civilian leaders. Civilian fears of military pressure in bureaucratic battles should be no more alarming than fears of any other pressure group within government if there is no danger that the group will usurp ultimate authority.

When Huntington wrote in 1957, the potential for significant civil-military conflict seemed greater than it does now. At that time the proto-garrison state born in World War II was barely fifteen years old, and the National Security Act and the Department of Defense were only ten. The military had eclipsed the State Department in the policymaking process during World War II; General George Marshall had run both the State and Defense departments in the years following; and General Eisenhower became the most powerful political leader in the Western world. The Truman-MacArthur controversy, involving clear insubordination by a top commander who had more prestige in public opinion than the president, was only a half-dozen years in the past; today it is more distant in time than the Spanish-American War was then. Today, the United States has lived with a large military establishment for more than seventy years. There have been episodic military challenges to civilian authority since 1957, but they are minor compared with that posed by MacArthur.

Tensions simmered closest to the boiling point in the early 1960s, when a youthful president, a technocratic secretary of defense, and a brashly confident clique of defense intellectuals came to manage a military establishment

led by officers who had already been generals in World War II. The worst
moments were in the Cuban Missile Crisis, when Chief of Naval Operations George Anderson tangled angrily with Secretary of Defense Robert
McNamara, and the other chiefs grumbled that the civilian leaders were
irresolute. The military leadership was certainly restive, but not as rebellious as legend has suggested. For example, the sources on which Graham
Allison relied in the original edition of *Essence of Decision* claimed that the
navy failed to implement the president's orders to draw the blockade line
closer to Cuba, orders intended to allow Khrushchev more time to decide
to halt the Soviet ships, and that Admiral Anderson resisted explaining to
McNamara what procedures the navy would use when intercepting the
first ship to approach the line. Others claimed that civilian leaders were not
aware that U.S. antisubmarine warfare (ASW) operations were using depth
charges to force Soviet submarines to surface, raising the risk of inadvertent war.[25] Subsequent research indicated that these stories were incorrect.
Indeed, as Joseph Bouchard shows, McNamara actually ordered ASW procedures that were *more* aggressive than the ones standard in peacetime.
Harried civilian leaders may not have fully comprehended the implications
of all these technical measures, or may later have had second thoughts,
but the relevant procedures and initiatives did not escape their review and
approval.[26]

The Kennedy administration was a turning point. It was then, in crisis discussions over intervention in Laos, Cuba, and Vietnam, that the rift
between civilians and military over limited versus decisive use of force
emerged again. Limited war in Korea had been controversial, but military
leadership then was divided and was if anything more in favor of limitation
(for fear of diverting resources that would be needed if war broke out in
Europe). With Kennedy and later, civilian initiatives to make war in small
doses usually provoked united military recommendations for overwhelming force. This then inhibited the civilians' interest in using force or frustrated the military when intervention proceeded with less force than they
recommended.

The gap in mutual understanding, respect, and trust between soldiers
and political leaders in the early 1960s was greater than in decades before
or since. In the 1950s President Eisenhower had directed military personnel to participate in educating the public about the danger of communism,
an initiative that led to formal collaboration between military institutions
and right-wing organizations;[27] such official links did not occur in later decades. With the start of the new administration in the early 1960s, it was a

harsh jolt for the leaders of the military's World War II generation to move overnight from answering to five-star General Eisenhower to taking orders from Lieutenant Kennedy. The civilian whiz kids on McNamara's staff were seen as usurpers, and McNamara's insistence on assessing programs in terms of their comparative advantage for combat missions rather than the service requesting them struck at the traditional essence of military organization. Visibly contemptuous chiefs such as Curtis LeMay and George Anderson came close to kicking over the traces, but their rebellions were successfully contained, and none of the men who followed as service chiefs or field commanders in later years made as much trouble for their civilian masters. Ones who might have were simply not selected by the politicians or avoided appointment when it seemed clear that they were being set up to be co-opted or ignored. For example, General John Vessey was passed over for army chief of staff after an interview in the Carter administration when he said that he disagreed with the policy of withdrawing U.S. ground forces from Korea (although President Reagan later appointed him JCS chairman), and Marine Corps Commandant James Jones declined to be considered for the chairmanship of the JCS under Secretary of Defense Rumsfeld (and was later appointed assistant to the president for national security affairs by President Obama).[28]

After the 1962 missile crisis, the military posed no significant obstacle to presidents' preferences on policy toward the Soviet Union, the main issue of consistent importance through the remainder of the Cold War. In arms control negotiations, the Joint Chiefs of Staff bargained for offsetting programs but supported the treaties that resulted.[29] On the most important issue concerning the use of force, the Vietnam War, military leaders remained equally compliant, despite strong reservations about the limitations imposed by the Johnson administration. They grumbled mightily sub rosa, and there is an unconfirmed legend that the JCS aborted a plan to resign en masse in 1967.[30] The fact remains that they did not resign or otherwise protest in public. Their compliance, in fact, was what enraged critics like McMaster.

Neither Johnson nor his successors ever faced a McClellan or MacArthur. Since Huntington wrote, no general or admiral has ever flirted with running for president while on active duty, as MacArthur did in 1944, or has gone directly from uniformed service to political candidacy against the party in power, as Eisenhower did in 1952. Westmoreland did venture into politics, but not to oppose national policymakers, and with results that made any threat of a "man on horseback" look pathetic: years after leaving Vietnam and the position of army chief of staff, he lost the Republican primary for governor of South Carolina to a right-wing dentist. The few flag officers who have ventured into high-level electoral politics have fared no better, and their attempts do more to mock the threat of a man on horseback than to warn of it: Major General Edwin Walker finished sixth and last in the Texas gubernatorial primary in 1962 after being relieved of his command by the Kennedy administration; General Curtis LeMay ran as the vice presidential nominee of George Wallace's losing American Independent Party in 1968; Admiral Elmo Zumwalt lost in his bid as the Democratic candidate for the Senate from Virginia in 1976; Vice Admiral James Stockdale humiliated himself in debate as Ross Perot's running mate in 1992; and General Wesley Clark finished several notches down in the Democratic primaries for president in 2004. Admiral Joe Sestak served in Congress but was not an antagonist of civilian leadership on national security policy and lost his bid for the Senate in 2010. John McCain was a candidate who benefited from his status as a military hero, but he ran for president only after a lower-level career of three decades in politics (and he had not been a flag officer before retirement from the navy).

Every president except Clinton and Obama in the decades since World War II has been a veteran, but almost all of the citizen-soldier type. The only professional officer to run successfully for president since Ulysses S. Grant, apart from Dwight Eisenhower, was Jimmy Carter, and he had left the navy as a young lieutenant. In any case, Carter hardly represented militarism to anyone. The one general who had a good chance of unseating a president, Colin Powell, decided not to try in 1996. Of the thirty-four presidents who had served when Huntington wrote, one-third were military heroes, and of those, six were career professional officers. (Huntington does not count Washington as a professional. If we do, a full one-fifth of presidents by 1957 had been professional generals.)[31] Of the nine presidents who have followed in the past half-century, however, only Kennedy and Bush I might possibly be counted as military heroes, and not a single one has been a general or an admiral. In modern times, a military takeover via "One Day in November" appears no more a threat than the fictional *Seven Days in May*.

## POWELL AND PETRAEUS

In the wars since Vietnam, military leaders have been no harder to handle than they were then, with the possible exception of the Afghanistan policy review in 2009. In the first war against Iraq there was no conflict because the politicians did not resist the military preference for overwhelming force. (That did not mean that the civilians were pushovers. Secretary of Defense Dick Cheney fired Air Force Chief of Staff Michael Dugan without a qualm in the midst of the Operation Desert Shield buildup, and civilian policy-makers readily challenged and changed Central Command's "straight up the middle" war plan.) There was much muttering and tearing of hair behind the scenes on Bosnia, on Kosovo, and during the initial planning for the second war against Iraq, but in each case the generals fell into line, their objections unheard outside the Washington Beltway, and they posed no significant political problems for presidents. They did inhibit the intervention enthusiasts in the Reagan administration, who chomped at the bit to use force in Central America, and in the Clinton and Obama administrations, where the civilian leadership was nervous about its political credibility and standing on military matters. Two soldiers whose behavior provoked civilian critics to worry about danger to civilian control were General Colin Powell, who spanned the time of Bush I and Clinton, and General David Petraeus, who spanned Bush II and Obama. They were charged with opposite excesses—too much energy in both opposition to and promotion of American use of force.

In 1993 JCS Chairman Powell prompted Secretary of State Madeleine Albright's irritated question, "What's the point of having this superb military you're always talking about if we can't use it?" (Powell later commented, "I thought I would have an aneurysm.")[32] Clintonites in particular were cowed because the men in uniform were a constant reproach to their own strategic amateurism and privileged absence from service in their generation's war.[33] And if military leaders constrained decisions by the substance of their intramural arguments, this was in no way an illegitimate wielding of influence. They did not block presidents who finally decided that they wanted to use force, as in Bosnia by 1995 or Kosovo four years later. Civil-military relations in the Clinton administration were not good, but they were not dangerous. The imbalance in the equation was due primarily to self-inflicted deficiencies in the sociology of the administration's leadership. The one and only legal affirmative action category that the administration failed abysmally to honor in hiring for Schedule C appointments was that of Vietnam era veterans, who would have been three times as numerous among Clinton personnel if they had been appointed in proportion to their percentage of the American population.[34] At the highest level the symbolism got worse:

during Clinton's first term, four of the five civilian members and statutory advisors of the National Security Council—all but the president himself— were veterans: Vice President Al Gore, Secretary of State Warren Christopher, secretaries of defense Les Aspin and William Perry, and Director of Central Intelligence James Woolsey. By the second Clinton term, only the vice president was.

In arguing strenuously for using force decisively and without ambivalence, or not at all, Powell did more to constrain Clinton than the JCS of the mid-1960s did Johnson. Was this a blow to civilian control or a good thing resulting from healthy debate within the government? Powell was not shy about pushing his strategic preferences with political skill. Critics made much of his 1992 *New York Times* op-ed article discussing reasons to avoid limited intervention in the Balkans, as if it represented subversion of civilian leadership, but the article was approved in advance by the secretary of defense and NSC staff.[35] The argument that it was improper rests on its appearance during an election campaign in which the out-party candidate was hinting at the desire to intervene. Perhaps this discredits Powell's publication, but if so, it is hard to see justification in any instance for a career government official to publish an opinion on how a hypothetical policy initiative could raise operational problems that might call the policy into question.

In the 2002 run-up to the assault on Iraq, when the military acted more like Wheeler and Westmoreland than like Powell, was this a progressive return to good norms or a tragic failure of the sort mourned by McMaster? The lack of publicly audible protest when Rumsfeld steadily whittled down the size of the 2003 invasion force was a deafening silence to observers who knew anything about the preferences of the army and the marine corps. Not only did the generals not resist: they were induced to make the formal decisions themselves, so that Rumsfeld could later say disingenuously, but without literally lying, that his generals had not asked for more.

If Powell was criticized for publicly opposing a policy favored by out-of-office Democrats, a comparable controversy in reverse involved the September 2007 report to Congress on Iraq by General Petraeus. In this case, however, the criticism was not that the field commandeer was slipping his leash, MacArthur-like, but that he was *too* cooperative with his civilian commander in chief. War opponents charged that Petraeus, in making the case for the strategy he was applying in Iraq, was acting as a military shill for the Bush administration. There is no question that his stance put him on the side of the president and against Democratic critics. But what is Petraeus or any military commander to do if not to make the case for his own strategy? If he does not believe in the strategy, he should ask the president to relieve him and appoint someone who can pursue the plan with a clear conscience. If the president insists on having him remain despite his opposition—a hypothetical but hardly plausible possibility—then he could legitimately refuse to testify in favor of the strategy because the testimony would be false. But obviously Petraeus and Bush were aligned on the question, as is to be expected in war except in unhealthy or outright destructive situations like the McClellan-Lincoln or Truman-MacArthur controversies. Those on the left who would have been happy to see Petraeus oppose the president while remaining in command would have to say that MacArthur, too, had been within his rights, which none of them would believe. So what else could a field commander have done that would have been more proper for civil-military relations?

This situation was complicated, again in a manner reminiscent of the Korean War, since the military leadership in Washington did not entirely share Petraeus's views. Some, such as Army Chief of Staff George Casey, reportedly feared the drain and damage to other military missions imposed by the burden of maximizing effort in Iraq and favored larger and faster withdrawals than did Petraeus.[36] This raises other questions, of how far Congress should go in demanding that military leaders publicly voice their disagreements with their commander in chief, but it does not provide grounds for charging Petraeus with crossing a line into improper political behavior.

In Obama's first year the president and his confidants reportedly felt that the Joint Chiefs of Staff and field commanders were offering only high-end options for effort in Afghanistan, still failed to provide a better set of choices when pressed, and compelled the president to lay the law down to get a compromise with which he could live. Later Petraeus was criticized for trying to box the president in with statements that withdrawals planned for 2011 might be negligible, and that the American war might go on for a generation or more.[37]

Whatever pressure the soldiers may have attempted to exert undoubtedly came from their desire to avoid jumping halfway across the ditch. In a way disturbingly reminiscent of 1965, however, Obama and the generals as well seemed to do just that. The president chose neither to withdraw from the war nor to escalate to a level the military considered high enough;

he announced a troop increase at the same time that he announced that withdrawals would begin little more than a year later; he determined that he could not lose in Afghanistan but could also not provoke the base of the Democratic Party; and in the natural way of democracy, he chose compromise. Equally reminiscent of 1965, no one at the top of the military was apparently willing to consider recommending withdrawal from a war already under way, even if they could not get what they considered necessary for victory. Instead, when the president explicitly asked them whether they definitely approved his chosen course, they said yes. The wisdom of the 2009 decisions remains to be seen, but if they reflected problems in civil-military relations, they were normal political problems of trying to square the circle when participants in the process disagree, not dangerous challenges to civilian authority.

With few exceptions, overt challenges to civilian supremacy in the past half-century have been limited to promptly disciplined minor incidents involving officers below the top level, such as Major General Edwin Walker's attempt to indoctrinate his division on matters of domestic politics in 1961, and Major General John Singlaub's public disagreement with Carter administration plans to withdraw U.S. troops from Korea. More troublesome, because they reflected widespread animosity within the ranks, were scattered incidents of speech disrespectful to President Clinton early in his administration.[38] These were understandable, given Clinton's record—not simply the first of ten presidents since World War II never to have served in uniform, but one who had actively evaded the draft and had made common cause with antimilitary activists. But these incidents were effectively suppressed. They were worrisome in terms of ideal notions of harmony and good order, but not when considered from the perspective of realistic expectations about interactions between chief executives and civilian institutions of the permanent government. Critical remarks about President Obama and civilian officials by General Stanley McCrystal and his staff reported in 2010 posed no serious problem because the general resigned promptly and was replaced in the Afghanistan command by the more prestigious Petraeus.

There were three recognized exceptions to the inconsequential nature of such infractions during the past half-century, but even these were not challenges to civilian control of the military. One was General John Lavelle's apparent conduct of unauthorized bombing raids on North Vietnam in the early 1970s, under the cover of phony "protective reaction" strikes that the rules of engagement permitted if U.S. aircraft were attacked. Evidence uncovered years later indicated that Lavelle's operations were not unauthorized after all and that he took a fall for President Nixon. At the time Lavelle was fired and retired at lower rank but not prosecuted. A congressional investigation exonerated him, and the president's right-hand man, John Ehrlichman, claimed that Nixon had secretly circumvented Secretary of Defense Melvin Laird and directed the raids.[39] Subsequent evidence uncovered by journalists led Secretary of Defense Robert Gates and President Obama to clear Lavelle's name.[40] The second exception was serious and would count as criminal behavior if the perpetrators had not gotten off on legal technicalities, but it was not military insubordination. This was the role of two officers detailed to the NSC staff in the Reagan administration, Vice Admiral John Poindexter and Lieutenant Colonel Oliver North, in executing the plot to divert funds illegally from sale of arms to Iran to support of the Contra rebels in Nicaragua. These actions were the most blatant betrayals of the Constitution by military officers in modern memory, but Poindexter and North were not serving in military positions, asserting military demands, acting as military officers in any way, or resisting presidential authority when they committed their crimes. Indeed, they were promoting the policy objectives of the civilian administration they served, even if Reagan did not direct the illegal actions. The third exception was resistance of the military leadership to President Clinton's plan to allow homosexuals to serve openly in the armed forces. On this the generals simply made known their opposition; the real leverage came from Congress, which supported the military opposition and forced a compromise with the president (the "Don't Ask, Don't Tell" law, eventually repealed in 2010). This was just an example of the bare-knuckled form of what Huntington called "the lobbying functions of Congress."[41] None of these exceptions was trivial, but none posed a major challenge to civilian political control.

The main initiative of the past half-century that inhibited civilian political control may be one not usually recognized in that light, and which turned out to have unanticipated consequences. It was also one in which, ironically, the professional military tried to align itself with the societal imperative. This was the reorganization of the army in the 1970s under Chief of Staff Creighton Abrams that integrated reserve and National Guard units with active forces in war plans, to create the "total force."[42] According to folklore, Abrams's aim was to avert a repetition of the Vietnam experience, in which few reserve units were ever mobilized, allowing the political leadership to avoid demanding the national commitment to war that a call-up would have symbolized. There is no clear evidence that the army undertook the reorganization deliberately to subvert civilian control: indeed, it was prompted first by Secretary of Defense Laird and was designed primarily to get more forces out of limited resources. The effect of the change, nevertheless, was to constrain the options of the commander in chief. As Secretary of Defense Schlesinger put it, "the military sought to fix the incentives so that the civilians would act appropriately."[43] General John Vessey, then on the army staff, often heard Abrams say, "They're not taking us to war again without calling up the reserves."[44] This constraint did not prove to be a problem, however, until more than two decades later because the only war of consequence was the one against Iraq in 1991, a short and popular one.

Rigging the system in this manner did not lead to trouble until the prolonged peacekeeping deployments in the Balkans and then, especially, the second war against Iraq. In the planning stage for the latter, Rumsfeld steadily browbeat the leadership of the ground forces into chopping down the size of the invasion force, and he disrupted the Time Phased Force Deployment List (TPFDL).[45] As a result, the conventional phase of the war ended with no government functioning in the country and barely 150,000 American troops covering an area with 25 million people. If three times as many American forces had been available after the fall of Baghdad to impose "shock and awe" not just in the invasion but in the occupation as well, it is not certain that history would have turned out better, but that alternative was the only one with a chance of avoiding the anarchy that gave would-be insurgents a green light. Rumsfeld's concerns, however, had been motivated in part by desire to fight the war with reduced reserve mobilization. In this way, his micromanagement was the counter to the thirty-year-old scheme that would have forced civilian leaders to confront the full implications of war.

As it turned out, the requirements of the long counterinsurgency campaign after 2003 made unprecedented demands on the reserves and National Guard—prolonged and repeated tours of active duty in combat zones—but without energizing society on behalf of the war effort. This revealed the downside of any military plot there may have been in the 1970s to manipulate the weekend-warrior system as a political forcing mechanism. Those who saw the Abrams reorganization as such a mechanism did not quite grasp that the bigger measure of a nation's commitment is willingness to send conscripts to fight its wars, which only comes into play with reliance

on a large active force. Thus the Bush II administration never had to face
the intensity of domestic political opposition that the Vietnam draft caused
for Johnson and Nixon. Reliance on reserves has not proved to be as potent
a forcing mechanism as Cold War conscription was. Indeed, inhumane as
it proved for the civilians who joined the reserves, the system allowed other
American families to avoid any material stake in the war. The war became
highly unpopular in public opinion polls but provoked nothing like the
mass demonstrations and unruly active opposition of the Vietnam antiwar
movement. In contrast to the 1960s, the Bush administration demanded no
sacrifice whatever—not even war taxes—from those civilians who did not
elect to join the military in any of its forms. If there was any Abrams plot,
it backfired. The integrated active-reserve organization did limit the president's options, but in a way that allowed him to fight an unpopular war, and
failed to prevent him from doing so with underwhelming force.

## EQUAL DIALOGUE AND UNEQUAL AUTHORITY

Civil-military relations have been a problem, but less than might have been
anticipated in the shadow of MacArthur, and not a severe one as problems
in politics and government go. Recent frictions between political leaders
and professional soldiers do not seem especially severe compared with
protests from professionals in the Environmental Protection Agency about
distorted editing of scientific reports on global warming by nonexpert political appointees of the Bush II administration, or with administration
concerns that professionals in the Central Intelligence Agency were trying
to subvert Bush policies on Iraq, or with Republican concern about liberal
bias among National Public Radio personnel. Those who worry more about
the civil-military problem would say that comparisons to other areas of
public policy, such as public broadcasting, set the standard too low because
the stakes in military affairs are higher. The examples from conflict between
politicos and professionals over crucial issues such as global warming and
intelligence warnings about Iraq, however, refute that argument. Yet no coherent literature of concern on professional-political relations on other vital
matters rivals the amount of analytical hand-wringing about civil-military
relations.

Conflict between technical specialists and political generalists is natural in democratic government. Experts risk undermining policy objectives
by narrow application of professional formulas that ramify in the policy

realm with unanticipated negative consequences; politicians risk deranging operations by imposing requirements meant to safeguard higher concerns but whose implementation creates dangers of which only specialists would be aware. Conflict between the camps can be constructive if it is well managed, destructive if either denies the purview of the other. The principle of objective control still accords the military profession less autonomy than most others: certainly less than lawyers, doctors, or professors.

Civilian leaders have often received less support or enthusiasm from the generals and admirals than they would have liked, and military preferences have sometimes been wrong and difficult for civilians to handle. But civilian preferences have sometimes been wrong too, yet have carried the day because civilian authority is, when the last word is said, unchallenged. Presidents always get their way unless another civilian branch of government—Congress—supports the military's preferences. When this happens, we are just witnessing good old checks and balances, the essence of constitutional constraint on executive power, and civilian control of a sort, just not executive supremacy. To observers horrified to find that presidents and civilian managers in the Pentagon sometimes bend to bureaucratic resistance or compromise with conflicting preferences of other constituencies, one can only say that this is utterly typical of American government. This leaves two main overlapping questions for judging Huntington's models of civilian control: first, whether a line should be drawn between the legitimate spheres of authority of military professionals and of political leadership, and if so, where it should be; and second, whether either the professionals or the politicos have had too much influence in the equation.

One could make the case that for ideal integration of objectives, strategy, operations, and tactics, civilians and military should be equally conversant in each others' terms of reference and should participate equally at all stages. In the end, however, few would deny that there is some level of high politics at which soldiers should be silent, and some level of tactical specificity or micromanagement where civilians should keep their hands off. Huntington himself was not as explicit as he might have been about where exactly the lines should be drawn. At one point he cited Hitler's intervention in the chain of command to direct battalion-level operations as clearly beyond the line.[46] If this were the standard for objective control, at least in wartime, would many oppose it? Similarly, at the other end of the range, one can surmise that Huntington would endorse Roosevelt's overruling Army Chief of Staff Marshall in order to divert American weapons to aid Britain before U.S. entry in the war.

Even the extreme tactical limit suggested above might have exceptions. For near-war crisis management, to avoid 1914-type escalation, civilian monitoring of standard operating procedures like the execution of the 1962 blockade of Cuba may be valid. This is risky because there can be negative unintended consequences from civilian interference, just as from unthinking military application of drill-book procedures. For example, in the Cuban Missile Crisis, civilian monitors were oblivious to the way their attempts to keep abreast of all relevant details in the military operation wound up clogging naval communication channels and delaying transmission of important messages down the chain of command. (In this light, efforts of Admiral Anderson and Admiral Denison, head of the Atlantic Command, to keep civilians at arm's length from the command-and-control system become more understandable, even if still unjustified.)[47] The vital importance of avoiding accidental war in the nuclear age is one *The Soldier and the State* did not really engage, and it gives grounds for more fusion of military and political judgment than the objective control model implies.

In wartime, when crisis management is less of a concern, the case becomes stronger for bowing to the military norm of overwhelming force. As Clausewitz said at the beginning of *On War*, "the mistakes which come from kindness are the very worst."[48] (This idea should not be confused with approval of indiscriminate force or indifference to collateral damage.) The norm of overwhelming force is also a direct response to Clausewitz's warning against jumping halfway across a ditch. The norm can be wasteful, as military estimates of requirements may sometimes prove excessive. But that mistake is better than the reverse—undertaking combat with a level of effort that proves indecisive and that squanders blood and treasure to no purpose. Would the world have been worse off if the invasion of Iraq in 2003 had immediately installed an occupation force of several hundred thousand, as Army Chief of Staff Eric Shinseki had advised? Or if in 1993 Secretary of Defense Les Aspin had authorized the requested dispatch of tanks to Somalia before the "Blackhawk Down" incident, in which American soldiers had to fight their way out of enemy territory in Mogadishu on foot? Or if the Air Force's 94 Target Plan—the only scheme for bombing that the service claimed would be effective—had been implemented against North Vietnam in 1965, rather than in gradual increments over the succeeding years?

More overwhelming force in these cases might not have succeeded. Cohen rightly points out that criticism of civilian leadership on Vietnam "would be infinitely stronger if one could adduce evidence that Johnson's professional military advisers had a better idea of how to fight the war," but he also concedes that the gradualist rationale for the air war, which the JCS did firmly oppose, proved "calamitously false."[49] On Vietnam, neither camp had a recipe for success, and the worst mistake of the JCS was their unwillingness to see withdrawal from the war as preferable to acceptance of the civilians' strategy for stalemate. But if the overwhelming-force alternative for the air war had been tried, at least the fact and price of failure would have been evident sooner and the choices for policymakers clearer, diminishing the temptation to forge ahead with continued slow bleeding.[50]

The contrast between the results of the first and second American wars against Iraq makes McMaster's concerns more salient. Because the chiefs adhered to the silence outside the confines of the Pentagon and White House that critics would insist upon, professional military opposition to the Johnson administration's planned strategy for Vietnam was unknown to the public. This in turn reduced the constraints on Johnson, made it easier for him to avoid the choice between the extremes of withdrawal and overwhelming force, and facilitated the descent into disaster that did not end until a decade later, at a price far higher than a choice of either of the extremes in 1965 would have cost.

It is quite true, as Cohen suggests, that at the outset of wars professional soldiers cannot claim superior expertise about which uses of force will work to achieve political objectives. Westmoreland, Wheeler, and company were not fonts of strategic wisdom. There were also very powerful reasons that Johnson had to avoid risky escalation and that compelled him to follow a middle course. The point is simply that the luxury of hindsight shows civilian political leaders to be no wiser in the end than the soldiers.

Cohen's portrait of four civilian war leaders whose intervention in military planning and operations turned out well points to a different verdict. He does not demonstrate, however, that these four were a representative sample of intrusive hands-on political managers, rather than just four he came to know and admire. He does not compare the lessons of their cases with ones in which the civilian impulse to meddle deep in the chain of command produced bad military results, such as Hitler's armchair commands in World War II, and he does not indicate how one should decide whether the effects of such meddling are more often good than bad. (Nor does he indicate whether he approves of the records of activist secretaries of defense McNamara and Rumsfeld in managing peacetime programs, the supreme examples of the demanding management style he endorses in chief executives in wartime.) It is possible that a systematic survey would show that political leaders are usually wiser than their uniformed subordinates about operational-level matters, but it is no less possible that military advisors would prove more prescient about strategic-level matters than their civilian masters. Military autonomy often leads to bad results, but so does civilian meddling. With this reality, muddier than the intellectually clean ideal types of objective and subjective control, practical solutions will not embrace either one unequivocally, but they should tilt toward Huntington's old preference.

Critics of objective control sometimes skirt the question of why subjective control should be preferable. They might argue against the polarity Huntington poses, denying that subjective control need be the alternative. If it is not the alternative—if presidents do not concede military leaders any autonomy but also do not try to ensure that those leaders share the administration's views—the only plausible third alternative is one in which the professional military have no influence at all: where their advice is so unimportant that civilians do not care who gives it. This would not be an unequal dialogue but a superfluous one. Otherwise, opposition to objective control must imply some measure of preference for what Huntington calls fusion, in which military leaders are politicized in the mold of their masters, lest the soldiers resort to political maneuvering against civilian preferences.

Subjective control does not mean civilianizing the military in the sense that Morris Janowitz saw happening ineluctably in the postwar period as the military adapted to modern society. Janowitz described civilianization as a process of bureaucratization, assimilation of noncombat functions, ascendancy of a managerial rather than heroic ethos, and reduced physical isolation from the rest of society.[51] Huntington's concept of fusion involves more direct politicization of the military. For example, the replacement of the commanding general of the army by a chief of staff under Secretary of War Elihu Root's reforms of the early twentieth century made the military leader's term coextensive with the president's. "Under this system, the Chief of Staff became a part of the administration in power. He was not simply the spokesman for permanent military interests. He was also political. . . . His position was, in effect, that of an undersecretary in an executive department."[52] Had this system endured, defense policy would probably have witnessed increasingly explicit partisan activity by ambitious officers. Which set of problems would be more worrisome: tension between the professional military elite and political leaders, or competition among Republican and Democratic officers for appointments and advancement?

The main critique of objective control does not fully engage Huntington's concern about subjective control. For example, Cohen quotes Huntington's line that in World War II, "so far as the major decisions in policy and strategy were concerned, the military ran the war," but Cohen then says, "And a good thing too, he seems to add." The page in *The Soldier and the State* where the quoted line appears, however, says something rather different. The line is actually followed by Huntington's lament that the military accomplished this dominance through fusion, "only by sacrificing their military outlook" and becoming one with the liberal society, with bad effects on the peace that followed the war.[53]

How should the dialogue be made equal? Clausewitz recommended that the top commander be in the cabinet, to ensure that policymakers understood the limitations of military options and the ramifications of their choices at each point.[54] U.S. practice does not go that far; the chairman of the Joint Chiefs of Staff is a statutory advisor, but not an official member, of the National Security Council. This is good enough, as long as the chairman and the chiefs are as free as the regular members to discuss their views. It is also only realistic to expect presidents to pay some attention to whether top military appointees have views that are minimally compatible with their own aims. Having Curtis LeMay as a member of the JCS under Kennedy and Johnson served no one's interests. But this does not mean looking for clones. It may mean exerting close control of military appointments at the four-star, or occasionally the three-star, level, but not vetting all general officer promotions, as critics believed Rumsfeld did.

A better way to balance the equation is desirable, but probably not achievable. The principle endorsed by Cohen—the "unequal dialogue"—is not literally apt. Inequality of authority between civilian and military executives is as it should be, and if checks on executive authority are a problem, blame the Founders. But the proper inequality of authority makes it all the more important for the dialogue between the camps to be equal. Subjective control that keeps bruising dialogue limited to the bureaucratic level within the Defense Department by appointing accommodating officers at the top has not served the functional imperative. Equality in strategic discussion does not compromise the civilians' ultimate primacy. Presidents have the right to be wrong in the end, but generals should have every chance to prevent error before that end.

In *The Soldier and the State*, Huntington posed two stark ideal types of civilian control and endorsed one. In *The Common Defense*, which covered a much broader set of problems, he presented a more complex and richer set of ways to understand military policy. That book made clear that the genius of the American system was not its consistent adherence to planned courses of action, but its robust ways of muddling through, thereby implying how civil-military relations might work satisfactorily without always embodying the pure form of objective control. He ends *The Common Defense* by describing Fisher Ames's 1795 address in the House of Representatives:

> A monarchy or despotism, Ames suggested, is like a full-rigged sailing ship. It moves swiftly and efficiently. It is beautiful to behold. It responds sharply to the helm. But in troubled waters, when it strikes a rock, its shell is pierced, and it quickly sinks to the bottom. A republic, however, is like a raft: slow, ungainly, impossible to steer, no place from which to control events, and yet endurable and safe. It will not sink, but one's feet are always wet.[55]

In American civil-military relations the water never gets chin-deep. In the worst of times it splashes up toward knee level. Our feet are always wet, but the water rarely gets above our ankles. Democracy can nevertheless yield disaster, as in the compromise decisions that propelled American forces halfway across the ditch of Vietnam. In 2011 the verdict is still out on whether that might happen in Afghanistan. When it does happen the result is tragic, but the tragedy flows from the political logic of democratic compromise, not from the unique nature of civil-military relations.

# 10 PLANS AND RESULTS
## IS STRATEGY AN ILLUSION?

Strategy is the essential ingredient for making war either politically effective or morally tenable. It is the link between military means and political ends, the scheme for how to make one produce the other. Without strategy, there is no rationale for how force will achieve purposes worth the price in blood and treasure. Without strategy, power is a loose cannon and war is mindless. Mindless killing can only be criminal. Politicians and soldiers may debate which strategic choice is best, but only pacifists can doubt that strategy is necessary.

Because strategy is necessary, however, does not mean that it is possible. Those who experience or study many wars run into strong reasons to doubt that strategists can know enough about causes, effects, and intervening variables to make the operations planned produce the outcomes desired. To skeptics, effective strategy is often an illusion because what happens in the gap between policy objectives and war outcomes is too complex and unpredictable to be manipulated to a specified end. When this is true, war cannot be a legitimate instrument of policy.

This chapter surveys ten critiques that throw the practicability of strategy into question. It pulls together many arguments that emerge in bits and pieces from a variety of sources. Some are my own formulation of skepticism implicit but unformed in others' observations; few analysts have yet attacked the viability of strategy head-on. The notion that effective strategy could be an illusion emerges cumulatively from arguments that strategies cannot be evaluated because there are no agreed criteria for which are good or bad; there is little demonstrable relationship between strategies and outcomes in war; good strategies can seldom be formulated because of policymakers' biases; if good strategies are formulated, they cannot be executed because of organizations' limitations; and other points explored below. Unifying themes include the barriers to prediction and control imposed by political and military complexity; the pervasive undertow of goal displacement in the behavior of governments and militaries that reverses the canonical relationship between ends and means; the implementation gap (how confusions and breakdowns in the process of turning decisions into outcomes confound intentions); and the greater difficulty of strategies of coercion, which aim to change adversaries' policies, as compared with strategies of control, which impose the objective by destroying capabilities to resist.

Strategy is defined here as a plan for using military means to achieve political ends, or, as Clausewitz put it, "the use of engagements for the object of the war."[1] Strategy is the *bridge* between the higher level of policy and the lower level of operations, the scheme by which the application of military force is designed to produce a stipulated political result. If effective military strategy is to be real rather than an illusion, one must be able to devise a rational scheme to achieve an objective through combat or the threat of it; implement the scheme with forces; keep the plan working in the face of enemy reactions (which are anticipated in the plan as much as possible); and achieve something close to the objective. Rational strategic behavior should be value maximizing, choosing appropriate means according to economistic calculations of cost and benefit.

Two potential confusions should be clarified. First, this chapter is most concerned with strategy as a cause of victory that can be distinguished from raw power. The distinction is blurred when the strategy is simple attrition, direct application of superior resources to defeat the enemy by having the last man standing. Attrition meets the definition of strategy when it is used by a strong power against a weak one, and circumstances sometimes make it the right choice. In those cases, however, strategy is not interesting because it does not tell us more than we could estimate from the distribution of power. Strategy is most important when it provides added value to resources, functions as a force-multiplier, offers a way to beat an adversary with equivalent resources, or minimizes the cost of defeating an inferior.

Second, strategies are chains of relationships among means and ends that span several levels of analysis, from the maneuvers of units in specific engagements, through larger campaigns, whole wars, grand strategies, and foreign policies. The reader is forewarned that this chapter blithely moves back and forth across these levels. Considering examples at different levels of analysis is reasonable as long as the focus remains on the *linkages* in the hierarchy of policy, strategy, operations, and tactics, where the logic at each level is supposed to govern the one below and serve the one above. A scheme for how to use a particular operation to achieve a larger military objective and a foreign policy decision that requires certain military actions are both strategic matters at different levels in the chain between means and ends. Strategy is derailed when some link in the planned chain of cause and effect from low-level tactics to high-level political outcomes is broken, when military objectives come to be pursued for their own sake without reference to their political effect, or when policy initiatives depend on military options that are infeasible. The issue for strategy is whether choices at any level do or do not maintain a logical consistency with levels above and below, and ultimately a consistency between political ends and military means.

Why is a long essay on this question necessary? Because many people are insensitive to the issue. Among practitioners, politicians often conflate strategy with policy objectives (focusing on what the desired outcome should be, simply assuming that force will automatically move the adversary toward it), while many soldiers conflate strategy with operations (focusing on how to destroy targets or defeat enemies tactically, assuming that positive military effects automatically serve policy). The connection is never automatic, but policymakers and soldiers both have more than they can handle, working around the clock, to deal with the demanding problems in their respective realms, with neither focusing intently on the linkage—the bridge between objectives and operations, the mechanism by which combat will achieve objectives. Strategy becomes whatever slogans and unexamined assumptions occur to them in the moments left over from coping with their main preoccupations.

Among analysts, many do not take seriously the barriers to effective strategy. A generation ago students were more immersed in literature that emphasized nonrational patterns of decision, implementation, and outcome. The brief vogue of bureaucratic politics theory in the 1970s was fed by disillusionment over U.S. policy in Vietnam: it seemed impossible that the civilian and military leaders who produced that disaster could have known what they were doing. Soon, though, the pendulum swung back. Rationalist theories returned to the fore and remained ascendant. Political science has emulated economics, where realistic behavioral economics has only recently challenged the profession's fixation on rationalist assumptions. Political science no longer encourages operational analysis as a prime mission for ambitious scholars. Thus few of them anymore learn enough about the processes of decision making or military operations to grasp how hard it is to implement strategic plans, and few focus on the conversion processes that open gaps between what government leaders decide to do and what government organizations implementing those decisions actually *do* do. Rationalist models provide the best normative standards for what strategists ought to try to do, but they are only heuristic beginnings for real strategies that, by definition, must be demonstrably practical. "The question that matters in strategy is: Will the idea work?" as Brodie writes. "In that respect it is like other branches of politics and like any of the applied sciences, and not at all like pure science, where the function of theory is to describe, organize, and explain and not to prescribe."[2]

The chapter groups four sets of critiques. In the first set, critique 1 argues that strategy cannot reasonably be judged in advance because anything goes: virtually any choice—even one that later proves disastrous—can be justified before it is tried. Critique 2 is that we cannot use hindsight to select model strategies because experience shows that nothing goes: the record of strategies played out reveals so little correspondence between plans and outcomes that strategic choice proves to be seldom more than a shot in the dark. In the first criticism, strategy is no better than a crapshoot; in the second, it is not even that, but instead a "random walk."

Critiques 3–10 explore why it is so hard to use strategy to integrate ends and means: psychological impediments from unconscious emotions, cognitive processes, and cultural differences between antagonists; operational complexity and friction, organizational process and goal displacement, and the interactive dynamics of war; and the antistrategic effects of democratic pluralism and compromise. Several cases are used recurrently as illustrations; using different facets of a single case underlines the multiplicity of barriers to strategic effectiveness.

Following each critique below is a response that tries to refute or mitigate it. The aim of the responses is to salvage the practice of strategy against the cumulative weight of the criticisms. The chapter is not meant to be a screed against strategy, and I do not accept the pacifism that is the only legitimate alternative to belief in the possibility of strategy. But the salvage mission succeeds only in part. The chapter concludes with reflections on the implications of a dismal view of what strategy can do: an abstemious view of the use of force—especially limited coercive force—for foreign policy.

## RISK, UNCERTAINTY, AND PREDICTION: ANYTHING GOES IN FORESIGHT, NOTHING GOES IN HINDSIGHT

Strategies can be judged looking backward, but they must be chosen looking forward. If any choice of action can be deemed strategically reasonable beforehand, or none can be afterward, strategy cannot be meaningful.

CRITIQUE 1: Luck Versus Genius. *Strategy is an illusion because it is impractical to judge in advance which risk is reasonable or which strategy is less justifiable than another. The illusion persists because observers confuse what they know about results of past strategic choices with what they can expect strategists to know before the choices are tested. Almost any strategy can be rationalized and no rationale falsified at the time that a strategy must be chosen.*

If strategy is to be useful, there must be adequate criteria for judging between smart and stupid strategies and between reasonable and excessive risks. This must be done in terms of what decision makers know when they choose strategies, not what proves out after strategies are tried. Successful strategy must also achieve an objective at acceptable cost in blood and treasure. The best strategy does so not just effectively but efficiently as well—at the lowest cost of any option. Acceptable cost cannot be determined easily or precisely because there is no unit of account for weighing objectives and prices in the way that money provides for market exchange. Notions about acceptable cost may also prove volatile, as political circumstances change or costs accumulate. Economists know that sunk costs should not influence decisions, but psychologists know that they do. There must be some judgment about acceptable cost, however imprecise it may be, or there is no basis on which to decide why some causes are worth fighting for and others not.

Because strategic choices depend on estimates about risks and subjective judgments about the value of the stakes, they are gambles. If there is scant danger of failure, counterproductive results, or excessive cost, the strategic problem is not challenging. If strategic decisions are gambles, however, it is hardly reasonable to judge one as foolish simply because hindsight shows that it failed. The wisdom of a choice of action also depends on the objective it is meant to serve. Strategy may be immune to criticism if the objective could not fail to be achieved. For example, American officials declared that the objective of Operation Desert Fox—the four-day bombing of Iraq in 1998—was to "degrade" Saddam Hussein's capabilities. *Any* combat action at all would do that. Strategy cannot be faulted, however, just because the objective it serves is dubious to the observer, if it makes sense in terms of a different value of concern to the one making the decision. If the decision maker puts the priority on a moral value that conflicts with material welfare (for example, honor), even self-destructive behavior can be strategic. These qualifications put assessment on a slippery slope, where it becomes difficult to discredit *any* strategic choice and the concept of strategic behavior degenerates into indeterminacy and nonfalsifiability.[3]

What amount of risk is strategically sensible? Without hindsight—knowledge of who won and who lost—it proves hard to distinguish calculated risks from shots in the dark. Judgment is often contaminated by hindsight as good fortune is mistaken for strategic foresight. Before the fact, what kind of a gambler should a respectable strategist be: a percentage player or a high-roller? It is not easy to prescribe the cautious percentage-player model even if we want to, because it is never as clear what the odds of military success or failure are before the fact as it seems to be once hindsight is available. Success makes the estimable odds before the fact seem better than they were, and failure makes them seem worse. Even if odds are calculable in advance, what do we make of a strategist who has a 30 percent chance and wins, compared to one who has a 40 percent chance but loses? Can we call the first wise and the second wrong, or both wrong or right? By what standards can one say which choices are reasonable gambles that do not pan out and which are egregious miscalculations, which ones reflect strategic genius and which simply good luck? *Among practitioners and observers of military affairs there is no consensus whatever on the absolutely fundamental question of what degree of risk is acceptable.*

Adolph Hitler, Winston Churchill, and Douglas MacArthur all gambled more than once, and all won some and lost some. Hitler rolled the dice several times against the advice of prudent generals and won stunning victories until his two big mistakes in 1941, attacking the Soviet Union and declaring war on the United States. Churchill's risk propensity contributed to the disaster of Gallipoli in 1915 but also to Britain's finest hour in 1940. In 1950 MacArthur overrode the fears of U.S. military leaders that a landing at

Inchon would be a fiasco and scored a stunning success, then took a similar gamble in splitting his force on the march to the Yalu and caused a calamity. In hindsight most judge Hitler to be strategically foolish, Churchill brilliant, and MacArthur either one, depending on the observer's political sympathies. Do the strategies chosen warrant such differing verdicts? Or are the prevalent judgments really not about these leaders' strategic sense, but about the higher values for which they stood?

Consider Churchill more carefully, since Britain's resistance alone after the fall of France ranks among the epochal decisions of the past century. Only after the fact did it seem obvious that the British should have continued to fight after June 1940, risking invasion and occupation (or at least a draining war of attrition they could not win), rather than make peace when Hitler was willing to "partition the world" with them.[4] The gamble made sense if there were good odds that the Soviet Union or the United States would save the day, but in 1940 either eventuality was a hope, not a probability. It was hardly terrible for Foreign Secretary Lord Halifax to say, as he did on May 26, that "if we could obtain terms which did not postulate the destruction of our independence, we would be foolish if we did not accept them."[5]

The rationales in 1940 for how Britain could win rested on underestimation of the German economy, ungrounded faith in strategic bombing, and overestimation of the U.S. inclination to intervene. Nor did most British leaders believe that Hitler would attack the USSR until a few weeks before he did. Churchill's decision seems less risky if the British knew for sure that the Germans lacked the amphibious capability to invade and would lose the Battle of Britain and Battle of the Atlantic. These are many ifs and still would not offer a chance of *defeating* Germany—the only thing that would make continued combat and losses, as opposed to negotiated peace, worthwhile. Churchill's poor excuse for a victory strategy, apart from the hope of rescue by the Americans and Russians, was to peck at the periphery of *Festung Europa*, foment insurrection in the occupied countries, and pray for a coup in Berlin. As David Reynolds concludes, "in 1940 Churchill and his colleagues made the right decision—but they did so for the wrong reasons."[6] This is another way of saying, "Thank God for bad strategy."

None of this means that the British should not have made the gamble. Who can quarrel with the result? It does suggest, however, that the decision should be approved on grounds other than strategic logic. Churchill's odds were not clearly better than Hitler's. Hitler had rationales for invading the

USSR and declaring war on the United States: attacking the Soviets was preventive, since their power was increasing; the British would not come to terms as long as they held out hope for Russian assistance; the Soviet Army was less formidable than the French; American entry into the war was inevitable, but it would take at least a year for American power to be applied, by which time the war would be over and the continent secured; declaring war on the United States kept faith with treaty obligations to the Japanese and increased the chances that they would divert Soviet as well as American power. Hitler also had inadequate intelligence on the strength of Soviet forces, at the same time that the string of German victories in Poland, Norway, France, Greece, and Yugoslavia did nothing to discredit the image of Wehrmacht invincibility. Only in hindsight should those rationales seem riskier than Churchill's.[7]

Apart from the fact that Churchill's gamble against the odds paid off, few are willing to challenge it because it is obvious how crucial it was to the survival of liberalism in Europe and perhaps the world.[8] That is, the ambit for functional rationality is widened by considerations of higher rationality—the values at stake. Many feel comfortable endorsing the risk because of a visceral conviction that a value higher than life was at stake. How else to justify Churchill's chilling declaration, "If this long island story of ours is to end at last, let it end only when each one of us lies choking in his own blood upon the ground"?[9] This was grisly, absolutist, nationalist idealism.

High risk does not in itself discredit a strategy. The logic of choice depends on expected utility. If the interest at stake is great enough and the anticipated costs of failure low enough, a gamble can be sensible even if its odds of success are low. In cases we have been discussing, the interests at stake were large but the prospective costs of failure were large as well. Moreover, there is little evidence that many decision makers think in terms of specific gradations of utility or likelihood. As the subsequent discussion of cognitive processes notes, they often think categorically rather than probabilistically and see the interest at stake as close to absolute.

Can any values or interests be excluded as legitimate grounds for choice if we are considering the logic of strategy rather than judging the values themselves? If not, virtually any action can be rationalized, even suicide. Everything works for something. Once moral values like honor or ideology are allowed to trump material values of survival and prosperity, any long-shot scheme can be justified. There is always some preference function by which a choice seems valid—especially since policymakers juggle numerous values and are seldom clear about their rank order. If the strategist's logic proves faulty in selecting means appropriate to ends, the fault can usually be attributed to imperfect information. If the problem is that the ends are wrong, we are in the realm of policy and values, not strategy. As General Henry Pownall confided to his diary in 1940, Churchill was useful, but "also a real danger, always tempted by the objective, never counting his resources to see if the objective is attainable."[10]

Churchill's willingness to have the English choke in their own blood was functionally rational as long as "death before dishonor" defined the priority to be served by strategy. But this sentiment is not far from Hindenburg's comment that he preferred "an honorable end to a shameful peace," which most would see as evidence of "the mentality of a military caste that attached little importance to the nation's vital interests."[11] Only the difference in the moral background of these two invocations of honor, not the strategic logic attached to either, can account for why we endorse one and not the other.

Nor is Churchill's rationale that far from the willingness of Japan's leaders in 1941 to risk annihilation by attacking the United States. Some judge that decision to be rational even in standard terms of national security calculations, given the economic strangulation that Tokyo faced and the cabinet's hope that limited war could end in negotiated peace (which before December 7 was a possibility that American military leaders envisioned as well).[12] Others reject this interpretation, seeing Japanese culture at the time as romantically antistrategic, or decision makers as simply unthinking and unrealistic. "Japanese values appeared to decree the rejection not merely of mercantile rationality but of strategy itself," writes MacGregor Knox, who goes on to quote accordingly: "'Calculating people are contemptible . . .' ran the *Way of the Warrior*, an eighteenth-century distillation of the samurai ethic widely popular in the 1930s and 1940s; 'common sense will not accomplish great things. Simply become desperate and "crazy to die."'"[13] Churchill simply may have had better luck than Tojo.

RESPONSE 1. Issues entwined in assessing a strategic choice include chances of success, costs of failure, value of the objective, alternate strategic options, and acceptability of the consequences of not fighting. After the value of the stakes is assessed, the fundamental question is the degree of acceptable risk in operations designed to secure them. It is more reasonable to gamble against high odds in a situation where the objective is truly vital, in the strictest sense (meaning literally necessary to life), and there is no satisfactory alternative option, than it is if the interest is not absolute or another, less risky course of action might suffice. Even if real strategists rarely reason carefully in all these terms, we can use them as a basis for judgments about strategy in principle. This is a defense against the notion that in strategy anything goes. Facing the full implications, however, will leave many uneasy.

These standards, together with the principle that we must judge according to what was reasonable before the fact rather than in light of what becomes known afterward, would require condemning some successes and excusing some failures. If we reject the advance to the Yalu, we may also have to reject the magnificent assault on Inchon as well. Apart from MacArthur, military leaders opposed the landing because an overwhelming number of factors made it appear foolhardy.[14] One cannot say there was no choice. Other options offered less risk of catastrophic failure. Army Chief of Staff Lawton Collins preferred to use the seventy thousand men earmarked for Inchon to support the breakout from the Pusan perimeter or for an amphibious flanking operation closer to Pusan.[15] These alternatives implied a more costly campaign of attrition back up the peninsula. The success of the long shot at Inchon averted these costs and yielded one of the most impressive coups de main of the century. With the comfort of hindsight, one may celebrate that roll of the dice. To see it as strategic genius rather than a stroke of luck, however, or to see it as less reckless than the operations near the Yalu, requires the prop of hindsight that strategic planners do not have.

By criteria of forecasting rather than hindsight it is also unreasonable to be more critical of Churchill's promotion of the Gallipoli campaign than of his persistence in 1940. There were errors at the highest level of command in 1915, but they did not doom the campaign. The critical mistakes were operational and tactical choices—failures to adapt—by the men on the spot.[16] As to alternative options, the obstacles to success in the Dardanelles were not overwhelming, and success might have yielded a decisive shift in the fortunes of war years earlier than 1918. Do we give better marks for 1940 because the stakes were so much higher and thus deserving of absolute commitment? Yes, but because of the moral imperative behind the strategy, not the economistic standards of strategy itself.

It is hard to keep clear the distinctions between material and moral standards for strategic choice because in practice it is hard to have any but a seat-of-the-pants estimate of the odds for a strategy's success or its relative costs and benefits, or to know the counterfactual (what would happen if a different option were chosen). It is especially easy for many to endorse high-risk commitments on behalf of subjective values like national honor because it is often unclear how the implications differ from a material standard of interest. Material standards are most often identified with realist theories of international politics, but while generally better than the alternatives for diagnosing problems and constraints, realism is quite underdetermining. It prescribes objectives like security, wealth, and power but does not prescribe what strategies work best to attain them.[17] For insight into which strategies work, it is necessary to resort to hindsight.

CRITIQUE 2: Randomness Versus Prediction. *Strategy is an illusion because results do not follow plans. Complexity and contingency preclude controlling causes well enough to produce desired effects. Hindsight reveals little connection between the design and denouement of strategies. The problem before the fact appears to be estimating risk (probability of failure), but the record after the fact suggests that the real problem is pure uncertainty (insufficient basis for estimating any odds).*

To skeptics, the odds against a strategy working are very high. First, half of all strategies—the losers'—must fail by definition. Second, many strategies in the other half do not work either. Some winners win not because of their strategies, but because of their superior power; contending strategies may cancel each other's effects more easily than an imbalance of capability can be overcome by strategy. Third, some win their wars but lose the peace, or they achieve acceptable outcomes but not ones they set out to achieve through the war. Either case invalidates strategy since the purpose of strategy is to achieve stipulated aims.

Without believing in some measure of predictability, one cannot believe in strategic calculation. For strategy to have hope of working better than a shot in the dark, it must be possible to analyze patterns of military and political cause and effect, identify which instruments produce which effects in which circumstances, and apply the lessons to future choices. Unless strategists can show that a particular choice in particular circumstances is likely to produce a particular outcome, they are out of business. Disenchantment with all prediction implies the darkest view—a strategic nihilism that should make war morally indefensible for any but powers so overwhelmingly superior that they could not lose even if they tried. (There are some situations where overweening American power makes this the case.)

Historians suspicious of theory and generalization are more susceptible to skepticism about prediction and control than are social scientists. One example is Tolstoy's sweeping view that individuals cannot control events, that history is "a succession of 'accidents' whose origins and consequences are, by and large, untraceable and unpredictable."[18] Ronald Spector sees a dismal record in history:

> Rulers and politicians have a difficult time in making war or prepara-
> tion for war serve the ends of statecraft. For every case of England un-
> der Pitt or Germany under Bismarck where success is achieved through
> careful orchestration of military and political means, there are a dozen
> other cases of countries, such as Spain in the seventeenth century, Rus-
> sia in 1904, and Austria-Hungary in 1914. . . . Even more common are
> those governments who find that having fought a harrowing and costly
> war, and having strained and distorted their economies to achieve a mili-
> tary success, they are scarcely better off than before. Spain and France in
> the sixteenth century, Britain and Holland in the seventeenth century,
> France and Britain in the eighteenth century.[19]

Thoughtful strategic initiatives sometimes fail while thoughtless ones work. Richard Nixon and Henry Kissinger were consummate strategists, but the grand strategy of détente with Moscow that they carefully crafted crumbled within a few years and gave way to a reborn Cold War. Bill Clinton, Madeleine Albright, and Sandy Berger, on the other hand, were widely regarded as bunglers when they launched a limited air war against Serbia, with no strategic rationale supported by historical experience, and were enveloped in a cataclysm for which they were unprepared. Yet in the end they did achieve their primary objective. Berger was even proud of his nonstrategic cast of mind.[20]

Some strategies prove successful in the short term, only to prove counterproductive soon afterward. The United States armed and trained Afghan guerrillas against Soviet forces in the 1980s, but after the Soviets withdrew the Taliban took over and gave the country a government more oppressive and unfriendly to the West than the Marxists had been, and mujaheddin veterans like Osama bin Laden turned against the United States in acts of terrorism. The opposite sequence, losing the war but winning the peace, is also possible. In the 1970s U.S. strategy failed in Vietnam and the long bloody war that had been fought in large part to contain China was lost. Yet soon after Saigon fell, Southeast Asia was more stable than it had been for half a century and Washington was in a cordial entente with Beijing.[21]

In other cases, strategy has no certifiable impact independent of the pre-war balance of power. One of Sun Tzu's alluring differences with Clausewitz is his relative emphasis on stratagem and strategy as substitutes for mass, frontal assault, and artless attrition. But how often in modern war is the outcome more attributable to strategic wizardry than to superiority in money, men, and matériel? In combat, the side with the big battalions usually wins.[22] In the American Civil War Lincoln lost faith in ingenious strategy and won by letting grinding attrition take its toll. Generals and the public "'have got the idea in their heads that we are going to get out of this fix, somehow, by strategy!,'" Lincoln fulminated. "'That's the word—strategy! General McClellan thinks he is going to whip the rebels by strategy. . . .' Lincoln had developed a contempt for what he scornfully called 'strategy.' What he thought was needed was not more maneuvering but assault after assault on the Confederate army."[23] U.S. Grant did not shrink from that conclusion and led the Union—enjoying more than a four-to-one superiority in manpower and industrial production over the Confederacy—to victory.

Doubts about governments' capacity to cause intended effects through strategy are reinforced by "chaos theory," which emphasizes how small, untraceable events produce major changes. Weather forecasting captures this in the Butterfly Effect, the idea that a butterfly's flapping wings in Brazil can trigger a tornado in Texas.[24] Analysts typically look at war as a linear system and assume that outputs are proportional to inputs, the whole is the sum of the parts, and big questions can be solved by solving the component parts. Chaos theory, in contrast, sees war as a nonlinear system that produces "erratic behavior" through disproportionate relationships between inputs and outputs or synergies "in which the whole is not equal to the sum of the parts."[25] In reality, most systems are nonlinear, but scientists have psychologically trained themselves "not to see nonlinearity in nature."[26] Skeptics believe that a healthier appreciation of chaos reveals what Barry Watts sees as the "Laplacian" foolishness of trying to analyze war with enough mechanical precision to predict its course.[27] Robert Jervis emphasizes many other ways in which pervasive complexity and unintended consequences frustrate the purposeful use of action.[28]

To some the connection between intended and actual outcomes over time seems virtually random.[29] Experts' predictions prove scarcely better than those of amateurs. (At the outset, how many strategists would have predicted better than laypeople the length of the Korean War, the outcomes of the wars in Vietnam or Kosovo, or the number of U.S. casualties in the Persian Gulf War?) Some strategies seem to work in some cases and not others; evidence about efficacy is too mixed to command enough consensus on a verdict to qualify as proof; or there are too few comparable cases to provide lessons applicable to future choices.

To skeptics, the illusion of strategy is abetted by the tendency of observers to confuse acceptable results with intended results, and to overestimate the effect of deliberate strategy as opposed to luck. Wars considered successful may turn out in ways quite different from initial strategic expectations. War turned out better for Churchill than for Hitler not because Churchill's strategic choices were wiser, but because of events and influences that neither understood better than the other and simply turned up on the roll of the dice. In this view, military strategy is like the "random walk" theory of the stock market: despite mythology, and all the expertise and analysis brought to bear, those who pick stocks by strategy do no better on average than those who pick them randomly.[30] A few fund managers outperform the market consistently, but they present only the illusion of brilliance and control because statistically their streaks are really luck as well; when thousands of players continually spin a roulette wheel, a few of them will win a dozen times in a row. With such statistical knowledge in mind, the best investment strategy is no active strategy; rather, it is an index fund.

RESPONSE 2. Chaotic nonlinearity is common but neither absolute nor pervasive. Sometimes there can be enough method in the madness to make resort to force a means likely to achieve a given goal. If chaos theory really meant that no prediction is possible, there would be no point in any analysis of the conduct of war. Those who criticize social science approaches to strategy for false confidence in predictability cannot rest on a rejection of prediction altogether without negating all rationale for strategy. Yet critics like Watts do not reject the possibility of strategy. Any assumption that some knowledge, whether intuitive or explicitly formalized, provides guidance about what should be done is a presumption that there is reason to believe the choice will produce a satisfactory outcome—that is, it is a prediction, however rough it may be. If there is no hope of discerning and manipulating causes to produce intended effects, analysts as well as politicians and generals should all quit and go fishing.[31]

Jervis mitigates the thrust of his own argument against prediction by noting, "As Albert Hirschman has stressed, straightforward effects are common and often dominate perverse ones. If this were not the case, it would be hard to see how society, progress, or any stable human interaction could develop."[32] No model succeeds in forecasting weather two weeks ahead, but near-term forecasting can often work.[33] Some phenomena *are* linear, but predictability declines with complexity and time. So effective strategy is not impossible, but complex strategies with close tolerances are riskier than simple ones with few moving parts, and strategies that project far ahead and depend on several phases of interaction are riskier than ones with short time horizons. This limited confidence comports with the tension in Clausewitz between, on one hand, his emphasis on the prevalence of chance and unpredictability and the folly of faith in calculation in war and on the other, his stern warning of how imperative is "the need not to take the first step without considering the last."[34] Clausewitz recognized nonlinearity, but he still believed in strategy.

Attrition is comparatively simple in concept, so if simplicity is important, its status as strategy should not be brushed aside. How attrition is accomplished matters. First, the actions needed to get an inferior force to expose itself to attrition are not artless. Grant did it by initiatives such as threatening Richmond. Commanders facing agile guerrilla forces are sometimes never able to do it. Second, even when clear superiority in the balance of forces foreordains victory, efficient exploitation conserves blood and treasure.

In many wars, it is not clear before the fact that one side has superiority. Indeed, if it were, there would be fewer wars because the weaker would more often capitulate without a fight.[35] Where capabilities are nearly even, strategy provides the only alternative to stalemate. There are cases in which countries that lack clear superiority do use strategy to gain the edge; for example, Israel against the Arabs in 1967; Arabs against Israel in 1973; Britain against Argentina in 1982; North Vietnam against the United States, in 1965–75. And although northern mass did wear down the Confederacy, the South held out and actively threatened the North for several years. Had higher political and diplomatic components of southern grand strategy worked (the hope to induce war-weariness in the North and British intervention), southern military strategy would look brilliant.

The random walk analogy is limited as well. In one sense it misrepresents the nature of the problem. The evidence supporting the random walk view comes from interactions in a market price system, where sellers and buyers naturally converge toward an equilibrium. Military strategy, in contrast, seeks *dis*equilibrium, a way to defeat the enemy rather than to find a mutually acceptable price for exchange. War is more like the contest of two firms to dominate sales. One cannot invest in war, or dominate a particular market, without any strategy. For combat, in this sense, there is no counterpart to an index fund.

In a different sense, as a general view of how to cope with risk or uncertainty when strategizing, the random walk notion suggests that attrition may be the analog to an index fund. Complex strategizing is like active stock picking: it is risky, offers high potential return, but requires exceptional people—a Buffett or a Bismarck—to work. Attrition is like indexing: it works slowly but surely if the underlying trend—a rising market, or a superior military power position—is favorable. Avoiding war, in turn, is like staying out of the market: the right decision if one is not a Buffett or Bismarck, *and* the underlying trend is adverse.

## Deflecting Calculation: Psychology and Culture

The conventional Western standard of rationality is a universal economistic calculus based on conscious maximization of benefit relative to cost. Military strategy does not operate with a single currency of exchange to make goods and prices clear to all parties of a bargain. Unconscious emotions, unclear motives, and cognitive and cultural impulses to misperception prevent strategy from integrating means and ends.

Critique 3: Psychoanalysis Versus Conscious Choice. *Strategy is an illusion because leaders do not understand what motives drive them, and they delude themselves about what they are really trying to do. They use war not for manifest political purposes but for subliminal personal ones, so the link between political ends and military means is missing at the outset.*

The rational standard assumes that the strategist at least *tries* to select instruments and plans that will work toward a selected goal, that logic will drive choice. To keep the logic disciplined, assumptions of rationality apply "the criterion of consciousness," whereby "a non-logical influence is any influence acting upon the decision maker of which he is unaware and which he would not consider a legitimate influence on his decision if he were aware of it."[36] In real life, strategic decisions are awash in nonlogical influences.

The deepest of these is the individual's emotional unconscious. To psychoanalysts who emphasize mental displacement of motives, strategic analysis cannot even get off the ground in applying military means toward higher ends because political leaders deceive themselves about what their real goals are. Military grammar cannot be summoned by political logic because policymakers start from pseudo-logic. Not realizing that they are really driven by subliminal concerns of personal security, they pretend to be grappling with national security. Their emotional imperatives are psychically displaced into war, and consciously articulated national aims are but a metaphor for personal urges. From this perspective, strategy can be the opposite of economistic rationalism. Franco Fornari presents an extreme version of this argument:

> [War] serves to defend ourselves against the "Terrifier" as an internal, absolute enemy similar to a nightmare, through *a maneuver which transforms this terrifying but ultimately unaffrontable and invulnerable entity into an external, flesh-and-blood adversary who can be faced and killed.* . . . [War's] most important security function is not to defend ourselves from an external enemy, but *to find a real enemy.* . . . *outward deflection of the death instinct.* . . . war could be seen as an attempt at therapy. . . . Conflicts connected with specific historical situations reactivate the more serious conflicts which each of us has experienced in infancy, in the form of fantasies, in our affective relationships to our parents.[37]

Fornari's explanation of the origins of war verges on a caricature of Freudian interpretation, but Fornari is no fringe figure (he was president of the Italian Psychoanalytic Society and director of the Institute of Psychology at the University of Milan). Although it seems ridiculous to most political scientists, and psychoanalysis is out of favor within psychology, this sort of approach persistently resonates with intellectuals. One popular example traces the origins of war to primordial ritual sacrifices reenacting "the human transition from prey to predator"![38] Even some sober observers of military affairs take highly subjective explanations seriously. Bernard Brodie wrote respectfully of the Freudian notion of "filicide": "the reciprocal of the well-known Oedipus complex . . . the unconscious hatred of the father for the son. . . . And what better way . . . of finding expression for filicide than by sending the youth out to die in a war?"[39] John Keegan embraced anthropological interpretations of primitive war as ritual, the continuation of sport by other means, or symbolic activity rather than a political phenomenon.[40] If war serves latent psychic functions rather than manifest policy, strategic rationalizations must be phony.

Psychoanalytical interpretations support the critical view of Churchill's strategic thinking. Storr diagnoses Churchill as clinically depressed during much of his public life, an "extraverted intuitive," a "cyclothmic temperament" with extreme mood swings, suffering from compensatory aggressiveness and a compulsive sense of mission due to being deprived of love in childhood. "Although he had brilliant ideas, he was hardly susceptible to reason and could not follow a consecutive argument when presented to him by others. . . . He was never good at looking at all the implications of any course he favoured."[41] After the fall of France he could hope that something would turn up to let England prevail, but there was no solid reason to bet the country's life on such hope. Churchill did so, in Storr's view, because of an irrational optimistic streak:

> When all the odds were against Britain, a leader of sober judgment might well have concluded that we were finished. . . . in 1940, [Churchill's] inner world of make-believe coincided with the facts of external reality in a way which very rarely happens to any man. . . . In that dark time, what England needed was not a shrewd, equable, balanced leader. She needed a prophet. . . . his inspirational quality owed its dynamic force to the romantic world of phantasy in which he had his true being. . . . England owed her survival in 1940 to . . . an irrational conviction independent of factual reality.[42]

RESPONSE 3. Much in this critique is simply wrong because of naïve psychologism—a common but erroneous assumption that politics is nothing more than individual impulses writ large.[43] Because strategy is made by humans, psychology cannot help but affect it. It is hard to know, however, whether it does so in ways more often deranging than constructive because it is difficult to pin down evidence of the independent effect of subjective factors on decisions or actions.

There is also confusion of psychological expertise and political opinion in many diagnoses. Much psychological literature on war betrays a bias about policy that depreciates the significance of conflict of interest in international relations.[44] (In a 1932 letter to Einstein, Freud admitted the pacifist bias in his own thinking.)[45] The resilience of psychoanalytic interpretations reflects more than anything the premise that war itself must be irrational, so strategy must be rationalization. Few analysts can bring themselves to differentiate what *they* consider foolish political stances from irrationality, or correct political views from psychic health and logical calculation. Consider John Foster Dulles. Was he the rigid, ideologically blinded, obtuse Calvinist moralist portrayed by Townsend Hoopes, or, as Michael Guhin argued with comparably respectable evidence, a flexible, crafty realist who only pretended to be unsubtle and who posed U.S. policy in deliberately simplified terms precisely because he feared subtlety could cause misperception in Moscow and Beijing?[46] Either diagnosis would be more persuasive if it did not happen to coincide with the biographer's partisan identity (Hoopes being a Democrat, Guhin a Republican). How easy is it to know when we see evidence of psychology rather than ideology?

Keegan's dismissal of Clausewitzian rationality falls of its own weight. It simply confuses what politics, the proper driver of strategy, is. Consider his astounding statements that "Politics played no part in the conduct of the First World War worth mentioning," or that Balkan wars "are apolitical."[47] Keegan is a respectable historian of military operations but a naïf about politics, so he cannot render a verdict on the strategy that connects them.

CRITIQUE 4: Cognition Versus Complex Choice. *Cognitive constraints on individual thought processes limit strategists' ability to see linkages between means and ends, or to calculate comprehensively.*

Psychoanalytic psychology suggests that leaders do not know what urges really drive their choices. Cognitive psychology suggests that even if they do, conscious calculation can be nonrational. Even if aims are not displaced within the mind, strategic selection of appropriate means is still deformed by the physiology of perception. Normal mental functions cause false rationalization because the mind imposes consistency on observations in order to maintain the stability of existing belief structures. The mind resists facing trade-offs among conflicting values by convincing itself that the values really go together. (In this view, even detached analysts observing irrational decision processes convince themselves that they are not.)[48] Cognitive biases also predispose strategists to see their adversaries' behavior as "more centralized, disciplined, and coordinated than it is," and to assume that their own benign intentions are obvious to the adversary.[49]

Whereas the rational model of calculation implies that "complexity should breed indecisiveness," cognitive mechanisms allow confidence by filtering complexity out of perception. Whereas the rational model handles unknowns by probabilistic inference, cognitive processes respond to uncertainty with firm, categorical, either-or beliefs. Thus the Hitlers, Churchills, and MacArthurs do not explicitly estimate odds but simply forge ahead with confidence once they have decided what should be done. The refraction of observed information through cognitive biases allows it to be seen as consistent with expectations even when it is not.[50] In short, strategists tend to see what they expect to see.

RESPONSE 4. Cognitive theory runs into problems outside of laboratory experiments. As with other psychological explanations, it proves hard to distinguish cognitive pathologies from differences of political opinion. Whereas psychoanalyst critics may confuse their professional diagnosis with their political prejudices, cognitive critics may confuse the psychological diagnosis with their empirical analysis of strategic logic. Analysts who attribute errors in calculation to misperception necessarily use a standard of objectivity against which to measure the deviation. In politics, however, it is seldom possible to differentiate such a standard from what analysts themselves consider to be the real logic of value tradeoffs, and these are matters of opinion too.

For example, one cognitive theorist illustrates his models with a case study of policy on nuclear sharing in NATO, arguing that the strategy promulgated ignored the contradiction between the values of alliance solidarity and deterrence. This assumes, as Robert McNamara did, that deterrence required centralizing control of nuclear release in the hands of the American president, but this assumption was not universally shared. The civilian leadership of the Defense Department at the time was promoting a doctrine of graduated escalation, which theoretically required carefully orchestrated control of nuclear strikes, rather than independent capabilities to launch nuclear forces. That doctrinal ambition of a coterie of theorists was never fully accepted within the American government, less so by the alliance, and was soon even rejected by McNamara himself. Many others believed that diffusing the option to initiate escalation would be more logical for deterrence since it coped with the danger that a rational Washington would renege on the commitment to escalate and thus raised the credibility of the principle that escalation would still occur if a Soviet attack on Western Europe succeeded at the conventional level of combat. Were proposals on nuclear sharing evidence of cognitive distortion in handling a "two-value problem"? Or normal political compromises in a situation where interests and beliefs diverge? Or the least irrational strategic choices available for a problem that had no good rational solution? The real two-value problem was the combined U.S. and West European interest in deterrence as an end, and their divergent interests in using conventional, tactical nuclear, and intercontinental nuclear forces as means—divergence imposed by the geography that protected the United States but not the Europeans from the ravages of conventional or tactical nuclear war.[51]

That case study does not necessarily validate a diagnosis of psychological dysfunction in policymaking more than it reflects the author's own strategic judgment. If a policymaker resists the logic and supporting evidence of the argument that forms the analyst's standard of rational strategy, is she evincing cognitive dissonance, or is the analyst suffering from hubris about his own logic? What should give analysts confidence that they can assess value tradeoffs more objectively than the officials whose cognitive facility they are judging? As Verba says, "when faced with a decision made by an individual or group as highly trained and sophisticated as he is, the outside observer is probably no more able to judge whether the resulting decision meets the criteria of rationality than are the actual decision makers. Their frailty is his frailty too."[52]

CRITIQUE 5: Culture Versus Coercion. *Coercive strategies aimed at an adversary's will depend on communication. Cultural blinders prevent the common frames of reference necessary to ensure that the receiver hears the message that the signaler intends to send.*

Even if psychology does not prevent leaders from understanding themselves, the collective personality traits of a culture may prevent them from understanding their adversaries. Strategic calculations can be logical within their own cultural context but founder on the difference in the opponent's mind-set. Thus even if both parties are rational in their own terms, strategic interaction becomes a dialogue of the deaf.

Soon after U.S. bombing of North Vietnam began in 1965, Schelling discussed its logic in terms of effects not on North Vietnamese capability but on Chinese perceptions: "America's reputation around the world . . . for resolve and initiative, was at stake. . . . the military action was an expressive bit of repartee. The text of President Johnson's address was not nearly as precise and explicit as the selection of targets and timing of attack."[53]

Schelling said nothing about whether or why the Chinese should assess the signals the way he did. The foundation of his thinking on strategy was that "the assumption of rational behavior is a productive one" because "it permits us to identify our own analytical processes with those of the hypothetical participants in a conflict."[54] Since then research by a bicultural scholar has shown how American and Chinese statesmen utterly misread each others' aims, calculations, and tactics in Cold War confrontations because of societal differences in values and axioms. The American concept of crisis saw it only as a danger, which led to methods of crisis management aimed only at resolving crises rather than exploiting them, while the Chinese concept emphasized that crises are also opportunities; U.S. officials considered "military killing capacity as the key to deterrence," while the Chinese emphasized the masses who operate the weapons, and social cohesion rather than weapons themselves; and American leaders saw the prospect of human casualties as inherently negative, while the Chinese saw the sacrifice of lives as a necessary price for progress and evidence that political gains were being achieved.[55]

RESPONSE 5. This critique effectively indicts sophisticated signaling strategies meant to induce compliance without forcing it. The response does not contest that indictment. The argument against subtle signaling, however, does not necessarily negate strategies aimed at destroying enemy capabilities to resist. Nor does it preclude all effective signaling between adversaries. Many messages can be transmitted and understood across cultures if they are stark rather than subtle—for example, "Surrender or die."

Culture, like psychology, can matter in strategy without discrediting it. Johnston defines strategic culture as "historically imposed inertia on choice that makes strategy less responsive to specific contingencies."[56] This represents an impediment to efficiency, not a denial of efficacy.

## DEFLECTING IMPLEMENTATION: ORGANIZATION, FRICTION, AND GOAL DISPLACEMENT

The previous three critiques are about how individuals misunderstand what is at issue in a war—what their own or their adversaries' objectives are—and thus cannot choose strategies that optimize their aims. The three critiques in this section are about barriers to applying means effectively even when policymakers are clear about what is at issue. Critique 6 concerns constraints on coercive communication imposed by technical problems in coordinating decisions and implementation. These problems can block timely orchestration of signals even if the executing organizations are faithfully attuned to higher strategy. Critique 7 concerns constraints that emerge from preoccupations and professional interests within those organizations. Critique 8 adds to the mix the effects of feedback from war, the interactive dimension of strategy after plans are put in motion and the adversary counters them.

The critiques in this vein complement critique 5 to argue against subtlety or sophistication in strategy, making game-theoretic schemes designed to influence an opponent seem inevitably too clever. In this view, because subordinate organizations prove unable or unwilling to do what strategists at the top direct, and schemes for affecting the adversary's calculations go awry because the variables in play are more complex than those in the strategists' model, the only strategies that work are unsubtle and blunt ones that conform to the traditional military KISS principle (Keep It Simple, Stupid). But while simplicity may increase the controllability of a strategy's execution, simple strategies will be no more effective in achieving an objective if the objective or the target is not simple.

CRITIQUE 6: Friction Versus Fine-Tuning. *Even if cultural blinders do not foreordain a dialogue of the deaf when coercive signals are sent, normal operational friction delays execution of plans and decouples signals from the events to which they are meant to respond. Strategy that depends on coupling then collapses.*

Consider again the bombing of North Vietnam. Even if different mindsets would not have prevented mutual understanding, limitations of organizational agility did. Actual as opposed to intended coupling of events in the theater made U.S. policy seem more provocative than political leaders meant it to be at some times, and more timid than intended at others. In the 1964 Tonkin Gulf crisis the patrol in which the U.S. destroyer *Maddox* was attacked while collecting electronic intelligence coincided by happenstance with an attack on two North Vietnamese villages by Laotian aircraft and covert paramilitary operations against North Vietnamese territory in the vicinity of the *Maddox*; when there was a strategic interest in *not* having the North Vietnamese believe these actions were coordinated, they probably believed they were.[57] Later in the year, in contrast, intended links were obscured. Washington warned Hanoi against provocation but then did not respond to an attack on Bien Hoa airbase (indeed, the B-57 aircraft that had made Bien Hoa a target were withdrawn) and after that did not retaliate for the bombing of the Brink officer quarters.

Meanwhile, interagency contingency planning in 1964 pitted the Joint Chiefs of Staff and air force against the State Department and the Pentagon's Office of International Security Affairs. The military favored a quick and massive bombing campaign (the 94 Target Plan) aimed at capitalizing on simultaneity to smash North Vietnamese capabilities. The civilians favored a "slow squeeze" approach that sounded as if it was plagiarized from an early draft of *Arms and Influence*. Abstemious bombing was to signal U.S. resolve, remind the North Vietnamese of what they had left to lose from further attacks, and induce them to desist and negotiate. Bombing began in February 1965 with the FLAMING DART raids, conceived as tit-for-tat reprisals for communist attacks in South Vietnam.[58]

Careful correlation of events in Hanoi, Washington, and South Vietnam demonstrates how the rationale for FLAMING DART was negated by its implementation. Timing problems, prior context, and technical complications in the theater made it impossible to convey the message that U.S. policymakers had in mind. If any message was read in Hanoi, it was probably the opposite of what was intended by Washington. When threatened retaliation did occur after the February 1965 raid on Pleiku, it was weak: "the mildest attack option (three targets) was selected, but bad weather forced many sorties to abort, with the result that only one target . . . was struck in force." Later U.S. strikes in the FLAMING DART raids were not coordinated with the provocations to which policymakers in Washington meant to respond, thus vitiating the intended signal. "In situations in which members of the target state's government have been arguing that the coercer will not intervene in strength, a coercive strategy based upon 'graduated pressures' may serve only to 'convince' the opponent that low-level pressures are all that will be attempted."[59] Thies's reconstruction of the sequence of events discredits elaborate signaling strategies by showing that "there may be significant discrepancies both between the actions intended by senior officials on Side A and the actions undertaken by A and between the message intended for transmission to B by A's leaders and the message read into A's actions by senior officials on Side B."[60]

RESPONSE 6. There is no good response to this critique. Cultural and operational complications simply compound each other in raising the odds against tacit bargaining through symbolic combat. One might conclude simply that policymakers chose the wrong strategy. There is no reason to believe, however, that the Air Force's preferred 94 Target Plan, aimed at capabilities rather than will, would have fared better in inducing North Vietnam to stop supporting the ground war in the South. Heavy bombing in the 1972 LINEBACKER campaigns, often credited with making Hanoi accept the Paris Peace Accords, did not do that either; those accords permitted the North Vietnamese Army to remain in South Vietnam.

CRITIQUE 7: Goal Displacement Versus Policy Control. *Organizational processes deflect attention from policymakers' priorities to implementing organizations' habits of operation and institutional interests. Means may be applied effectively toward goals, but to instrumental goals of the operators rather than the higher political objectives meant to govern strategy.*

Critique 6 showed why organizations trying to implement strategy may fail because of problems in the operating environment (such as weather delays). Professional guilds also have inbuilt tendencies to resist direction from political leaders, and thus in effect not even to try to implement chosen strategies. Cybernetic and organizational process models liken behavior to working according to a recipe. Military organizations operate from a limited repertoire, in a prescribed sequence of previously rehearsed actions, and monitor only a few reactions. In contrast to the rationalist model, which assumes that actors face constraints but try within them to optimize results with explicit calculations, cybernetic and organizational theories presume that decision processes simplify the problem to make it amenable to the repertoire and avoid dealing with unfamiliar aspects on their merits. Organizations become oriented not to the larger political aims they are enlisted to pursue, but to their own stability. Instead of engaging in comprehensive search, weighing of alternatives, and analytical selection, they pay attention to a few variables and shunt most incoming information aside.[61]

The chronic result is goal displacement: "Rules originally devised to achieve organizational goals assume a positive value that is independent of the organizational goals."[62] Organizations shift attention from original missions to internal methods and instruments developed as means to pursue those missions. The means become the organization's ends, even when they cease to be consistent with the larger purposes of the political leadership.[63] Individual military services, which normally provide components for a trans-service combined arms strategy, tend to identify their own instruments and priorities with strategy as a whole and identify whatever military task they can accomplish as the achievement of strategic goals.

Elements of the military may in effect subvert overall military strategy in order to maximize their parochial priorities. For example, in the 1991 Persian Gulf War the allocation of airpower assets was centralized in the daily Air Tasking Order (ATO) of the Joint Force Air Component Commander (JFACC), Air Force General Horner. The ATO allocated air force, navy, and marine corps aircraft to various missions in accord with an overall strategic plan. This created tensions between JFACC and the service components, who worried about covering targets of special concern to their forces. "Some Marines would later say that their planners 'gamed' the ATO by overbooking it with sorties to give them flexibility."[64] The effect of overbooking would be to reduce resources available for higher strategic purposes in order to increase them for lower tactical purposes.

Civilian strategists may take a nonpartisan approach to integrating service priorities for a combined strategy, but very few know enough about operations and logistics to be as informed about the underpinnings of strategy as military professionals. When civilians override service objections, they risk promoting strategies that prove tactically insupportable. If not thus made militarily unrealistic, national strategy remains hobbled by organizational parochialism, inflexibility, and incremental change. Leaders can disturb organizational behavior but can rarely control it.[65]

The ground war in Vietnam illustrates the problem. U.S. Army operations were never as encumbered with civilian tinkering for purposes of diplomatic signaling as were air force and navy air operations. In the view popular within the postwar U.S. Army, however, strategy failed because ground forces concentrated on the wrong operations—counterinsurgency—rather than conventional warfare against North Vietnamese regular units.[66] The more convincing argument is the reverse: strategy was *too* conventional, as the army was allowed to indulge institutionally preferred operational concepts designed for its primary mission in Europe. This approach unleashed punishing firepower against the very South Vietnamese population whose loyalty was what was mainly at stake in the war.[67] One result: strategic judo. Meanwhile, the operational standard of advantageous attrition ratios substituted for strategy, despite the fact that communist Vietnamese demography allowed them to keep replacing losses and stay in the field, while the asymmetry of interests ensured that they would be willing to keep bleeding longer than the United States would.

RESPONSE 7. Cognitive, cybernetic, and organizational barriers to rational plans imply that wise strategists should limit their choices to options provided by predictable standard operating procedures (SOPs). This would let the tail wag the dog. Such extreme conclusions are unnecessary, however, where the strategy's subtlety and inbuilt potential for faulty implementation and misperception are less extreme than in the air war against North Vietnam, or where the obstacles to success of *any* plausible strategy are lower than in the ground war in South Vietnam.

Organization theory points in more than one direction. Bureaucracies are not always as irresponsible as implied by literature that assumes "institutions to be dumber than their members"; indeed, they can be smarter. Even a rational individual free of cognitive blinders can focus on only one thing at a time, while organizations can multiply centers of attention, focus on numerous parts of a problem at once, and alleviate the limitations on information processing that cognitive theory cites as blocking rationality in a single mind.[68] Division of labor fosters deeper expertise. Critics worry about parochialism, but compared with high-level decision makers who discipline them, experts can rely "less on ordinary folk heuristics, with their attendant biases, and more on scientifically based inferences, with their lower rates of error."[69]

This more positive Weberian view of bureaucracy as a rationalizing force is consistent with the erosion of data that used to be cited from the Cuban Missile Crisis to support the more negative view. Several of the examples that originally illustrated the antistrategic impact of organizational processes have not held up. Subsequent research does not support suggestions in the first edition of the classic work on the subject that: the navy disobeyed orders to tighten the blockade line and delay interception of Soviet ships; aggressive antisubmarine warfare was undertaken without the knowledge of the secretary of defense; the Tactical Air Command deceived the president in arguing that a "surgical" air strike was infeasible; or the bureaucracy failed to implement an earlier presidential order to get U.S. missiles removed from Turkey.[70] (These points, however, do not mean that SOPs produced no dangerous events in the crisis—other chilling examples have turned up.)[71]

Trying to make strategy realistic by gearing it to predictable SOPs that limit organizational actions in cybernetic fashion could be as wrongheaded as assuming frictionless implementation of subtle schemes. The internal logic of Allison's organizational model does not lend itself to predicting military interactions because chaos theory demonstrates how a handful of simple rules can yield a pattern of behavior "so complex as to appear ran-dom, even though the rule itself is completely deterministic." Allison likens the constraints on leaders' choice of options to working within the limited rules of a chess game, but "chess is a paradigmatic example of a choice situ-ation that involves only a handful of basic rules yet exhibits truly Byzantine strategic complexity. . . . when we compare chess to the strategic maneuver-ings of two real military forces . . . the odds are that chess is *simpler*."[72]

Another limitation of cybernetic and organization theory is that they help to explain continuity, but not innovation. Yet strategic innovations do occur. They may happen despite the conservatism of professional organiza-tions, in which case the organizations' constraining effect is not determina-tive, or they may happen because organizations are more adaptable than the negative strands of organization theory imply.[73]

Organizational goal displacement or concentration on the wrong strat-egy are not the main reasons that the United States lost in Vietnam. Neither the Summers nor the Krepinevich view provides enough of the answer. Al-though Krepinevich is right about army goal displacement, conventional operations ultimately did determine the end of the war (in 1975, as Sum-mers noted, "it was four North Vietnamese Army corps, not 'dialectical materialism,' that ultimately conquered South Vietnam"),[74] and much ef-fort *was* invested in counterinsurgency along the way. The United States pushed *both* strategies (and not entirely at cross purposes), but both were not enough to win. A string of American tactical victories failed to serve policy because Saigon could not survive the withdrawal of American force, even after seven years of devastating U.S. combat against its enemy. U.S. strategies never came to terms with the inability of the South Vietnamese political leadership to overcome the fundamental asymmetry in the war. The center of gravity throughout was the political loyalty of the Vietnamese population—in the country as a whole, *both* South and North. This contest was always uneven, fought only within half of the country, South Vietnam. The North was pounded by bombs, but not by political competition. If the Saigon government had been able to match Hanoi in mobilizing and con-trolling population, the ocean of material resources supplied by the United States would have carried the day in the conventional war, Saigon would have been no more dependent on allies to provide combat troops than Ha-noi and the Viet Cong were, and Hanoi would have been as vulnerable to anticommunist insurgency within North Vietnam as the Saigon govern-ment's control of its villages was to the Viet Cong.

The asymmetry of social mobilization and political control capacity within Vietnam as a whole was the crucial factor. The Thieu government did not capitalize on the tremendous destruction of communist forces after the 1968 Tet Offensive by creating its own disciplined political organization in the countryside, never eliminated the communist infrastructure in the South, and never mounted any comparable challenge to the rear security of the Hanoi regime. Summers denies that the war was a civil war, thus doing what his idol Clausewitz warns against: losing sight of what the war was about—which Vietnamese political group would govern South Vietnam. Summers focuses on the disjunction between politics and strategy in *American* policy—the failure of President Johnson to mobilize the public for a real war—but not on the political essence of the war in the country about which it was fought. The main problem was not that U.S. strategy was too conventional or not conventional enough, but that no U.S. effort could make up for the asymmetry in political motivation, mobilization, and organization between the Vietnamese communists and noncommunists. That difference meant that the war could not be won by any primarily *American* strategy at an acceptable price. Sensible strategies are available for some problems but not all.

CRITIQUE 8: War Versus Strategy. *Strategy is an illusion because practice reverses theory. In theory, strategy shapes the course of war to suit policy. In actual war, the target resists strategy and counters it, confounding plans, and redirecting strategy and policy to suit the unanticipated requirements for operational success. This puts the cart before the horse and negates the rational basis for strategy.*

A proper sequence for relating means to ends is commonly assumed: first, political objectives are determined; second, the optimal military strategy for achieving the objectives is deduced; third, the forces and operating doctrines necessary to implement the strategy are fielded. But war rarely unfolds according to expectations because the target of strategy—which has as much ingenuity as those applying the strategy—finds ways to frustrate it and forces revisions that ramify upward to alter policy itself. Policy is not a tyrant and "must adapt itself to its chosen means . . . yet the political aim remains the first consideration."[75] If the strategist does not keep control throughout, however, the second half of that point is lost—means take on life of their own and change initial objectives. To paraphrase Clausewitz, the *purpose* of war is to serve policy, but the *nature* of war is to serve itself.[76]

In the absence of great wisdom and firmness at the top, military grammar overwhelms political logic. Russell Weigley concludes darkly that "War in the twentieth century is no longer the extension of politics," and war works "not as the servant but as the master of politics."[77]

In the professional military establishments entrusted to execute strategy, many officers claim to crave policy guidance yet prove utterly hostile to it when it is serious enough to impinge on operational autonomy.[78] Military professionals often accept the primacy of political objectives in principle and then cast it aside in practice, with Moltke's rationale that politics reigns *until* war but not *during* it, when military necessity takes over.[79] The operational imperative becomes the driver, strategy the rider.[80] Then there is nothing to prevent operational genius from serving strategic stupidity, as "the understanding of war is displaced by the competitive management of military action."[81]

The premier example is Germany after Bismarck. The Schlieffen Plan designed an operational success that required unprovoked attack on Belgium, which in turn helped bring Britain into the war. To deal with Britain the Germans launched unrestricted submarine warfare, which further expanded the coalition against them by bringing in the United States. To cope with declining prospects on the battlefield, Ludendorff and Hindenburg introduced tactical reforms that required high social mobilization, which in turn spurred the escalation of war aims. Strategy came to shape politics, and strategy "no longer calculated instrumentally, but sought to inspire and direct people in an unlimited war effort. . . . Escalatory strategy thrived on ideology rather than on instrumental rationality. . . . mobilization of means began to determine the goals of the war."[82]

In the interwar period a realistic General Beck was isolated by younger officers. "He complained that they had never learned to evaluate operations within the context of a coherent strategy. . . . They were technocrats rather than strategists." The blitzkrieg doctrine that emerged produced stunning tactical success—and strategic success as well until the invasion of the Soviet Union—but "the very means of achieving victory rendered German military and political leaders unable to gauge the limits of success," and increasing conquests again increased the countering coalition. "Every operational success, for military commanders rewarding and a goal in itself, raised the odds for the strategist."[83]

Strategy may also be revised not because it fails in the face of resistance, but because it works too easily. In early 1942 the Japanese succumbed to "victory disease" and undertook more ambitious conquests in the Pacific that overextended them and made it easier for the Americans to strike back.[84] Thus either failure or success may derange strategy.

RESPONSE 8. The ideal sequence of policy, strategy, and operations is not sacrosanct. Rather, it should be conceived not as a sequence but as an organic interrelationship. There are many good reasons for feedback from the lower levels to adjust the higher ones, most notably the simple fact that means are more unwieldy than ends. Lead times for change in military capabilities are long, while political objectives can change quickly. Most modern wars can only be fought with forces of size and type decided years in advance, when economic, political, and technological expectations may have been very different. Strategy or even policy then have to adjust to mediate the difference between capability and objective.[85]

Nor is goal displacement, the tyranny of means, all that disrupts strategy. Letting policy be the tyrant may have the same effect. Because strategy *mediates* between ends and means, obsessive concentration on either one without constraint by the other can prevent rational integration of the two. Means should be subordinate to ends, but rational strategy requires that ends that cannot be achieved by available means must be changed. This is when the strategically responsible military experts must insist not, "Let us do it our way," but instead, "We can't get there from here."

That the German military substituted operational excellence for strategy was only half of their problem. The other half was the political objective that force was called on to serve. Hitler was utterly clear in his own mind about the linkage of means and ends. Everything he did was focused on making Germany the dominant power in Europe and conquering territory for *lebensraum* in the East. It was the unlimited, millennialist quality of Nazi ideology that did itself in. It led Hitler to take high risks, and its Social Darwinist logic led him to sacrifice his country. "For someone with such a mentality, strategy was a concept from a bygone age."[86]

## DEMOCRACY VERSUS STRATEGY: POLITICS, COMPROMISE, AND EFFECTIVENESS

Although there is no consistent evidence that autocracies do better, many skeptics believe that democratic pluralism—in either the body politic or the competition of organizational interests within government—fosters incoherence in strategy. The essential logic of democracy is compromise, but compromise often undermines strategic logic.

CRITIQUE 9: Democracy Versus Consistency. *The logic of strategy depends on clarity of preferences, explicitness of calculation, and consistency of choice. Democratic competition and consensus building work against all of these.*

Rational strategic calculation implies that if values conflict, they are ranked, and ones of greater importance take precedence. For governments, especially democracies, this is an unnatural act. Governments are groups, not individual calculators. As two rational-choice theorists argue, "individuals are rational, but a group is not, since it may not even have transitively ordered preferences."[87] Democracies serve disparate constituencies with competing objectives. Decisions to rank values are not only hard to make, but politically dysfunctional if they are made. The model of rationality that dominates theory about strategy assumes the maximization of economic gain, but in politics the issue is "maximization of any and all values held by the individual or the group." The more rigorously straightforward a proposal is in terms of means-ends rationality, the less likely it is to be accepted in policy because it will provoke "opposition among members of the foreign policy coalition whose value preferences are different."[88] In particular, signaling strategies based on models of individual rationality and interpersonal relations founder on the collective character of politics. Governments attempting coercion speak "with many voices at once." In the target government, officials who have to decide to concede to the enemy may destroy their careers, something not captured in "dispassionate references to 'affecting the enemy's will.'"[89]

To some critics this pluralism is what blocks rationality, and what must be overcome by forceful political leadership. The crucial problem is not figuring out external military strategy against the country's adversaries, but internal political strategy to control fractious groups with their own agendas and special interests. "What percentage of the work of achieving a desired governmental action is done when the preferred analytic alternative has been identified?" Graham Allison once asked. He answered, "my estimate is about 10 percent in the normal case."[90] Thinking up the right national security strategy is comparatively easy, but making it come out at the other end of government is awesomely hard. By the standard of coherent, consistent, individualistic value-maximization enshrined in the ideal type of strategic rationality, political pluralism is pathological.

RESPONSE 9. One may accept that decentralization, separation of powers, and checks and balances make democracy constitutionally antistrategic. But one may also assume that the procedural norms of constitutional democracy are, at least for the United States, the highest national security value, ranking above particular substantive values that come and go in policy. In that case it is possible to hold out a different standard of collective rationality by which muddled decisions and strategies meet the test. This standard assumes that the pulling and hauling that some bureaucratic politics literature sees as dysfunctional for rational strategy are a wise constraint on the naïve arrogance of anyone who presumes to know what is good for everyone; a little incoherence is a good thing. Exemplars of this view of bureaucratic politics, in contrast to the negative view of Neustadt, Allison, and Halperin, would be Charles Lindblom and Samuel Huntington.

To Lindblom, an attempt to impose the ideal type of rational strategy on a complex political system is wrongheaded in practice because it will not work and in principle because it risks big mistakes. In public policy, means and ends are too complex for values to be ranked consistently, or for the relations between choices and outcomes to be predicted accurately. Limited search, blurring of distinctions between means and ends, and incremental change are desirable because they are safer, more manageable, and more effective. If they yield policy that is suboptimal for all particular substantive values and interest groups, that is still the best way to match ends and means if the alternative is not efficient application of means to one end, but large mistakes due to the impossibility of comprehensive calculation.[91] In this sense strategy is a metaprocess that links ends and means effectively but not efficiently. Huntington supports this view when he discusses "executive legislation" of strategy: "the major problem is not to discover rationally what is required to bring forth the 'desired result' but rather to reconcile conflicting views of what results are desirable."[92]

This political logic can also be summoned to depreciate the danger of organizational goal displacement. Competing organizational interests may compensate for each other's mistakes. For example, critique 7 presented the marines' gaming of the ATO in the 1991 war against Iraq as subverting higher-level air strategy. For those who lacked faith in the strategic wisdom of the air force—which controlled the ATO—subverting that strategy was the right thing to do. The ground forces believed that the ATO was shortchanging the targets they needed to be attacked in preparation for the ground war. (Two weeks into the air war, only 17 percent of the targets nominated by the army had been included in the ATO, and only 12 percent struck.) When the marines stopped cooperating with the air force planners, they were supporting a sensible ground strategy.[93]

CRITIQUE 10: Compromise Versus Effectiveness. *Compromise between opposing preferences is the key to success in politics but to failure in military strategy. Since political leaders have the last word on strategy in a democracy, they tend to resolve political debates about whether to use force massively or not at all by choosing strategic half-measures that turn out to serve no good objectives at all.*

In the optimistic view, pluralist political competition produces equilibrium as the marketplace of ideas winnows out bad calculations and weak strategies. Consensus is forged by satisficing, combining second-choice strategies that produce a "good enough" result—ideal for none but acceptable to all. The underside of pluralism, however, is that when applied to grappling with an external adversary it can produce compromise that vitiates the logic of both opposed alternatives, leaving a military action that is less costly than the more ambitious option, but still quite costly, yet not costly enough to buy peace. This is the kind of compromise that kills for no good purpose—the worst consequence of jumping halfway across Clausewitz's ditch.

Vietnam exemplified Lindblom's logic and the bad form of compromise. Half-measures and incrementalism avoided defeat for many years at the price of ultimate disaster. Later examples were interventions by the United States in Beirut in 1983, and by the United Nations in Bosnia until mid-1995 (this holds in abeyance how NATO strategy in Bosnia should be judged after the Dayton Accords). In both cases the main problem was unsettled objectives and deep confusion about how military means could help. Compromise was the middle ground between doing nothing and doing something effective. In Beirut, marines were deployed to signal U.S. involvement, but not to impose control in the city. Their mission became just to be there and draw fire. After taking hundreds of casualties the marines were withdrawn, having achieved no worthwhile strategic objective, and leaving terrorists heartened by what they saw as a victory over a superpower. In Bosnia in the early 1990s the UN mandated itself to defend Bosnia's sovereignty but would not ally itself with the Bosnian government and engage its enemy in combat. UN troops on the ground then became part of the problem instead of the solution, as their vulnerability made them hostages and inhibited military action against the Serbs. In 1995 diplomatic compromises led the UN to declare "safe areas" without the intent to defend them, only with the hope that rhetoric and symbolic presence would deter Serb attacks. Then as a Dutch UN contingent exercising presence stood by, Serb forces overran the phony safe area of Srebrenica and committed mass murder.

In both Beirut and Bosnia, military forces were committed because of a conviction that it was necessary to "do something," but without a sensible strategic notion of how, or of what costs were acceptable. The argument that either doing nothing or doing much more would be a lesser evil than doing something in between did not register. These cases resembled the logic of compromise in the apocryphal decision in Ruritania to switch from driving on the left side of the road to the right. Fearful of too radical a change overnight, the transportation minister decreed that it would be done gradually: trucks would switch to driving on the right in the first week, and cars would switch over the following week. When politicians feel compelled to do something without being willing to do anything decisive, strategy goes out the window. Policymakers overlook the gap between moral imperatives and material action, confuse the difference between objectives and strategy, and take military half-measures that yield costs without benefits.

RESPONSE 10. A different kind of compromise can be strategically functional. An example of what works is the strategy of the grand alliance in World War II. Western strategy proved a great success even though it emerged from compromises that left many less than fully pleased and was later roundly criticized from both the right and the left.[94] Moreover, with the exception of the invasion of North Africa, political considerations almost always gave way to military expediency. At first glance this seems anti-Clausewitzian, but it actually represented "the height of political wisdom." This was because the one objective that would not shatter the solidarity of Washington, London, and Moscow was the total defeat of the enemy; it was "the only ground on which a coalition with disparate political interests could be held together."[95]

The compromises in World War II worked as strategy because they were mainly about where and when offensive campaigns would occur, not about how much of an effort to make or the ultimate objective of unconditional surrender. In the later U.S. wars over Korea, Kuwait, and Kosovo, the scale of effort was limited, but still sufficient to achieve primary objectives, which were also limited. One may criticize the policy, and doubt whether the main objectives were worth the price, or argue that they should have been more ambitious, but those objectives were achieved—the criterion for success of strategy. It is also not inevitable that success defeats itself by generating victory disease. The Bush administration resisted this temptation in 1991, settling for a stunning partial victory that liberated Kuwait at low cost but did not move on to Baghdad.

If there is virtue in the benign notion of pluralist rationality and the wisdom of compromise in strategy, it depends on clear delineation of which type of compromise is at issue. Compromise is more likely to work where objectives are relative or continuous and can be achieved partially—where if you end up only half as far as you wanted to get you are still ahead of the game. Compromise is likely to spend lives for no good purpose where the stakes are absolute or dichotomous, matters of all or nothing—where getting halfway to the goal is no better than getting nowhere—as in jumping halfway across Clausewitz's ditch. For example, control of territory is a relative objective (borders can be pushed incrementally in one direction or another by conventional military action), while control of a regime is more often absolute (one party in a civil war gets to constitute the government throughout the country).

Strategy that follows from compromise of the ends may also be more often likely to work than one that compromises the means. Reducing an objective raises the odds that a constrained effort can achieve it. Reducing the means used to pursue an uncompromised objective raises the risk of failing to achieve it at all; that sort of compromise drops strategy between the stools of inaction and effectiveness. Compromising the ends sets sights lower; compromising the means fires short. Too often the drawbacks of the former seem clearer to political leaders than the risks of the latter.

## STRATEGY WITHOUT CONFIDENCE

Strategy is not always an illusion but it often is. The defenses of strategy offered in the responses to each critique above are valid but wobbly. A few of the critiques are weaker than their popularity would suggest (for example, the Freudian view in critique 3), but most are stronger than generally realized. All the critiques are valid in some cases, yet strategy does sometimes work. The answers about strategy that politicians and generals have to find lie in the gray area between confidence and nihilism. How much do the problems of strategy matter? How can effective strategy be practical more often?

In some cases the weakness of strategy may not matter much; an artless use of force may be effective nonetheless. This happens most easily for a superior power that confronts an enemy too weak to counter that superiority. Uninventive assault and attrition may suffice. The United States can find itself in that position often; it could hardly have failed against Grenada or Panama however it chose to apply its military capacity. Even for a superior power, however, simple attrition does not guarantee success at acceptable cost. Reliance on attrition may still pose high costs if the opponent, though weaker, is not helpless. The United States proved willing to bear very high costs to subdue the Confederacy, Germany, and Japan because the stakes were high. It proved willing to bear moderate costs against Korean and Vietnamese communists when they appeared to be the wedge for worldwide Leninism, and it was prepared to take thousands of casualties against Iraq when it threatened Western oil supplies. Few causes after the Cold War, however, present stakes that seem important enough to accept much two-sided attrition. The United States was not willing to bear even low costs against barracks bombers in Beirut in 1983 or a Somali warlord ten years later. Effective exploitation of an advantage in attrition also requires the ability to find, fix, and target the adversary. This is easier in a conventional engagement than in irregular warfare, where the weaker enemy can use strategy to raid, evade, and subvert. Irregular combat is more typical of contemporary conflict than are set-piece conventional battles.

Except for the least difficult military challenges, there is no alternative but to engage in strategy unless one is willing to give up the use of force as an instrument of policy. To develop strategy despite the many obstacles surveyed requires care in assuming the links between the ultimate political objectives sought and the military objectives set out in a campaign plan. In this it matters a great deal whether political objectives are absolute—achieved wholly or not at all—or can be achieved by degree, in proportion to effort. Another important general distinction is between types of strategy: those whose aim is to control an outcome, by conquest, or to coerce the adversary, by torture.[96] Objectives that can be achieved partially or by coercion sometimes tempt policymakers because they seem susceptible to limited investment of force; those that are absolute or achieved by elimination of enemy capability are often preferred by military officers because they leave fewer ambiguities about results and do not depend on changes in enemy will. But it is hard to eliminate a tenacious enemy's capability to resist without waging total war, and most wars by far are limited.

The challenge is particularly great when a government pursues an absolute objective with a limited coercive strategy. An assumption that simply hurting an adversary will achieve a desired result is sure to fill the bill only if the objective is to punish past behavior rather than control future behavior. Pain does not automatically lead to submission, and the mechanisms by which force influences the will of its targets are poorly understood.[97] Contrasting examples include the American bombing of North Vietnam and of Serbia. These campaigns aimed to induce Hanoi and Belgrade to cease military action against South Vietnam and Kosovo, by inflicting pain on their home territories without invading and subduing them. The result in Kosovo surprised most observers of military strategy because it did not repeat the failures to compel surrender of most past cases of coercive bombing. Figuring out precisely why Milosevic surrendered when he did would help to specify mechanisms by which bombing does coerce successfully and does not.

Sensible strategy is not impossible, but it is usually difficult and risky, and what works in one case may not in another that seems similar. Indeterminacy suggests some cautions.

First, given the big obstacles to manipulating military causes to produce political effects, resort to force should be rare in cases where the estimated balance between benefits and costs is close. (That balance was not close for Britain in 1940, for example, but it was for the United States in Vietnam in the 1960s.) This does not mean force should necessarily be the last resort, as the Weinberger/Powell Doctrine maintained. Nor does it mean that passivity is the natural default option; whenever a situation is bad enough that combat comes into consideration, there will be costs from inaction (as in the failure to intervene in Rwanda in 1994). But when deliberate killing is at issue—as it is in any significant decision to use military force—it is important to have some well-founded reason to believe that the plan for killing will achieve results worth the lives. The one thing worse than doing nothing is doing the wrong thing. Action is preferable to inaction only where policymakers think seriously beyond the objective and to the logic by which military means will take them there. Whatever the costs of refraining from war may be, they can seldom be greater than those from killing without strategy.

This is not just a pious truism. In periods when military disasters fade in memory, reliance on force becomes more popular in the United States. This happened in the post–Cold War hiatus as Vietnam was forgotten and Munich remembered, pseudo-pristine airpower was idealized, and Americans sought once again to make the world safe for democracy. Results were mixed. With low confidence in capacity to control outcomes, force should be used only where the interests at stake are high or the costs of combat are certain to be low.

Second, while analyses of cause and effect should become more careful, strategies should be kept simple. Simplicity does not guarantee success, but complexity begs for failure. There is a chain of causes and effects among policy, strategy, operations, and tactics to political outcomes. Since a chain is as strong as its weakest link, the more links there are in the chain, the higher the odds are that something will go wrong. Large-scale force is seldom more than a blunt instrument. That is apparent to most experienced military professionals but was obscured for some civilians in the generation of policymakers whose image of war was formed by videotapes of bombs riding laser beams smartly down Iraqi and Serbian airshafts. Any policymaker who hears a suggestion for "surgical" military action needs a second opinion. In the age of enthusiasm for a revolution in military affairs, it became harder to suppress faith in precision, flexibility, and mastery by remote control. It took new setbacks in Iraq and Afghanistan to renew skepticism.

Third, civilian policymakers need more understanding of military operations. For strategy to bridge policy and operations, civilian and military professionals on either side of the divide need more empathy with the priorities and limitations that those on the other side face. If the professional military take on the main responsibility for bridging the gap, they trigger concern with military usurpation of political functions. If civilians take on more of the bridging function, they trigger resentment among the military about meddling, but this is a more manageable tension since all accept the principle of civilian supremacy. Civilians cannot do this responsibly, however, unless they acquire much more empirical knowledge of tactics, logistics, and operational doctrines than is normal for top-level staff.

Fourth, the objectives by which strategic logic is measured should be limited as far as possible to material interests. If the prospective ratio between costs and benefits is low enough, this can include the interests of foreigners. (Humanitarian intervention is a moral interest for the United

States but a material interest for the beneficiaries.) Subjective values like "credibility" lend themselves too easily to visceral commitments that elude discipline by calculation. There are few clear standards to prevent credibility from becoming an excuse for showing who's boss in any and every conflict of interest, and this makes the defense of credibility a recipe for overextension. Credibility is most impressive when power is husbanded and used undiluted. Credibility is most threatened when the United States resorts to force but fails to use it decisively.

Credibility is the modern antiseptic buzzword now often used to cloak the ancient enthusiasm for honor. But honor's importance is always more real and demanding to national elites and people on home fronts than it is to the nineteen-year-olds put into the point of the spear to die for it. In rare cases a threat to national honor may also be a threat to national survival. Perhaps Churchill understood this better in 1940 than critics who would have made the case for negotiated peace. Great powers do not find themselves in this position often.

Strategy fails when the chosen means prove insufficient to the ends. This can happen because the wrong means are chosen or because the ends are too ambitious or slippery. Strategy can be salvaged more often if peacetime planning gives as much consideration to limiting the range of ends as to expanding the menu of means.

# 11 | A DISCIPLINED DEFENSE
## REGAINING STRATEGIC SOLVENCY

Halfway through the Obama administration brakes were put on the U.S. defense budget, but only lightly. Early in 2010 Secretary of Defense Robert Gates declared the need to economize and make hard choices. He planned cuts in certain programs, but in order to free funds for others, not to reduce total military spending. Contrary to claims of right-wing critics, the administration's FY 2011 budget requested a real increase in defense spending of more than 2 percent, and the future plan at the time still envisioned annual increases of 1 percent, not reductions. The avalanche of demands for budget cutting after the fall 2010 elections finally halted the long climb, and the FY 2012 budget requested an actual modest reduction in defense spending.

What is most striking is how very long it took to reverse the long climb in military spending that had begun less than a decade after limited post–Cold War reductions, even before the shock of September 11th. That climb of more than a dozen years was steeper and more sustained than in any period between the Korean War and the opening of the Berlin Wall. The military budget doubled in real terms after 1997, a period still defined by unipolarity that should have made the United States more secure than at any time in history. Instead, the level of effort implied a security situation as parlous as the Cold War.

Consider the FY 2008 budget, the last before the election that brought Obama to power. If Rip Van Winkle had fallen asleep in the Pentagon twenty years earlier and awoke when that budget was being submitted, his first reaction would have been that nothing had changed. George W. Bush had asked for $505 billion for the peacetime military establishment in 2008—almost exactly the amount, in real dollars, that Ronald Reagan requested for 1988. Rip would start scratching his head, however, when he discovered that the Soviet empire and the Soviet Union itself had imploded more than fifteen years earlier, and that Washington was spending almost as much for military power as the entire rest of the world combined, and more than five times as much as all its potential enemies combined. Rip would have lost his bearings completely when told that despite all this, Pentagon planners were worried about overstretch and presidential candidates were vying to see who could pledge even higher budgets and larger forces.

The strains on resources and forces have been due to the wars in Iraq and Afghanistan. But the costs of those wars were not included in the half-trillion dollar baseline figure. They were covered by a supplemental request for an extra $142 billion, bringing the total 2008 military budget request to $647 billion—more than 25 percent larger, in real terms, than it had been forty years earlier at the height of combat in Vietnam, a much bigger and bloodier conflict than any the United States has seen since. And even that total figure did not include the $46 billion budget of the Department of Homeland Security (DHS), whose functions would be handled by the Defense Ministry in many other countries. Rip would not have been brought back to earth when the Democrats took power. Military spending continued to climb under Obama—and right-wing critics complained that it was still too low.[1] By FY 2012 the budget requests in billions were approximately $553 billion for the base, $118 billion for the wars, and $57 billion for DHS. Only the surge of hysteria in 2011 over ballooning national debt finally made a turnaround in defense spending politically respectable in both parties.

So what has been going on? For one thing, everything costs more these days, thanks to advanced technology and weapon system costs that accelerate above the rate of inflation, higher personnel costs in a volunteer as opposed to conscripted force, including huge bonuses needed to induce re-enlistments, disproportionately increased bills for military health care, and other reasons. Most to the point, one might note that military spending was taking up less of GDP than it did during the Cold War—4.2 percent in 2008 and 4.7 percent in 2010, as opposed to 5.8 percent in 1988 and 9.4 percent in 1968. The main reason that Washington has spent so much yet still feels so insecure, however, is that policymakers lost the ability to think about defense efforts in perspective.

Since September 11th, American national security policy has responded to a visceral sense of threat spawned by the frightening intentions of enemies rather than to sober estimates of those enemies' capabilities and what it would take to counter them effectively. The United States faces real threats today and potentially bigger ones in the future. Too many Americans, however, have lost sight of the fact that they are not threats that can be tamed by the most expensive components of military power but must be met largely by means other than high-tech military forces.

Political leaders, meanwhile, forgot the craft of balancing commitments and resources. Barely anyone still alive can remember a peacetime America without vast standing armed forces—even though that was the norm for the first 165 years of the Republic—so the post–Cold War situation has not seemed as odd as it should. Corporate interests that live off the defense budget also became more adept at engineering political support by spreading subcontracts around the maximum number of congressional districts and stoking pork-barrel politics. Most of all, the traditional constituencies for restraint in spending in both major political parties evaporated, removing the obstacles to excess.

At the same time, ambitious ventures to reshape the world according to American preferences proceeded without considering the full costs and consequences of grandiose visions, and until setbacks in Iraq, too often under the illusion that they could be achieved with lean and surgical application of force. As a result, defense spending came to fall between two stools: more than needed for basic national security, but less than would be necessary to eliminate the villainous governments and groups of the world. Defense policy was left in a state of insolvency. As Walter Lippman and James Chace reminded us long ago, this means that objectives and commitments, on one hand, and resources applied to implementing them, on the other, are out of alignment.[2] Policymakers have looked to the wrong historic benchmarks for military spending and would do well to take some lessons from how the issue was handled in the more dangerous time of the Cold War.

## HOW SOON WE FORGET

Armchair field marshals assume that nations decide what their foreign policy objectives are and subordinate everything else to achieving them. Real life is more complicated. Threats, opportunities, and risks are always uncertain, but the economic costs of maximum preparedness are definite. Political leaders in a democracy have to pay for other things besides defense and prevent military commitments from outstripping economic resources.

Solvency is an equation with several elements, and during the Cold War American presidents tilted in various directions to make the balance of resources and commitments come out right. Kennedy and Reagan tried to close gaps between ambitious objectives and limited resources by raising defense spending. Nixon closed the same sort of gap the opposite way, trimming military commitments through burden sharing and diplomatic realignments. Eisenhower wanted to cut spending while maintaining the commitments he inherited, and he did so by adapting strategy and accepting greater risk (choosing to defend NATO through the doctrine of massive nuclear retaliation rather than through large conventional forces).

So far in the twenty-first century supporters of increased military spending make their case by pointing out that current levels of effort, measured by share of GDP devoted to defense, are well below those of the Cold War. This is both true and irrelevant. It focuses on only one component of the equation—spending—ignoring that the scope of commitments, the choice of strategy, and the degree of risk accepted might all be adjusted as well. It also draws the wrong lesson from history, which, properly interpreted, suggests that today's lesser threats could be handled more adeptly.

During the Cold War the U.S. armed forces were constantly preparing for World War III. U.S. military strength was geared to readiness for battle against an opposing superpower with numerous allies. Yet even in the early phases of the conflict, when tensions were highest and fears greatest, the value of economization was not forgotten. Defense spending was kept in check by the limits on revenues, the extent of other government spending, and a serious commitment to balancing the budget. Truman and Eisenhower calculated military spending using the "remainder method": they started with tax revenues, subtracted domestic spending, and gave whatever was left over to defense.[3] Truman did this before the shock of the Korean War caused him to unleash a military buildup, and Eisenhower did it to preserve a healthy domestic economic base for strategic competition over the long haul. The remainder method was a strategically arbitrary means of limiting expenditures and was not used for very long. It would not make sense to resurrect it now. But neither does it make sense to benchmark current defense spending against any other phase of the Cold War, given that the Cold War is over.

The last time the United States faced a multipolar international system, in the decades prior to World War II, its peacetime defense spending was usually no more than 2 percent of GDP—only 1.4 percent in 1939, the last year before mobilization for World War II began in earnest.[4] Such a level of effort was certainly too low, and Americans learned that lesson for good after Pearl Harbor. But on what grounds can we conclude that the current level should be three times or more as high? Not because of any actual threats that American armed forces can plausibly be expected to have to counter. U.S. military capabilities need to be kept comfortably superior to those of present and potential enemies. But they should be measured relatively, against those enemies, not against the limits of what is technologically possible or some vague urge to have more.

## FACING THREATS

As a practical matter, the Pentagon will have a hard time confronting the underlying problems in defense spending until the United States works its way back from the demands of Afghanistan and Iraq. The wars pushed parts of the U.S. armed forces close to the breaking point. Soldiers were forced to do extended and repeated combat tours, and reservists had to do repeated deployments that disrupt their lives for years on end. To a degree that disgraces strategic planning, a small number of volunteers paid an outsized price for their political leaders' miscalculations.

Despite the Bush II administration's attempts to conflate the second war against Saddam Hussein with the war on terror, the two conflicts were not the same. (Indeed, it was the U.S. invasion that brought Al Qaeda into a new base in Iraq, where Saddam Hussein's effective repression had excluded it.) The groups and individuals inspired by Al Qaeda will remain a challenge around the world after the United States has extricated itself from Iraq. But the notion that Osama bin Laden's legions are as awesome as Josef Stalin's, a notion hyped by neoconservatives and instinctively plausible to young people with short memories, is an inflation of the threat that reflects amnesia about the scope of past challenges.

Washington opened the sluice gates of military spending after the September 11th attacks not because it was necessarily the appropriate thing to do strategically, but because it was something it *could* do at a time when something had to be done. With rare exceptions, however, the war against terrorists cannot be fought by army tank battalions, air force F-22 wings, or navy fleets—the large conventional forces that drive the defense budget. The main challenge is not killing the terrorists but finding them, and the capabilities most applicable to this task are intelligence and special operations forces. Improving U.S. capabilities in these areas is difficult. It requires recruiting, training, and effectively deploying a limited number of talented and bold people with relevant skills. But it does not require over a half-trillion dollars worth of conventional and nuclear forces.

The other major potential threats to the United States are the spread of nuclear and biological weapons and a hostile full-grown China. The spread of WMD cannot be stopped by large and expensive conventional forces unless they are used for preventive war. This is not a promising option on the merits, as chapter 6 argued, since it is likely to trigger strategic judo, inflaming the opposition it is meant to counter. If chosen anyway, the option offers no assurance of solving the problem short of unlimited war that invades and occupies the offending country—in which case even the high level of military spending of recent years is unlikely to be enough to sustain the effort.

A new Cold War with a stronger China would indeed mandate high levels of military effort. For the moment, however, U.S. policy should try to defuse the security dilemma with China and avoid making all-out confrontation a self-fulfilling prophecy—something that premature or immoderate military initiatives targeted on China could do. There is time yet before feverish competition need be unleashed. China's forces have been improving impressively, but the United States is still well ahead in airpower and seapower, the capabilities that war in the Taiwan Strait would test. While fighting China's large army on the ground of the Asian mainland would be difficult, that will always be the case. The answer is a strategy that avoids engaging on the mainland in the first place (with the exception of Korea, where geography makes a defensible front feasible).

The correct way to hedge against the long-term China threat is by adopting a mobilization strategy: developing plans and organizing resources now so that military capabilities can be expanded quickly later if necessary. This means a carefully designed system of readiness to get ready. Beyond maintaining a limited but potent standing force, emphasis would be on research, development, experimentation, and testing of new technologies rather than production of large quantities of advanced weapons; maintenance of skeletal and embryonic units primed for expansion on short notice; organization, training, and advanced schooling of professional cadres and staffs more than full-strength formations; careful reserve arrangements to preserve design teams and other support functions; preparation of standby facilities for rapid conversion to industrial action; and planning and exercises.[5]

The decision to shift mobilization into high gear should be held off until genuine evidence indicates that the margin of American military superiority is not just eroding but slipping into equality. Waiting to surge military production and expansion until then would avoid the mistake of sinking hundreds of billions of dollars into weaponry that may become technologically obsolescent before a threat actually materializes. (The United States waited too long—until 1940—to mobilize against Nazi Germany and imperial Japan. But starting to mobilize in, say, 1930 would have been no wiser, since a crash program in aircraft production back then would have yielded thousands of ultimately useless biplanes.) As a practical matter there will always be debate about whether U.S. superiority is in doubt, but accepting the worst estimates will accelerate the drift to a new cold war.

## EMPIRE AND EFFORT

If the current U.S. defense budget is larger than necessary to counter existing and plausible future threats, it is smaller than necessary to support an effective role for the United States as a genuine global policeman or overseer of an altruistic empire. The globocop mission aims to protect other peoples from immediate threats, not to guard Americans themselves. Some advocates of a new domino theory would claim that it involves not altruism, but enlightened self-interest—since the immediate threats to others can eventually become immediate threats to Americans if allowed to grow unchecked. Contract out Middle Eastern stability to local tyrants and let Afghanistan become a safe haven for terrorists, the argument runs, and the result is September 11th. It is according to such logic that preventive war became considered a legitimate instrument of national security policy.

The biggest problem with this concept is that attempts at running the world generate resistance. Local actors rarely see the dominant power's actions as benign or disinterested; external interventions often provoke resentment and nationalist reactions; praise for good results is accorded stingily but blame for problems freely. If Americans are credited with molding world order, they get blamed for whatever injustices others see in that order—such as the Israeli-Palestinian conflict. As a result, muscular military activism tends to multiply enemies, where sound strategy should try to reduce and divide them.[6]

The second problem is that domestic support for humanitarian intervention tends to be wide but shallow, popular as long as it is assumed to be quick and cheap. Success on the ground, however, tends to depend on its being sustained and expensive. Washington flirted hesitantly with the globocop role after the Cold War, holding back in cases where it risked any cost in American lives. Political leaders rarely suggest spending a great deal of national blood and treasure on remote problems, and if experience in the Balkans did not reinforce their skepticism about doing so, Iraq and Afghanistan probably will.

These two problems reinforce each other. To rule a benign empire credibly, the United States would need to be more consistent in enforcing international law, overthrowing murderous regimes, preventing governments from acquiring dangerous weapons, and so forth. But the burden of doing so would be huge, requiring national mobilization and exertion (including conscription) far beyond what even the most ardent interventionists asked for after the Cold War. But if Washington chooses to keep costs low by backing up its universal rhetoric with limited actions in only a few easy cases, then its policies will appear arbitrary and capricious, driven largely by material interests. The recent level of American military power is more than necessary to protect national security directly, and nowhere near enough to implement the more ambitious vision consistently. In the end, therefore, an imperial role is both unaffordable and unwise, and the fact that Washington does not at present have the capabilities to sustain it should not be considered a problem. Direct use of force for humanitarian purposes should be reserved for the most egregious case, such as Rwanda in 1994, and explained as ad hoc emergency action, not a universal civilizing project.

## IMPOSING POLITICAL DISCIPLINE

So just how should U.S. policymakers balance their various concerns and arrive at strategic solvency? Truman's and Eisenhower's remainder method of budgeting had the merit of limiting costs but the defect of accepting higher risks (of capabilities proving inadequate if put to the test) than one should want to accept. The approaches that replaced it after the 1950s, however, have been uncertain improvements. John Kennedy and Ronald Reagan came to power after campaigning against predecessors' failure to do enough for national security, and they claimed that the United States would spend whatever was necessary. The problem in both those cases and since, however, is that there is simply no objective way to calculate how much is enough to guard against potential threats, even when aims and strategies are clear. Analysts with green eyeshades can highlight tradeoffs and efficiencies, but politics always determines whose vision of what is needed prevails.

A significant virtue of a fixed budget ceiling before the 1960s, moreover, was that it forced the Joint Chiefs of Staff to make difficult choices about program priorities. Despite the Kennedy administration's rhetorical claims about being willing to spend whatever was necessary, budget ceilings were actually still imposed. But because of the official fiction that there were no arbitrary limits, the size of the pie as a whole (and not simply the proportions of its slices) became a subject of contention. Unable to throw up their hands and say that more money was unavailable, civilian managers could reject military program requests only by saying that more money was unnecessary—insulting the professionals by saying in effect that the civilians' judgment of military requirements was more accurate than the soldiers', turning budget discussions into a test of civil-military relations. Giving up arbitrary budget caps thus inadvertently crippled a prime means of civilian control, the ability to divide and conquer the services and force military professionals to make tradeoffs among programs themselves. Given the official principle that spending would be determined by the threat rather than by economic limits, the services could present a united front, endorsing each other's programs, often getting support in Congress and weakening presidential control.[7]

The managerial reforms of the 1960s that tried to rationalize resource decisions did not only create new difficulties for civilian control; they also contributed indirectly to higher defense spending in the long run by feeding the image of Democrats as antimilitary. Democrats had regularly favored higher defense budgets than Republicans during the first phase of the Cold War. Beginning with the McGovern campaign of 1972, however, the party became identified with opposition to military spending and use of force and developed a reputation for strategic fecklessness. When this image became a political liability, the party tried to counter it by stopping its push for military economization. By the 1990s Bill Clinton was spending more on defense than Bush I's final plans had proposed, and in the 2000 campaign Al Gore promised to add another $80 billion over the following decade. Bill Bradley was the only major candidate that year to oppose more increases in defense.[8] After that mainstream Democrats tripped over themselves trying to prove they were as promilitary as anyone. Neither Kerry nor Obama recommended defense spending cuts in subsequent campaigns.

Meanwhile, Republicans had given up their traditional fixation on fiscal responsibility. That fact is easy to forget in a time of Tea Party fulmination and mainstream Republican rhetoric trumpeting the imperative of budget cutting. But it has been a long time since reality matched rhetoric. Truman and Eisenhower had favored the remainder method because they felt a need to balance the federal budget. Republicans gave that priority up in practice if not in principle, beginning with Richard Nixon's 1971 statement that "We are all Keynesians now." They kept up the talk about frugality but abandoned the substance behind it, putting far more effort into cutting taxes than cutting spending, and letting budgets swing out of balance as a result. Reagan and both Bushes claimed to want a balanced budget but never once submitted one to Congress. Bush II even expanded the deficit by demanding tax cuts without asking for comparable expenditure cuts, and embracing additional spending in prescription drug coverage. Under Obama, most Republicans demanded radical cuts in discretionary domestic spending, a small portion of the total budget, and wanted to exempt defense as well as popular entitlement programs.

Between these trends in both parties, over the years the strong political base for constraining defense spending that had existed previously eroded and was blown away completely on September 11, 2001. The result was a defense budget that rose every single year but one after 1997, at an average rate of more than 6 percent annually for most of that time. This was a record of expansion unmatched in any other dozen-year period since World War II, even during the wars in Korea and Vietnam. (In the 1960s, which included Kennedy's military buildup and the worst years of the Vietnam War, the average defense budget increase was 2.5 percent.) During the Cold War defense spending fluctuated around a plateau established during the Korean War, never rising or falling for more than a few years in a row.

## STRATEGIC SOLVENCY

To ask whether the United States can afford higher levels of military spending is silly—it can, and if necessary it would. The question is only at what price to other objectives. There are other important things the United States wants too, and a dollar spent on one thing cannot be spent on another, or to pay off debt. Defense spending thus has to be balanced not simply against presumed military needs, but against all other needs as well. This is utterly obvious, yet the partisan stalemate that prevented hard choices over the past three decades made deficit spending the path of least resistance. Economic crisis and public debate since Obama's election made clear that nonmilitary priorities loom larger than in the years just after September 11th.

Competition includes not only bedrock domestic programs such as Social Security and Medicare entitlements, which are imperiled by uncontrolled annual deficits and mounting total debt, but also other expenditures affecting national security. The State Department, for example, has been comparatively starved. Despite an increase of about 25 percent in the administration's request between FY 2008 and 2011, the department struggles to staff embassies and project the American message around the world with a Foreign Service of only a few thousand officers and a requested operating budget for 2012 of less than $15 billion. Its total budget request for 2012—including all foreign aid, all contributions to international organizations and peacekeeping missions, and operations in Iraq and Afghanistan—comes to just under $53 billion, or less than 8 percent of the funding asked for the Pentagon. (And the State Department request was immediately targeted for cuts on Capitol Hill.) For a global power dealing with a world in which many threats stem from political and economic instability and anti-American sentiment, and in which the U.S. government has great trouble communicating at the grassroots level abroad, those numbers appear unbalanced. Even the secretary of defense proposed shifting funds from the military budget to State.

Even if there were infinite resources available to support them, military capabilities would still be useful for only some purposes. The ability to use military power to regulate the world according to American values is more limited than post–Cold War optimism assumed. Imperial policing in the literal sense is feasible where the problem consists of individuals or gangs of thugs rather than organized and trained armed forces. In most cases, however, imposing political order against resistance requires waging war, a much bloodier and more involved enterprise. The professional military understand this, which is why they rarely press for such operations and usually argue for strategies that rely on overwhelming force.

By 2011 the stars had realigned to make military restraint popular. Regaining strategic solvency, however, will take time, and there is good reason not to cut the defense budget drastically. Arguments for restraint, moreover, will go out the window if future catastrophic attacks revive the notion prominent in public opinion after September 11th that terrorism is an epochal threat. Should that not happen and should the case for a more modest national security strategy gain ground, it will become easier to limit defense spending and focus it on the threats that merit the most concern. Democrats will have to get over their long battle against the wimp image, and Republicans will have to rediscover the virtues of fiscal responsibility in practice as well as principle.

Powerful armed forces are necessary for American national security, but they should be tailored to counter particular threats and vulnerabilities the country actually faces, not to ambitions of remaking the world. Ideally the government should make these decisions through a process of calculation less arbitrary than Truman's and Eisenhower's and less constrained than Nixon's. But if the choice were only between those clumsy efforts and recent profligacy, one could do worse than to follow the old models.

Translating a change of direction into specific spending cuts of more than token size would involve hard choices, rough bargaining, and much blood on the floor of the political arena but should flow as much as possible from sensible strategic and operational analysis. The sentiment in favor of defense increases after September 11th was so broad, however, that few organizations associated with mainstream policy thinking offered systematic options for reduction. Even the Institute for Policy Studies, usually considered far to the left of the mainstream, offered a recommendation as late as 2007 that would have brought the baseline defense budget down by only about 12 percent, and total military spending down less than 9 percent—a far cry from the McGovern campaign's excessive call for a one-third defense cut in the late stages of our last unpopular war.[9]

Marshalling the political will for restraint was an uphill battle until panic over deficits put all government functions on the table for reassessment. Modest reductions for a few years, and a steady defense budget eroded by inflation for a few more, could get the system's belt tightened without seeming to slash national security. But not even that course yet commands consensus a dozen years into the twenty-first century. The case for cuts can be made on the principle that the U.S. armed forces should be designed to cope with evolving threats—not to maintain a size and status to which they have become accustomed over time, or to nurture individual service priorities, or to acquire whatever capabilities become possible on the technological frontier, or to consume resources that happen to be politically available.

# 12 CONCLUSION
## SELECTING SECURITY

American power reached a peak in the 1940s, was then compromised by bipolarity for almost half a century, and peaked again at the end of the twentieth century. Capability to impose preferences by force is one aspect of that power but varies according to the quality and scale of resistance. The purposes and places for which force should be committed—either passively in deterrence or actively in combat—are the main issues in national security policy.

"National defense" is the catch-all term used to define these purposes, but it has become a legitimizing bromide rather than an accurate description. Especially since the Cold War it does not take much to ensure national defense in the strict sense: protection of the United States itself from invasion, destruction, or crippling coercion. This situation of extraordinary inherent security did not apply when thousands of Soviet nuclear weapons were a constant threat, and it came into question on September 11, 2001. For more than two decades, however, U.S. territory has confronted no enemy that poses a credible danger of devastating attack. Russia, China, and a few countries with nuclear forces have the capability but, at present, no plausible intent. Al Qaeda has the intent but, so far, little capability; September 11th was a major tragedy, but still on a modest scale in normal military terms.

Americans long ago became thoroughly conditioned to think of national defense in terms of missions far from home. The consensus took root after 1945, when the lesson was that the United States had erred in withdrawing from the European balance of power after World War I. The expansive conception of national security carried over from the Cold War, when it was necessary, to the unipolar world, when it was tempting. Today an aggressive forward strategy is still logical in regard to the problem of counterterrorism, but not in regard to much else. Instead of standing down from global military engagement when the global struggle with Marxism-Leninism ended, the United States conflated the idea of national defense with liberal empire. Fitful attempts to enlarge and nurture liberal world order and democracy and human rights inside benighted countries ran up against obstacles that sometimes proved more trouble than policymakers had counted on. Manipulating armed force to control political developments has usually proved more difficult than anticipated, but especially so in cases where the stakes were lower than in the Cold War, and where the obstacles were underestimated.

Throughout the post–Cold War era force was applied frequently but inconsistently. It has been used for humanitarian purposes, but in a select number of cases that a naïve observer might consider random. Why Haiti, Bosnia, Kosovo, and Libya, but not Rwanda, Sudan, Congo, Syria, or other places where suffering was more acute? Force has been used to prevent a tyrant from deploying weapons of mass destruction and to liberate his country from oppression. But why Saddam Hussein's Iraq and not Kim Jong-Il's North Korea? Force was used to deprive Al Qaeda of the base of operations provided by the Taliban in 2001, but the U.S. campaign in the country continued, at far higher cost, after a decade in which Al Qaeda had as much purchase in other countries as in Afghanistan.

Of course there are reasons for inconsistency. Before the fact, humanitarian intervention looked like an easy venture in the places where it was undertaken, but high costs could be foreseen in the places that were left to stew in their own juices; Iraq in 2003 seemed like low-hanging fruit because it had no friends, while China stands with North Korea; and once hip-deep in a mess like Afghanistan, it is harder to climb out than to refrain in the first place. Using the military instrument where it can be exploited cheaply is a reasonable standard for choice, in principle, but in practice estimates of low cost too often proved wrong. This record does not necessarily discredit the use of force. Benefits may justify high costs. But the record does suggest that force should be reserved for cases in which the anticipated benefit, moral or material, is high. The benefit from forcible action may simply be avoiding the cost of *in*action, losses if force is withheld. But the more uncertain the prospective effectiveness of force at low cost, the higher the anticipated benefit should be.

Earlier chapters argued for less ambitious uses of force for world ordering in the near term, present concentration on forceful counterterrorism and nonforcible counterproliferation, and otherwise focusing national security priorities on threats that lie in the future. The highest premium should be on prior planning and clear decision on commitments where threats worth countering can be foreseen. Wars over Korea and Kuwait might have been avoided altogether if their possibility had been considered and U.S. willingness to fight had been determined and declared in advance. Foreseeing all crucial contingencies is not possible, but most attention should be paid to threats that could increase the demands on defense more than in the past twenty years.

## DANGERS WITHOUT DELUSIONS

Several potential threats that stand out seem improbable, yet not less probable than some past threats have seemed before they burst forth. However unlikely they may be, the severity of their consequences should put the following at the top of the list for countermeasures, above the minor threats that preoccupied policy during the post–Cold War hiatus.

*Terrorists' acquisition of usable weapons of mass destruction.* Typical terrorism has a fearsome psychological impact, but it actually inflicts few casualties compared with even small wars and does not pose a serious material threat in itself. If terrorists could deploy nuclear or efficient biological weapons, however, the potential casualties would be far higher. Unless U.S. intelligence could find, fix, and pounce on such weapons, there is little chance of preventing their use since terrorists are not easily subject to deterrence. Acquisition of WMD by dangerous regimes like North Korea or Iran is also a severe threat, but at least is more manageable since rogue states have a return address and thus *are* more subject to deterrence.

What to do? For counterterrorism, first, business as usual (which means energetic intelligence collection and special operations), and second, better civil defense preparations. For dealing with nuclear proliferation by states, diplomatic and economic carrots and sticks, and covert action to disrupt and retard nuclear development programs where it can be effective. None of these actions assures success, but more ambitious efforts at overt preventive war are likely to accelerate the threat more than suppress it.

*A World War IV against a coordinated international coalition of revolutionary Islamist regimes.* After September 11th neoconservative pundits hyped the Islamist threat, claiming that World War IV was under way (the Cold War having been World War III).[1] This image exaggerates the threat so far. Radical "jihadist" Islamists remain mostly stuck at the level of episodic low-casualty terrorism, with the exception of larger-scale unconventional warfare in Afghanistan and Iraq (the second of which the United States unnecessarily inflicted on itself). Even those wars are small. As long as anti-Western militants are only subnational secretive groups, armed only with regular weapons, they are a serious threat to some American allies, but a minor threat to the United States itself. All that could elevate them to a level of epochal importance would be growth and coordination on a grand scale: a worldwide radicalization of important Islamic countries in addition to Iran—from Egypt to Saudi Arabia, the Persian Gulf states, Indonesia, Nigeria, and Pakistan—and an organized alliance of the radicalized regimes. This would dramatically increase the power of the movement, most obviously in the potential to cripple the West by withholding oil supplies.

As this book goes to press in early 2011, a wave of revolts is sweeping the Arab world, and it is yet unclear what the results will be when the dust settles—benign outcomes as in the Philippines after Marcos and Eastern Europe after the Cold War, or bad ones as in Iran after the shah or China after the Tianmen Square massacre. Initially the popular movements against authoritarian regimes in Tunisia, Egypt, Bahrain, Yemen, and Libya seemed remarkably democratic and uncompromised by anti-Western radicalism. If revolutions can remain democratic and moderate, the World War IV threat will not emerge. This is a huge "if," however, far from a safe bet for American strategists. And democratic Muslim governments are likely to be less cooperative with Washington than their despotic predecessors were.

What to do? At this point there may be little the United States can do other than offer assistance, or that is not already too late to counter anti-American impulses. Washington should support democratic revolutions as long as they do not degenerate, it but cannot avoid seeming late or disingenuous in doing so, since it has had to befriend and do business with most of the authoritarian regimes that are replaced. U.S. support for democratization makes sense on balance for several reasons, and with much luck could foster amicable relations, but it cannot be counted on to undercut anti-Americanism—it may unleash it.

*Morass-like wars from which it is hard to extricate, like the recent ones in Iraq and Afghanistan.* Avoiding messy, inconclusive wars that cannot be terminated satisfactorily should be easier after the cautionary experience in Iraq and Afghanistan. It took more than a generation after Vietnam for American leaders to risk such ventures, and it should take another generation before history repeats, if the risk is recognized. But leaders rarely risk descent into a military morass deliberately; Vietnam was an exception.[2] The danger is combat action that leaders undertake expecting a clear beginning and quick end but which proves more complicated and intractable than anticipated.

What to do? Avoid initiating combat operations that cannot be sure to stay at the conventional level of warfare, unless Americans are willing to risk a long and dirty little war, and avoid limited punitive combat actions that Washington cannot afford to back away from if they fail to coerce. Either caution is easier said than done as long as the United States itches to control politico-military developments in other regions.

*Conflict with a great power, especially China.* This is the big one, the potential danger of greatest consequence. A new cold war between the United States and China or Russia is not inevitable and should be prevented if possible. Contrary to common assumptions, however, economic interdependence does not make it an improbable development that can occur only if government leaders are more foolish than usual. Rather, it will take hard work and hard choices to avoid it. Historically, when a new power rises, conflict with the reigning dominant power is the default option.[3] Statesmen will have to be wiser than usual.

What to do? Fish or cut bait: make clear whether the United States will fight to defend Taiwan against forcible reincorporation with the PRC, or not. Ambiguity is good for deterrence if the answer is no (because it encourages caution without bluffing), but bad if the answer is yes (because it raises the chances of miscalculation and accidents). If Americans do not want to abandon Taiwan to its fate and do not want to risk inadvertent war, reinvigorating the defense guarantee to Taipei explicitly is the lesser evil. The price of reducing the risk of war by clarifying deterrence, however, would be indefinite tension and confrontation, and sustained damage to the U.S.-China relationship. If Americans do not want a new cold war with China and do not want the risk of inadvertent war that goes with ambiguity, declaring that we will keep military hands off a conflict between Taipei and Beijing would be the lesser evil. (Cutting Taiwan off completely would be safest for the United States, but reserving the option to supply arms would be a reasonable compromise.) If neither choice is acceptable to Washington, continued betting on indefinite forbearance by the PRC, and acceptance of the risks of unplanned and inadvertent escalation of an unanticipated crisis, are the necessary price.

The preceding dangers grow out of milder challenges confronted in recent years and discussed in earlier chapters. There are also well-recognized and important dangers not examined in this book, but which belong on the list of high-priority threats. The problem with the two mentioned here is that resistance to the most appropriate policies is deeply entrenched in American domestic politics.

*Energy dependence.* As long as the American economy runs on huge imports of oil, the lifestyle national security policy must protect is the nation's main vulnerability, one largely self-inflicted. Americans remain unwilling to readjust domestic priorities and habits—for example, by hefty taxes on gasoline and inefficient consumption—to increase incentives for conservation and exploitation of energy resources other than petroleum. Instead Americans have chosen to invest in military power oriented to securing oil by force if necessary. (As early as the mid-1990s, Eric Nordlinger liked to point out that the U.S. military force oriented to combat in the Persian Gulf was costing almost three times as much annually as the oil imports it was to protect.)[4] The blood-for-oil option should never be out of the question, but it should not be the first option, preferred to domestic belt-tightening. Failure to adjust consumption simply makes immediate gratification a higher priority than long-term security.

*The Middle East cauldron and revolutions in crucial countries.* The Middle East and Southwest Asia are the most obvious regions of risk. The Israel-Palestine conflict is an indirect source of the revolutionary Islamist campaign against the United States. It may not be the main reason for Muslim hostility to the United States, but it is always up in the top three. Revolutions in Arab countries could raise the costs from supporting Israel, since democratic regimes may prove less willing or able to suppress popular solidarity with the Palestinians. Renewal of interstate war between Israel and Arab countries, which may also become less unthinkable with the passing of cynical dictators, could also implicate the United States, as in 1973. Revolutions that turn out like Iran in 1979 will generate crises. Radicalization of Saudi Arabia (controller of a large share of world oil resources) or Pakistan (with nuclear weapons) would be the worst cases and, if coupled with similar disasters in other major Muslim states, could push the World War IV scenario closer.

Heading off any of these events, or preparing for their consequences, would take sacrifice, energy, or concentrated attention. The American political system does not facilitate hard choices and subordination of short-term comfort to long-term security, even when most thoughtful analysts and officials recognize the need in principle. On energy consumption and support of Israel, moreover, interest groups opposed to major course changes are strong.

A different basic problem is that there are just too many plausible dangers for top-level policymakers to keep in mind. Human beings are incapable of giving careful thought to more than three things at one time. But complexity, bureaucracy, inertia, and an overloaded agenda mean that decisive action to alter course on any given problem is unlikely unless policymakers at the top level weigh in on it—and they usually do not until a crisis thrusts the question upon them. As a result, the odds are stacked in favor of a reactive policy for all but the most obvious threats. Well-recognized dangers may be contained by countermeasures deployed in advance, but the contingencies that redefine priorities are usually surprises. This highlights the last and potentially most important danger:

*Wild card: a yet unknown and unanticipated threat.* Identified problems may not dominate the agenda. Paradoxically, the least likely threat may be most likely. Since 1945 the biggest turning points in U.S. national security have come from surprise contingencies that blindsided the national security establishment, crises in countries or on issues that had been on no high-level policymaker's radar screen.

Anyone willing to rest national security planning on well-recognized threats should ponder that record: In May 1950, who would have predicted that America's next war would be in a place called Korea? At the end of the Korean War, who would have predicted that America's next war would be in Vietnam? In 1988, who would have predicted (without being sent to a mental hospital) that within three years the Berlin Wall would open, the Cold War would end, the Soviets' East European empire would be liberated, and the Soviet Union itself would cease to exist? In early 1990, who would have predicted that America's next war would be against Iraq? In mid-1991, who would have predicted that fifteen years later Iraq would be looking like Vietnam? When the Soviets left Afghanistan in 1989, who would have dreamed that the Americans would be filling their place twenty years later? These rhetorical questions underline two points: major upheavals in U.S. national security policy are usually unpredicted, and they happen much more often than once in a lifetime. The one thing that should be no surprise is that we will be surprised.

## STRATEGY DESPITE DILEMMAS

The inconstancy of the American political system precludes strategy that is refined, coherent, and consistent. Any general plan that relies on tight control of causes and effects, by adept orchestration of many moving parts, is likely to fail. Acting at their best, leaders may stipulate a vague grand strategy at the level of a bumper sticker—such as containment and deterrence from Truman onward, or détente and triangular diplomacy under Nixon, or engagement and enlargement under Clinton—and prod the pulling and hauling of the decision and implementation process to produce specific programs that move results roughly in the direction announced.

A bumper sticker for a sensibly recast American strategy would be "soft primacy and burden-shifting." It would be nonsensical to want to shed primacy, in the sense of number one status in the international system. There is an important difference, however, between having primacy and reaping its passive benefits, on one hand, and trying to milk it forcefully to control world order, on the other. Primacy provides an important reserve of power in many dimensions, but no guarantee that power is fungible across all issues, or sufficient to control outcomes at acceptable cost. Primacy means having more power than anyone else, but not necessarily having enough power for all purposes, or for spendthrift use. Primacy should be a cushion, not a driver.

Soft primacy means fielding superior American military power but using it sparingly, keeping it in the bank for a truly rainy day. Military restraint is not isolationism, any more than European countries can be called isolationist. It is perfectly feasible to be energetically engaged with the world economically, diplomatically, and ideologically, marketing soft power, without often pushing U.S. preferences for political order at the point of a gun. Soft primacy would mean activism, but military caution: economically, interaction as open as that of European countries and Japan; politically, promotion of democracy and human rights not only by rhetoric but by occasional manipulation of aid or other economic incentives; and militarily, robust maintenance of defensive alliances, military assistance programs in some places, and aloofness in others.

This book has not developed the full case for which military alliances should be maintained or how. Most of that answer was well established in the Cold War and continues, even though the requirements of proper maintenance have declined. More detailed analysis would justify a list that includes the following.

*NATO.* This is the most important alliance in principle, given history and the sanctity of the institution, although in practice there is no direct military threat to European countries that makes the task a real problem. Fear of going out of business should not drive NATO out of area. As it is, NATO's role in helping the United States in Afghanistan is half a fiction, since most of the nineteen countries of the organization did not participate significantly and the multilateral aspect of the enterprise has really been a coalition of the willing. In a sensible reformulation the regular military function of NATO should now be considered a reserve capacity to be reactivated if the world changes.

*The U.S.-Japan Mutual Security Treaty.* In reality this is not at all mutual, since the defense guarantee only runs one way. The U.S. commitment is nonetheless a cheap way to underwrite stability in Asia, by enabling Japan to abjure the normal military role of a great power. This has prevented a Japanese buildup that would alarm other Asian countries, aggravating a regional security dilemma. The commitment is cheap because island geography eases the military measures necessary to prevent conquest, and Japan's own short-range capabilities can handle most of the mission of direct defense. The main U.S. contribution is the "nuclear umbrella" to substitute for autonomous Japanese deterrence. This unequal alliance commitment is the one very big and important exception to the objective of burden shifting, or even burden sharing. U.S. efforts to get Japan to do more militarily made sense in the Cold War, when the burden of countering communist power worldwide was heavy, but are unnecessary in a unipolar world.

*The Republic of Korea.* South Korea's resources far outclass those of North Korea, and now make it technically capable of taking full responsibility for self-defense. North Korea has been wild and crazy enough, however, that the U.S. deterrent could remain the key ingredient in ensuring against Pyongyang's adventurism, and thus a benefit worth the cost. This was true even before North Korea developed nuclear weapons and renewed military provocations with attacks on a South Korean ship and island town. U.S. retrenchment that would make economic and military sense would be misread as bowing to North Korean bravado. With reduced anti-American sentiment in South Korea after provocations in 2009 and 2010, the political costs of continuing American military presence in the country abated.

So change in U.S. strategy is unwise unless North Korea can be induced to negotiate its nuclear weapons away or South Korean popular opposition to American military presence grows again.

In the event of either of those developments, a revised U.S. strategy should be considered to (1) sap some of the popular South Korean resentment of the U.S. presence in the country and thus fortify the foundation of the alliance; (2) reduce peacetime costs; and (3) preserve ample capacity to defend South Korea in the event of war.[5] The change would withdraw U.S. ground forces from South Korea, leaving stockpiles of equipment behind to allow rapid reinforcement in a crisis. To compensate militarily, U.S. war plans would rely on air power for direct combat in support of South Korean ground forces in the initial phase of war, until U.S. ground forces could return to the peninsula. Jimmy Carter planned such a shift at the beginning of his administration. It was a thoroughly bad idea then and was thankfully abandoned. Today, more than thirty years later, four considerations make it the right idea.

First, the risk that obtrusive American presence in South Korea could be strategically counterproductive is higher now than it was then because of increased anti-American sentiment concentrated in the younger generation. Second, the substitution of air power for ground forces was militarily much riskier at that time. Since then the maturation of precision targeting has made clear that air attacks are devastating against any mechanized units that move on the ground. It is hard for aircraft to destroy enemy armor when it is dug in and hidden, but easy when it is exposed in attack mode. Third, the Cold War is over, North Korea long ago lost the military aid it used to have from Moscow and Beijing, and its forces are huge but threadbare. Without nuclear weapons, the low quality of North Korean military forces negates the edge that high quantity used to give them. Fourth, with the Cold War over, the implications of potential conquest of South Korea for the worldwide balance of power and American security are less important, so there is no good reason that the responsibility for fully funding and manning the defense line against North Korea should not be borne by the far richer and more populous South Korea—whose level of military effort, in terms of percentage of GDP devoted to military expenditures, is little more than half that of the United States. Unless North Korean nuclear weapons go away, however, the United States needs to accept a disproportionate military burden for deterrence in order to keep Seoul from getting nuclear weapons too.

Even if nuclear weapons go away, a revised U.S. strategy would risk being mistakenly characterized as retreat, alarming Korean conservatives and feeding North Korean hubris. Revision would have to be done in active collaboration with Seoul and with plenty of rhetoric and actions to make credible the explanation that it is a shift toward strategic efficiency, not a change of commitment toward military disengagement. It would be analogous to the U.S. military infrastructure in Kuwait between the two wars against Iraq—practical preparations for war without overwhelming presence in peacetime. One element of credible reassurance would be amplified exercises in which U.S. ground force units are flown into the country, break out stored equipment, and move to wartime positions, to test and signal the speed with which U.S. power can be brought back in the event of war. This would be similar to the old annual REFORGER (for "Reinforcement of Germany") exercises in NATO during the Cold War. If this infuriates Pyongyang as annual exercises did in the past, all the better for deterrence of the adversary and reassurance of the ally.

*Conditional defense of Israel.* In the hypothetical event of a general peace settlement in the Middle East, if based roughly on the 1967 borders and an unencumbered Palestinian state, the United States should be willing to provide a formal guarantee to Israel proper against attack by Arab countries. This would be risky, since unconventional warfare against Israel, or terrorism that provokes Israeli retaliation against bases of operation in neighboring countries, would be likely to continue despite a treaty and could implicate the American alliance in uncomfortable ways. The United States is partially responsible for the tragic situation as it has evolved, however, having backed and funded Israel for almost half a century, and is morally obligated to contribute to maintenance of a solution if the locals can agree. Otherwise, a U.S. military role in the Middle East should be limited, relying on offshore assets rather than permanent bases in the region, which cause as many strategic problems as they solve. Revolutions in Arab countries make an explicit U.S. defense commitment to Israel more important at the same time that they intensify the reasons to avoid stationing American forces on the ground in the region.

Military aloofness in most areas apart from the above alliances means not contesting regional arrangements for stability that do not depend on American force. These could be either local balances of power, if they can be kept stable, or spheres of influence by single dominant powers in their neighborhoods. Local hegemony may not be desirable, but it is likely to be less threatening than in the age of imperialism, when states competed for direct rule of territory for economic reasons that seldom drive military policies today (Iraq's invasion of Kuwait in 1990 is one big exception, but notable for its uniqueness in the postcolonial era).

Selective aloofness goes with burden shifting, the natural implication of standing down from empire. American force should be promised to allies for their defense against major threats, not to manage rebellions or disorders that they are capable of handling on their own. There was no logical necessity for the United States to weigh in on the Balkans in the 1990s, any more than for European countries to help Americans intervene in the Western Hemisphere. If a formal multilateral enterprise was needed to impose a solution, the European Union, not NATO, should have served as the vehicle.

The area where aloofness would make the most important difference is East Asia outside Japan and Korea. It would be undesirable for all the countries with claims on islands in the South China Sea to have to roll over belly up in the face of Chinese counterclaims, and it would be undesirable for countries like Vietnam or Mongolia to be under China's thumb. But standing down from empire means living with a number of undesirable conditions. Planning to insert American forces into a fight over the Spratlies, or promising to defend Vietnam militarily, would demand more from the United States than its real interests or public opinion yet warrant. Once China is a full-grown superpower, the price of peace may be that smaller neighboring countries on the Asian mainland grudgingly accept what used to be called "Finlandization"—or what Beijing might consider Chinese "leadership"—as much as Caribbean or Central American countries have had to bow to U.S. preferences.[6]

Recognizing a Chinese sphere of influence would not make the regional international system as stable as that in the Western Hemisphere since there are other major powers in the region. But even if Japan remains an abnormal great power, disengaged militarily from other countries—as we should hope it will—the issues that involve Indian and Russian interests should be manageable by New Delhi and Moscow. Burden shifting should not rely on Japan to take up slack but should be a good option for Washington when applied to most other major states.

The question on which U.S. aloofness would raise the most controversy is Taiwan. This is the occasion for miscalculation to which we keep coming back. As strategy now stands, the United States is ambiguously committed to stand in the way of forcible resolution of the Chinese civil war. This is not a major issue only because Beijing has not made it so. If the Taiwan issue never comes to crisis, ambiguity is not a problem, and perhaps a help, in giving China reason for caution. A crisis over Taiwan, however, would trigger a great debate about what the United States should do, just when either action or restraint would be most urgent and most fraught. Arms transfers to Taiwan in the event of conflict would be a reasonable risk, but the United States should avoid direct combat against a nuclear-armed China over a territorial issue in which Beijing has a far bigger stake than Washington. Explicit abandonment of Taiwan to its fate is not an option yet pushed by any significant constituency in American policy debate, but neither has war with China been explicitly considered as an acceptable option. Leaving all this in abeyance, until a time when it is too late to make decisions and select options with proper time and care, is one of the biggest continuing risks in U.S. strategy.

## Resort to Force

The United States needs to stand down from the condition of permanent war that has characterized the twenty-first century so far, and to be more selective than it was in the 1990s in using armed forces for small-scale stability operations. But things will come up and force will be applied at some time or other. No rule should be absolute, and particular circumstances may throw up a case where the following recommendations should be rejected. But with pragmatic allowance for an appropriate exception, two norms should inform U.S. plans for combat commitments.

*Avoid bluffs.* For some reason adversaries in the post–Cold War period often misjudged the United States as a paper tiger, underestimating American willingness to fight them effectively. They looked to withdrawals from Vietnam in 1975, Beirut in 1983, and Somalia in 1993 as characteristic, rather than focusing on dogged American willingness to engage in heavy combat and accept nearly sixty thousand fatalities over seven long years in Vietnam for a stake of minor value, or on the decisive assaults on Panama in 1989 and Iraq in 1991. Hesitancy after muscular posturing in some cases sometimes fed adversaries' misapprehension, especially during the Clinton administration.[7]

The sort of initiative that should be avoided was the dispatch of the U.S.S. *Harlan County* to Port au Prince, Haiti, in October 1993, with American personnel assigned to implement a UN peacekeeping mission. When Haitian thugs demonstrated at the port, Washington directed the ship to back away and return, lest violence occur. This inevitably appeared as a craven retreat, despite the intrinsic unimportance of the event. If the United States decides to intervene in a country without the approval and good offices of local forces, it should be prepared to follow through with force. Credibility should not be a fetish, nor an excuse in its own right for using force, but it should not be squandered unnecessarily. The more often it is risked, the more it will suffer.

*All-in or stay out.* After the Cold War the United States used force frequently but not intensely. In the future that pattern should be reversed. If force is to be used, it should normally be used decisively, to impose American will. In a few cases this could be for limited punitive purposes, simply to show that adversaries cannot attack American interests for free. In such rare cases retaliatory bombing, without attempting to control who rules on the ground, could be sensible. But when the purpose of American force is to compel a change in policy by coercion, or to impose a political solution by conquest or intervention, force will more often fail if it is too light than if it is too heavy. This skepticism about limited uses of force for purposes of signaling contradicts economic logic and popular academic theories of coercion. Empirical evidence about application of signaling theories, however, is not encouraging.[8]

This does not mean that force should be used indiscriminately, or more destructively than is required to impose control; needless casualties do not improve military effectiveness. The dilemma between attrition and strategic judo in unconventional warfare underlines good reasons that massive use of force can be counterproductive. This means that when the United States is considering involvement in a revolutionary situation, a careful decision must be made about whether any combat action at all should be undertaken. If it is, the need to avoid collateral damage suggests that "all-in" should mean a military presence that is massive but passive—counterinsurgency work through a very high force-to-population ratio, with emphasis on civic action, patrolling, and reaction to attack rather than initiation of strikes on targets that risk strategic judo. Making the effort massive is the lesser risk because American politics cannot be relied on to provide enough time for a more gradual, measured expansion of effort akin to the oil-spot model. In Afghanistan the U.S. Army practiced goal displacement, the typical malady of complex organizations, for the first seven years of involvement. It mistook progress in the operations that are its forte—attrition of the enemy—for progress toward policy objectives. Generals McCrystal and Petraeus understood that mistake and reoriented strategy toward facilitating secure governance. But after seven years American patience had worn thin, and the generals had lost the option for a counterinsurgency effort that would require another ten years.

Since Americans may tolerate a long war, but not one that begins to appear endless, "all-in" for counterinsurgency privileges intensity over duration in strategy. In this spirit it may also mean heavy reliance on economic aid and construction projects to win hearts and minds. The best counterinsurgency may use force as a reserve option for emergencies rather than as the first line of action. If the United States is to invest large amounts of resources in a country's reconstruction and development, without having the effort short-circuited by theft and corruption or hijacked by the enemy, it would need to deploy an army of auditors, monitors, and project shepherds to track and control the distribution of aid. This would be a green-eyeshade peace corps, in effect, and probably infeasible, but a strategic initiative that makes sense in principle. If measures of this sort are more impractical than unleashing expensive firepower, decision makers have another reason to reconsider resort to force and prefer "stay out."

The trouble with the all-in or stay out norm is that it asks politicians to commit an unnatural act: to make hard choices rather than compromise between the risks of either extreme by limited action, to accept certain costs in the near term rather than uncertain costs in the long term. Politicians must survive in the short term or they will have no long term. Most successful political leaders feel compelled to compromise because choosing either extreme alienates a constituency that favors the opposite. Any such constituency can seem necessary to keep a majority. This dilemma is not easily avoided before initiating a venture, but the costs of facing it then are lower than they are after getting stuck in stalemate.

The presumption in favor of massive force or none at all can only be a guideline, not a rule. There will be an appropriate exception to the rule sometime. As a tentative rule of thumb it helps by fixing attention on the odds that costs of combat will turn out higher than anticipated, and encouraging more careful assessment of whether the benefits of action compensate for the uncertainty about results. If a gamble on limited force makes sense, it should still be done with a plan in reserve for massive action to bail it out if the limited action fails. If policymakers cannot stomach high costs, they need greater certainty about outcomes than is usually available.

For most of the post–Cold War period American force was applied with too much breadth and too little depth—in more cases than were politically necessary, but with less decisiveness than would have been militarily sensible. The first tendency, excessive assertiveness, crested late in the Bush II administration. The second tendency, trying to keep the profile of force low when it is applied, remained a temptation, as in the 2009 haggling over how many additional forces should be sent to Afghanistan. The first tendency may come back, if economic pressures and international constraints become more permissive and regenerate a sense of opportunity, or if a concatenation of small disasters panics Americans into overreaction. What should be of greatest concern, however, is the potential emergence of genuinely serious threats, rather than the small threats faced in the past twenty-odd years. Some serious threats, such as the transfer of WMD to Al Qaeda, may warrant the kind of decisive force missing in some past cases. Others, such as military confrontation with China, may require restraint, to hold back the risk of catastrophic escalation. There will be no formula to relieve American leaders of the need for judgment.

Such hedged conclusions will not satisfy visionaries of any stripe, but they are more realistic than any consistent simplicities. These conclusions may strike opponents of American military activism as too equivocal, muddying the arguments for restraint that animate earlier chapters. To them the answer is that sharp arguments are useful for bringing essential problems, priorities, and misconceptions into focus, but not for selecting specific solutions. Real life in international politics is muddy, too complicated for absolute consistency. Enthusiasts for military activism, on the other hand, will reject the message as waffling at best, or a counsel of fear and passivity. To them the answer is that the only thing worse than doing nothing is doing the wrong thing. To do the right thing for American interests or values, American force must first do no harm to them.

# NOTES

## 1. INTRODUCTION: FROM COLD WAR TO HOT PEACE

1. Alexander B. Downes, *Targeting Civilians in War* (Ithaca, N.Y.: Cornell University Press, 2008), 8. See also Stephen Peter Rosen, "Blood Brothers: The Dual Origins of American Bellicosity," *The American Interest* 4, no. 6 (July/August 2009).

2. Andrew J. Bacevich, *Washington Rules: America's Path to Permanent War* (New York: Metropolitan Books, 2010).

3. Michael Mandelbaum, "Foreign Policy as Social Work," *Foreign Affairs* 75, no. 1 (January/February 1996).

4. Martin Rees, *Our Final Hour: A Scientist's Warning: How Terror, Error, and Environmental Disaster Threaten Humankind's Future in This Century—On Earth and Beyond* (New York: Basic Books, 2003). I thank Stephen Van Evera for bringing this sobering book to my attention.

5. Fred Charles Iklé, *Annihilation from Within: The Ultimate Threat to Nations* (New York: Columbia University Press, 2006).

6. Carl von Clausewitz, *On War*, eds. and trans. Michael Howard and Peter Paret (Princeton: Princeton University Press, 1976), 598.

7. This term follows what Daniel Ellsberg called "revolutionary judo" in "Revolutionary Judo: Working Notes on Vietnam No. 10" (Santa Monica, Calif.: RAND Corporation, January 1970) (declassified October 2005); what Gene Sharp called "political *jiu-jitsu*," in *The Politics of Nonviolent Action* (Boston: Porter Sargent, 1973), 110, 453, 807; and what Samuel L. Popkin called "political judo" in "Pacification: Politics and the Village," *Asian Survey* 10, no. 8 (August 1970), and Popkin, "Internal Conflicts—South Vietnam," in *Conflict in World Politics*, ed. Kenneth N. Waltz and Steven Spiegel (Cambridge: Winthrop, 1971).

8.  For example: Andrew J. Bacevich, *American Empire: The Realities and Consequences of U.S. Diplomacy* (Cambridge: Harvard University Press, 2002); Barry R. Posen, "The Case for Restraint," *American Interest* 3, no. 2 (November/December 2007); Stephen M. Walt, *Taming American Power: The Global Response to U.S. Primacy* (New York: Norton, 2005); and Eric A. Nordlinger, *Isolationism Reconfigured: American Foreign Policy for a New Century* (Princeton: Princeton University Press, 1995).

## 2. POLICY MILESTONES: COLD WAR ROOTS OF CONSENSUS

1.  See Hubert Zimmerman, "The Improbable Permanence of a Commitment: America's Troop Presence in Europe During the Cold War," *Journal of Cold War Studies* 11, no. 1 (Winter 2009).

2.  The different approaches both have a long tradition and were evident before the outbreak of the Cold War. Arthur Schlesinger, Jr., discussed the clashing views as "universalist," based on international organization, and "spheres of influence," based on balance of power. Schlesinger, "Origins of the Cold War," *Foreign Affairs* 46, no. 1 (October 1967): 26, 36–38.

3.  The table of contents to *A National Security Strategy of Engagement and Enlargement* (Washington, D.C.: The White House, July 1994) includes fourteen entries for nonmilitary interests—for example, "The Environment," "Partnership with Business and Labor," "Promoting Sustainable Development Abroad," and "Promoting Democracy"—as many as for traditional security concerns like "Maintaining a Strong Defense Capability," "Combatting Terrorism," and "Strong Intelligence Capabilities." On the alleged "Minor Role of Military Force," see Robert O. Keohane and Joseph S. Nye, *Power and Interdependence* (Boston: Little, Brown, 1977), 27–29. Keohane and Nye modified this argument in the afterword to second and third editions in 1989 and 2001.

4.  John Gerard Ruggie, *Winning the Peace: America and World Order in the New Era* (New York: Columbia University Press, 1996), chaps. 3, 4.

5.  See David A. Baldwin, "The Concept of Security," *Review of International Studies* 23 (1997).

6.  Kenneth N. Waltz, *Theory of International Politics* (Reading, Mass.: Addison-Wesley, 1979), 94, 96.

7.  Walter Russell Mead, *Special Providence* (New York: Knopf, 2001), chaps. 2, 6, 7; William Schneider, "Public Opinion: The Beginning of Ideology?" *Foreign Policy* no. 17 (Winter 1974–1975).

8.  Louis Hartz, *The Liberal Tradition in America* (New York: Harcourt, Brace, 1955). Rationalizing the conflation of interest with virtue, and national security with international security, is an old habit in the Anglo-American tradition. More

than a century ago British diplomat Eyre Crowe wrote in his famous memorandum: "the national policy of the insular and naval State is so directed as to harmonize with the general desires and ideals common to all mankind, and more particularly . . . is closely identified with the primary and vital interests of a majority, or as many as possible, of the other nations. . . . England, more than any other non-insular Power, has a direct and positive interest in the maintenance of the independence of nations, and therefore must be the natural enemy of any country threatening the independence of others, and the natural protector of the weaker communities." Eyre Crowe, "Memorandum on the Present State of British Relations with France and Germany," January 1, 1907, in G. P. Gooch and Harold Temperley, eds., *British Documents on the Origins of the War, 1898–1914*, vol. 3: *The Testing of the Entente, 1904–6* (London: His Majesty's Stationery Office, 1928), 402–3.

9. Reported in "Answers to the FP Quiz," *Foreign Policy*, no. 178 (March/April 2010): 110.

10. Carl von Clausewitz, *On War*, ed. and trans. Michael Howard and Peter Paret (Princeton: Princeton University Press, 1976), 128 (emphasis deleted).

11. Robert O. Keohane, *After Hegemony: Cooperation and Discord in the World Political Economy* (Princeton: Princeton University Press, 1984), 136–37.

12. On intelligence activities that skirted or violated U.S. law, see U.S. Senate Committee to Study Governmental Operations with Respect to Intelligence Activities, *Final Report*, book 2: *Intelligence Activities and the Rights of Americans*, 96–104, 139–65; and book 3: *Supplementary Detailed Staff Reports on Intelligence Activities and the Rights of Americans*, 94th Cong., 2d sess., 1976. The main case of a covert operation abroad that violated U.S. law was the Iran-Contra scandal in the 1980s. David Fagelson argues that covert action may be unconstitutional because Congress does not appropriate funds to the CIA in the constitutionally stipulated manner: "The Constitution and National Security: Covert Action in the Age of Intelligence Oversight," *Journal of Law and Politics* 5, no. 2 (Winter 1989): 294. The courts have not endorsed this interpretation.

13. Waltz, *Theory of International Politics*, 152.

14. On the difference between collective security and collective defense (alliance), see G. F. Hudson, "Collective Security and Military Alliances," in *Diplomatic Investigations*, ed. Herbert Butterfield and Martin Wight (Cambridge: Harvard University Press, 1968), 176–78; Arnold Wolfers, *Discord and Collaboration* (Baltimore: Johns Hopkins Press, 1962), chap. 12.

15. Joseph M. Jones, *The Fifteen Weeks* (New York: Viking, 1955), 6–11, 59–76, 92–94.

16. Robert A. Pollard, *Economic Security and the Origins of the Cold War, 1945–1950* (New York: Columbia University Press), 244; Walter Millis, ed., with the collabo-

ration of E. S. Duffield, *The Forrestal Diaries* (New York: Viking, 1951), 350–51.
On strategic comparative advantage, see Michael I. Handel, *Masters of War:
Classical Strategic Thought*, 3d ed. (London: Cass, 2001), 114.

17. Arthur B. Darling, *The Central Intelligence Agency: An Instrument of Government,
to 1950* (University Park: Pennsylvania State University Press, 1990), 245–65 (this
is the declassified publication of the CIA's official history originally compiled in
1953); U.S. Senate Select Committee to Study Governmental Operations with
Respect to Intelligence Activities, *Final Report*, book 4: *Supplementary Detailed
Staff Reports on Foreign Aid and Military Intelligence*, "History of the Central Intelligence Agency," 94th Cong., 2d sess., 1976, 25–31; Gregory Treverton, *Covert
Action* (New York: Basic Books, 1987), 20–21, 34–36.

18. Dean Acheson, *Present at the Creation: My Years in the State Department* (New
York: Norton, 1969), 280.

19. Robert E. Osgood, *NATO: The Entangling Alliance* (Chicago: University of Chicago Press, 1962), 32.

20. George F. Kennan, *Memoirs: 1925–1950* (Boston: Atlantic-Little, Brown, 1967),
358, 407–12.

21. NSC 68, "A Report to the President Pursuant to the President's Directive of January 31, 1950," April 7, 1950, chaps. 5, 7–9, in *Foreign Relations of the United States,
1950*, vol. 1: *National Security Affairs; Foreign Economic Policy* (Washington, D.C.:
Government Printing Office, 1977), 245–52, 262–87.

22. Samuel P. Huntington, *The Common Defense: Strategic Programs in National
Politics* (New York: Columbia University Press, 1961), 52.

23. Paul Y. Hammond, "NSC-68: Prologue to Rearmament," in *Strategy, Politics, and
Defense Budgets*, ed. Warner R. Schilling, Paul Y. Hammond, and Glenn H. Snyder (New York: Columbia University Press, 1962), 362.

24. Marc Trachtenberg and Christopher Gehrz, "America, Europe, and German Rearmament, August–September 1950: A Critique of a Myth," in *Between Empire
and Alliance: America and Europe During the Cold War*, ed. Marc Trachtenberg
(Lanham, Md.: Rowman and Littlefield, 2003), 8–9, 11–14.

25. Marc Trachtenberg, *A Constructed Peace: The Making of the European Settlement,
1945–1963* (Princeton: Princeton University Press, 1999), 148.

26. Douglas S. Blaufarb, *The Counterinsurgency Era: U.S. Doctrine and Performance*
(New York: Free Press, 1977), 52.

27. Henry A. Kissinger, *White House Years* (Boston: Little, Brown, 1979), 223–25.

28. Acceptance of the *condition* of mutual assured destruction did not mean shifting
to a *strategy* defined by it. Contrary to the mistaken inferences of dovish observers on the outside at the time, U.S. nuclear war plans remained oriented to coun-

terforce targeting, even though they could no longer promise great limitation of damage to the United States.

29. William W. Kaufmann, *Planning Conventional Forces, 1950–80* (Washington, D.C.: Brookings Institution, 1982), 4–17; Alain C. Enthoven and K. Wayne Smith, *How Much Is Enough? Shaping the Defense Program, 1961–1969* (New York: Harper and Row, 1971), 214.

30. Zbigniew Brzezinski, *Power and Principle: Memoirs of the National Security Adviser*, rev. ed. (New York: Farrar, Straus, Giroux, 1985), 456.

31. John S. Duffield, *Power Rules: The Evolution of NATO's Conventional Force Posture* (Stanford: Stanford University Press, 1995), 60–61.

32. NSC 162/2, October 30, 1953: "Basic National Security Policy," in *Foreign Relations of the United States, 1952–1954*, vol. 2: *National Security Affairs* (Washington, D.C.: Government Printing Office, 1984), 593.

33. Jane Stromseth, *The Origins of Flexible Response: NATO's Debate over Strategy in the 1960s* (London: Macmillan, 1988); Ivo Daalder, *The Nature and Practice of Flexible Response: NATO Strategy and Theater Nuclear Forces Since 1967* (New York: Columbia University Press, 1991).

34. Duffield, *Power Rules*, 112–14, 121–30; Trachtenberg, *A Constructed Peace*, 188–89.

35. Francis J. Gavin, "The Myth of Flexible Response," *International History Review* 23, no. 4 (December 2001): 859–61; Duffield, *Power Rules*, chap. 5.

36. J. Michael Legge, *Theater Nuclear Weapons and the NATO Strategy of Flexible Response*, R-2964-FF (Santa Monica, Calif.: RAND Corporation, April 1983), chap. 2; David N. Schwartz, *NATO's Nuclear Dilemmas* (Washington, D.C.: Brookings Institution, 1983), 152–85. A superb graphical representation of the chilling theoretical sequence of escalation in flexible response is in Carl H. Amme, Jr., *NATO Without France* (Stanford: Hoover Institution, 1967), 18.

37. The requirement to consult is conditioned by the qualification "time and circumstances permitting," and "the NATO Defense Planning Committee is not responsible for approving a nuclear release request . . . its function is to act as a channel for conveying the views of the allies to the nuclear power concerned." Legge, *Theater Nuclear Weapons*, 23.

38. Schwartz, *NATO's Nuclear Dilemmas*, 158–60.

39. Robert S. McNamara, "The Military Role of Nuclear Weapons: Perceptions and Misperceptions," *Foreign Affairs* 62, no. 1 (Fall 1983): 79.

40. Fred Kaplan, "JFK's First-Strike Plan," *Atlantic* Monthly 288, no. 3 (October 2001); Kaplan, *Wizards of Armageddon*, chap. 20; Richard K. Betts, *Nuclear Blackmail and Nuclear Balance* (Washington, D.C.: Brookings Institution, 1987),

91–102; Desmond Ball, *Politics and Force Levels* (Berkeley: University of California Press, 1980), 189–201; William W. Kaufmann, *The McNamara Strategy* (New York: Harper and Row, 1964), chap. 2.

41. Christopher Layne, "The Unipolar Illusion Revisited: The Coming End of the United States' Unipolar Moment," *International Security* 31, no. 2 (Fall 2006): 26n68.

42. Secretary of Defense William S. Cohen, *Report of the Quadrennial Defense Review* (Washington, D.C.: Department of Defense, May 1997), 9 (emphasis added).

43. Quoted in David M. Halbfinger, "Shedding Populist Tone, Kerry Starts Move to Middle," *New York Times*, May 8, 2004, A14.

44. Quoted in Mark Landler, "In a Speech on Policy, Clinton Revives a Theme of American Power," *New York Times*, September 9, 2010, A8.

45. G. John Ikenberry, *After Victory: Institutions, Strategic Restraint, and the Rebuilding of Order After Major Wars* (Princeton: Princeton University Press, 2001), 220, 221.

46. Thomas Risse-Kappen, *Cooperation Among Democracies: The European Influence on U.S. Foreign Policy* (Princeton: Princeton University Press, 1995).

47. "From Pentagon's Plan: 'Prevent the Re-Emergence of a New Rival,'" *New York Times*, March 8, 1992, 14.

48. Patrick Tyler, "Pentagon Drops Goal of Blocking New Superpowers," *New York Times*, May 24, 1992, 1, 14.

49. Press Release: "The Clinton Administration's Policy on Reforming Multilateral Peace Operations," U.S. Mission to the United Nations, n.d.; Eric Schmitt, "U.S. Set to Limit Role of Military in Peacekeeping," *New York Times*, January 29, 1994, 1, 5; Paul Lewis, "U.S. Plans Policy on Peacekeeping," *New York Times*, November 18, 1993, A7.

50. The phrase "militarization of enlargement" was suggested by Anne-Marie Slaughter.

51. Trachtenberg, *A Constructed Peace*, 147–56 (Eisenhower quoted on p. 147).

52. Ibid., 166–73, 213–15, 298n46.

53. Consider SACEUR Wesley Clark's experience in NATO's first war, over Kosovo in 1999. He was sandwiched between conflicting pressures from European diplomats and U.S. political and military leaders and provoked ire in the Pentagon when he did not truckle completely to his military colleagues' preferences. However, he did not resist demands from the American commander in chief, as reflected, for example, in the fact that the Clinton White House insisted on approving all bombing targets. See Wesley K. Clark, *Waging Modern War* (New York: PublicAffairs, 2001), 124–27, 178, 224, 278.

54. By 1958 De Gaulle told Eisenhower and British Prime Minister Harold Macmillan that it was "essential for Paris to participate directly in the political and strategic decisions of the alliance, decisions which were in reality taken by America alone with separate consultation with England." When Eisenhower tried to convince him to accept nuclear weapons from the United States, but with the Americans controlling the key to them, De Gaulle replied, "'If Russia attacks us, we are your allies and you are ours. But . . . we want to hold our fate in our own hands. . . . you Americans certainly have the means of annihilating the enemy on his own territory. But he has the means to blow you to pieces on yours. How could we French be sure that, unless you yourselves were bombed directly on your own soil, you would invite your own destruction. . . . I know, as you yourself know, what a nation is. . . . It can help another, but it cannot identify itself with an-other." When Kennedy visited and promised that the general could count on the United States to use nuclear weapons to defend Europe, De Gaulle later wrote, "But in answer to the specific questions I put to him, he was unable to tell me at what point and against which targets, far or near, strategic or tactical, inside or outside Russia itself, the missiles would in fact be launched. 'I am not surprised,' I told him. [American] General Norstad, the Allied Commander-in-Chief . . . has never been able to enlighten me on these points." Charles de Gaulle, *Memoirs of Hope: Renewal and Endeavor*, trans. Terence Kilmartin (New York: Simon and Schuster, 1971), 202–3, 213–14, 257–58.

55. Mary N. Hampton, "NATO at the Creation: U.S. Foreign Policy, West Germany, and the Wilsonian Impulse," *Security Studies* 4, no. 3 (Spring 1995): 616.

56. *Countering the Changing Threat of International Terrorism*, Report of the Na-tional Commission on Terrorism, Pursuant to Public Law 277, 105th Congress (n.p. [Washington, D.C.], n.d. [2000]), 9–12; *The 9/11 Commission Report: Final Report of the National Commission on Terrorist Attacks upon the United States* (New York: Norton, n.d. [2004]), 74–80.

57. Jones, *The Fifteen Weeks*, 177; James T. Patterson, *Mr. Republican: A Biography of Robert A. Taft* (Boston: Houghton Mifflin, 1972), 386.

3. CONFUSED INTERVENTIONS: PUTTERING WITH PRIMACY

1. Virginia Page Fortna, *Peace Time: Cease-Fire Agreements and the Durability of Peace* (Princeton: Princeton University Press, 2004), chaps. 3, 5, 6 and appendix A; Fortna, *Does Peacekeeping Work? Shaping Belligerents' Choices after Civil War* (Princeton: Princeton University Press, 2008), chaps. 5, 7, and appendix A. The verdict depends on discounting for the fact that peacekeepers are usually sent to the places where peace seems most likely to fail. The overall record is at best

a glass half-full: "Peace fell apart eventually in about 60% of the cases in which unarmed monitoring missions were present, and in almost 40% of the cases with armed peacekeeping forces, as compared to only about 20% of cease-fires with no peacekeeping." Fortna, *Peace Time*, 189.

2.   Referring to Congo, Doyle and Sambanis write: "One has to go back more than forty years to find a successful UN effort to impose a peace on recalcitrant parties who lacked a peace treaty or framework of agreement. Even so, that success produced one of the most corrupt and tyrannical regimes in post-independence Africa, and the peace crumbled in renewed fighting soon after the UN departed." Michael W. Doyle and Nicholas Sambanis, *Making War and Building Peace: United Nations Peace Operations* (Princeton: Princeton University Press, 2006), 172.

3.   See Michael Mandelbaum's scathing criticism, "A Perfect Failure: NATO's War against Yugoslavia," *Foreign Affairs* 78, no. 5 (September–October 1999); and the Clinton administration's rebuttal: James Steinberg, "A Perfect Polemic: Blind to the Reality on Kosovo," *Foreign Affairs* 78, no. 6 (November–December 1999).

4.   "Overwhelming" statistical evidence from cases in the 1990s shows that "peace is much more likely to last, and to last longer, when peacekeepers have deployed than when belligerents are left to their own devices." Fortna, *Does Peacekeeping Work?*, 116.

5.   General Wesley K. Clark, *Waging Modern War: Bosnia, Kosovo, and the Future of Combat* (New York: PublicAffairs, 2001), xxiii.

6.   Quoted in Gwen Ifill, "Conflict in the Balkans," *New York Times*, April 24, 1993, 6; and *Public Papers of the Presidents of the United States: William J. Clinton, 1993*, book 1 (Washington, D.C.: Government Printing Office, 1994), 488.

7.   Chuck Sudetic, "U.N. Warns Bosnians to End Shelling Violations," *New York Times*, August 11, 1994, A10.

8.   Michael Maren, "Leave Somalia Alone," *New York Times*, July 6, 1994, A19.

9.   Jeffrey Gettleman and Neil MacFarquhar, "Congo Rebels Advance; Protesters Hurl Rocks at U.N. Compound," *New York Times*, October 28, 2008, A6; "A Captive's Pain in the Strife of Eastern Congo," *New York Times*, November 24, 2008, A11; Stephanie McCrummen, "Meltdown in Darfur," *Washington Post National Weekly Edition*, July 14–20, 2008, 17, 18; Lynda Polgreen, "Darfur Peacekeepers Robbed by Militia in Army Uniforms," *New York Times*, May 24, 2008, A8; Polgreen, "Dozens Are Killed in Raid on Darfur Camp," *New York Times*, August 26, 2008, A9; "Sudan Asks Peacekeepers to Leave a Town," *New York Times*, February 2, 2009, A7.

10. United Nations Security Council Resolution 1244, June 10, 1999, Preamble (emphasis in original), and Resolution 1244, paragraph 10, and Annex 2, paragraph 5 (emphasis added). Lawyers tasked to justify the legality of independence might argue that it was implicit in the clauses of the resolution that included the condition, "taking into account the Rambouillet accords," which had envisioned a referendum in Kosovo that would almost certainly have approved independence. The fact remains that such reasoning was still inconsistent with the explicit references to Yugoslavia's sovereignty and integrity.

11. Richard K. Betts, "The Lesser Evil: The Best Way Out of the Balkans," *The National Interest* no. 64 (Summer 2001): 54. Kimberly Zisk Marten picks up this theme in more detail in *Enforcing the Peace: Learning from the Imperial Past* (New York: Columbia University Press, 2004), chap. 3.

12. Laurinda Zeman et al., *Making Peace While Staying Ready for War: The Challenges of U.S. Military Participation in Peace Operations* (Washington, D.C.: Congressional Budget Office, December 1999), 39–49.

13. Ivo H. Daalder, *Getting to Dayton* (Washington, D.C. Brookings Institution Press, 2000), 180.

14. Barry R. Posen, "The War for Kosovo: Serbia's Political-Military Strategy," *International Security* 24, no. 4 (Spring 2000): 79.

15. Michael Slackman, "U.N. Force Is Treading Lightly on Lebanese Soil," *New York Times*, September 25, 2006, A1, A12.

16. Radha Kumar, "The Troubled History of Partition," *Foreign Affairs* 76, no. 1 (January/February 1997).

17. Chaim Kaufmann, "Possible and Impossible Solutions to Ethnic Civil Wars," *International Security* 20, no. 4 (Spring 1996); and Kaufmann, "When All Else Fails: Ethnic Population Transfers and Partitions in the Twentieth Century," *International Security* 23, no. 2 (Fall 1998).

18. "Cypriots frequently overran UNFICYP's [United Nations Peacekeeping Force in Cyprus] posts, manhandled UN troops, and refused to comply with orders issued by UN commanders." One of the few exceptions to the UN force's passivity was its 1972 interdiction of arms supplies from Czechoslovakia to Greek Cypriots meant for police to fight EOKA-B, a subversive paramilitary organization, but this "significantly diminished the GC [Greek Cypriot] government's ability to fight terrorists." Doyle and Sambanis, *Making War and Building Peace*, 273, 276.

19. Quoted in Clark, *Waging Modern War*, 394. Clark feared that if Russia took control of a sector in the North, "Kosovo would be effectively partitioned" (p. 377).

That might actually have been desirable, since it would have made the independence of the rest of Kosovo more tolerable to the Serbs. More Russian forces were prevented from moving in when neighboring countries denied overflight permission.

20. Patrice C. McMahon and Jon Western, "The Death of Dayton," *Foreign Affairs* 88, no. 5 (September/October 2009); Craig Whitlock, "'We Must Not Let Things Fall Apart,'" *Washington Post National Weekly Edition,* August 31–September 6, 2009, 20; Neil MacFarquhar, "Serb Wins Bid to Review Independence of Kosovo," *New York Times,* October 9, 2008, A10.

21. Ivo H. Daalder and Michael E. O'Hanlon, *Winning Ugly: NATO's War to Save Kosovo* (Washington, D.C.: Brookings Institution Press, 2000), 216.

22. John Mueller, "The Banality of Ethnic War," *International Security* 25, no. 1 (Summer 2000).

23. Ambassador Richard Holbrooke believed the refugees generated would cause huge problems and peace would not follow—interstate war would simply replace intrastate war. See his *To End a War* (New York: Modern Library, 1999), 365.

24. Richard K. Betts, "Wealth, Power, and Instability," *International Security* 18, no. 3 (Winter 1993/94): 41.


4. New Threats of Mass Destruction:
   Capabilities Down, Intentions Up

1. WMD should be considered to be those that can inflict Hiroshima-level casualties—tens of thousands—at one blow. This conception has sometimes been confused by depreciation in official usage, for example, when the Nigerian "underwear bomber" who attempted to blow up an airliner on Christmas Day 2009 was legally charged with using a weapon of mass destruction.

2. Fred C. Iklé, "Nuclear Explosion," *Wall Street Journal,* August 5, 2005.

3. For perspectives on how these less quantifiable factors trump standard compilations of personnel, units, and equipment as measures of capability, see Stephen Biddle, *Military Power: Explaining Victory and Defeat in Modern Battle* (Princeton: Princeton University Press, 2004), chaps. 2, 3, 10; Kenneth M. Pollack, *Arabs at War: Military Effectiveness, 1948–1991* (Lincoln: University of Nebraska Press, 2002), 2–12, 552–83; and Bruce Newsome, *Made, Not Born: Why Some Soldiers Are Better than Others* (Westport, Conn.: Praeger Security International, 2007), chaps. 2, 3.

4. Quoted in George Quester and Victor Utgoff, "No-First-Use and Nonproliferation: Redefining Extended Deterrence," *Washington Quarterly* 17, no. 2 (Spring 1994): 107.

5.  Thomas L. McNaugher, "Ballistic Missiles and Chemical Weapons: The Legacy of the Iran-Iraq War," *International Security* 15, no. 2 (Fall 1990); Steve Fetter, "Ballistic Missiles and Weapons of Mass Destruction: What Is the Threat? What Should be Done?," *International Security* 16, no. 1 (Summer 1991): 15–22, 24–28.

6.  Scott D. Sagan, "The Commitment Trap: Why the United States Should Not Use Nuclear Threats to Deter Biological and Chemical Weapons Attacks," *International Security* 24, no. 4 (Spring 2000).

7.  U.S. Congress, Office of Technology Assessment, *Proliferation of Weapons of Mass Destruction: Assessing the Risks*, OTA-ISC-559 (Washington, D.C.: Government Printing Office, August 1993), 54.

8.  Kathleen C. Bailey, *Doomsday Weapons in the Hands of Many* (Urbana: University of Illinois Press, 1991), chap. 7.

9.  Keir A. Lieber and Daryl G. Press, "The End of MAD? The Nuclear Dimension of U.S. Primacy," *International Security* 30, no. 4 (Spring 2006).

10.  John F. Sopko, "The Changing Proliferation Threat," *Foreign Policy* no. 105 (Winter 1996–97): 18; Lawrence J. Korb and Sean E. Duggan, "Putting the Coast Guard Out to Sea," *New York Times*, February 27, 2010, A21.

11.  For the full version of this argument, see Richard K. Betts, *Enemies of Intelligence: Knowledge and Power in American National Security* (New York: Columbia University Press, 2007), chap. 7.

12.  Siobhan Gorman, "FAA's Air-Traffic Networks Breached by Hackers," *Wall Street Journal*, May 7, 2009.

## 5. TERRORISM: THE SOFT UNDERBELLY OF PRIMACY

1.  John Mueller, *Overblown: How Politicians and the Terrorism Industry Inflate National Security Threats, and Why We Believe Them* (New York: Free Press, 2006), 13.

2.  *Countering the Threat of International Terrorism,* Report of the National Commission on Terrorism Pursuant to Public Law 277, 105th Congress (Washington, D.C., 2000), 1–2, 5.

3.  Thomas L. McNaugher, "Ballistic Missiles and Chemical Weapons: The Legacy of the Iran-Iraq War," *International Security* 15, no. 2 (Fall 1990): 8–15. Despite their frightening psychological impact, the German V-1 and V-2 missile programs were not at all cost-effective in material terms, providing a very low military return relative to investment. Williamson Murray and Allan R. Millett, *A War to Be Won: Fighting the Second World War* (Cambridge: Harvard University Press, 2000), 333. Perhaps because ballistic missiles, being supersonic, give no

warning, they seemed more fearsome than bombers or regular artillery, which both cause far higher casualties.

4.  Mueller, *Overblown*, chaps. 1–2. For rebuttal, see Richard K. Betts, "Maybe I'll Stop Driving," *Terrorism and Political Violence* 17, no. 4 (Autumn 2005).

5.  Mueller, *Overblown*, 4 (emphasis added).

6.  Ibid., 5.

7.  *National Strategy for Combating Terrorism* (Washington, D.C.: The White House, February 2003), 10.

8.  Mueller, *Overblown*, 22–23.

9.  For a survey of types, see Christopher C. Harmon, "Five Strategies of Terrorism," *Small Wars and Insurgencies* 12, no. 3 (Autumn 2001).

10. Suicide terrorism in particular has been tightly correlated with resistance to foreign intervention or occupation. Robert A. Pape, *Dying to Win: The Strategic Logic of Suicide Terrorism* (New York: Random House, 2005), chap. 4.

11. "Full Transcript of bin Ladin's Speech," October 30, 2004, http://english.aljazeera .net/NR/exeres/79C6AF22–98FB-4A1C-B21F-2BC36E87F61F.htm. In December 2010 a suicide bomber did strike in Stockholm, but this was after Sweden had sent a small troop contingent to Afghanistan.

12. "We issue the following fatwa to all Muslims: The ruling to kill Americans and their allies—civilians and military—is an individual duty for every Muslim who can do it in any country in which it is possible to do it. . . . comply with allah's order to kill the Americans and plunder their money whenever they find it." Shaykh Usamah Bin-Muhammad Bin-Ladin et al., "Jihad Against Jews and Crusaders: World Islamic Front Statement," February 23, 1998, http://www.fas.org/ irp/world/para/docs/980223-fatwa.htm.

13. Washington did exert pressure on Israel at times. The Bush I administration, for example, threatened to withhold loans for housing construction, but this was a marginal portion of total U.S. aid. There was never a threat to cut off the basic annual maintenance payment of several billion dollars to which Israel became accustomed decades ago.

14. The United States has also given aid to friendly Arab governments, but this does not counterbalance the aid to Israel in effects on Muslim opinion. Radical Islamists have seen the regimes in Cairo (under Mubarak for thirty years) and Amman as American toadies, complicit in betrayal of the Palestinians.

15. Samuel P. Huntington anticipated this in his 1962 analysis of the differences between symmetrical intergovernmental war and asymmetrical antigovernmental war. See "Patterns of Violence in World Politics," in *Changing Patterns of Military Politics*, ed. Huntington (New York: Free Press of Glencoe, 1962), 19–21.

16. Eric Frank Russell, *Wasp* (London: Victor Gollancz, 2000 [originally published 1957]), 7.

17. The Royal Air Force gave up on precision bombing early and focused deliberately on night bombing of German cities, while the Americans continued to try precision daylight bombing. Firestorms in Hamburg, Darmstadt, and Dresden, and less incendiary attacks on other cities, killed several hundred thousand German civilians. Over Japan, the United States quickly abandoned attempts at precision bombing when weather made it impractical and deliberately resorted to an incendiary campaign that burned most Japanese cities to the ground and killed at least 300,000 civilians (and perhaps more than half a million) well before the nuclear attacks on Hiroshima and Nagasaki, which killed another 200,000. Michael S. Sherry, *The Rise of American Air Power: The Creation of Armageddon* (New Haven: Yale University Press, 1987), 260, 413n43.

18. The threat of deliberate nuclear escalation remained the bedrock of NATO doctrine throughout the Cold War, but after the Kennedy administration the flexible response doctrine made it conditional and included options for nuclear first-use that did not involve deliberate targeting of population centers. In the Eisenhower administration, however, all-out attack on the Soviet bloc's cities was integral to plans for defense of Western Europe against Soviet armored divisions.

19. Quoted in "Bin Ladin's Words: 'America Is in Decline,' the Leader of Al Qaeda Says," *New York Times*, December 28, 2001, B2.

20. Soft power is "indirect or cooptive" and "can rest on the attraction of one's ideas or on the ability to set the political agenda in a way that shapes the preferences that others express." It "tends to be associated with intangible power resources such as culture, ideology, and institutions." Joseph S. Nye, Jr., "The Changing Nature of World Power," *Political Science Quarterly* 105, no. 2 (Summer 1990): 181. See also Nye, *Soft Power: The Means to Success in World Politics* (New York: PublicAffairs, 2004).

21. For example: Bruce Hoffmann, *Inside Terrorism* (New York: Columbia University Press, 1998); Richard A. Falkenrath, Robert D. Newman, and Bradley A. Thayer, *America's Achilles Heel: Nuclear, Biological, and Chemical Terrorism and Covert Attack* (Cambridge: MIT Press, 1998); and Paul R. Pillar, *Terrorism and American Foreign Policy* (Washington, D.C.: Brookings Institution, 2001).

22. The ripple effects include strategic judo. Creating a phony rebel organization leads the enemy security apparatus to turn on its own people. "If some Sirians could be given the full-time job of hunting down and garroting other Sirians, and if other Sirians could be given the full-time job of dodging or shooting down the garroters, then a distant and different life form would be saved a few

unpleasant chores. . . . Doubtless the military would provide a personal body-guard for every big wheel on Jaimec; that alone would pin down a regiment." Russell, *Wasp*, 64, 26, 103.

23.  Study by the Milken Institute discussed in "The Economics: Attacks May Cost 1.8 Million Jobs," *New York Times*, January 13, 2002, 16.

24.  "Full Transcript of bin Ladin's Speech," 4.

25.  See "Problems of Strategy in China's Revolutionary War" (especially chap. 5), in *Selected Works of Mao Tse-Tung* (Peking: Foreign Languages Press, 1967), vol. 1; and "Problems of Strategy in Guerrilla War Against Japan," in *Selected Works*, vol. 2 (1967). Much of the Western analytical literature grew out of British experience in the Malayan Emergency and France's in Indochina and Algeria. For example: Franklin Mark Osanka, ed., *Modern Guerrilla Warfare* (New York: Free Press, 1962); Roger Trinquier, *Modern Warfare: A French View of Counterinsurgency*, trans. Daniel Lee (New York: Praeger, 1964); David Galula, *Counterinsurgency Warfare: Theory and Practice* (New York: Praeger, 1964); George Armstrong Kelly, *Lost Soldiers: The French Army and Empire in Crisis, 1947–1962* (Cambridge: MIT Press, 1965), chaps. 5–7, 9–10; Sir Robert Thompson, *Defeating Communits Insurgency* (New York: Praeger, 1966); Richard L. Clutterbuck, *The Long Long War: Counterinsurgency in Malaya and Vietnam* (New York: Praeger, 1966); W. P. Davison, *Some Observations on Viet Cong Operations in the Villages* (Santa Monica: RAND Corporation, 1968); and *Guerrilla Strategies: An Historical Anthology from the Long March to Afghanistan*, ed. Gerard Chaliand (Berkeley: University of California Press, 1982). See also Douglas S. Blaufarb, *The Counter-Insurgency Era: U.S. Doctrine and Performance, 1950 to the Present* (New York: Free Press, 1977); D. Michael Shafer, *Deadly Paradigms: The Failure of U.S. Counterinsurgency Policy* (Princeton: Princeton University Press, 1988); and Timothy J. Lomperis, *From People's War to People's Rule: Insurgency, Intervention, and the Lessons of Vietnam* (Chapel Hill: University of North Carolina Press, 1996).

26.  Huntington, "Patterns of Violence in World Politics," 20–27.

27.  Robert Jervis, "Cooperation under the Security Dilemma," *World Politics* 30, no. 2 (January 1978); Jack L. Snyder, *The Ideology of the Offensive: Military Decision Making and the Disasters of 1914* (Ithaca: Cornell University Press, 1984); George Quester, *Offense and Defense in the International System*, 2d edition (New Brunswick, N.J.: Transaction Books, 1988); Sean Lynn-Jones, "Offense-Defense Theory and Its Critics," *Security* Studies 4, no. 4 (Summer 1995); Charles L. Glaser and Chaim Kaufmann, "What Is the Offense-Defense Balance and Can We Measure It?" *International Security* 22, no. 4 (Spring 1998); and Stephen Van

Evera, *Causes of War: Power and the Roots of Conflict* (Ithaca: Cornell University Press, 1999), chaps. 6–8.

28. For critiques, see Jack S. Levy, "The Offensive/Defensive Balance of Military Technology," *International Studies Quarterly* 28, no. 2 (June 1984); Richard K. Betts, "Conventional Deterrence: Predictive Uncertainty and Policy Confidence," *World Politics* 37, no. 2 (January 1985); Scott D. Sagan, "1914 Revisited," *International Security* 11, no. 2 (Fall 1986); Jonathan Shimshoni, "Technology, Military Advantage, and World War I: A Case for Military Entrepreneurship," *International Security* 15, no. 3 (Winter 1990/91); and Richard K. Betts, "Must War Find a Way?" *International Security* 24, no. 2 (Fall 1999).

29. Jerry Schwartz, Associated Press dispatch, October 6, 2001, quoted in Brian Reich, "Strength in the Face of Terror: A Comparison of United States and International Efforts to Provide Homeland Security," ms., Columbia University, December 2001, 5.

30. Stephen E. Flynn, "The Unguarded Homeland," in *How Did This Happen? Terrorism and the New War*, ed. James F. Hoge, Jr., and Gideon Rose (New York: PublicAffairs, 2001), 185.

31. Ibid., 185–86.

32. Ibid., 193–94.

33. Thomas L. Friedman, "Naked Air," *New York Times*, December 26, 2001, A29.

34. See Steven Simon and Daniel Benjamin, "America and the New Terrorism," *Survival* 42, no. 1 (Spring 2000): 59, 66–69, 74.

35. Estimates in the 1960s indicated that even combining ABM systems with counterforce strikes and fallout shelters, the United States would have to counter each Soviet dollar spent on ICBMs with three U.S. dollars to protect 70 percent of industry, assuming highly effective ABMs (0.8 kill probability). To protect up to 80 percent of population, far higher ratios would be necessary. Fred Kaplan, *The Wizards of Armageddon* (New York: Simon and Schuster, 1983), 321–24.

36. For an appropriate list of recommendations, see *Countering the Changing Threat of International Terrorism*. This report holds up very well in light of September 11th.

37. Quoted in Douglas Jehl, "After Prison, a Saudi Sheik Tempers His Words," *New York Times*, December 27, 2001, B4.

38. Michael Walzer, *Just and Unjust Wars: A Moral Argument with Historical Illustrations*, 4th ed. (New York: Basic Books, 2006), chap. 16.

39. See data in the study by Barry M. Blechman and Tamara Cofman Wittes, "Defining Moment: The Threat and Use of Force in American Foreign Policy," *Political Science Quarterly* 114, no. 1 (Spring 1999).

40. Quoted in Simon and Benjamin, "America and the New Terrorism," 69.

41. Pillar, *Terrorism and U.S. Foreign Policy*, 130.

42. Ibid., 231.

43. "Perhaps terrorism is most likely to occur precisely where mass passivity and elite disaffection coincide. . . . Terrorism may thus be a sign of a stable society rather than a symptom of fragility and impending collapse. Terrorism is the resort of an elite when conditions are not revolutionary." Martha Crenshaw, "The Causes of Terrorism," *Comparative Politics* 13, no. 4 (July 1981): 384. The second part of this diagnosis applies more to the typical terrorism of the Cold War than to the radical Islamist terrorism of recent years.

44. Rohan Gunaratna, *Inside Al Qaeda: Global Network of Terror* (New York: Columbia University Press, 2002), 185; Pillar, *Terrorism and U.S. Foreign Policy*, 233. Terrorists also tend to attack democracies: Robert A. Pape, *Dying to Win: The Strategic Logic of Suicide Terrorism* (New York: Random House, 2005), chap. 4.

45. See, for example, Lawrence Wright, *The Looming Tower: Al Qaeda and the Road to 9/11* (New York: Knopf, 2006), chap. 1 and pp. 186–87.

46. Michael Mousseau, "Market Civilization and Its Clash with Terror," *International Security* 27, no. 3 (Winter 2002/03): 26.

47. "Full Transcript of bin Ladin's Speech."

48. Martha Crenshaw, "The Logic of Terrorism: Terrorist Behavior as a Product of Strategic Choice," in *Origins of Terrorism: Psychologies, Ideologies, Theologies, States of Mind*, ed. Walter Reich (Washington, D.C.: Woodrow Wilson Center Press, 1998); Marc Sageman, "Jihadi Networks of Terror," in *Countering Modern Terrorism: History, Current Issues and Future Threats*, ed. Katharina von Knop, Heinrich Neisser, and Martin van Creveld, Proceedings of the Second International Security Conference, Berlin, December 15–17, 2004 (Bielefeld, Germany: W. Bertelsmann Verlag, 2005).

49. Jerrold M. Post, "Terrorist Psycho-Logic: Terrorist Behavior as a Product of Psychological Forces," in *Origins of Terrorism*, ed. Reich, 25, 27–28, 35 (emphasis in original).

6. STRIKING FIRST: WELL-LOST OPPORTUNITIES

1. See Michael W. Doyle et al., *Striking First: Preemption and Prevention in International Conflict* (Princeton: Princeton University Press, 2008).

2. Ibid., 55: "The likelihood of less imminent threats that justify preventive action is shaped by a change in military capabilities that produces a significant rise in threatening power, a change in regime that produces a significant shift in ex-

pected intentions, *or* a change in an actor's behavior; *each* may trigger a justifiable preventive war if the threats are sufficiently certain and large" (emphasis added). Then on p. 63: "The overall set of standards that I propose is systemic; *each is necessary* and all are interrelated. We can think of them as multiplicative, not additive. . . . That is, if one standard measures in at zero, no preventive action is justified" (emphasis added).

3. For example, to justify the Israeli attack on Iraq's nuclear reactor in 1981 as preemptive, which is generally recognized as more legitimate than preventive attack: "Imminence, according to this view, involves more than merely the temporal immediacy of the threat itself; it is a function of the temporal opportunity for carrying out the preventive action, as well as the seriousness of the feared harm." Alan M. Dershowitz, *Preemption: A Knife That Cuts Both Ways* (New York: Norton, 2006), 96.

4. The prevalent view that realpolitik is amoral rests on a narrow concept of morality. If morality means rightness or wrongness of an action, absolute principles are not the only moral standard in politics, and utilitarian or consequentialist considerations must apply. This is Machiavelli's essential message in his arguments for why a prince must sometimes do evil in order to do good.

5. Doyle, *Striking First*, 30; Allen Buchanan and Robert O. Keohane, "The Preventive Use of Force: A Cosmopolitan Institutional Proposal," *Ethics & International Affairs* 18, no. 1 (2004): 3.

6. Lee Feinstein and Anne Marie Slaughter, "A Duty to Prevent," *Foreign Affairs* 83, no. 1 (January/February 2004).

7. Abraham D. Sofaer, "The Best Defense? Preventive Force and International Security," *Foreign Affairs* 89, no. 1 (January/February 2010): 114, 116.

8. On the differences between preventive and preemptive war and incentives for either, see Richard K. Betts, *Surprise Attack: Lessons for Defense Planning* (Washington, D.C.: Brookings Institution, 1982), 141–46, 168, 233–34, 262, and Betts, "Surprise Attack and Preemption," in *Hawks, Doves, and Owls*, ed. Graham T. Allison, Albert Carnesale, and Joseph S. Nye, Jr. (New York: Norton, 1985).

9. Dan Reiter, "Exploding the Powder Keg Myth: Preemptive Wars Almost Never Happen," *International Security* 20, no. 2 (Fall 1995).

10. Jack L. Snyder, *The Ideology of the Offensive: Military Decision Making and the Disasters of 1914* (Ithaca: Cornell University Press, 1984); and Stephen Van Evera, *Causes of War: Power and the Roots of Conflict* (Ithaca: Cornell University Press, 1999), chap. 7.

11. Russell D. Buhite and Wm. Christopher Hamel, "War for Peace: The Question of an American Preventive War Against the Soviet Union, 1945–1955," *Diplo-*

*matic History* 14, no. 3 (Summer 1990); Marc Trachtenberg, *History and Strategy* (Princeton: Princeton University Press, 1991), 103–18, 132–46; William Burr and Jeffrey T. Richelson, "Whether to 'Strangle the Baby in the Cradle': The United States and the Chinese Nuclear Program, 1960–64," *International Security* 25, no. 3 (Winter 2000/01); Robert S. Litwak, "The New Calculus of Pre-emption," *Survival* 44, no. 4 (Winter 2002–03): 61–62.

12. Robert M. Lawrence and William R. Van Cleave, "Assertive Disarmament," *National Review* (September 10, 1968).

13. Nigel Nicolson, ed., *Harold Nicolson Diaries and Letters, 1907–1964* (London: Weidenfeld & Nicolson, 2004), 363. I thank Gideon Rose for calling this entry to my attention.

14. This section draws on Richard K. Betts, "The Osirak Fallacy," *The National Interest*, no. 83 (Spring 2006). I subsequently discovered that Dan Reiter makes similar points in "Preventive Attacks Against Nuclear Programs and the 'Success' at Osiraq," *Nonproliferation Review* 12, no. (July 2005).

15. For several reasons—see Richard K. Betts, "Suicide for Fear of Death?" *Foreign Affairs* 82, no. 1 (January/February 2003).

16. Malfrid Braut-Hegghammer, "Revisiting *Osirak*: Air Strikes and Domestic Drivers of Nuclear Proliferation," ms., 2009.

17. Amos Perlmutter, Michael Handel, and Uri Bar-Joseph, *Two Minutes Over Baghdad* (London: Corgi, 1982), 149.

18. Even Israel, with more constraints than the U.S. Air Force, could strike known targets in Iran effectively. Even assuming that Iran does not have a full, undiscovered parallel program, uncertainty about intelligence on targeting remains a reason against assuming complete effectiveness of an attack. Whitney Raas and Austin Long, "Osirak Redux? Assessing Israeli Capabilities to Destroy Iranian Nuclear Facilities," *International Security* 31, no. 4 (Spring 2007): 9, 31, and passim.

19. Amrom H. Katz, "The Fabric of Verification: The Warp and Woof," in *Verification and SALT: The Challenge of Strategic Deception*, ed. William C. Potter (Boulder, Colo.: Westview Press, 1980), 212.

20. Quoted in C. L. Sulzberger, *An Age of Mediocrity* (New York: Macmillan, 1973), 463.

21. Carl von Clausewitz, *On War*, ed. and trans. Michael Howard and Peter Paret (Princeton: Princeton University Press, 1976), 80. See also Michael I. Handel, *Masters of War: Classical Strategic Thought*, 3rd ed. (London: Frank Cass, 2001), 196–201.

22. Karl P. Mueller et al., *Striking First: Preemptive and Preventive Attack in U.S. National Security Policy* (Santa Monica, Calif.: RAND Corporation, 2006), xviii.

## 7. BIG SMALL WARS: IRAQ, AFGHANISTAN, AND VIETNAM

1. The first President Bush later denied the green light by noting that Washington had made clear it "did not condone aggression," and he explained away Ambassador April Glaspie's statement to Saddam Hussein that the United States did not have a position on the territorial dispute as "standard State Department language" that "has been grossly misconstrued as implying we would look the other way." George Bush and Brent Scowcroft, *A World Transformed* (New York: Knopf, 1998), 311. Nevertheless, Glaspie made the statement, and conveyed no threat that the United States would respond militarily to an attack on Kuwait.

2. Joseph E. Stiglitz and Linda J. Bilmes, *The Three Trillion Dollar War: The True Cost of the Iraq Conflict* (New York: Norton, 2008).

3. For additional reasons, see Richard K. Betts, "Suicide from Fear of Death?" *Foreign Affairs* 82, no. 1 (January/February 2003); and "War with Iraq Is Not in America's National Interest," the manifesto by thirty-three scholars of strategic studies on the op-ed page of the *New York Times*, September 26, 2002.

4. David Kilcullen, quoted in Thomas E. Ricks, *The Gamble: General David Petraeus and the American Military Adventure in Iraq, 2006–2008* (New York: Penguin, 2009), 163.

5. Jason Lyall and Isaiah Wilson III, "Rage Against the Machines: Explaining Outcomes in Counterinsurgency Wars," *International Organization* 63, no. 1 (Winter 2009): 69, 73–77. The success rate declined over time, running at 70–95 percent in the nineteenth century and 40 percent in the third quarter of the twentieth, according to Lyall and Wilson; they argue that the higher failure rate of more recent times occurred because mechanization supplanted foraging and isolated armies from interaction with populations. Revision of American counterinsurgency doctrine in the twenty-first century pushes practice back away from such separation. Determining the scorecard for success and failure is a slippery task and depends on how cases are defined and ambiguous results in some are counted. In a tally contrasting with Lyall and Wilson's, for example, counterinsurgents won in just over two-thirds of cases since 1945. Seth G. Jones, *In the Graveyard of Empires: America's War in Afghanistan* (New York: Norton, 2009), 154–55. For criticism of Lyall and Wilson, see Niel A. Smith and Nathan W. Toronto, "It's All the Rage: Why Mechanization Doesn't Explain COIN Outcomes," *Small Wars and Insurgencies* 21, no. 3 (September 2010).

6.  Michael A. Cohen, "The Myth of a Kinder, Gentler War," *World Policy Journal* (Spring 2010).

7.  J. B. Firth, "The Guerrilla in History," *Fortnightly Review* (ed. W. L. Courtney) 70, New Series (July–December 1901): 806–8, 811.

8.  See, for example, Carline Elkins, *Imperial Reckoning: The Untold Story of Britain's Gulag in Kenya* (New York: Henry Holt, 2005); Brian McAllister Linn, *The Philippine War 1899–1902* (Lawrence: University Press of Kansas, 2000), 212–13, 220–24.

9.  Col. C. E. Callwell, *Small Wars: Their Principles and Practice*, 3d ed. (London: HMSO, 1901), 40, 42.

10. Martin van Creveld, "On Counterinsurgency," in *Countering Modern Terrorism: History, Current Issues and Future Threats*, ed. Katarina von Knopp, Heinrich Neisser, and Martin van Creveld, Proceedings of the Second International Security Conference, Berlin, December 15–17, 2004 (Bielefeld: W. Bertelsmann Verlag, 2005), 119–21.

11. Research indicated that in Iraq, with high population density, accidental killing of civilians reduced people's willingness to give information to counterinsurgent forces, and in Afghanistan it increased insurgent recruitment. Collateral damage inflicted by insurgents also generated less public outrage than accidental killing by counterinsurgents. Luke N. Condra, Joseph H. Felter, Radha K. Iyengar, and Jacob N. Shapiro, *The Effect of Civilian Casualties in Afghanistan and Iraq*, Working Paper no. 16152 (Cambridge, Mass.: National Bureau of Economic Research, July 2010), 2, 2n, 4, 30.

12. Quoted in Robert Shaplen, *The Lost Revolution: The U.S. in Vietnam, 1946–1966* (New York: Harper and Row, 1966), 48.

13. Quoted in Michael I. Handel, *Masters of War: Classical Strategic Thought*, 3d ed. (London: Frank Cass, 2001), 159.

14. T. E. Lawrence, "Science of Guerrilla Warfare," *Encyclopedia Britannica*, 14th ed., 1929, 10:952. "How would the Turks defend all that—no doubt by a trench line across the bottom, if the Arabs were an army attacking with banners displayed . . . but suppose they were an influence, a thing invulnerable, intangible, without front or back, drifting about like a gas? Armies were like plants, immobile as a whole, firm-rooted . . . the Arabs might be a vapour. . . . The next step was to estimate how many posts they [the Turks] would need . . . sedition putting up her head in every unoccupied one of these 100,000 square miles. They would have need of a fortified post every four square miles, and a post could not be less than 20 men. The Turks would need 600,000 men . . . they had 100,000 men available" (951).

15. Mao Tse-tung, *Selected Military Writings*, quoted in Handel, *Masters of War*, 366.

16. Sir Robert Thompson, *Defeating Communist Insurgency: The Lessons of Malaya and Vietnam* (New York: Praeger, 1966), 48. Thompson's estimated ratios included police and Home Guard forces on the government side.

17. Michael R. Gordon and General Bernard E. Trainor, *Cobra II: The Inside Story of the Invasion and Occupation of Iraq* (New York: Pantheon, 2006), 468–69, 477. The numbers look better if civilian contractors, who have taken over many logistical functions previously handled by military personnel, are counted in the force ratios.

18. L. Paul Bremer III, *My Year in Iraq* (New York: Simon and Schuster, 2006), 356.

19. James T. Quinlivan, "Force Requirements in Stability Operations," *Parameters* 25, no. 4 (Winter 1995–96): 65.

20. David Galula, *Counterinsurgency Warfare: Theory and Practice* (New York: Praeger, 1964), 72.

21. Quoted in John A. Nagl, *Learning to Eat Soup with a Knife: Counterinsurgency Lessons from Malaya and Vietnam* (Chicago: University of Chicago Press, 2005), 27.

22. Thompson, *Defeating Communist Insurgency*, 35.

23. Douglas Pike, *Viet Cong: The Organization and Techniques of the National Liberation Front of South Vietnam* (Cambridge: MIT Press, 1966), 155.

24. Quinlivan, "Force Requirements in Stability Operations," 63–64.

25. Jeffrey A. Friedman, "Boots on the Ground: The Significance of Manpower in Counterinsurgency," ms., Kennedy School of Government, Harvard University, May 2010, 8, 12, 17.

26. Steven M. Goode, "A Historical Basis for Force Requirements in Counterinsurgency," *Parameters* 39, no. 4 (Winter 2009–10): 45–47, 52.

27. Antonio Giustozzi, *Koran, Kalashnikov, and Laptop: The Neo-Taliban Insurgency in Afghanistan* (New York: Columbia University Press, 2008), 237.

28. "In Marja, Marines Try to Win Trust," *New York Times*, March 1, 2010, A10.

29. Richard Clutterbuck, *The Long, Long War: The Emergency in Malaya 1948–1960* (London: Cassell, 1966).

30. Seth G. Jones, *Counterinsurgency in Afghanistan* (Santa Monica, Calif.: RAND Corporation, 2008), 10.

31. Leslie H. Gelb with Richard K. Betts, *The Irony of Vietnam: The System Worked* (Washington, D.C.: Brookings Institution, 1979).

32. Samuel P. Huntington, "Patterns of Violence in World Politics," in *Changing Patterns of Military Politics*, ed. Huntington (Glencoe, Ill.: Free Press, 1962), 29.

33. Thomas C. Thayer, *War Without Fronts: The American Experience in Vietnam* (Boulder, Colo.: Westview Press, 1985), 157, 160, 163; Shaplen, *Lost Revolution*, 137, 139; William R. Corson, *The Betrayal* (New York: Norton, 1968), 84, 87.

34. Thayer, *War Without Fronts*, 165–67.

35. Richard A. Hunt, *Pacification: The American Struggle for Vietnam's Hearts and Minds* (Boulder, Colo.: Westview Press, 1995), 200–201.

36. Jeffrey Race, *War Comes to Long An: Revolutionary Conflict in a Vietnamese Province* (Berkeley: University of California Press, 1972), xiv, xvi; Douglas Blaufarb, *The Counterinsurgency Era: U. S. Doctrine and Performance 1950 to the Present* (New York: Free Press, 1977), 270–73; Pike, *Viet Cong*, 110 and chap. 10; Alan Goodman and Douglas Pike, cited in Timothy J. Lomperis, *The War Everyone Lost—and Won: America's Intervention in Viet Nam's Twin Struggles* (Baton Rouge: Louisiana State University Press, 1984), 104; Kevin M. Boylan, "The Red Queen's Race: Operation Washington Green and Pacification in Binh Dinh Province, 1969–70," *Journal of Military History* 73, no. 4 (October 2009): 1201, 1203–4, 1226–27.

37. On the Phoenix program, see Mark Moyar, *Phoenix and the Birds of Prey: The CIA's Secret Campaign to Destroy the Viet Cong* (Annapolis: Naval Institute Press, 1997; new ed. University of Nebraska Press, 2007); Thayer, *War Without Fronts*, 208–16; William Rosenau and Austin Long, *The Phoenix Program and Contemporary Counterinsurgency* (Santa Monica, Calif.: RAND Corporation, 2009), chaps. 2, 3.

38. Dexter Filkins, "U.S. Delays Setting Up More Anti-Taliban Militias," *New York Times*, January 23, 2010, A3.

39. Alissa J. Rubin, "Afghan Program Adds Local Units to Resist Taliban," *New York Times*, July 15, 2010, A1.

40. Corson, *The Betrayal*, 108.

41. John T. McAlister, Jr., *Viet Nam: The Origins of Revolution* (New York: Knopf, 1969), 7–8.

42. Kilcullen, *Accidental Guerrilla*, 51.

43. Austin Long, "The Anbar Awakening," *Survival* 50, no. 2 (April/May 2008): 82.

44. A few of the following paragraphs draw on Richard K. Betts, "Blowtorch Bob in Baghdad," *The American Interest* 1, no. 4 (Summer 2006): 39–40, 36–37.

45. Ricks, *The Gamble*, 31; and Steven Metz, cited by Ricks, 165.

46. Samuel P. Huntington, *Political Order in Changing Societies* (New Haven: Yale University Press, 1968); Edward D. Mansfield and Jack Snyder, *Electing to Fight: Why Emerging Democracies Go to War* (Cambridge: MIT Press, 2005); Jack L. Snyder, *From Voting to Violence: Democratization and Nationalist Conflict* (New York: Norton, 2000).

47. Robert W. Komer, *Bureaucracy at War: U.S. Performance in the Vietnam Conflict* (Boulder, Colo.: Westview Press, 1986), 12, 35, 81, 99. This book was the commercially published version of Komer's RAND monograph, better known inside the Washington Beltway: *Bureaucracy Does Its Thing: Institutional Constraints on U.S.-GVN Performance in Vietnam*, R-967-ARPA (Santa Monica, Calif.: RAND Corporation, August 1972).

48. Komer, *Bureaucracy at War*, 163.

49. "U.S. Debates Afghan Leader's Role in Corruption Fight," *New York Times*, September 15, 2010, A12.

50. Komer, *Bureaucracy at War*, 10, 12, 35, 70, 136.

51. Ibid., 22, 24, 160.

52. Clausewitz, *On War*, 92.

53. Stephen Biddle, "Is It Worth It?," *The American Interest* 4, no. 6 (July/August 2009): 11.

## 8. THE MAIN EVENTS: CHINA'S RISE AND RUSSIA'S RESURGENCE

1. Robert Gilpin, *War and Change in World Politics* (New York: Cambridge University Press, 1981), 13–15, 48–49, 186–204. With the exception of passages noted that were written by Christensen, the first half of this chapter draws on the portions written by Betts in Richard K. Betts and Thomas J. Christensen, "China: Getting the Questions Right," *The National Interest* no. 62 (Winter 2000/01).

2. Michael Pillsbury, ed., *Chinese Views of Future Warfare* (Washington, D.C.: National Defense University Press, 1997), part 4.

3. Susan L. Shirk, *China: Fragile Superpower* (New York: Oxford University Press, 2007); Lester Thurow, "A Chinese Century? Maybe It's the Next One" *New York Times*, August 19, 2007, BU4.

4. Thomas J. Christensen, "Posing Problems without Catching Up," *International Security* 25, no. 4 (Spring 2001).

5. Quoted in Helene Cooper and Martin Fackler, "U.S. Is Not Threatened by the Success of China, Obama Tells the Japanese," *New York Times*, December 14, 2009, A6.

6. Richard Rosecrance, *The Rise of the Trading State* (New York: Basic Books, 1986), 146–47. See also Helen Milner, "Trading Places: Industries for Free Trade," *World Politics* 40, no. 3 (April 1988): 350–76.

7. G. John Ikenberry, "The Rise of China and the Future of the West," *Foreign Affairs* 87, no. 1 (January/February 2008). Cautious examples of institutionalist optimism are James Shinn, *Weaving the Net: Conditional Engagement with*

*China* (New York: Council on Foreign Relations, 1996); and David Shambaugh, "China Engages Asia: Reshaping the Regional Order," *International Security* 29, no. 3 (Winter 2004/05). A constructivist version is Alastair Iain Johnston, *Social States: China in International Institutions* (Princeton: Princeton University Press, 2008).

8.   Andrew Scobell, "Is There a Civil-Military Gap in China's Peaceful Rise?" *Parameters* 39, no. 2 (Summer 2009): 10, 12.

9.   Michael W. Doyle, "Liberalism and World Politics," *American Political Science Review* 80, no. 4 (December 1986).

10.  Most of this paragraph and some of the next was written by Christensen, in Betts and Christensen, "China: Getting the Questions Right," 24.

11.  Fareed Zakaria, "The Rise of Illiberal Democracy," *Foreign Affairs* (November/ December 1977): 22–43.

12.  John M. Owen IV, *Liberal Peace, Liberal War: American Politics and International Security* (Ithaca, N.Y.: Cornell University Press, 1997).

13.  Edward D. Mansfield and Jack L. Snyder, "Democratization and the Danger of War," *International Security* 20, no. 1 (Summer 1995): 5–38.

14.  David Martin Jones and Michael L. R. Smith, "Making Process, Not Progress: ASEAN and the Evolving East Asian Regional Order," *International Security* 32, no. 1 (Summer 2007).

15.  Ikenberry, "The Rise of China," 31.

16.  Statements in Scobell, "Is There a Civil-Military Gap in China's Peaceful Rise?" 10–11; Joseph Kahn, "Chinese General Threatens Use of A-Bombs if U.S. Intrudes," *New York Times*, July 15, 2005; and *China, Nuclear Weapons, and Arms Control* (New York: Council on Foreign Relations, 2000), 31n.

17.  This paragraph is by Christensen, in Betts and Christensen, "China: Getting the Questions Right," 27–28.

18.  Alexis de Tocqueville, *The Old Regime and the French Revolution*, trans. Stuart Gilbert (New York: Doubleday, 1955), part 3, chap. 4; and J. C. Davies, "Toward a Theory of Revolution," *American Sociological Review* 27, no. 1 (February 1962): 6.

19.  Andrew E. Kramer, "Russia Claims Its Sphere of Influence in the World," *New York Times*, September 1, 2008, A6. Medvedev said, "Russia, like other countries in the world, has regions where it has privileged interests. . . . the border region, but not only."

20.  Richard K. Betts, "Systems for Peace or Causes of War? Collective Security, Arms Control, and the New Europe," *International Security* 17, no. 1 (Summer 1992): 17–20, 23–26.

21.  Patrick E. Tyler, "Russia and China Sign 'Friendship' Pact," *New York Times*, July 17, 2001, A1, A8; Yong Deng, "Remolding Great Power Politics: China's Stra-

tegic Partnerships with Russia, the European Union, and India," *Journal of Strategic Studies* 30, nos. 4–5 (August–October 2007): 870–72, 874–76. Restrained views of the potential for the two countries' collaboration are Jennifer Anderson, *The Limits of Sino-Russian Strategic Partnership*, Adelphi Paper no. 315 (London: International Institute for Strategic Studies, 1997); and Nebojsa Bjelakovic and Christina M. Yeung, *The Sino-Russian Strategic Partnership: Views from Beijing and Moscow* (N.p.: Defence R&D Canada, Centre for Operational Research and Analysis, September 2008).

22. Keir A. Lieber and Daryl G. Press, "The End of MAD?," *International Security* 30, no. 4 (Spring 2006); Lieber and Press, "U.S. Nuclear Primacy and the Future of the Chinese Deterrent," *China Security* (Winter 2007): 66–67, 74–75.

## 9. CIVIL-MILITARY RELATIONS: A SPECIAL PROBLEM?

1. Samuel P. Huntington, *The Soldier and the State: The Theory and Politics of Civil-Military Relations* (Cambridge: Harvard University Press, 1957).

2. Richard H. Kohn, "Out of Control: The Crisis in Civil-Military Relations," *National Interest* no. 35 (Spring 1994); and Kohn, "Coming Soon: A Crisis in Civil-Military Relations," *World Affairs* (Winter 2008).

3. Samuel P. Huntington, *The Common Defense: Strategic Programs in National Politics* (New York: Columbia University Press, 1961), 1.

4. Huntington, *The Soldier and the State*, 2–3.

5. The six principles of the Weinberger Doctrine were that commitment of U.S. forces to combat should be undertaken only on behalf of vital interests; "wholeheartedly, and with the clear intention of winning"; with "clearly defined political and military objectives"; if objectives and force requirements are "continually reassessed and adjusted"; with "the support of the American people and their elected representatives in Congress"; and as "a last resort." Secretary of Defense Caspar W. Weinberger, "The Uses of Military Power," speech to the National Press Club, November 28, 1984, http://www.pbs.org/wgbh/pages/frontline/shows/military/force/weinberger.html.

6. Regarding the decision on Laos in 1961, Roger Hilsman recalled: "Not all of the Joint Chiefs fully subscribed to the 'Never Again' view, but it seemed to the White House that they were at least determined to build a record that would protect their position and put the blame entirely on the President no matter what happened. The general thrust of their memoranda seemed to imply that they were demanding an advance commitment from the President that, if they agreed to use American force and there were any fighting at all, then there would be no holds barred whatsoever—including the use of nuclear weapons." Roger Hilsman, *To Move a Nation* (Garden City, N.Y.: Doubleday, 1967), 129.

7.  Colin Powell with Joseph E. Persico, *My American Journey* (New York: Random House, 1995), 558.

8.  Richard K. Betts, *Soldiers, Statesmen, and Cold War Crises*, 2d ed. (New York: Columbia University Press, 1991), 19–20, 254; General Wesley K. Clark, USA (Ret.), *Waging Modern War: Bosnia, Kosovo, and the Future of Combat* (New York: PublicAffairs, 2001), 312–13; Thomas E. Ricks, *The Gamble: General David Petraeus and the American Military Adventure in Iraq, 2006–2008* (New York: Penguin Press, 2009), 52–54, 57, 61, 99–100, 104, 111–14.

9.  Graham T. Allison, *Essence of Decision: Explaining the Cuban Missile Crisis* (Boston: Little, Brown, 1971), and Graham Allison and Philip Zelikow, *Essence of Decision*, 2d ed. (New York: Longman, 1999); Barry R. Posen, *The Sources of Military Doctrine: France, Britain, and Germany Between the World Wars* (Ithaca, N.Y.: Cornell University Press, 1984); Eliot A. Cohen, *Supreme Command: Soldiers, Statesmen, and Leadership in Wartime* (New York: Free Press, 2002).

10. The second edition of Allison's book was more measured in its emphasis on errors due to organizational process and renamed the model "organizational behavior." Allison and Zelikow, *Essence of Decision*, chap. 3.

11. Cohen, *Supreme Command*, 4–8, 174–75, 226–29.

12. H. R. McMaster, *Dereliction of Duty: Lyndon Johnson, Robert McNamara, the Joint Chiefs of Staff, and the Lies That Led to Vietnam* (New York: HarperCollins, 1997).

13. The JCS in 1965 may have pulled punches more than they should have in telling civilian leaders they were wrong, but they did clearly recommend far more massive and speedy application of force in the air war and presented estimates within the Defense Department that victory would require half a million men or more on the ground. They were not frank about their views in congressional testimony, as they should have been, because of a misguided notion that their responsibility to the commander in chief canceled out responsibility to the legislative branch of government. Their biggest mistake was in not forthrightly arguing in both arenas that withdrawal and acceptance of defeat were preferable to the weaker civilian strategy they opposed. They were complicit with the strategy because it was all they could get, and by 1965 the idea of giving up the fight was unthinkable to them, as it was to everyone of consequence in the American government except George Ball. Ibid., 309–12, 328–31; Betts, *Soldiers, Statesmen, and Cold War Crises*, 228–30; Leslie H. Gelb with Richard K. Betts, *The Irony of Vietnam: The System Worked* (Washington, D.C.: Brookings Institution, 1979), chap. 4. The mistake is clear only in hindsight, after the full calamitous costs of the venture came due. In the context of the time none could realistically have expected soldiers to endorse defeat.

14. Morris Janowitz, *The Professional Soldier: A Social and Political Portrait*, 2d ed. (New York: Free Press, 1971), 260–61.

15. Drone strikes in Pakistan are not a strategic bombing campaign and do not involve the disagreements between civilians and military about limitations on targets that characterized the air war against North Vietnam.

16. Previously they had been the link between the secretary of defense and the commanders in chief (CINCs) of the unified and specified commands.

17. Peter D. Feaver and Christopher Gelpi, *Choosing Your Battles: American Civil-Military Relations and the Use of Force* (Princeton: Princeton University Press, 2004), chap. 3.

18. Samuel P. Huntington, "The Defense Policy of the Reagan Administration, 1981–1982," in *The Reagan Presidency: An Early Assessment*, ed. Fred I. Greenstein (Baltimore: Johns Hopkins University Press, 1983), 85.

19. From the 1930s into the 1960s, Democrats "favored a higher level of military effort than did the Republicans. . . . In every year of the Eisenhower Administration except 1957, congressional Democrats attempted to increase the military budget." Huntington, *The Common Defense*, 252–53, 255, 261.

20. Richard K. Betts, "The Political Support System for American Primacy," *International Affairs* (London) 81, no. 1 (January 2005): 5–6, 12.

21. By the time of the Vietnam War, social representativeness was reduced, as large portions of the highly educated escaped service. Lawrence M. Baskir and William A. Strauss, *Chance and Circumstance: The Draft, the War, and the Vietnam Generation* (New York: Knopf, 1978), 5–11, 29–32.

22. See Peter D. Feaver and Richard H. Kohn, *Soldiers and Civilians: The Civil-Military Gap and American National Security* (Cambridge: MIT Press, 2001).

23. For example, see Kathy Roth-Douquet and Frank Schaeffer, *AWOL: The Unexcused Absence of America's Upper Classes from Military Service—and How It Hurts Our Country* (New York: Collins, 2006).

24. In 1960, Janowitz reported, "the concentration of personnel with 'purely' military occupational specialties has fallen from 93.2 per cent in the Civil War to 28.8 per cent in the post–Korean Army and to even lower percentages in the Navy and Air Force." *Professional Soldier*, 9.

25. Allison, *Essence of Decision*, 129–32; John D. Steinbruner, "An Assessment of Nuclear Crises," in *The Dangers of Nuclear War*, ed. Franklyn Griffiths and John C. Polanyi (Toronto: University of Toronto Press, 1979), 38.

26. Dan Caldwell, "A Research Note on the Quarantine of Cuba," *International Studies Quarterly* 22, no. 4 (December 1978): 625–33; Scott D. Sagan, "Nuclear Alerts and Crisis Management," *International Security* 9, no. 4 (Spring 1985): 112–18; Richard K. Betts, *Nuclear Blackmail and Nuclear Balance* (Washington, D.C.:

Brookings Institution, 1987), 118–19; Scott D. Sagan, "Rules of Engagement," *Security Studies* 1, no. 1 (Autumn 1991): 91–93; Joseph F. Bouchard, *Command in Crisis: Four Case Studies* (New York: Columbia University Press, 1991), 111–12, 120–28; transcript of Cabinet Room meeting, October 22, 1962, in Ernest R. May and Philip D. Zelikow, eds., *The Kennedy Tapes: Inside the White House During the Cuban Missile Crisis* (Cambridge: Harvard University Press, 1997), 212. The second edition of Allison's book omitted the stories in question and substituted a milder account of the notorious confrontation between McNamara and Anderson in the Navy Flag Plot: Allison and Zelikow, *Essence of Decision*, 232–36.

27.  In 1961 Senator J. W. Fulbright reported the 1958 NSC directive that led to these links. Daniel Bell, "The Dispossessed (1962)," in *The Radical Right*, ed. Bell (New York: Anchor, 1963), 5–8.

28.  Bob Woodward, *State of Denial: Bush at War, Part III* (New York: Simon and Schuster, 2006), 54.

29.  John Newhouse, *Cold Dawn: The Story of SALT* (New York: Holt, Rinehart and Winston, 1973), 124, 129.

30.  Betts, *Soldiers, Statesmen, and Cold War Crises*, xii.

31.  Huntington, *The Soldier and the State*, 158–59, 158n.

32.  Powell, *My American Journey*, 576.

33.  David Halberstam, *War in a Time of Peace: Bush, Clinton, and the Generals* (New York: Touchstone, 2002), 246–47: "Powell did not believe that on those issues where the military power of the United States might be employed, Clinton's people had thought things out carefully. They were almost vague in their attitudes toward the use of force and its consequences. . . . They in turn, sensed his disdain for them. . . . 'You could feel it in the way he looked at us. We were doves, people who had sat out the war while he had fought it, people who had never really paid a price for what we had attained,' one senior member of the Clinton administration said."

34.  David S. Broder, "No Veterans Preference in This Administration," *Washington Post*, December 26, 1993, C7.

35.  Powell, *My American Journey*, 559.

36.  David S. Cloud and Steven Lee Myers, "Generals Differ on the Timing of Troop Cuts," *New York Times*, August 25, 2007, A1; David S. Cloud, "Why Well-Placed Officers Differ on Troop Reduction," *New York Times*, September 14, 2007, A11.

37.  Bob Woodward, *Obama's Wars* (New York: Simon and Schuster, 2010).

38.  See the incidents reported in Kohn, "Out of Control," 3.

39.  See Betts, *Soldiers, Statesmen, and Cold War Crises*, 262–63n30.

40. Craig Whitlock, "Honor Restored for General Blamed After Nixon Denied Authorizing Vietnam Bombing," *Washington Post*, August 5, 2010.

41. Huntington, *The Common Defense*, 135–46.

42. For the story of the reorganization, see Suzanne Nielsen, "Preparing the Army for War: The Dynamics of Peacetime Military Reform," Ph.D. dissertation, Harvard University, 2003, chap. 4.

43. Interview with Lewis Sorley, quoted in ibid., 224n185.

44. Quoted in Lewis Sorley, *Thunderbolt: General Creighton Abrams and the Army of His Times* (New York: Simon and Schuster, 1992), 364.

45. Michael R. Gordon and General Bernard E. Trainor, *Cobra II: The Inside Story of the Invasion and Occupation of Iraq* (New York: Pantheon, 2006), chap. 3 and 96–100; Tom Ricks, *Fiasco: The American Military Adventure in Iraq* (New York: Penguin Press, 2006), pp. 70–71, 75, 83–84.

46. Huntington, *The Soldier and the State*, 77.

47. Bouchard, *Command in Crisis*, 96–97, 100.

48. Clausewitz, *On War*, 75. "If one side uses force without compunction, undeterred by the bloodshed it involves, while the other side refrains, the first will gain the upper hand. That side will force the other to follow suit; each will drive its opponent toward extremes, and the only limiting factors are the counterpoises inherent in war" (75–76).

49. Cohen, *Supreme Command*, 177.

50. Betts, *Soldiers, Statesmen, and Cold War Crises*, 211.

51. Janowitz, *Professional Soldier*, passim.

52. Huntington, *The Soldier and the State*, 253.

53. Cohen, *Supreme Command*, 229; Huntington, *The Soldier and the State*, 315–17.

54. As the editors clarify, "Clausewitz emphasizes the cabinet's participation in military decisions, not the soldier's participation in political decisions." Clausewitz, *On War*, 608, 608n1.

55. Huntington, *The Common Defense*, 447.

## 10. Plans and Results: Is Strategy an Illusion?

1. Carl von Clausewitz, *On War*, trans. and ed. Michael Howard and Peter Paret (Princeton: Princeton University Press, 1976), 128 (emphasis deleted), 181.

2. Bernard Brodie, *War and Politics* (New York: Macmillan, 1974), 452–53 (emphasis deleted).

3. "If, on one hand, the investigator superimposes a clear and definite pattern of tastes on economic actors and assigns a clear and definite mode of rationality to them, then the possibility of determinate theoretical explanations is increased.

If, on the other hand, tastes and modes of rational action are regarded as idiosyncratic and variable from actor to actor, then theoretical determinacy is lost as analysis moves in the direction of relativism of tastes and a phenomenological conception of the actor." Neil J. Smelser, "The Rational Choice Perspective: A Theoretical Assessment," *Rationality and Society* 4, no. 4 (October 1992): 399; see also 398, 400–401, 403. These problems apply to strategies for preventing wars as well as fighting them. "One disturbing possibility lies at the intersection of the nonfalsifiable character of the weak model [of deterrence] and the difficulty of testing any proposition about the nature of deterrence empirically. . . . history rarely presents evidence that unambiguously falsifies the weak version of rational deterrence theory." George W. Downs, "The Rational Deterrence Debate," *World Politics* 41, no. 2 (January 1989): 227.

4.  The deal would have been to let Britain keep its empire while Germany kept Europe. Klaus Hildebrand, *The Foreign Policy of the Third Reich*, trans. Anthony Fothergill (Berkeley: University of California Press, n.d.), 93–94; Norman Rich, *Hitler's War Aims*, vol. 1: *Ideology, the Nazi State, and the Course of Expansion* (New York: Norton, 1973), 157–58; Wilhelm Deist, "The Road to Ideological War: Germany, 1918–1945," in *The Making of Strategy: Rulers, States, and War*, ed. Williamson Murray, MacGregor Knox, and Alvin Bernstein (New York: Cambridge University Press, 1994), 388.

5.  Quoted in John Lukacs, *Five Days in London: May 1940* (New Haven: Yale University Press, 1999), 117.

6.  "Churchill and the British 'Decision' to Fight on in 1940," in *Diplomacy and Intelligence During the Second World War*, ed. Richard Langhorne (New York: Cambridge University Press, 1985), 147, 154–55, 156–60, 163, 167. "A belief which is unjustified . . . may well be instrumentally useful, but it seems odd to call it rational. Rationality . . . is a variety of intentionality. For something to be rational, it has to be within the scope of conscious, deliberate action or reflection. Useful false beliefs obtain by fluke, not by conscious reflection upon the evidence." Jon Elster, *Solomonic Judgments* (New York: Cambridge University Press, 1989), 7. Churchill's rationale for confidence in the defensibility of England is set out in his June 18, 1940, speech in the House of Commons. See "Their Finest Hour," in *Winston S. Churchill: His Complete Speeches, 1897–1963*, vol. 6, ed. Robert Rhodes James (New York: Chelsea House, 1974), 6231–38.

7.  Richard K. Betts, *Surprise Attack* (Washington, D.C.: Brookings Institution, 1982), 130–33.

8.  In terms of imperial interests, which were a powerful motive at the time, the result is different. Churchill declared, "I have not become the King's First Min-

ister in order to preside over the liquidation of the British Empire," but that is more or less what he did—a reason that reactionary revisionists criticize his failure to consider a deal with Berlin. John Charmley, *Churchill: The End of Glory* (London: Hodder and Stoughton, 1993), chaps. 37, 38 (quotation on 431); and Charmley, *Churchill's Grand Alliance* (New York: Harcourt Brace, 1995), chaps. 5, 19–20.

9.  Quoted in Martin Gilbert, *Finest Hour: Winston S. Churchill, 1939–1941* (London: Heinemann, 1989), 420.

10. Quoted in Lukacs, *Five Days in London,* 23–24.

11. Wilhelm Deist, "The Road to Ideological War," in Murray, Knox, and Bernstein, eds., *The Making of Strategy,* 356.

12. Scott D. Sagan, "Origins of the Pacific War," in *The Origin and Prevention of Major Wars,* ed. Robert I. Rotberg and Theodore K. Rabb (New York: Cambridge University Press, 1989), 345–47.

13. Quoted in MacGregor Knox, "Conclusion," in Murray, Knox, and Bernstein, eds., *Making of Strategy,* 634. See also Masao Maruyama, *Thought and Behavior in Modern Japanese Politics* (New York: Oxford University Press, 1963), 84–85, 95.

14. Richard K. Betts, "Strategic Surprise for War Termination: Inchon, Dienbienphu, and Tet," in *Strategic Military Surprise,* ed. Klaus Knorr and Patrick Morgan (New Brunswick, N.J.: Transaction Books, 1983), 148–53. The advance to the Yalu was not MacArthur's decision alone.

15. Clay Blair, *The Forgotten War* (New York: Times Books, 1987), 224–26.

16. B. H. Liddell Hart, *The Real War, 1914–1918* (Boston: Atlantic-Little, Brown, 1930), 143–74; Eliot A. Cohen and John Gooch, *Military Misfortunes* (New York: Free Press, 1990), chap. 6. Churchill was also less responsible for the land operation at Gallipoli than for the naval attack in the Dardanelles. Winston S. Churchill, *The World Crisis,* vol. 2 (New York: Scribner's, 1923), chaps. 2, 7–8; Alan Moorehead, *Gallipoli* (London: Hamish Hamilton, 1956), 45–47; Robert Rhodes James, *Gallipoli* (London: B. T. Batsford, 1965), 41; Martin Gilbert, *In Search of Churchill* (New York: HarperCollins, 1994), 56–58.

17. "Defenders of realism might argue that the theory is intended to be probabilistic rather than determinative. . . . Nevertheless, when the range of possible outcomes extend from appeasement to preventive war, one is justified in asking whether alternative approaches might do better." Matthew Evangelista, "Internal and External Constraints on Grand Strategy," in *The Domestic Bases of Grand Strategy,* ed. Richard Rosecrance and Arthur Stein (Ithaca: Cornell University Press, 1993), 167.

18.  Isaiah Berlin, *The Hedgehog and the Fox* (New York: Clarion, 1970), 18–19; see also 13, 17. Tolstoy believed "there is a natural law whereby the lives of human beings no less than those of nature are determined; but that men, unable to face this inexorable process, seek to represent it as a succession of free choices, to fix responsibility for what occurs upon persons endowed by them with heroic virtues or heroic vices, and called by them 'great men'" (read, great strategists). Ibid., 27.

19.  "Discussion," in *Security Studies for the 1990s*, ed. Richard Shultz, Roy Godson, and Ted Greenwood (New York: Brassey's, 1993), 109.

20.  "In 1991, he said . . . that most 'grand strategies' were after-the-fact rationales developed to explain successful ad hoc decisions. He said in a recent conversation that he prefers to 'worry about today today and tomorrow tomorrow.'" R. W. Apple, "A Domestic Sort with Global Worries," *New York Times*, August 25, 1999, A10.

21.  For arguments that outcomes of strategy always confound initial calculations and are usually counterproductive, even for the victor, see Kenneth J. Hagan and Ian J. Bickerton, *Unintended Consequences: The United States at War* (London: Reaktion Books, 2008).

22.  Only at first glance do Vietnam and Afghanistan contradict this notion. The Vietnamese communists won only after American forces left the country and Saigon's forces were outnumbered. The Soviets never committed more than a tiny fraction of their army to Afghanistan, and they withdrew without being defeated on the battlefield. Attrition worked for the victors in these cases, not tactically, but by sapping the will of the more powerful adversaries to persevere.

23.  David Herbert Donald, *Lincoln* (New York: Simon and Schuster, 1995), 389, 499. In his docu-novel about Gettysburg, Michael Shaara has his favorite Confederate general put it this way: "'God in heaven,' Longstreet said . . . 'there's no strategy to this bloody war. What it is is old Napoleon and a hell of a lot of chivalry.'" *The Killer Angels* (New York: McKay, 1974), 267.

24.  Edward N. Lorenz, *The Essence of Chaos* (Seattle: University of Washington Press, 1993), 181–84. See also James Gleick, *Chaos* (New York: Viking, 1987), 8–31.

25.  Alan Beyerchen, "Clausewitz, Non-Linearity, and the Unpredictability of War," *International Security* 17, no. 3 (Winter 1992/93): 62.

26.  James Gleick and J. Franks, quoted in Stephen H. Kellert, *In the Wake of Chaos: Unpredictable Order in Dynamical Systems* (Chicago: University of Chicago Press, 1993), 138.

27.  Barry D. Watts, "Ignoring Reality: Problems of Theory and Evidence in Security Studies," *Security Studies* 7, no. 2 (Winter 1997/98): 119–22, 125–27. See also Watts,

*Clausewitzian Friction and Future War*, McNair Paper no. 52 (Washington, D.C.: National Defense University Press, 1996), chap. 10; Roger Beaumont, *War, Chaos, and History* (Westport, Conn.: Praeger, 1994).

28. Robert Jervis, *System Effects* (Princeton: Princeton University Press, 1997).

29. For the extreme argument of unpredictability, see Nassim Nicholas Taleb, *Fooled By Randomness: The Hidden Role of Chance in Life and in the Markets*, 2d ed. (New York: Random House, 2005); and Taleb, *The Black Swan: The Impact of the Highly Improbable*, 2d ed. (New York: Random House, 2010).

30. Peter L. Bernstein, *Against the Gods* (New York: Wiley, 1996), 144–50; Burton G. Malkiel, *A Random Walk Down Wall Street* (New York: Norton, 1999).

31. "Watts asserts . . . that there are no meaningful regularities in social events. If this were true, it would render all efforts to study social events—including war—futile. . . . if we really had no ability to predict consequences of our actions with some degree of confidence better than mere chance, then no intelligent choices could be made in any realm of social behavior. . . . there would be no point in studying history, and there could be no such thing as meaningful expertise, including military expertise." Robert A. Pape, "The Air Force Strikes Back," *Security Studies* 7, no. 2 (Winter 1997/98): 196–97.

32. Jervis says of his own work, "books like this select a biased sample of cases; when things work out, we do not study or even notice them." *System Effects*, 68.

33. Lorenz, *Essence of Chaos*, 183.

34. Clausewitz, *On War*, 584.

35. Geoffrey Blainey, *The Causes of War*, 3d ed. (New York: Free Press, 1988), 109–14; James Fearon, "Rationalist Explanations for War," *International Organization* 49, no. 3 (Summer 1995).

36. Sidney Verba, "Assumptions of Rationality and Non-Rationality in Models of the International System," in *The International System*, ed. Klaus Knorr and Sidney Verba (Princeton: Princeton University Press, 1961), 108, 94.

37. Franco Fornari, *The Psychoanalysis of War*, trans. Alenka Pfeifer (Bloomington: Indiana University Press, 1974), xvi, xvii, xxvi (emphasis in original).

38. Barbara Ehrenreich, *Blood Rites: Origins and History of the Passions of War* (New York: Henry Holt, 1997), 22. See also Vamik Volkan, *The Need to Have Enemies and Allies: From Clinical Practice to International Relationships* (Northvale, N.J.: Jason Aronson, 1988); Daniel Pick, *War Machine: The Rationalization of Slaughter in the Machine Age* (New Haven: Yale University Press, 1993), chap. 15.

39. Brodie, *War and Politics*, 311.

40. Keegan, *A History of Warfare*, especially chaps. 1–2.

41. Anthony Storr, "The Man," in *Churchill Revised,* ed. A.J.P. Taylor (New York: Dial Press, 1969), 231, 234–35, 240, 247, 250, 239.

42. Ibid., 230, 274, 251.

43. On deficiencies in psychological explanations, see Kenneth N. Waltz, *Man, the State, and War* (New York: Columbia University Press, 1959), chaps. 2–3.

44. Robert Jervis, *Perception and Misperception in International Politics* (Princeton: Princeton University Press, 1976), 4.

45. Sigmund Freud, "Why War?" in Freud, *Civilization, War and Death,* ed. John Rickman (London: Hogarth Press and Institute of Psycho-Analysis, 1953), 97.

46. Townsend Hoopes, *The Devil and John Foster Dulles* (Boston: Atlantic/Little, Brown, 1973); Michael Guhin, *John Foster Dulles* (New York: Columbia University Press, 1972).

47. Keegan, *A History of Warfare,* 21, 58.

48. Critics charge that rationalist theorists "lapse into tautology to prevent this everyday experience [of irrationality] from becoming compelling evidence *against* the notions. The result is to identify the fact of adaptation with the notion of rationality and to further anchor that notion in our habits of mind. The only evidence against rationality thus becomes behavior which seems obviously maladaptive. Since adaptation is so closely related to survival itself, maladaptive behavior is *perforce* a rare event." John Steinbruner, *The Cybernetic Theory of Decision* (Princeton: Princeton University Press, 1974), 50n (emphasis in original). Rationalists argue that critics rely on simplistic or dated conceptions of rationality, and that Graham Allison's model is now "seriously out of date." Jonathan Bendor and Thomas Hammond, "Rethinking Allison's Models," *American Political Science Review* 86, no. 2 (June 1992): 302–7, 319. A revised edition has updated the model since Bendor and Hammond wrote but does not address criticisms in literature of rational choice theory head-on: Graham Allison and Philip Zelikow, *Essence of Decision,* 2d ed. (New York: Longman, 1999).

49. Robert Jervis, "Hypotheses on Misperception," *World Politics* 20, no. 3 (April 1968): 475; Jervis, *Perception and Misperception,* chap. 4.

50. Steinbruner, *Cybernetic Theory of Decision,* 89 and chap. 4.

51. Richard K. Betts, "Compound Deterrence vs. No-First-Use: What's Wrong Is What's Right," *Orbis* 28, no. 4 (Winter 1985).

52. Verba, "Assumptions of Rationality and Non-Rationality," 109–10. Verba does nevertheless argue that detached research is more objective. For a good example of psychological interpretation that recognizes the difference between political judgment and mental dysfunction, see Barbara Rearden Farnham, *Roosevelt and the Munich Crisis* (Princeton: Princeton University Press, 1997).

53. Thomas Schelling, *Arms and Influence* (New Haven: Yale University Press, 1966), 142, 171ff, 186–88.

54. T. C. Schelling, "The Retarded Science of International Strategy," *Midwest Journal of Political Science* 4, no. 2 (May 1960): 108.

55. Shu Guang Zhu, *Deterrence and Strategic Culture: Chinese-American Confrontations, 1949–1958* (Ithaca, N.Y.: Cornell University Press, 1992), 279–82.

56. Alastair Iain Johnston, *Cultural Realism* (Princeton: Princeton University Press, 1995), 2.

57. At the time, two attacks on U.S. destroyers were alleged. Subsequent investigation established that the first definitely occurred but the second probably did not.

58. *The Senator Gravel Edition: The Pentagon Papers* (Boston: Beacon Press, 1971), 3:106–15, 269–71, 299–306, 315, 342, 628.

59. Wallace Thies, *When Governments Collide* (Berkeley: University of California Press, 1980), 42–44, 56–57, 77–82, 85–89, 124–27, 144, 265. Robert Pape, *Bombing to Win* (Ithaca: Cornell University Press, 1996), extends this criticism to discredit nearly all attempts to use strategic bombing for political coercion.

60. Thies, *When Governments Collide*, 392 (emphasis deleted).

61. Steinbruner, *Cybernetic Theory of Decision*, 55–56, 64–66, 74–75; Allison and Zelikow, *Essence of Decision*, chaps. 3–4.

62. James G. March and Herbert A. Simon, with collaboration of Harold Guetzkow, *Organizations* (New York: Wiley, 1958), 38.

63. Philip Selznick, *Leadership in Administration* (New York: Harper and Row, 1957), 12, 74–76; Anthony Downs, *Inside Bureaucracy* (Boston: Little, Brown, 1967), 19, 100; Perry McCoy Smith, *The Air Force Plans for Peace: 1943–1945* (Baltimore: Johns Hopkins Press, 1970). See also Robert Merton, "Bureaucratic Structure and Personality," in *Reader in Bureaucracy*, ed. Merton et al. (Glencoe, N.Y.: Free Press, 1952); Charles Perrow, "Goals in Complex Organizations," *American Sociological Review* 26, no. 6 (December 1961); Herbert Simon, "Bounded Rationality and Organizational Learning," *Organizational Science* 2, no. 1 (February 1991).

64. Lt. Gen. Royal Moore, cited in Thomas A. Keaney and Eliot A. Cohen, *Revolution in Warfare? Air Power in the Persian Gulf* (Annapolis: Naval Institute Press, 1995), 131.

65. Allison and Zelikow, *Essence of Decision*, 143.

66. Harry Summers, *On Strategy* (Novato, Calif.: Presidio Press, 1982), 85.

67. Andrew F. Krepinevich, Jr., *The Army and Vietnam* (Baltimore: Johns Hopkins University Press, 1986). See also Douglas Blaufarb, *The Counterinsurgency Era* (New York: Free Press, 1977), 65, 80–87, 218–30, 251, 270–73, 277–78.

68. Bendor and Hammond, "Rethinking Allison's Models," 309, 312.

69. Ibid., 312 (quoting Robin Hogarth).

70. Joseph F. Bouchard, *Command in Crisis* (New York: Columbia University Press, 1991), 111–12, 120ff; Scott D. Sagan, "Nuclear Alerts and Crisis Management," *International Security* 9, no. 4 (Spring 1985); Dan Caldwell, "A Research Note on the Quarantine of Cuba October 1962," *International Studies Quarterly* 22, no. 4 (December 1978); Richard K. Betts, *Soldiers, Statesmen, and Cold War Crises*, 2d ed. (New York: Columbia University Press, 1991), 155–56.

71. Scott D. Sagan, *The Limits of Safety* (Princeton: Princeton University Press, 1993), chaps. 2–3.

72. Bendor and Hammond, "Rethinking Allison's Models," 310 (emphasis in original). Although final outcomes may not be predicted, there are many ways to predict next moves in chess.

73. Posen, *Sources of Military Doctrine*; Stephen Peter Rosen, *Winning the Next War* (Ithaca, N.Y.: Cornell University Press, 1991).

74. Summers, *On Strategy*, 85.

75. Clausewitz, *On War*, 87.

76. This is what he means by his discussion of "absolute" war, which so many of his critics misread. The political object comes to the fore as the tendency to extremes wanes. "Were it a complete, untrammeled, absolute manifestation of violence (as the pure concept would require), war would of its own independent will usurp the place of policy the moment policy had brought it into being; it would then drive policy out of office and rule by the laws of its own nature." Ibid., 80, 87. The apt paraphrase that the nature of war is to serve itself is from Richard Henrick, *Crimson Tide* (New York: Avon, 1995), 75.

77. "Political and Strategic Dimensions of Military Effectiveness," in Millett and Murray, eds., *Military Effectiveness*, 3:341.

78. See Bernard Brodie on "The Traditional Military Depreciation of Strategy," in his *Strategy in the Missile Age* (Princeton: Princeton University Press, 1959), 11–19.

79. Helmuth von Moltke, "Doctrines of War," in *War*, ed. Lawrence Freedman (New York: Oxford University Press, 1994), 218–20.

80. Michael Howard, "War as an Instrument of National Policy," in Herbert Butterfield and Martin Wight, eds., *Diplomatic Investigations* (Cambridge: Harvard University Press, 1968), 198; Brodie, *War and Politics*, 11; Williamson Murray and Mark Grimsley, "Introduction," in Murray, Knox, and Bernstein, eds., *The Making of Strategy*, 3; Edward N. Luttwak, *Strategy* (Cambridge: Harvard University Press, 1987), 219–94.

81. Michael Geyer, "German Strategy in the Age of Machine Warfare, 1914–1945," in *Makers of Modern Strategy*, ed. Peter Paret (Princeton: Princeton University Press, 1986), 591.

82. Ibid., 548–49; see also 531–47, 550. Decisions to antagonize third parties may sometimes be a necessary choice—for example, the British attack on the French fleet at Oran after Paris surrendered in 1940, or the Anglo-American invasion of Vichy territory in North Africa two years later. These initiatives, however, did not seem likely to move France into full combatant alignment with Germany.

83. Ibid., 572, 581–82, 575.

84. Samuel Eliot Morison, *Strategy and Compromise* (Boston: Atlantic-Little, Brown, 1958), 71–74.

85. "What remains peculiar to war is simply the peculiar nature of its means. War . . . is entitled to require that the trend and designs of policy shall not be inconsistent with these means. That, of course, is no small demand; but however much it may affect political aims in a given case, it will never do more than modify them." Clausewitz, *On War*, 87. Nor is Michael Howard rejecting strategy when he notes that "the strategy adopted is almost always more likely to be dictated rather by the availability of means than by the nature of ends." "British Grand Strategy in World War I," in *Grand Strategies in War and Peace*, ed. Paul Kennedy (New Haven: Yale University Press, 1991), 32. See also Selznick, *Leadership in Administration*, 77–78.

86. Deist, "The Road to Ideological War," 380.

87. Kenneth A. Shepsle and Mark S. Bonchek, *Analyzing Politics* (New York: Norton, 1997), 71.

88. "This may also explain why rationality models have been used in international relations largely in connection with the problems of nuclear deterrence. . . . the relevant goals within this limited sphere are less ambiguous . . . and easier to place in a hierarchy." Verba, "Assumptions of Rationality," 110–11n, 115–16.

89. Thies, *When Governments Collide*, 13–14, 355.

90. This appeared in the first edition of Graham T. Allison, *Essence of Decision* (Boston: Little, Brown, 1971), 267. For other reductions of national strategy to bureaucratic politics see Richard E. Neustadt, *Alliance Politics* (New York: Columbia University Press, 1970); and Morton Halperin and Priscilla Clapp with Arnold Kanter, *Bureaucratic Politics and Foreign Policy*, 2d ed. (Washington, D.C.: Brookings Institution, 2006), 102, which says, "Conventional analyses of foreign policy usually assume that the actions of other nations are the major stimulus for foreign policy decisions. . . . they are only one stimulus, and not even the most

frequent one. Most decisions are responses to domestic pressures, and the actions of other nations often figure merely as devices for argument."

91. Charles E. Lindblom, "The Science of 'Muddling Through,'" *Public Administration Review* 19 (Spring 1959).

92. "Criticism of strategy-making . . . is directed at the appearance in the strategy-making process of characteristics pervasive in American government. . . . dispersion of power and authority in American government insures the representation of all claims but the priority of none." Samuel P. Huntington, *The Common Defense* (New York: Columbia University Press, 1961), 169, 173. The benign view of pluralism was a theme in Robert Art's review of the bureaucratic politics literature that appeared after Huntington: "Bureaucratic Politics and American Foreign Policy: A Critique," *Policy Sciences* 4, no. 4 (December 1973).

93. Michael Gordon and Bernard Trainor, *The Generals' War* (Boston: Little, Brown, 1995), 319–20.

94. See Morison, *Strategy and Compromise*. Revisionists on the right criticized the strategy for allowing Soviet power into the heart of Europe and preventing the reestablishment of a traditional balance of power. Hanson W. Baldwin, *Great Mistakes of the War* (New York: Harper, 1950), parts 1, 2. This assumes a dubious counterfactual case for the success of either an earlier cross-channel invasion, or a Balkan campaign. Moreover, it would have cost the Western allies far more casualties to beat the Russians into Eastern Europe (ironically, it was Moscow and left-wing revisionists who charged Western strategy with cynically delaying a second front in order to bleed the Russians dry), unless the critics' preferred strategy included a separate peace that allowed the Germans to keep fighting the Soviets. In that case one of the greatest achievements of the unconditional surrender policy, the democratization of most of Germany, would have been lost. By the same token, there is no reason to assume that reestablishing a multipolar balance in Europe would have produced a safer postwar world than the bipolar Cold War standoff did.

95. Kent Roberts Greenfield, *American Strategy in World War II: A Reconsideration* (Baltimore: Johns Hopkins Press, 1963), 14, 16, 23.

96. Ernest R. May, *"Lessons" of the Past* (New York: Oxford University Press, 1973), 126. The problem with coercive strategy based on a model of torture ("do what I demand and the pain will stop") is that the target government is not a person; political authorities are not on the rack themselves. They can persevere, secure in bunkers with caches of caviar, while the population bears the pain of losing homes and lives.

97. Pape, *Bombing to Win*, 329–30.

11. A Disciplined Defense: Regaining Strategic Solvency

1.  See, for example, Mackenzie Eaglen, *U.S. Defense Spending: The Mismatch Between Plans and Resources*, Backgrounder no. 2418 (Washington, D.C.: Heritage Foundation, June 2010).

2.  Walter Lippmann, *U.S. Foreign Policy: Shield of the Republic* ((Little, Brown, 1943); James Chace, *Solvency: The Price of Survival* (Random House, 1981).

3.  Glenn H. Snyder, "The 'New Look' of 1953," in *Strategy, Politics, and Defense Budgets*, ed. Warner R. Schilling, Paul Y. Hammond, and Glenn H. Snyder (Columbia University Press, 1962), 440–43; Samuel P. Huntington, *The Common Defense* (Columbia University Press, 1961), 42, 75, 221.

4.  "Introduction," in *Arms, Politics, and the Economy: Historical and Contemporary Perspectives*, ed. Robert Higgs (New York: Homes and Meier, 1990), xvii.

5.  For detailed discussion of mobilization strategy, see Richard K. Betts, *Military Readiness: Concepts, Choices, Consequences* (Washington, D.C.: Brookings Institution, 1995), chap. 8.

6.  See Frederick H. Hartmann, *The Conservation of Enemies: A Study in Enmity* (Westport, Conn.: Greenwood Press, 1982).

7.  Arnold Kanter, *Defense Politics: A Budgetary Perspective* (Chicago: University of Chicago Press, 1979), 24–28. See Huntington, *The Common Defense*, part 6, chaps. 28–30, on how interservice rivalry served civilian control.

8.  Lawrence J. Korb, "U.S. Defense Spending After the Cold War: Fact and Fiction," in *Holding the Line: U.S. Defense Alternatives for the Early 21st Century*, ed. Cindy Williams (Cambridge: MIT Press, 2001), 37, 43.

9.  *Report of the Task Force on a Unified Security Budget for the United States, FY 2008* (Washington, D.C.: Institute for Policy Studies, April 2007), 21–25.


12. Conclusion: Selecting Security

1.  Eliot A. Cohen, "World War IV: Let's Call This Conflict What It Is," *Wall Street Journal*, November 20, 2001; Norman Podhoretz, *World War IV: The Long Struggle Against Islamofascism* (New York: Doubleday, 2007).

2.  Leslie H. Gelb with Richard K. Betts, *The Irony of Vietnam: The System Worked* (Washington, D.C.: Brookings Institution, 1979).

3.  Robert Gilpin, *War and Change in World Politics* (New York: Cambridge University Press, 1981).

4.  Eric Nordlinger, *Isolationism Reconfigured* (Princeton: Princeton University Press, 1995), 87.

5.  The following three paragraphs are drawn from Richard K. Betts, "The United States and Asia," in *Strategic Asia 2008–09: Challenges and Choices*, ed. Ashley J.

Tellis, Mercy Kuo, and Andrew Marble (Seattle and Washington, D.C.: National Bureau of Asian Research, 2008), 57–58.

6. See Richard K. Betts, "Vietnam's Strategic Predicament," *Survival* 37, no. 3 (Autumn 1995).

7. See the summary of case studies in Barry M. Blechman and Tamara Cofman Wittes, "Defining Moment: The Threat and Use of Force in American Foreign Policy," *Political Science Quarterly* 114, no. 1 (Spring 1999), especially 5, 27–29.

8. Wallace J. Thies, *When Governments Collide: Coercion and Diplomacy in the Vietnam Conflict 1964–1968* (Berkeley, CA: University of California Press, 1980); Robert A. Pape, *Bombing to Win: Air Power and Coercion in War* (Ithaca, NY: Cornell University Press, 1996).

# INDEX

Abkhazia, 190, 192

Abramo, Creighton, 223 225

Acheson, Dean, 142, 148

action vs. inaction, choice of, 13, 269–270

Afghanistan: corruption scandals in, 166, 168; mujaheddin trained and armed by U.S., 243–244; self-government by, 161, 168; Soviet Union war with, 243, 332n22

Afghanistan, war in (2002): attrition and, 298, 332n22; as backfired retaliation, 114–115; and breaking point of U.S. forces, 276; capping costs of failure, 167; and civil-military relations, 221–222; and collateral damage, 13, 168; as combination of conventional war and counterinsurgency, 85, 149, 150, 158, 332n22; and compromise, 222, 231; and control, U.S. vs. local, 16–17; costs of, 16, 24, 116, 167, 273; and defense budget supplemental request, 273; as direct self-defense of U.S., 148; and force ratios, 156, 157, 167–168; goal displacement in, 297–298; and "government as competent and honest" strategy, 160–161; and ideological power, 164; independent Afghan government and, 17; Islamists and, 287; and local security forces, development of, 157, 160, 168; multilateral aspect of, 292; and neighboring countries providing support, 165, 168; Barack Obama and, 167–168, 221–222; obstacles to success, 168; opium economy and, 168; persis-

tence of U.S. in, 123, 165, 166–168; and primacy, 122; and public pressure, lack of, 158; Sweden and, 312n11

Afghan National Army (ANA), 157

Ahmadinejad, Mahmoud, 135, 142

Aideed, Mohammed Farah, 57, 63

air-breathing delivery systems, 95

air strikes, allure of, 95, 137, 139–140

Air Tasking Order (ATO), 257, 264–265

air traffic control, hackers and, 98

air travel and airline security, 107, 118–119

Albanians, 60–61, 62, 72, 76, 78, 192. See also Kosovo

Albright, Madeleine, 67, 219, 243

Algeria, 123, 214

alliances important to maintain: Israel, conditional defense of, 294; military aloofness in most other areas, 294–296; NATO, 292; with South Korea, 292–294; U.S.-Japan Mutual Security Treaty, 292

all-in or stay out norm, 297–299

Allison, Graham T., 206, 212, 216, 259, 263, 264, 334n48

Al Qaeda: and deterrence, 120; as first strike, 143; funding of, 120; growth of, 285; in Indonesia, 125; in Iraq, 276; as main focus, 209; motives of, 110; in Pakistan, 165; retaliation against, as backfiring, 114–115; and risk of new spectacle, 107; and self-rule of Iraq, 161; Taliban harboring, 114, 120, 148, 285; and WMD, 83, 86, 108, 109. See also September 11, 2001; terrorism